REPRESENTING CONSUMERS

Voices, views and visions

Edited by Barbara B. Stern

London and New York

First published 1998
by Routledge
11 New Fetter Lane, London EC4P 4EE

Simultaneously published in the USA and Canada
by Routledge
29 West 35th Street, New York, NY 10001

Typeset in Baskerville by
J&L Composition Ltd, Filey, North Yorkshire
Printed and bound in Great Britain by
Biddles Ltd, Guildford and King's Lynn

British Library Cataloguing in Publication Data
A catalogue record for this book is available from the British Library

Library of Congress Cataloging in Publication Data
Representing consumers: voices, views and visions/
edited by Barbara Stern
p.   cm.
Includes bibliographical references and index.
1. Consumers–Research–Methodology.   I. Stern, Barbara B.
HF5415.32.R47   1998
381.3–dc21   98–11171
CIP

ISBN 0-415-18413-4 (hbk)
ISBN 0-415-18414-2 (pbk)

REPRESENTING CONSUMERS

Disciplinary deba... es of
collecting, analyz... ailing
orthodoxy by exa... away
from the issue of... is to
investigate repres... ruct-
ing the consume... ches,
drawing from mo... inary
inquiry rooted in... ojects
covered include:

- the crisis in ...
- construction ...
- qualitative a...
- multimedia ...
- narrative co...
- poetry and ...
- reassessment ...

The internationa... umer
research: Eric J.... dson
Escalas, Kent G... Dawn
Iacobucci, Linda... usan
Spiggle, Barbara ...

Barbara B. Ste... eting
Department at R...

ROUTLEDGE INTERPRETIVE MARKET RESEARCH SERIES

Edited by Barbara B. Stern, *State University of New Jersey,* and Stephen Brown, *University of Ulster, Northern Ireland*

Recent years have witnessed an "interpretive turn" in marketing and consumer research. Methodologies from the humanities are taking their place alongside those drawn from the traditional social sciences. Qualitative and literary modes of marketing discourse are growing in popularity. Art and aesthetics are increasingly firing the marketing imagination.

This series of scholarly monographs and edited volumes brings together the most innovative work in the burgeoning interpretative marketing research tradition. It ranges across the methodological spectrum from grounded theory to personal introspection, covers all aspects of the postmodern marketing "mix", from advertising to product development, and embraces marketing's principal sub-disciplines.

REPRESENTING CONSUMERS
Voices, views and visions
Edited by Barbara B. Stern

ROMANCING THE MARKET
Edited by Stephen Brown, Anne Marie Doherty and Bill Clarke

CONTENTS

CONTENTS

CONTENTS

PLATES

FIGURES

TABLES

POEMS

CONTRIBUTORS

Eric Arnould, an anthropologist by training, is Associate Professor of Marketing at the University of South Florida. He has taught at Odense University in Denmark, California State University, Long Beach, and the University of Colorado at Denver. Dr Arnould's work appears in the three major U.S. marketing journals, and other social science periodicals and books. His recent work has focused on consumer rituals (holidays, leisure, disposition), service encounters, marketing channels in West Africa, and issues associated with multimethod research.

Russell W. Belk is N. Eldon Tanner Professor in the David Eccles School of Business at the University of Utah. He has taught there since 1979 and has had previous appointments at the University of Illinois, Temple University, the University of British Columbia, the University of Craiova, Romania, and Edith Cowan University, Perth, Australia. His Ph.D. is from the University of Minnesota. He is past president of the Association for Consumer Research, and a fellow of the American Psychological Association, the Society for Consumer Psychology, and the Association for Consumer Research. He is past recipient of the University of Utah Distinguished Research Professorship and a Fulbright Fellowship. He currently edits *Research in Consumer Behavior*, and has been Advisory Editor for the *Journal of Consumer Research* and Associate Editor for the *Journal of Economic Psychology* and *Visual Sociology*. He has also served on the editorial review boards of twenty-five journals, has written or edited fifteen books or monographs, and has published over two hundred articles and papers. His research primarily involves the meanings of possessions and materialism and his methods have been increasingly qualitative and cross-cultural.

Stephen Brown is Professor of Retailing at the University of Ulster, Northern Ireland. He is an aspirant pseudo-intellectual, peppers his papers with lots of big words, most of which he doesn't understand, and goes all misty-eyed when anyone mentions Baudrillard, Bakhtin or Derrida.

Jennifer Edson Escalas is Assistant Professor of Marketing at the University of Arizona, Tucson. She earned her Ph.D. in business administration from Duke University in 1996. She has published articles in the *Journal of Public Policy & Marketing* and *Advances in Consumer Research*. Her dissertation, "Narrative processing: building connections between brands and self," received an honorable mention in the Alden G. Clayton Doctoral Dissertation Competition. Her research focuses on the use of narrative processing to create brand meaning, the relationship between brands and consumers' self-concepts, and the role of affect in both of these conceptual areas.

Kent Grayson is Assistant Professor of Marketing at the London Business School, where his research focuses on deception and truth in marketing and on network marketing (or pyramid selling) organizations. He has published articles in the *Journal of Consumer Research*, the *Journal of Consumer Psychology*, and *Sloan Management Review*.

Elizabeth C. Hirschman is Professor of Marketing in the Faculty of Management at Rutgers, the State University of New Jersey. She has published articles in a wide variety of social science and business journals. She is past president and Treasurer of the Association of Consumer Research and past vice president of the American Marketing Association. Her primary research interests are philosophy of science, interpretive research methods, and the semiotic analysis of cultural media.

Morris B. Holbrook is W.T. Dillard Professor of Marketing, Graduate School of Business, Columbia University, New York, where he teaches courses in communication and in consumer behavior. Besides his articles in various marketing journals, his research has appeared in publications devoted to research on consumer behavior, semiotics, cultural economics, the arts, aesthetics, psychology, organizational behavior, communication, leisure, and related topics. Recent books include *Daytime Television Game Shows and the Celebration of Merchandise: The Price is Right*; *The Semiotics of Consumption*; *Interpreting Symbolic Consumer Behavior in Popular Culture and Works of Art* (with Elizabeth C. Hirschman); *Postmodern Consumer Research: The Study of Consumption as Text* (with Elizabeth C. Hirschman); and *Consumer Research: Introspective Essays on the Study of Consumption*.

Dawn Iacobucci is Professor of Marketing at the Kellogg Graduate School of Management, Northwestern University. She joined Kellogg in 1987 after receiving her M.Sc. in statistics and her M.A. and Ph.D. in quantitative psychology from the University of Illinois at Urbana-Champaign. Her two research streams focus on the modeling of dyadic interactions and social networks, and the conceptualization and measurement of customer satisfaction and service quality. She has published in a variety of journals including the *Journal of Consumer Psychology*, the *Journal of Marketing*, the *Journal of Marketing Research*, *Psychometrika*, *Psychological Bulletin*, and *Social Networks*.

Linda L. Price is Professor of Marketing at the University of South Florida. She has published over fifty research papers in areas of marketing and consumer behavior in major marketing and management journals such as the *Journal of Marketing*, the *Journal of Consumer Research* and *Organization Science*. She has been the invited speaker for national organizations, businesses, state and local business chapters, and state universities. She serves on the editorial boards of major marketing, tourism, and business journals and is also an active member of the American Marketing Association and the Association for Consumer Research. Her research focuses on consumers as emotional, imaginative, and creative agents and on the relational dimensions of consumer behavior.

Jonathan E. Schroeder is Associate Professor of Marketing and Honors Faculty Fellow at the University of Rhode Island. He received his Ph.D. in social psychology from the University of California, Berkeley, and continued his training in visual studies at the Rhode Island School of Design. His research focuses on the production and consumption of images, and it has appeared in marketing, psychology, and design journals. He is interested in introducing visual theory and art criticism into the study of consumption issues such as patronage, representation, and ethics. He enjoys teaching his seminar course, "Advertising in society: Art, images and meaning." He was recently awarded a senior research fellowship at the Wesleyan University Center for the Humanities to conduct research on culture and visual representation.

John F. Sherry, Jr., Professor of Marketing at Northwestern University's Kellogg School, is an anthropologist who studies both the socio-cultural and symbolic dimensions of consumption and the cultural ecology of marketing. He is President-Elect of the Association for Consumer Research and former Associate Editor of the *Journal of Consumer Research*.

Susan Spiggle is Associate Professor and Department Head, Department of Marketing, University of Connecticut. She has published in the *Journal of Consumer Research* and the *Journal of Marketing*. She serves on the editorial review board of the *Journal of Consumer Research* and is currently working on two phenomenological research projects – one on philanthropic giving and one on consumption experience.

Barbara B. Stern is Professor of Marketing and Vice-Chair of the department at Rutgers, the State University of New Jersey. She has published articles in the *Journal of Marketing, Journal of Consumer Research, Journal of Advertising, Journal of Current Research in Advertising* and other publications. She is on the editorial boards of the *Journal of Consumer Research, Journal of Advertising, Journal of Consumer Marketing, Journal of Promotion Management*, and *Consumption, Culture, and Markets: A Journal of Critical Perspectives*. Her research has introduced principles of literary criticism into the study of marketing, consumer behavior, and advertising. Additionally, she has focused on gender issues from the perspective of feminist literary criticism, using deconstruction to analyze values encoded in advertising text.

Craig J. Thompson is Associate Professor of Marketing at the University of Wisconsin at Madison. He joined the UW-Madison faculty in 1991 after completing his doctoral work at the University of Tennessee. He has published articles in the *Journal of Consumer Research*, the *Journal of Public Policy & Marketing*, *Journal of Advertising*, *Psychology & Marketing*, the *International Journal of Research in Marketing*, and the *European Journal of Marketing Research*. He is on the editorial boards of the *Journal of Consumer Research*, the *Journal of Public Policy & Marketing*, and *Consumption, Culture, and Markets: A Journal of Critical Perspectives*. In very broad-brush terms, his research has sought to develop and apply hermeneutic approaches to the study of consumption meanings, with a particular focus on gender dynamics.

George M. Zinkhan is Coca Cola Professor of Marketing and Department Head at the University of Georgia. He has published more than 140 articles about advertising, promotion, and knowledge development in such publications as the *Journal of Marketing*, *Journal of Marketing Research*, *Journal of Consumer Research*, *Journal of Applied Psychology*, *Journal of Advertising*, *Strategic Management Journal*, *Journal of Social Psychology*, *Journal of Advertising Research*, and others. He has been named as one of the top twelve lifetime contributors to the advertising literature (in 1990, by the *Journal of Advertising*) and as one of the top twenty-five contributors to the marketing literature (in 1985, by the *Journal of Marekting Education*). Professor Zinkhan recently completed a four-year term as Editor of the *Journal of Advertising* and a three-year term as Book Review Editor for the *Journal of Marketing*. Among his consulting clients are Citicorp, Intermedics Inc., and the Federal Trade Commission, Division of Advertising Practice.

INTRODUCTION

The problematics of representation

Barbara B. Stern

In the past decade, much disciplinary debate in consumer research has centered on the most appropriate way to collect, analyze and report data. However, with some exceptions (Joy 1991; Stern 1990; Thompson 1990) this debate has focused on the way in which scholars *conduct* data-gathering rather than on the way in which they *represent* it. In Aristotelian terms, controversy has centered more on the "object" (that which is represented) than on the "manner" (the way in which it is represented) or the "medium" (the means or materials used in representation – numbers, words, music, pictures, cyberspace images, and so forth) (see Mitchell 1990).

Representation is simply taken as a "given" (something just there), not something that has to be studied. This does not reflect the "crisis of representation" throughout the social sciences (Marcus and Fischer 1986: 7), for little discussion of the way that consumer experience is to be "represented as an object for social thought" (ibid.: vii) has taken place. Despite the compelling argument that perception of a crisis acts as a stimulus for experimental forms of writing, consumer researchers continue to use traditional forms of writing even when representing innovative ideas. In other words, the crisis mentality has not yet hit home. Nonetheless, researchers must choose both the conventions and the materials that they use to represent reality, and representations shape what readers accept as reality. In consequence, it is time to begin analysis of the representational process and product from the vantage point of those who engage in it. The purpose of this book is to do so by "growing" disciplinary awareness of representation. The contributors aim at providing critical mass to focus on representation as a locus of assumptions, controversies, and decision rules central to the study of consumer behavior.

Representation, discourse, and dialogue: product versus process

Before we begin, we have to address the problem of terminology – what are we talking about when we talk about "representation"? Far from being opaque denotative signifiers, key terms such as "representation," "discourse," "dialogue," "narrative," "story," "reading," "writing," and "text" are often used interchangeably. Casual usage confuses not only denotative definition, but also connotative associations of power, persuasion, and author/subject/reader relationships encoded in usage. The codes have to be broken if we are to understand what users are talking about and engage in coherent discussion. Insofar as the term one uses to characterize a research product implies one's relationship to research, concept definition raises issues of self-reflexiveness not yet well-studied. Perhaps the most basic issue is the modernist privileging of "representation" versus the postmodernist privileging of "discourse" and "dialogue."

Representation

Representation is the most traditional term used to refer to symbols (words, pictures, musical notes) invented by humans to stand for or represent real-world things (Mitchell 1990). It is a classical construct derived from aesthetics – the criticism of art objects. Aristotle applied the term to the symbol systems of verbal (and, by implication, musical and visual) art, considered the repository of determinate or finite meaning. The values of accuracy (Aristotle's "imitation of life"), fixed meaning, and universally correct comprehension stem from the classical assumption that human superiority resides in the ability to devise, manipulate, and understand symbols. Aristotle praised symbol-creation as the characteristic that distinguishes humans from lower animals: "From childhood, men have an instinct for representation, and in this respect man differs from the other animals in that he is far more imitative and learns his first lessons by representing things" (*Poetics*, IV: 2). From classical times to the modern era, the language of representation dominated the scientific tradition of rationalism, which presumes that accurate representation gives rise to universal and singular meaning. Modern literary criticism, notably that of the American New Critics (see Ransom 1941) and the Russian formalists (Thompson 1971), follows this tradition.

The time-honored legacy of representation as a foundational concept facilitated its adaptation to disciplines other than aesthetics, including semiotics and political theory. In the latter, the notion of symbolic representation (things that stand for other things) was extended to political representation (people who act for other people). Recently, the New Historians – literary and cultural critics such as Greenblatt (1988, 1990), Althusser (1971), Montrose (1996), and McGann (1983) – have reiterated faith in representation as a key aspect of interpretation. They use the term to refer to written words as the ideological products of a particular era, based on the assumption that cultural constructs have fixed meaning at any given moment. The meaning is politically determined, for "representation is always *of* something or someone, *by* something or someone, *to* someone" (Mitchell 1990: 12).

Although representation is "an extremely elastic notion which extends all the way from a stone representing a man to a novel representing a day in the life of several Dubliners" (Mitchell 1990: 13), its use is often limited to language. The New Historians popularized the view of language as a product of the historical, social, and ideological context that serves "to reproduce, confirm, and propagate the power structures of domination and subordination which characterize a given society" (Abrams 1993: 248). In a particular era, finite meaning holds firm, for dominant power relationships sustain the bestowal of "meaning" on symbolic inventions.

Discourse

Discourse is fundamentally antithetical to "representation." Whereas the latter treats a verbal outcome as a closed product (a "work" or "object"), the former treats it as an open process. Since the 1970s, when "discourse analysis" (see Foucault 1972; Grice 1975) became influential in the social sciences, the term has been used to refer to language as an open-ended dynamic interaction among speakers (or writers) and listeners (or readers) in situation-specific contexts (Halasz 1988). However, poststructural critics use "discourse" more broadly as a generic referent to *all* communicative events in life and art rather than more narrowly as a specific referent to spoken interchanges between literary characters. Generalized usage rests on the postmodern blurring of boundaries between literature and non-literature, between one medium and another, and between one set of genre conventions and another. Blurring challenges such modernist hierarchies as the superiority of art versus science, of literary discourse versus non-literary discourse, and of poetry versus prose.

Postmodern critics exposed the implicit empowerment in hierarchical ranking and used "discourse" as a synonym for the power struggle encapsulated in the fluidity of language-in-use. Language is viewed as the expression of "linkages between power, knowledge, institutions, intellectuals, the control of populations, and the modern state as these intersect in the functions of systems of thought" (Bové 1990: 54–5). These linkages are arenas of conflict among various parties jockeying for power, which is always being negotiated and renegotiated. In postmodern work, "discourse" is the term of choice to describe communication that is fluid rather than fixed – an ensemble of voices, attitudes, and values activated by participants in the process.

Dialogue

Dialogue is a related concept, originally referring to verbal interchanges among literary characters (as did discourse) – that is, characters' spoken words, given written form in a dramatic script or a novel. The term acquired a postmodern flavor via the dialogic criticism of Mikhail Bakhtin, a Russian formalist whose major works were written in the inter-war period, but were not influential in English until the 1980s. Bakhtin defined dialogue as a polyphonic interchange among divergent voices, with each individual voice taking "shape and character in response to and in anticipation of other voices" (Bialostosky 1989: 215). He conceived of the "dialogic" novel as the opposite of the "monologic" one (Bakhtin

3

[1929] 1984). In monologic novels such as Tolstoy's, the author attempts to subordinate the characters' voices to his controlling purpose, whereas in dialogic novels such as Dostoevsky's, the author relinquishes control, allowing a multiplicity of independent and unmerged voices – his term is "polyphony" – to be heard. Despite the theoretical distinction, Bakhtin argued that novels cannot be purely monologic. The narrator's reports of the utterances of a character are inevitably "double-voiced," for the author's influence on the voice of the characters reinforces, alters, or argues with the characters' speech.

Bakhtin extended the concept of dialogic interaction from the novel to all language, viewed as a polyphonic conversation rather than as a series of univocally pronounced propositions (Bakhtin [1934–5] 1981). As such, "dialogue" has now come to mean an open-ended exchange among numerous voices (often called "polyvocality" in the social science literature), each having its own characteristic manner of expression (Abrams 1993). Although Bakhtin's theory elevates "dialogue" as the primary socio-verbal component of a work, the totality is not a determinate product of the medley of voices, social attitudes, and values that are articulated. Rather, the various voices and modes of communication are oppositional, contradictory, and irreconcilable.

Dialogic critics following Bakhtin ([1934–5] 1981; Bialostosky 1989; Todorov [1984] 1987) emphasize that all of language and culture is dialogic, in that readers (real, imagined, potential) shape the interchange, conceived of as a plurality of contending social voices that will never reach definitive resolution into a single monologic truth. In line with the perception of "the world of cultures" (Bialostosky 1989: 223) as open-ended, the dialogic critic is self-reflexive, evaluating his/her own works as merely an expression of one voice among many, all coexisting in a tension of opposition. To sum up so far, "representation" refers to the existence of a finished product in any media whose ostensibly "correct" meaning is accessible to all. "Discourse" and "dialogue" refer more narrowly to the transactive process in language whereby meaning is socially constructed by readers, writers, and those written about.

Story, plot, narrative, and rhetoric: research tellings

> So much of science proceeds by telling stories – and we are especially vulnerable to constraints of this medium because we so rarely recognize what we are doing. We think that we are reading nature by applying rules of logic and laws of matter to our observations. But we are often telling stories – in the good sense, but stories nonetheless.
>
> (Gould 1991: 251)

When we move from representation to story, the terminology gets even more slippery. Although "narrative" was originally used to describe non-dramatic written or spoken representation (the author speaks in his/her own person or takes on another persona) versus drama (the author presents all his/her characters, who speak in their own voice), it is now used interchangeably with both "representation" and "story." Some critics claim that differences between narratives and non-narratives relate to differences among media, with non-narratives considered "drawings, paintings, photographs – anything pictorial, in one frame" (Berger 1997: 6). Others claim that "narrative itself is a deep structure quite independent of its medium" (Chatman 1980: 117) – an organizational schema that can be actualized in words, pictures, dance, music, and so forth. Chatman and others use the term as a synonym for representation, applying it to any sequence of events that unfolds in time no matter the media.

In the consumer research discipline, narrative refers to a verbal structure that houses research prose. The assumption is that it is "so natural, so universal, and so easily mastered as hardly to seem a problematic region" (Miller 1990: 66). However, the voluminous and conflict-ridden body of attempts at construct definition indicates that nothing can be taken for granted (Miller 1990). A challenge to the field is to increase understanding of the way that research gets told by unpacking the term to demonstrate its controversial dimensions: truth/fiction (what is told); story/plot (how it is told); and researcher narrative/consumer narrative (who does the telling).

The told: truth/fiction

Positivist research is based on discovering a single universal truth, whereas non-positivist research seeks to discover multiple particular truths. Nonetheless, some version of truth is the goal of all social science research, for its business is not the creation of imaginative fictions. However, the Western preference for categorization and binary thinking diverts attention from the central issue – a permeable border between supposed oppositions. Insofar as narrative is virtually ubiquitous across domains, its classification is shaky. The term has been applied to the recounting of real-life events (history, biography, social science) as well as invented ones ("made up" is one meaning of the Latin "fingere," from which "fiction" derives). The complicating factor is that although all narratives are "made" or crafted in the sense that they impose structure on a multiplicity of details, only some (such as those in research) are assumed to be accounts of "things that really happened exactly as they really happened" (Miller 1990: 68). This complication is most evident in postmodern literary experimentation, which expands the notion of what "really happened" to include nearly everything. For example, the "non-fiction novel" (Truman Capote's *In Cold Blood*) fictionalizes real-life events, whereas the "documentary novel" (E.L. Doctorow's *Ragtime*) interpolates real-life events into fiction.

The mixture of truth/fiction is also present in consumer research accounts that present the consumer's own words, for polyvocality requires a multilevel structure

(Bal [1978] 1983; Genette [1972] 1980, [1983] 1988), with each narrator occupying a different position in terms of truth claims:

Level A (primary): researcher narrative – (objective truth)
Level B (secondary): consumer narrative – (subjective truth)
Level C (tertiary): consumer "tale-within-a-tale" – (possible fiction)

Each narrative level entails a different responsibility for making/making up material. Level A reflects the dominant social science research ideology of aiming at objective truth, with researchers permitted to "make" the total product by recording, transcribing, editing, and commenting on the consumers' words (Stanzel 1984), but not to "make up" any part of it. Although there are differences between positivist and non-positivist degrees of freedom in terms of relationships between the A and B levels (Belk 1986), researchers of all stamp are comparable to manufacturers expected to produce a trustworthy product out of consumer-generated raw materials.

The official research voice is negotiated in transactions with editor(s) and reviewers who form the social community that sets the expectations for the representation's truth claims (Lanser 1981). This community establishes norms that empower researchers to select material from levels B and C. However, the selection process inevitably includes the researcher's subjective decisions, for some things are put in and others are left out. In White's words, "every narrative, however seemingly 'full,' is constructed on the basis of a set of events that might have been included but were left out; this is as true of imaginary narratives as it is of realistic ones" (1987: 10). Thus, the notion of "pure" objectivity is fallacious, for the research narrator must invoke decision rules to enable him/her to make an account.

On the secondary and tertiary levels, consumers are expected to provide subjective material and to have the option of making up things, especially on level C, where they report the speech of others (Bakhtin [1934–5] 1981). That is, although both consumers and researchers make narratives, consumers can also make up things that other people say or think and perhaps even things that they themselves say or think. An important clue to the degree of narrative inventiveness is the mood of the verb (a formal indicator of the way that action is conceived). Let us look at an example of layered narration, paying special attention to the verbs, in a consumer story:

(A) While Joan values the sisters and the material things they provide, she is bothered by her lack of independence: (B) "I don't like having to be out all day. Not when I don't feel good . . ." (C) They [the sisters] can't make too many [exceptions] because then [some]one would say, "Well, she didn't [leave during the day]!"

(Joan's story, in Hill 1991: 304)

Level A is the researcher's narrative; level B is the consumer's (Joan's) narrative; and level C is Joan's anonymous informant ("someone"). On A, the researcher uses verbs in the historical present ("values" and "is bothered") to indicate that he is telling a universal truth about Joan and generalizing to all homeless women. His truth claim is introduced in the parenthetical comment that precedes the passage and labels the source ("from my field notes on these issues," p. 304), for field notes are assumed to be accurate recordings of what informants said. The colon after "independence" – a strong grammatical mark of equivalence – is the researcher's signal that what follows is to be taken as proof of what has gone before.

On level B (the material following the colon), Joan uses the historical present ("don't like" and "don't feel good") to indicate habitual action – she is referring to the way she generally feels, not to the way that she feels at that moment. Her quotation reinforces the researcher's claim to generalizability and universal truth by emphasizing her habitual response to feelings of dependency.

On level C (the material after the ellipsis), the shift to an indefinite pronoun and the subjunctive verb ("would say") reveals Joan's invented supposition – she provides an imaginative recreation of reported speech,[1] which is "distinctly and fundamentally different from dialogue" between the researcher and the subject (Bakhtin [1929] 1986: 215). Her "tale-within-a-tale" is an abbreviated dialogue in which she makes up a comment by an unnamed homeless woman who is not a real-life individual, but instead, "someone" who symbolizes all homeless women. The subjunctive verb expresses something that might have happened (a paraphrase reads, "If the sisters were to make exceptions, someone might say . . ."), not something that did happen. Thus, the passage as a whole shifts between three narratives (those of the researcher, Joan, and the symbolic homeless woman), with verbs indicating the made/made-up status of each one. Looked at this way, we see not a binary of truth/fiction but, rather, polyvocal narratives that range from the objective truth of a researcher's comments on the informant's subjective comments to the invented fiction of the informant's character. However, this is a comment neither on Joan's veracity – in Bohr's words, "When telling a true story, one should not be overinfluenced by the haphazard occurrences of reality" (Casimir 1986: 370) – nor on Hill's. Rather, it supports the argument that classification in accordance with modernist binaries is slippery, for the essential truth of a consumer's story cannot be judged by conformance to the literal truth (Belk 1986).

The telling: time and plot

Just as English verbs signify degrees of actual versus possible events, so too do they signify the temporal order in which events occur. The concept of chronological sequencing as necessary to stories stems from Aristotle, who identified temporal orderliness as one reason for their enjoyment. In the twentieth century, literary experimentalism veered away from linear time in favor of circularity (Joyce's *Finnegans Wake*), simultaneity (Woolf's *Mrs Dalloway*), stasis (Beckett's *Waiting for Godot*), and so forth. Nonetheless, faith in chronological time as an important aspect of human life remained strong, perhaps because of people's desire for a coherent universe that makes sense to them. Stories allow people to "order or reorder the givens of experience . . . [and] give experience a form and a meaning, a linear order with a shapely beginning, middle, end, and central theme" (Miller 1990: 69).

However, temporal order is necessary but not sufficient for research narratives, which require plot as well as story. Aristotle identified the attributes of plot in his *Poetics*: linear time progression – events with a beginning, middle, and end; parsimony (the unities) – no irrelevant material; and causation – motivation for the events. The requirements are grounded in classical and modern theory that affirms the superiority of *plot* to *story*. Stories may give pleasure, but plots provide instruction, teaching humans about themselves and others by demonstrating causes and effects. Whereas a story is merely a chronological string of events, a plot is a chronological sequence with causal structure and a purposeful goal. Causality in addition to temporality satisfies the human desire to learn, our most elevated aspiration. Despite the casual use of "story," "plot," and "narrative" as synonymous terms, the distinction between "story" and "plot" is crucial to understanding the role of the researcher in shaping the research narrative.

Let us use Hayden White's example and paraphrase a line in a historical chronicle to clarify the distinction (1987): "1056. The Emporer Henry died, and his son Henry became King." This is a story, for it has chronological sequence (one king after another) but no information about causality – why did the son follow the father as king? That is, the reader does not know anything about the nature of succession, the requirement of orderly transmission of authority, and the underlying purpose or causes. Readers simply learn that these events took place in time (see White 1973), not that they have one meaning rather than another.

When we turn to the actual entry in the chronicle, we see a plot, albeit a brief one: "1056. The Emporer Henry died; and his son Henry succeeded to the rule" (White 1987: 14). The final phrase states the relationships that imbue the events with meaning and integrate them into a whole. "Succeeded to the rule" tells us that the legal system encodes the principle of genealogical succession and the rule of regular transmission of authority from one generation to another (White 1987). The causality embedded in the chronicle plot is the need to pass authority from ruler to ruler in an orderly fashion.

In a more sophisticated way, research narratives impose "plot" on a variety of consumer "stories" (Durgee 1988; Forster [1927] 1954; Stern 1994). This is done by means of "double time structuring" (Chatman 1980: 118), the dimension of narrative based on two independent time orders: the first is the time sequence of the story events (the consumers' experiences), and the second is the causality of the plot (the researcher's account). From this perspective, the evaluation of "length to contribution" is a time measure, for it expresses the success (or failure) of the researcher's plot (length) in imposing meaning (contribution) on a plethora of stories.

Recall that narrative meaning is not restricted solely to meaning stated in words. Plots can be actualized in any medium capable of communicating two time orders (film, dance, opera, comic strips, interactive media, and so forth) and can be transposed from one medium to another. Although researchers are free to choose the media best suited to represent consumer phenomena (the object), for the most part, experiments with different media (Chatman 1978) have not been well received by the disciplinary community. Nonetheless, if the rich relationships between story time and plot time are to fulfill the potential of narrative, researchers should be encouraged to play with alternative means of telling, not discouraged by the constraints of journal publication or implied standards of propriety (prose is acceptable/poetry is not, and so forth).

The teller: narrative voice

Constraints and standards are now more open to reconsideration than in the past, for the classical and modern focus on events has given way to postmodern interest in the narrator (Stanzel 1978, 1984). The complex and controversial "relationships between author, narrator(s), characters, and audience" (Lanser 1981: 26) are treated in terms of topics such as the narrator's stance (point of view, intrusive/unintrusive), the mode of narrating (distance/closeness, stream-of-consciousness/interior mindscape), and the narratee's (Prince's term, 1973) responses (reader-response theory). Regrettably, the fierce controversies about formal differences between types of narration are difficult to follow because arguments are conducted in terminology so arcane and idiosyncratic that opinions are not easily comparable.[2] Various competing typological schemes span the gamut of twentieth-century literary criticism, and critical schools are "so many and diverse that it makes the mind ache to think of them all" (Miller 1990: 67).

The abundance of theories is not surprising, for discussion of the narrator has been going on for millennia. The classical division of literature into stories (with narrators) versus dramas (characters only, no narrators) dates from Plato's *Republic* (Book III), in which the perspectival axis is drawn between two "pure" or ideal poles: dramatic mimesis ('showing" of events by those taking part in them) versus epic diegesis ("telling" of events by an omniscient narrator) (Wells 1989). The narrative choice of telling versus showing is generally determined by the author's "philosophy of life or . . . ideology" (Stanzel 1984: 125), which applies to researchers as well as to novelists or playwrights. In this regard, David Lodge (1971) suggests an interesting correlation between conservative ideology (positivist, patriarchal, modern) and objective narration (omniscient researcher, superior to subjects in knowledge) versus liberal ideology (egalitarian, humanistic, and postmodern) and subjective narration (participatory researcher, knowledge bounded by relationships between researcher and researched).

Up until the 1970s, the preference for objectivity was reinforced by the rationalist bias in Western cultural criticism (Lanser 1981). Objective narration was awarded high critical praise on the ground that the more "transparent" the narrator (Cohn 1978, 1981), the better able the readers are to see the subjects' behavior directly. Subjective authorial interpolation was viewed as an old-fashioned remnant of Victorian intrusiveness, technically inferior to detached observation. Some critics (Banfield 1982; Lubbock 1957) claimed that the more absent the narrator/author, the closer language becomes to "objective knowledge" (Banfield 1982: 271) – universal truth, uncontaminated by any personal perspective. At the extreme of objectification, the disappeared narrator is said to allow events to unfold as they occurred with such fidelity to detail that the events appear to narrate themselves (Benveniste 1971).

James Joyce is generally credited with taking transparency to its outer limits by distancing the narrator such that he almost vanishes, in order to give readers the opportunity to get closer to his characters than they could to any others in literature. In *Ulysses*, Molly Bloom's soliloquy reveals her unconscious motivations with no narrative interpolation whatever. She pours out the raw material of her psyche without inhibition – or punctuation – and with such verisimilitude that the narrator/author appears to vanish. Joyce is acknowledged to have achieved his artistic aim: "The artist, like the God of the creation, remains within or behind or beyond or above his handiwork, invisible, refined out of existence, indifferent, paring his fingernails" (*A Portrait of the Artist as a Young Man*, [1916] 1957: 215). Nonetheless, whereas we know Molly Bloom in a way that we know no character before her, it is not clear whether we know her *better* than we know Jane Austen's Elizabeth Bennet or Chaucer's Wife of Bath.

The desire to understand human beings brings us full circle to consumer research, for it raises the question of how consumers are to be represented so that they may be best understood. The book's contributors show that consumers can be represented in a variety of ways: via subjective narration (Holbrook), objective narration (Iacobucci), layered narration (Arnould; Thompson), multimedia narration (Belk; Spiggle) and visual narration (Schroeder). Far from being a universally accepted closed form, narrative comprises a rich set of possibilities, some as yet not thought of. Although narration has been a cultural staple of all known communities, including the scholarly one, it has meant many different things to many people across time. Rather than perceiving differences as a threat, the elasticity of narrative should be seen as an opportunity for creative approaches that explore consumer behavior in innovative ways.

Rhetoric

Rhetoric is the source of a bundle of devices that research narrators can use to persuade audiences to accept their points of view. The term was originally associated with an orator's persuasive tactics, following Aristotle's distinction between poetry (imitation or representation of human life) and rhetoric (elicitation of audience responses). Beginning in the 1950s, "rhetorical critics" such as Wayne Booth ([1961] 1983), Kenneth Burke (1955), and M.H. Nichols (1963) began to erase the distinction. They pointed out that rhetorical devices ("figures of speech," see Corbett 1990) are used by literary authors as concerned with influencing reader responses as political orators are with acquiring votes. The implied stimulus–response model (see Booth [1961] 1983) rests on the presumption of authorial intention and its influence on reader responses. That is, authors of fiction are presumed to aim at imposing their fictive worlds on readers in an effort to inform them, capture their interest, guide emotions, or achieve imaginative consensus. Advertising shares these aims (McQuarrie and Mick 1992, 1996), using "a complex web of sociocultural signs and meanings" (McQuarrie and Mick 1996: 427) to persuade consumers to respond to figurative expressions. So, too, do authors of consumer research (Stern 1990), for anyone who survives the review process draws on an arsenal of persuasive tactics to coax reviewers into acceptance. Still, the rhetoric of research is especially worth attention in a field that has conspicuously failed to make explicit the persuasive aspects of author–reader relationships.

Reading, writing, and text

Reading

In the late 1960s and early 1970s, interest in the reading relationship shifted away from textual devices and the author's intention in using them, toward the reader's response. From this perspective, the author's intention is disavowed as the main influence on the reader, for most reader-response critics do not accept the idea that responses are author-driven. Instead, they view reading as a process of co-constructing meaning in which the reader processes information based on his/her pre-existing biases, expectations, and perceptions (Halasz 1988). Readers are presumed to "maneuver with the protagonist notably in the interest of comprehending the meaning of the work" (Halasz 1988: 6). What this implies is that no single "correct" meaning can be conveyed by language and transmitted to all readers alike. Nonetheless, meaning is generally agreed to be constrained by a range of possibilities situated in the historical, ideological, and socio-cultural nexus where the individual engages with the written word. That is, the "normal" reader is assumed to be responding to something on the page, for words (unlike ink-blots) control the potential meanings available in a specific culture.

Writing

Writing is now paired with reading, for meaning emerges out of a co-constructive negotiation between author and reader. Social science writing is no longer dominated by the conventions of "realism" that require an objective narrative stance on the part of the author and that convey "a clear, unmediated record of a knowable world" (Van Maanen 1995: 7). The product-orientation has been under attack in the U.S. for approximately a generation, since the dissemination of French poststructuralism. Barthes (1974) challenged the notion of the written product, instead conceiving of writing (*écriture*) as a process in which the author activates pre-existing language and literary conventions, and the readers interpret

11

the marks-on-a-page in accordance with socially determined meanings. That is, the written word is not considered a finite object in a universe of fixed meanings (problems/solutions, causes/effects, questions/answers), but instead is seen as a mediated bundle of diverse meanings in a universe of particularized interpretations (Abrams 1993).

To sum up, "narrative" in consumer research refers to prose accounts of consumption events in time, with consumers providing the raw materials that researchers record, organize, edit, and make public. Narratives have plot (chronological sequence, causality), one or more narrators, and readers who engage with the material. Research authors dig into the grab-bag of "rhetoric" for devices to persuade readers, but "reading" is the individually driven and culturally influenced process of interpretation that occurs regardless of the author's intention in "writing." The term does not refer to a finished and finite product, but to an activity that "disseminates into an open set of diverse and opposed meanings" (Abrams 1993: 285).

Text

Nonetheless, "an open set of diverse meanings" requires faith in the possibility of "meaning." When we get to the term "text" as used by the deconstructive critics (see Stern 1996), the concept of meaning is discarded. "Text" refers to "the manifestation of an open-ended, heterogeneous, disruptive force of signification and erasure that transgresses all closure" (Johnson 1990: 40). It is a catch-all term for any and all phenomena – the world is a text – and "writing" is considered merely the binary opposite of "speech." Both terms are conceived of as fields characterized by gaps, conflicts, and irreconcilable forces that play out to infinity. From this perspective, the written word's capacity to serve as a "representation" of things in the external world is an illusion, and language is a text that can only construct, reconstruct, and deconstruct itself. The written word as the locus of meaning is but a more sophisticated illusion, for when the claim that meaning is open-ended is taken to its logical conclusion, openness is infinite, not "ended" or endable.

One reason is that all language is nonlogical – ironically, rhetorical intent is doomed to fail because language is so endlessly rhetorical. The deconstructive interpretation of "rhetoricity" emphasizes not the ends (persuasion, eliciting audience effects), but the means used to achieve them (metaphor, allegory, symbol, and so forth). These figures – treated in both rhetorical and literary criticism – are said to be present in all language, including philosophy (de Man 1979; Derrida [1968] 1982), for all modes of communication depend on figurative usage that can never be reduced to literal meanings. On the contrary (see Ciardi and Williams 1975), ostensibly literal terms are metaphors whose metaphoric nature has often been forgotten, and language itself is a meta-allegory – an endless chain of significations.

The deconstructive insistence on infinite and indefinite signification positions text as an undecidable, non-referential, confrontational set of possibilities that "simultaneously asserts and denies the authority of its own rhetorical mode" (de Man 1979: 17). There is nothing outside the sequence of verbal signs, nothing independent of the language system, for all attempts to ground language in an absolute essence or center (God, Platonic Form, the intention of a speaker to signify something absolutely determinate in his/her consciousness at the moment of speech) are futile. Neither the author, merely an impersonal agent who inscribes the text in accordance with pre-existing linguistic and literary structures, nor the reader, merely the idiosyncratic interpreter of the text, makes meaning. Since there is nothing outside the text (one of Derrida's most famous pronouncements, [1967] 1976), and it fragments into the play of words, it is impossible even to conceive of meaning – don't ask. Postmodern researchers do not seek answers to a question but, rather, seek to understand why the question is being asked.

Derrida insisted that text comprised an indeterminate cycle of questions rather than a neatly finite series of questions and answers. Although his own work actualized his theory, most of his American followers argue that a provisional stopping-point is a practical necessity. De Man, perhaps the most influential American methodologist, is comfortable with the acceptance of a finite set of possible (although contradictory) meanings available at any given time. This provisional finiteness represents a middle way, somewhere between Derrida's completely open text and prior criticism's rigidly closed box of meaning. Berman summarizes the American epistemology: "For de Man, the author creates the text; for Derrida, there is no author, only text. For de Man, language must always mediate between self and world; for Derrida, self and world are generated by language; for de Man . . . truth cannot be grasped. For Derrida, truth cannot even be imagined" (Berman 1988: 246). De Man's pragmatic criticism empowers the adaptation of deconstructive readings to text viewed as a locus of provisional meanings.

In sum, the term for research that one uses announces one's belief that it is one kind of work (representation, discourse, dialogue, writing, narrative, text) rather than another. "Representation" empowers the Western preference for presence (finite meaning); "discourse" establishes the postmodern preference for fluidity (socially constructed meanings); "narrative" presumes authorial control over a written product; "reading" and "writing" return control to meaning co-constructed by author and audience; and "text" has been used so broadly that it can reference the absence of any decidable meaning as well as whatever meanings are present.

Overview of chapters

The book is organized into four parts in which the chapters reflect multiple approaches to representation and meaning. Part One, "Researchers and repre-sentation," consists of three chapters about symbols used to construct consumer reality. In Chapter One, Kent Grayson summarizes "icons" of consumer research such as equations, photographs, "F" values, and quotations that stand for the reality of consumer experience. He points out that each is a different kind of sign and classifies them using the semiotic categories of "icon," "index" and "symbol." In accordance with this scheme, icons represent reality via similarity, indices via causality, and symbols via conventional association.

Although none of these symbols is inherently preferable as a means of representing reality, researchers tend to rank them in an implicit hierarchy. Grayson explores the roots of this hierarchy from a semiotic perspective, drawing from semiotic theory to focus on "modality" or perceived level of congruence between a sign and the real world. His first conclusion is that the evaluation of modalities is subjective and highly dependent on the interpreter's knowledge structures regarding the semiotic status of certain symbols – what is an icon to some researchers is a symbol to others, and vice versa. His second conclusion is that preference ranking has an ideological basis, for the paradigm in which researchers are trained not only gives them great facility in seeing reality in certain types of signs, but also hinders their ability to see reality in other types of signs.

In Chapter Two, Dawn Iacobucci reviews the use of numerical indices as signs, summarizing quantitative tools in representation. She discusses the quantitative researcher's reliance on numerical modality based on congruence between numbers and what they represent. Her chapter examines the three primary quantitative tools relevant to representation: measurement, statistics, and modeling. Measurement is used to map numbers onto characteristics that researchers wish to represent so that the numbers behave roughly like the phenomenon being measured. The goal is convergence across multiple measures or raters, and some techniques are factor analysis and scaling techniques. Statistics are used in the social sciences to measure the probability of occurrence of predictable and replicable behaviors. Research hypotheses in relation to statistical null hypotheses are discussed in terms of the logic of Aristotle's syllogisms to understand validation versus falsification. Modeling by its very nature is intended to represent a phenomenon, albeit in a simplified version. However, she reminds us that models tend to be capricious in their assumptions, reflecting researcher decisions (that is, subjective decision rules) about the way the world operates to derive a parsimonious yet rich explanatory tool.

In Chapter Three, Barbara Stern turns from numerical data to verbal data. She presents a narratological analysis of the relationship between the research narrator and the consumer narrator, treating the prose account as the analytical object. Her chapter draws on narratology – a subdiscipline of literary criticism dealing with the identification of structural elements, the modes of combination, and the devices by which a narrative gets told (Abrams 1993) – for analytical methodology. She challenges claims of polyvocality, using a data set of articles published in the *Journal of Consumer Research* since 1987. These articles introduce the ethnographic, existential–phenomenological, and introspective traditions. Differences among these traditions are examined, and representational problems are exposed. She ends with suggestions for improved research representations based on clarification of narrative conventions, inclusion of silenced voices, and encouragement of innovative experiments.

14

Part Two, "Representation and verbal data," delves more deeply into verbal representation – the most common form of consumer research. Chapters Four and Five can be read as a unit, for they provide discussions of two popular approaches to consumers via their own words. In Chapter Four, Eric Arnould argues that consumer-oriented ethnographic research – the representation of cultural differences in consumption – provides multiple perspectives on consumer behavior. He discusses the strengths and limitations of the two main ethnographic methods – interviews and observations – each of which yields data that can be represented and interpreted to yield distinctive insights.

Arnould describes the capacity of ethnographic data to reveal four disjunctures in consumer behavior:

1   manifest behavior contrasted with ideal behavior;
2   observed behavior contrasted with consumer-articulated behavior;
3   recurrent patterns of action contrasted with consumers' representations of specific instances;
4   recurrent behavioral patterns contrasted with informants' representations of behavioral particularity.

In coming to understand these disjunctures, consumer-oriented ethnographers develop rich interpretations capacious enough to accommodate behavioral contrasts and alternative perspectives. Three of the most useful representational strategies are thick description, thick transcription, and thick inscription. Unlike conventional consumer research, consumer-oriented ethnography celebrates multiple divergent representations of consumer phenomenon rather than singular convergent representations. The chapter ends with a discussion of similarities and differences among related representational strategies.

In Chapter Five, Craig Thompson explores the "hermeneutic-phenomenological view," a vantage point from which the "crisis of representation" in consumer research appears to be "*déjà vu* all over again" – the same old crisis that researchers have always faced. He argues that for consumer researchers working in the spirit of the linguistic turn, the crisis is a function of its characteristic metaphor: the consumer-as-text. The metaphor attests to the wisdom that success sows the seeds of its own demise, for the growing legion of consumer researchers who uncritically and unreflexively embrace it foretells its destruction. Thompson reminds us that it was not so long ago that another metaphor – the consumer-as-computer (i.e. the rational information-processing unit) – appeared on the scene as a liberating and productive image for generating novel consumer research.

The linguistic turn challenged this metaphor, but in the challenge lies a warning – a productive metaphor can easily seduce researchers into believing that it is the essence of the research phenomena. This type of "ontological reification" encourages researchers to become so enamored of the complexities of their theoretical formulations that they become detached from the experiential foundations. When this occurs, the metaphor that was once productively novel becomes a conventionalized cliché, and innovative research gives way to the "narcissism of small differences." Thompson cautions researchers to avoid fomenting a crisis of representation, suggesting instead that we expend effort in grounding the implicit metaphoric model of the consumer-as-text in an explicit account of human experience.

The grounding that Thompson proposes is hermeneutic-phenomenology, a theoretical base on which to build a model of narrative structures that represents fundamental characteristics of the life-world. His chapter argues for the usefulness of hermeneutics in assessing the crisis of representation and in providing experiential grounding required by narratives rooted in the metaphor of the consumer-as-text. The chapter ends with a discussion of the implications of hermeneutic grounding for a variety of postmodern narratives based on the currently reigning metaphor.

In Chapter Six, Susan Spiggle turns attention from the created narrative to creating the narrative – the role of hypertext in the movement from product to process. Her chapter presents four interrelated perspectives on issues related to constructing the representation of voices in consumer research:

1 interactivity and iteration between analytic strategy, interpretive stance, and narrative strategy;
2 typological analysis of representation strategies used by consumer researchers in phenomenological, ethnographic, and other qualitative research;
3 an appropriate framework for guiding decisions about representation in crafting the narrative;
4 discussion of problems and opportunities in moving from text to hypertext in constructing the narrative.

Part Three, "Representation and pictorial data," consists of two chapters that expand the concept of representation in consumer research. In Chapter Seven, Jonathan Schroeder summarizes visual approaches to understanding the consumer. He points out that whereas the field of art criticism offers consumer researchers an astonishing array of tools with which to interpret and understand symbols and images, few studies within the field have taken advantage of an art-centered approach. This approach aims at understanding the historical, cultural, and representational contexts of visual text, applicable to consumption text as well. In this regard, he reminds us that discourse conducted via art is even more ancient than discourse via words, for visual symbols preceded verbal ones as a means of representation. Mining art criticism as a source of insights provides opportunities for more complete analysis of consumer behavior.

His chapter concentrates on the potential of visual consumer research via photography. After introducing photography as a dominant representational force in the lives of consumers, Schroeder reviews four research areas that demonstrate its potential as an approach to understanding the way that consumers use representation and the way that they are used by it. The areas are as follows:

1   photography as a research method in which photographs are used to generate data or as stimuli for research;
2   strategies for analyzing visual data such as content analysis, structural analysis, and formal analysis;
3   photography as an art form used by artists to represent consumer culture and to enrich understanding of how we "consume representation";
4   film, video, and television as prime sources of images for consumption.

The chapter concludes with a discussion of representation as an ethical issue and a way of framing experience.

In Chapter Eight, Morris Holbrook illustrates one visual approach by uniting the themes of introspection, auto-driving, and ethnoscopic stereography. He presents his subjective, personal, introspective insights concerning the transitional market economy found in the developing consumer culture of Kroywen – a society that has been little studied and remains poorly understood, in part because of the harsh and even dangerous conditions that exist therein. To overcome these barriers to investigation, Holbrook reflects on his long-term, immersive participant observation in the Kroywenese culture in the form of a *photo essay* (i.e. a photographically documented self-reflective account) that uses *stereography* (i.e. three-dimensional images) for purposes of *auto-auto-auto driving* or *auto^3-driving* (a self-expression of his own reactions to stereo pairs that he took) in order to construct a coherent *ethnoscopy* (i.e. a pictorial record of the relevant consumer culture). Hence, the example of Kroywen serves both to introduce and to illustrate an approach by means of the ethnoscopic, auto-driven, stereographic photo essay.

Holbrook's chapter leads into Part Four, "Pragmatics, innovation, and critical issues," six chapters that explore future directions for research on representation. In Chapter Nine, Jennifer Edson Escalas discusses the impact of advertising narratives on consumers. She accesses narrative research to show that people make sense of their lives by thinking about themselves and the events around them in story form. Advertising creatives tap into the human tendency to tell stories by presenting information about products and brands in story form. Escalas proposes that consumers respond by generating narrative thoughts to interpret the meaning of products and brands.

Her chapter enumerates different ways that advertising narratives influence viewers' cognitive, affective, and behavioral responses. She demonstrates several methods of quantifying the narrative structure of advertisements and the narrative structure of consumers' cognitive responses. She draws on theoretical constructs such as Bruner's (1986) narrative landscapes, Pennington and Hastie's (1986, 1992) episode schema, and Gergen and Gergen's (1986) narrative slopes.

Her chapter presents the findings of a content analysis of television advertisements designed to assess the number of narrative versus non-narrative commercials. Based on this analysis and prior research, she proposes the following effects of narrative form:

1 marketers can influence the degree to which viewers think narratively about their brand in response to a print advertisement;

2 when narratively structured thought is encouraged by advertising, consumers create meaning for the advertised brand, which leads to more favorable ad and brand attitudes and behavioral intentions;

3 different narrative structural elements in television ads lead to different effects on viewers' cognitive and affective responses.

Chapter Ten moves from the laboratory to the poet's study. George M. Zinkhan, John F. Sherry, Jr., and Barbara B. Stern argue for poetic representation as a valid modality of consumer experience. They begin with the question, "If poetry is about life, and life includes consumption, can poetry play a role in representing the consumer?" Their chapter claims that poetry has a unique contribution to make to research representation because of its power to evoke imaginative recreation of consumer experience by defamiliarizing (or "estranging") it. If representation is limited to prose – that is, if poetic offerings are not accepted into major research vehicles – the creativity that researchers are exhorted to cultivate will be stifled. The chapter claims that opening the concept of representation to include poetry as well as other creative art forms broadens the research canon. Like all poetry, the poetry of consumption provides an alternative perspective. It is one of the most subjective forms of representation, but in this respect differs more in degree than in kind from pictorial or verbal output. The chapter illustrates its "defense of poesy" with poems composed by George M. Zinkhan and John F. Sherry, Jr.

In Chapter Eleven, Russell W. Belk integrates many of the preceding strategies of representation in a discussion of multimedia approaches to data. He begins by noting that an increasing variety of observers in an increasing array of disciplines have pointed out that science, art, and culture, as well as everyday experience and understanding, are predominantly visual. Humans have found something compelling about visual images since at least the 100,000–year-old creation of the earliest surviving Australian rock art. Artwork, artifacts, photographs, film, television, audiotape, videotape, videodisks, computers, digital photography, CD-ROMs, and the World Wide Web, have vastly multiplied the possibilities for recording, storing, and presenting visual as well as oral information.

Belk emphasizes (as does Schroeder) that, with a few exceptions, consumer research is remarkably visually and orally illiterate, relying almost exclusively on the written word. His chapter draws on extant examples in consumer behavior research as well as in related fields to argue the need, potential, benefits, and limitations to incorporating multimedia data and presentations in order to understand the consumer and convey our understandings as well as our primary data to others. Belk uses Saint Exupéry's *Little Prince* to illuminate differences between the positivist and non-positivist views of consumer behavior. His chapter presents visual examples and critically questions the types of knowledge that can be captured and conveyed by means of multimedia representations.

In Chapter Twelve, Linda Price and Eric Arnould argue for the use of multiple methods associated with disparate paradigms in consumer research. They actualize the potential of multimethod research by drawing on examples that show the theoretical and practical importance of employing different assumptions about "doing science." They use the metaphor of conducting a choir to convey the assumptions and consequences of doing multimethod research. A choir is made up of multiple voices which, rather than being redundant, allow for a wide range of variations. The voices may sing in harmony, may sing partially overlapping melodic lines, may sing in different octaves, and may carry entirely different themes. Themes may be announced, disappear, recur, and be reworked. Interplay between the voices constitutes a whole that is greater than the sum of its parts and that cannot be achieved by the separate parts in isolation. When separated, partial parts may seem incongruous without the addition of other parts. Hence, simultaneity in performance of the parts is crucial to achieve desired musical effects. Price and Arnould explore three data-driven themes to exemplify the choir metaphor in terms of developing cross rhythms, echoes and interplays, and simultaneity in practice.

In Chapter Thirteen, Stephen Brown presents the view of someone stolen by the little people and still on loan to middle earth. This distinctive perspective allows him to see assumptions from odd angles, turning them into questions, arguments, attacks, and so forth. Brown begins by asking whether consumer research is caught up in a "crisis of representation or representations of crisis?" He turns Derridean, zooming in on "crisis" as a wonderful word that carries connotations of crying for help, purgatory, agonistics and all-purpose lachrymosity. In a rare combination of deconstruction and Swinburnian excess, he points out that the second sibilant syllable is redolent of vampires, Vincent Price and mustachioed villains of Victorian melodrama. Continuing the *fin de siècle* theme, Brown points out that "crisis" (we are still on the word itself) literally screams at us from the panic-stricken page. It deserves to be printed in scarlet or allowed to flash on and off like a literary lighthouse, the pulsar of prose, a textual patrol car in hot pursuit. Crisis, in short, is the intellectual equivalent of Pavlov's bell. On hearing it, scholars slaver uncontrollably, thinking of the self-aggrandizing opportunities arising from a serious disciplinary rupture.

Brown's chapter extends the possibilities of alliteration in research prose when he contends that the concept of crisis is in crisis. Crises have become a commonplace. They have been announced so often that the prospect of uninterrupted stability is much more disconcerting. In a massively blooming section, he asks: "What is it about crises? Why do we need them? What purpose, if any, do they serve? Are they a manifestation of pre-millennial tension?; an artifact of the academic avant-garde?; a cynical political ploy espoused by ambitious intellectuals?; a massive projection of the baby-boom's mid-life uncertainties?; or, as Kermode suggests, an instantiation of the innate human desire for the End?" Brown rejoicingly ends at the beginning, restating his meta-question: are we facing a crisis of representation or representations of crisis? His answer, needless to say, is both and neither.

In Chapter Fourteen Elizabeth Hirschman reflects on her thinking about representation, images, and meaning in consumer research. She reviews the changes in consumer research since the mid-1980s caused by the introduction of innovative methods of reading meaning. Her "afterwords" about the over-privileging of written words warn us that interpretive research can be as tyrannical as non-interpretive work. Her examples draw from her own life as well as from contemporary culture to illustrate the complexity of discerning what is real and what is hyperreal. Her emphasis on the visual and auditory – not simply the written – reinforces the importance of representation.

Notes

1   See Genette ([1983] 1988) for a discussion of the varieties of narrative speech. His terms for the authorial narrator are "narratized speech" (direct) and "transposed speech" (indirect) and for the characters, "reported speech" (direct) and "transposed speech" (indirect).

2   See Genette's tables ([1983] 1988: 119, 121) for a concise review of terminology and narrative types. Genette first used the terms "homodiegetic" versus "heterodiegetic" narration ([1972] 1980), and Lanser's "stance" reflects the diegetic to mimetic con-tinuum (1981). However, Genette ([1983] 1988) later used the terms *voice* ("who speaks?") and *vision* ("who sees?"). "Voice" relates to the narrator's perspective on the story, the time of narration, and narrative level. "Vision" relates to the focalization of the narrative, for the person who sees the events of the story need not be the persona who speaks. Stanzel's terms (1978, 1984) are "authorial" narrative (dominance of narrator) versus "figural" (dominance of character as reflector or focus of narrating). Cohn's terms (1978, 1981) for voice are "dissonant" and "consonant," which relate to Stanzel's "authorial" (dissonant, narrator-dominance) and "figural" (consonant, char-acter-dominance as focus of narrating).

References

Abrams, M.H. (1993) *A Glossary of Literary Terms*, 6th edn., New York: Holt, Rinehart and Winston.

Althusser, L. (1971) *Lenin and Philosophy, and Other Essays*, trans. B. Brewster, London: New Left Books.

Aram, V.H. (ed.) (1989) *The New Historicism*, New York: Routledge.

Aristotle ([4th cent. B.C.] 1927) *Poetics*, trans. W. H. Fyfe, Cambridge: Harvard University Press.

Bakhtin, M.M. ([1934–5] 1981) *The Dialogic Imagination: Four Essays*, trans. C. Emerson and M. Holquist, Austin: University of Texas Press Slavic Series.

—— ([1929] 1984) *Problems of Dostoevsky's Poetics*, ed. and trans. C. Emerson, Minneapolis: University of Minnesota Press.

Bakhtin, M.M. aka Volosinov, V.N. ([1929] 1986) *Marxism and the Philosophy of Language*, trans. L. Matejka and I.R. Titunic, Cambridge: Harvard University Press.

Bal, M. ([1978] 1983) "The Narrating and the Focalizing: A Theory of the Agents in Narrative," trans. J.E. Lewin, in *Style*, 17,2: 234–69.

Banfield, A. (1982) *Unspeakable Sentences: Narration and Representation in the Language of Fiction*, Boston: Routledge & Kegan Paul.

Barthes, R. (1974) *S/Z*, trans. R. Miller, New York: Hill and Wang.

Belk, R.W. (1986) "Art Versus Science as Ways of Generating Knowledge about Materialism," in D. Brinberg and R.J. Lutz (eds) *Perspectives on Methodology in Consumer Research*, New York: Springer-Verlag, 3–36.

Benveniste, E. (1971) *Problems in General Linguistics*, trans. M.E. Meek, Coral Gables: University of Miami Press.

Berger, A.A. (1997) *Narratives in Popular Culture, Media, and Everyday Life*, Thousand Oaks, CA: Sage.

Berman, A. (1988) *From the New Criticism to Deconstruction: The Reception of Structuralism and Post-structuralism*, Urbana: University of Illinois Press.

Bialostosky, D. (1989) "Dialogic Criticism," in G.D. Atkins and L. Morrow (eds) *Contemporary Literary Theory*, Amherst: University of Massachusetts Press, 214–28.

Booth, W.C. ([1961] 1983) *The Rhetoric of Fiction*, 2nd edn., Chicago: The University of Chicago Press.

Bové, P.A. (1990) "Discourse," in F. Lentricchia and T. McLaughlin (eds) *Critical Terms for Literary Study*, Chicago: The University of Chicago Press, 50–65.

Bruner, J.S. (1986) *Actual Minds, Possible Worlds*, Cambridge, MA: Harvard University Press.

Burke, K. (1955) *A Rhetoric of Motives*, New York: G. Braziller.

Casimir, H.B.G. (1986) "Mellem Spog og Alvor: Personal Recollections about Niels Bohr," in J. de Boer, E. Dal, and O. Ulfbek (eds) *The Lesson of Quantum Theory*, Amsterdam: Elsevier Science Publishers, 369–92.

Chatman, S. (1978) *Story and Discourse: Narrative Structure in Fiction and Film*, Ithaca: Cornell University Press.

—— (1980) "Novels and Films," in W.J.T. Mitchell (ed.) *On Narrative*, Chicago: The University of Chicago Press, 117–36.

Ciardi, J. and Williams, M. (1975) *How Does a Poem Mean?*, 2nd edn., Boston: Houghton Mifflin.

Cohn, D. (1978) *Transparent Minds: Narrative Modes for Presenting Consciousness in Fiction*, Princeton: Princeton University Press.

—— (1981) "The Encirclement of Narrative: On Franz Stanzel's *Theorie des Erzahlens*," *Poetics Today*, 2,2: 157–82.

Corbett, E.P.J. (1990) *Classical Rhetoric for the Modern Student*, New York: Oxford University Press.

de Man, P. (1979) *Allegories of Reading: Figural Language in Rousseau, Nietzche, Rilke, and Proust*, New Haven: Yale University Press.

Derrida, J. ([1967] 1976) *Of Grammatology*, trans. G. Chakravorty Spivak, Baltimore: Johns Hopkins University Press.

—— ([1968] 1982) *Margins of Philosophy*, trans. A. Bass, Chicago: University of Chicago Press.

Durgee, J.F. (1988) "Interpreting Consumer Mythology: A Literary Criticism Approach to Odyssey Informant Stories," in M.J. Houston (ed.) *Advances in Consumer Research*, vol. 15, Provo, UT: Association for Consumer Research, 531–6.

Forster, E.M. ([1927] 1954) *Aspects of the Novel*, New York: Harcourt, Brace, & World.

Foucault, M. (1972) *The Archaeology of Knowledge,* trans. A.M. Sheridan Smith, New York: Pantheon Books.

Genette, G. ([1972] 1980) *Narrative Discourse,* trans. J.E. Lewin, Ithaca: Cornell University Press.

—— ([1983] 1988) *Narrative Discourse Revisited,* trans. J.E. Lewin, Ithaca: Cornell University Press.

Gergen, K.J. and Gergen, M.M. (1986) *Social Psychology,* New York: Springer-Verlag.

Gould, S.J. (1991) *Bully for Brontosaurus: Reflections in Natural History,* New York: W.W. Norton.

Greenblatt, S. (1988) *Representing the English Renaissance,* Berkeley: University of California Press.

—— (1990) *Learning to Curse: Essays in Early Modern Culture,* New York: Routledge.

Grice, H.P. (1975) *Speech Acts,* P. Cole and J.L. Morgan (eds) New York: Academic Press.

Halasz, L. (1988) "Cognitive and Social Psychological Approaches to Literary Discourse. An Overview," in L. Halasz (ed.) *Literary Discourse: Aspects of Cognitive and Social Psychological Approaches,* Berlin: Walter de Gruyter, 1–37.

Hill, R.P. (1991) "Homeless Women: Special Possessions, and the Meaning of 'Home': An Ethnographic Case Study," *Journal of Consumer Research,* 18,3: 298–310.

Johnson, B. (1990) "Writing," in F. Lentricchia and T. McLaughlin (eds) *Critical Terms for Literary Study,* Chicago: The University of Chicago Press, 39–49.

Joy, A. (1991) "Beyond the Odyssey: Interpretations of Ethnographic Writing in Consumer Behavior," in R.W. Belk (ed.) *Highways and Buyways: Naturalistic Research from the Consumer Behavior Odyssey,* Provo: Association for Consumer Research, 216–33.

Joyce, J. ([1916] 1957) *A Portrait of the Artist as a Young Man,* New York: The Viking Press, 1916.

Lanser, S.S. (1981) *The Narrative Act: Point of View in Prose Fiction,* Princeton: Princeton University Press.

Lodge, D. (1971) *The Novelist at the Crossroads and Other Essays on Fiction and Criticism,* Ithaca: Cornell University Press.

Lubbock, P. (1957) *The Craft of Fiction,* New York: Viking Press.

Marcus, G.E. and Fischer, M.M. (1986) *Anthropology as Cultural Critique: An Experimental Moment in the Human Sciences,* Chicago: University of Chicago Press.

McGann, J.J. (1983) *The Romantic Ideology: A Critical Investigation,* Chicago: University of Chicago Press.

McQuarrie, E.F. and Mick, D.G. (1992) "On Resonance: A Critical Pluralistic Inquiry into Advertising Rhetoric," *Journal of Consumer Research,* 19,2: 180–97.

—— (1996) "Figures of Rhetoric in Advertising Language," *Journal of Consumer Research,* 22,1: 424–38.

Miller, J.H. (1990) "Narrative," in F. Lentricchia and T. McLaughlin (eds) *Critical Terms for Literary Study,* Chicago: The University of Chicago Press, 66–79.

Mitchell, W.J.T. (1990) "Representation," in F. Lentricchia and T. McLaughlin (eds) *Critical Terms for Literary Study,* Chicago: The University of Chicago Press, 11–22.

Montrose, L.A. (1996) *The Purpose of Playing: Shakespeare and the Cultural Politics of the Elizabethan Theatre,* Chicago: The University of Chicago Press.

Nichols, M.H. (1963) *Rhetoric and Criticism,* Baton Rouge: Louisiana State University Press.

Pennington, N. and Hastie, R. (1986) "Evidence Evaluation in Complex Decision Making," *Journal of Personality and Social Psychology,* 51,2: 242–58.

—— (1992) "Explaining the Evidence: Tests of the Story Model for Juror Decision Making," *Journal of Personality and Social Psychology*, 62,2: 189–206.

Prince, G. (1973) "Introduction to the Study of the Narratee," in J. Tompkins (ed.) *Reader-Response Criticism: From Formalism to Post-Structuralism*, Baltimore: Johns Hopkins University Press, 7–25.

Ransom, J.C. (1941) *The New Criticism*, Norfolk, CT: New Directions.

Stanzel, F.K. (1978) *Narrative Situations in the Novel*, trans. J.P. Pusack, Bloomington: Indiana University Press.

—— ([1979] 1984) *A Theory of Narrative*, trans. C. Goedsche, Cambridge: Cambridge University Press.

Stern, B.B. (1990) "Literary Criticism and the History of Marketing Thought: A New Perspective on 'Reading' Marketing Theory," *Journal of the Academy of Marketing Science*, 18,4: 329–36.

—— (1994) "Classical and Vignette Television Advertising Dramas: Structural Models, Formal Analysis, and Consumer Effects," *Journal of Consumer Research*, 19,4: 601–15.

—— (1996) "Deconstructive Strategy and Consumer Research: Concepts and Illustrative Exemplar," *Journal of Consumer Research*, 23,2: 136–47.

Thompson, C.J. (1990) "Eureka! And Other Tests of Significance: A New Look at Evaluating Interpretive Research," in M.E. Goldberg, G. Gorn, and R.W. Pollay (eds) *Advances in Consumer Research*, vol. 17, Provo, UT: Association for Consumer Research, 25–30.

Thompson, E.M. (1971) *Russian Formalism and Anglo-American New Criticism: A Comparative Study*, The Hague: Mouton.

Todorov, T. ([1984], 1987) *Literature and Its Theorists: A Personal View of Twentieth Century Criticism*, trans. C. Porter, Ithaca: Cornell University Press.

Van Maanen, J. (1995) "An End to Innocence: The Ethnography of Ethnography," in J. Van Maanen (ed.) *Representation in Ethnography*, Thousand Oaks: Sage, 1–35.

Wells, W.D. (1989) "Lectures and Dramas," in P. Cafferata and A.M. Tybout (eds) *Cognitive and Affective Responses to Advertising*, Lexington, MA: Lexington Books, 13–20.

White, H. (1973) *Metahistory: The Historical Imagination in Nineteenth Century Europe*, Baltimore: Johns Hopkins University Press.

—— (1987) *The Content of the Form: Narrative Discourse and Historical Representation*, Baltimore: Johns Hopkins University Press.

Part I

RESEARCHERS AND REPRESENTATION

1

THE ICONS OF CONSUMER RESEARCH

Using signs to represent consumers' reality

Kent Grayson

In consumer research – as in all types of human communication – there is an inevitable link between representation and deception. In articles, monographs, and books, consumer researchers seek to present consumer experiences, behaviors, and general tendencies to readers. However, because experiences, behaviors, and general tendencies cannot be presented directly to a reader, they must instead be *re*presented using words, tables, graphs, diagrams, formulae, and other signs. Thus, a great deal depends on the researcher's ability to choose the most representative signs because they are the only link that a reader has with what the researcher has examined. To the extent that the researcher chooses unwisely – or worse, chooses selectively in order to present a more convincing account – the reader will be left with an incorrect or distorted view of what was researched. Umberto Eco (1979: 59) summarizes this line of reasoning with the proposition that "every time there is signification, there is the possibility of using it in order to lie."

Are lies prevalent in consumer research? The answer depends on one's definition of a lie. Certainly when researchers choose signs to represent consumer experiences, they leave out some things and simplify others. Kenneth Burke suggests that this alone leads to misrepresentation and deception, saying that people search for:

> vocabularies that will be faithful *reflections* of reality. To this end, they must develop vocabularies that are *selections* of reality. And any selection of reality must, in certain circumstances, function as a *deflection* of reality (emphasis his).

> (Burke 1945: 59)

Perhaps it is unfair to call consumer research a lie if it "deflects reality" by omission or simplification. Readers undoubtedly would find fault with a consumer research article if it described every methodological detail, discussed every aspect of the raw data, or mentioned every possible exception to a general tendency. Yet, from the perspective of Burke's quotation, there is little difference between a researcher who does not report an outlier in order to make the write-up more general or easier to read, and a researcher who omits an outlier to make the write-up more convincing. Although the motives of these two researchers are different, both write-ups are misrepresentations, and both mislead the reader.

In Plato's "Republic" (1989), Socrates takes a similar perspective on the difficulty of accurately representing reality. Using the example of a painting of a couch, he argues that the painting is "far removed from truth" (Part X: 823) because it is neither an actual couch nor an imitation of a couch, but an imitation of how a couch appears, and thus twice removed from reality. Its inability to do justice to the reality of the couch is highlighted by the fact that it shows the couch from only one angle or perspective and therefore "touches or lays hold of only a small part of the object" (Part X: 823). Paradoxically, although it is twice removed from reality and shows only a small part of the couch, the painting leaves viewers with the impression that they have come to know the real couch, and more than just the small part shown in the picture. Thus, according to Socrates, the painting "associates with the part in us that is remote from intelligence" (Part X: 828). Socrates and Burke therefore make a more absolute connection than Eco: it is not that representation raises the possibility of deception, but that it cannot avoid deception.

As consumer researchers, we are representing not couches but consumer experiences and behaviors. And yet, like Socrates's proverbial painting, our research inevitably touches or lays hold of only a small part of the consumer experience we are studying. How can we maximize the representative power of the signs we use? How can we minimize their potential to deceive? In this chapter, I draw from semiotic theory to explore these questions. To do so, I begin by presenting some key elements of this theory, focusing particularly on the concept of truth in semiotic relationships. I then outline different ways in which truth can be achieved in representation, focusing particularly on the role of iconic representations. Then, using examples of representations from published articles in the *Journal of Consumer Research* and the *Journal of Marketing Research*, I explore the idea of iconic symbols in consumer research.

The triadic semiotic model applied to consumer research

Symbols form a bridge between our consciousness and the world beyond it. They help us to know what products can be found inside grocery-store packages, what sights can be seen in countries we may never visit, and what thoughts lie within the minds of others. We also use symbols to communicate our own experiences of the world to others. Symbols are such a pervasive and useful element of our lives that we do not – and in general, need not – think about how they work. Yet, in order to consider the proposition that symbols are often misleading, the semiotic process must be brought out from the background of experience. This is the purpose of semiotic models: to examine how ink on a page can successfully represent the price of a product, the proceedings of a seminar, or the response of a consumer to an advertising message.

This section describes the semiotic model developed by Charles Sanders Peirce, one of the thinkers who stand at the foundation of semiotic theory. Peirce's model differs from other semiotic models (e.g. Derrida 1976; Saussure 1959) in a number of ways. One of the most important of these differences is Peirce's proposition that a real world exists independently of human text, and that semiotic models need to take this real world into account (Peirce 1940: 38–9; Sheriff 1989; Silverman 1983; Tallis 1995). This is clearly a useful premise when examining how symbols may represent the behaviors of a real consumer in the real world. In this section, I outline the three elements of Peirce's semiotic model and describe how these elements interrelate. This will lay the groundwork for subsequent sections, which define an icon and explore its unique role in representation and in consumer research.

Peirce described the semiotic process in terms of three interacting elements, which are depicted in Figure 1.1. One element, a sign, is "something which stands to somebody for something in some respect or capacity" (Peirce 1940: 99). The "something" that the sign stands for is called the object, which can be an element of the real or social world; or can be just a possibility. In the mind of the "somebody" perceiving the sign, the sign prompts an idea or mental image called the interpretant. (Note that Peirce viewed an interpretant as being a sign in the mind's eye, and the term therefore differs somewhat from the term "interpretation" (Singer 1984: 66–9).) Applying these concepts to consumer research, the object of any research is ultimately consumer experiences or behaviors. These are represented by signs such as words, figures, equations, etc., which appear in

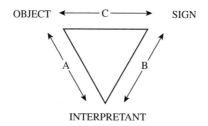

A = an (in)adequate relationship
B = an (in)correct interpretation
C = an (un)true connction

Figure 1.1 The triadic semiotic model
Source: Adapted from Peirce (1940) and Ogden and Richards (1923)

29

journal articles, monographs and books. These signs prompt in readers' minds interpretants (signs in the mind's eye) of the consumer experience being examined.

Most authors and/or readers of consumer research hope that the interpretants prompted by what they write or read will reflect as accurately as possible the consumer experience under examination. This is what Stierle describes as a desire to "fill the gap between word and world" (Stierle 1980: 84). Although researchers may differ in their methods for filling this gap and in their level of confidence in how well this gap can be filled, few (if any) researchers are in the business of making their texts *un*representative of the consumer experience. Thus, some researchers focus on achieving "construct validity" or "internal validity" (Cook and Campbell 1979), while others seek "findings that correspond to the consumption reality experienced by consumers" (Belk *et al.* 1988: 467) or interpetations that "illuminate, disclose, and reveal the lived experience" of the consumer (Hudson and Ozanne 1988: 515).

Peirce's semiotic model is useful for understanding how texts can be more or less successful in illuminating consumer experience. This utility is best illustrated by examining individually each of the three dyadic relationships in Peirce's triad. Although Peirce was clear in his later work that the elements of his triad "are bound together . . . in a way that does not consist in any complexus of dyadic relations" (1940: 100), he himself examined the relationships among the three dyads (1982: 79–80), illustrating (as this chapter will) that focusing on one dyadic link leads unavoidably to examining the others. The three links in Peirce's triad are marked in Figure 1.1 by the letters A, B and C. Ogden and Richards (1923: 11) respectively describe these links as referring to relationships of adequacy, correctness, and truth:

- Link "A" refers to the connection between the interpretant and the object. A common goal of consumer research is to prompt a symbol in the reader's mind that successfully represents or reflects the consumer experience. Because human communication and cognition always are inexact reflections of reality, the reader's impression of the consumer's experience always will be incomplete or distorted. However, the researcher, the reader, and to some degree even the consumer hope that this link is *adequate*, which means that the interpretant and object are similar enough that the reader gains knowledge about the reality of the consumer's experience.

- Link "B" refers to the relationship between the sign and the sign prompted in the reader's mind. If the reader misreads or misunderstands the signs used by the researcher, then the relationship between sign and interpretant will be threatened. However, researcher, reader, and consumer hope that this link is *correct*, which means that the sign has prompted the interpretant that was intended by the sign's user and/or that is dictated by well-established rules of sign reading.

- Link "C" is the connection between object and sign. Is this connection clear and unquestionable? If not, then even a correct interpretation of the sign can lead to a misperception of the consumer experience. However, researcher, reader, and consumer hope that the link between sign and object is *true*, which means that the sign is unequivocally connected with the consumer experience.

In an ideal semiotic process, each of the three relationships will function properly. However, it is important to note that the three links are independent of one another. For example, adequacy does not depend on truthfulness or correctness. To illustrate this, consider the example of a novice reader reading an article written by a novice researcher. The researcher has developed a scale to measure consumer experience "X" but, being a novice, does not realize that the scale is extremely vulnerable to method bias (for example, the items are all positive statements, measured using only four-point Likert scales, placed together on the survey, and so forth). The researcher reports that the Cronbach's Alpha for the scale is 0.93 and that responses to the scale are therefore an excellent indication of consumer experience "X." Given the strong method bias, the scale is not an excellent indication of the consumer experience, and so the researcher's statement (sign) is not true. However, the novice reader (being a bit overwhelmed by the technicalities in the researcher's report) misreads the article and comes away with the belief that the scale is not an excellent indication of consumer experience "X." The end result is that the researcher's sign is untrue (link "C"), and the reader's interpretation is incorrect (link "B"), but the reader's interpretant is adequate (link "A").

I have described this dysfunctional semiotic process to illustrate the point that each dyad in Peirce's semiotic triad depends on different conditions that can operate independently. Although the example is extreme, it highlights the importance of two issues. First, for the semiotic process to function properly, both the reader and the sign maker must have a level of knowledge about, if not an expertise in, the types of sign being used. This is an important issue that I will return to at the end of this chapter. Second, the researcher must be exceptionally good at ensuring that he or she chooses signs that accurately reflect the consumer experience under investigation (see, e.g. Shulman 1994). In Peircian terms, this is the relationship between sign and object, which can be either truthful or untruthful, and which is the topic of the next section.

Conditions for truth in consumer research

As compared with everyday or literary language, scientific language tends to place more emphasis on the relationship between sign and object. Focusing on sign and object directs attention away from the scientist, thus highlighting the perceived or desired objectivity of scientific activity (Baron 1984: 193, Potter 1996: 116). Most researchers admit that a perfect relationship between sign and object is impossible, yet many of us strive for a language that makes as firm a connection as possible. Peirce describes three types of relationship that can exist between a sign

31

and its object: iconic, indexical, and symbolic. In this section I outline the differences among the resulting three types of sign (icon, index, symbol), and then give careful attention to the first of these, the icon. The next section focuses on the icons of consumer research.

An icon is a sign that represents its object "mainly by similarity" (Peirce 1940: 105). For example, a realistic drawing of a dog is an iconic sign because, to the perceiver, the drawing looks like a dog. In contrast, an index is a sign that "refers to the Object that it denotes by virtue of being really affected by that Object" (Peirce 1940: 102) or because it "direct[s] the attention" to its object (Peirce 1940: 108). A dog's bark or its pawprint in the sand does not "look like" a dog, but it was affected by a dog, and thus has an indexical relationship with the dog. Lastly, a symbol is a sign that "refers to the Object that it denotes by virtue of a law" or convention (Peirce 1940: 102). The word "dog" represents a dog in English and the word "chien" represents a dog in French. Neither "dog" nor "chien" are icons because they do not resemble a dog, nor are they indices because they are not affected by a dog. Instead, they are symbols because they represent a dog simply because of the conventions of the English and French languages.

In many instances throughout his writing, Peirce presents icons, indices, and symbols as three separate and distinct types of sign. Nonetheless, he also softens this distinction by suggesting that no relationship between a sign and its object is purely iconic, indexical, or symbolic. For example, he notes that although a photograph is similar to the object that it represents, it is also caused by impressions of light on sensitive paper and is in that respect an index (1940: 106). He also writes that although a painting may be similar to the object it represents, it is "largely conventional in its mode of representation" (1940: 105) and is in that respect a symbol. More generally, Peirce writes that "It would be difficult, if not impossible, to instance an absolutely pure index, or to find any sign absolutely devoid of the indexical quality" (1940: 108). Thus, photographs can be both icons and indices; paintings can be both icons and symbols; and in fact, any sign – written, drawn, spoken etc. – has the capacity to be iconic, indexical and/or symbolic (Nöth 1995: 122; Pelc 1986).

Of Peirce's three potentially truthful signs, the icon is often experienced by viewers as having a particularly compelling relationship with its object because of its obvious similarity to it. However, the criterion of "obvious similarity" has been questioned by researchers in disciplines ranging from cognitive psychology to art theory. To illustrate the potential problem inherent in the concept of an icon, consider the two similar signs in Figure 1.2. Many viewers will say that sign (a) looks like a Christmas tree, and that sign (b) looks like an Egyptian pyramid. This undermines the general premise of an icon because both signs are so similar. How can such similar signs also be iconically similar to such different objects?

A potentially useful answer comes from Rosch's foundational work on categorization, which shows that human beings distinguish between objects based on a small and consistent subset of object attributes (e.g. Rosch et al. 1976). Based on this work, it could be argued that, for icons, it is the quality of similarity that

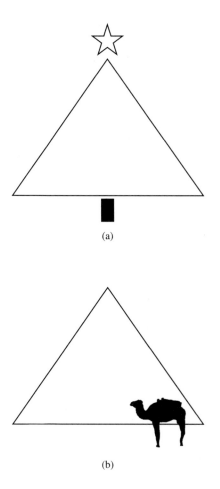

(a)

(b)

Figure 1.2 Two potential icons

matters, not the quantity. The star in sign (a) and the camel in sign (b) are small differences, but they could be such critical attributes that they prompt large differences in their respective signs' interpretants. In this light, an icon could be defined as a sign that resembles its object on those critical attributes necessary to define it as a member of a basic category. However, categorization research also suggests that when viewers differ in what they know about objects (for example, because of expertise or exposure to advertising), their criteria for distinguishing between objects can differ (e.g. Loken and Ward 1990: 124; Rosch *et al.* 1976: 430). If the key attributes for category resemblance can differ from person to person, then similarity (the key criterion for iconicity) is based not on objective criteria but on environmental context and cultural conventions (see also Eco 1979: 206).

Thus, a person raised in Cairo who has never seen a Christmas tree might see both sign (a) and sign (b) as icons of a pyramid. Sign (a) might be seen as a pyramid at night with a path leading to it, and (b) as a pyramid during the day with a camel in front of it. This possibility makes it difficult to deny that, to some people in some situations, anything triangular, from a church steeple to a piece of pie might stand as an icon for a pyramid. In fact, given the right perspective and choice of criteria, even non-triangular objects such as an automobile or a Florida orange could be icons for a pyramid. This is Bierman's (1962) criticism of the concept of an icon. Because similarity is in the eye of the beholder, "everything in the universe iconically denotes everything in the universe and . . . everything in the universe is iconically denoted by any other thing in the universe" (Bierman 1962: 245).

Surprisingly, Peirce himself (1940: 102) is willing to grant this extreme when he writes that "anything . . . can be an Icon of anything, in so far as it is like that thing and used as a sign of it." So how might an orange usefully serve as an icon of a pyramid? Imagine that a friend has just returned from researching consumer behavior near the Great Pyramids of Egypt, and that she has invited you over to hear about her experiences. To illustrate the different routes taken by tour guides around the pyramids, she grabs three oranges from a nearby fruit bowl and sets them on the table in relative locations that resemble the relative locations of the pyramids themselves. In this example, the oranges are icons in the sense that their visible physical relationships to one another are similar to the visible physical relationships of the actual pyramids to one another. In Peirce's (1940: 105) words, "there is an analogy between the relations of the parts of each." Such examples of icons only add ammunition to Bierman's attack. If an orange can be an icon of a pyramid then, indeed, anything in the universe can be an icon for anything, and an icon cannot be defined in terms of simple similarity.

Defenders of the icon might protest that the above example focuses on symbolic pyramids (not iconic ones) because the oranges represent their objects more by convention than similarity. Three oranges on a table mean nothing in relation to a friend's research in Egypt until she establishes the convention that each orange signifies a pyramid. In contrast, if someone displays a photograph or a realistic painting of a pyramid, no conventions are required. A photograph of a pyramid is a better example of an icon because it is so obviously similar to its object.

Gombrich (1959) counters this point in his classic book on representation. Viewers of art, he argues, may believe that some paintings, such as da Vinci's *Mona Lisa*, are self-evidently iconic while others, such as Picasso's *Guernica*, are more self-evidently symbolic. However, this distinction comes not from inherent qualities of the paintings themselves, but from viewers' understanding of how certain visual artists in their culture make semiotic decisions (see also Scott 1994a). For instance, in the West, a painting showing a side view of a bird is likely to show only one leg because Westerners are trained to understand that the bird's second leg is "hidden" by the one that is depicted. However, when the same bird picture is shown to an Australian Aborigine who is not trained in Western aesthetics, the image is described as being disturbingly unrealistic because a bird really has two legs, not one (Gombrich 1959: 119; see also Goodman 1976: 37). When we perceive a sign to be "obviously" similar to its object, this is only because the sign benefits from a culturally-based semiotic disguise: the masquerade of realistic conventions. These conventions are a masquerade because, unlike the explicit conventions needed to make an orange stand for a pyramid, the conventions of realistic representation are so implicit that we do not usually notice that they are operating.

The foregoing analysis reduces all icons to symbols, because all icons require conventions in order to be seen as icons. But all is not lost for the special status of icons. A useful solution comes from Ransdell (1986), who examines icons from the perspective of the viewer's experience, rather than from the detached perspective of the philosopher or art theorist (see also Baron 1984). Ransdell accepts that viewers must learn conventions in order to read a sign as an icon. However, he emphasizes that once users have learned these conventions, they habitually accept the iconic masquerade at face value. In his words, they have been trained to see the object "in the sign" instead of "separate from the sign," and seem not to be bothered by the idea that conventions, not similarity, lie at the roots of this semiotic experience. Ransdell's conclusion is that the learning required to see an object in a sign is not important to the definition of an icon. More important is the phenomenological fact that sign readers do have the experience of seeing the object in the sign, which is a different semiotic experience than seeing the object as separate from the sign (Ransdell 1986: 68; see also Merrell 1997).

A rudimentary example of Ransdell's "in the sign" versus "separate from the sign" can be found in Figures 1.3 and 1.4. In Figure 1.3, many readers will see a flower on a pedestal, while in Figure 1.4 they will see two English words. In each figure, the same long and thin sign plays different roles in its revelation of the object. We see it as a support in Figure 1.3 because we are familiar with certain conventions of line drawing. As a result, we are likely to see the pedestal as being to some extent on the very page we are examining. On the other hand, in Figure 1.4 we see the same sign as the subject of a sentence because we are familiar with the conventions of the English language. As an English word, this sign stands for something that we cannot see in the sign: the "I" (real or possible) who is saying the statement (Stern 1994).

Because all signs have the potential to be seen as an icon, index, or symbol, it must be admitted that neither Figure 1.3 nor Figure 1.4 are purely iconic or symbolic. However, my aim is not to establish a clearer distinction between the three types of sign than Peirce himself was willing to grant. Instead, I want to use Ransdell's (1986) approach to argue that when we speak of an icon, an index, or a symbol, we are not referring to objective qualities of the sign itself, but to a viewer's experience of the sign. It therefore might be more accurate to refer to iconic, indexical and symbolic experiences instead of iconic, indexical and symbolic signs.

Figure 1.3 Seeing the object "In the Sign"

Figure 1.4 Seeing the object "separate from the sign"

What is an iconic experience of a sign? By definition, seeing an icon is accompanied by a sense that in perceiving the sign we have had a sensual experience similar to seeing the object itself. Because we can see the object in the sign, we are often left with a sense that the icon has brought us closer to the truth than if we had instead seen an index or a symbol. This is what Bernstein (in Bollobás 1986: 279) describes as our "tacit acceptance of the visual as a brute reality." Hasenmuller (1981: 143–4) takes a similar view of religious icons: "An icon of the Virgin *is* the Virgin she is 'present' in it. This dimension of presence . . . consists in a special kind of value." Peirce himself writes that an icon is different from other signs because it reveals "unexpected truths" (1940: 105–6) and has "more to do with the living character of truth" than symbols or indices (Peirce 1991: 252). Peirce (in Ransdell 1986: 71) also describes the iconic experience of a painting saying that "there is a moment when we lose the consciousness that it [the painting] is not the thing," at which point "the distinction of the real and the copy disappears, and it is for the moment a pure dream" (in Ransdell 1986: 71). Even Eco (1979), who sides with Bierman (1962) in arguing against the theoretical usefulness of icons, recognizes the unique potential of an iconic experience:

> Maybe an "iconic" solution is not conventional when it is proposed, but it becomes so step by step, the more its addressee becomes acquainted with it. At a certain point the iconic representation, however stylized it may be, appears to be more true than the real experience, and people begin to look at things through the glasses of iconic convention.
>
> (Eco 1979: 204–5)

The enchanting potential of icons to become substitutes for their real objects is undoubtedly what gave Socrates such concern about the imitative arts, and what drives religions to place taboos on graven images (Mitchell 1986: 32). Iconic experiences promise such a compelling reflection of reality that, in their presence, it is easy to forget Burke's warning that all signs also entail an undeniable deflection of reality.

Textual icons and the icons of consumer research

Representation in science is different in many ways from representation in art. Yet, one of Peirce's main contributions is to highlight that a sign operates via the same mechanics, regardless of whether it represents everyday experience, religious experience, or consumer experience (Merrell 1997: 32). The connection between representation in art and in science is also extensively analyzed by Gadamer (1996), who argues that both modes of communication share a number of critical philosophical underpinnings. But until now my discussion of icons has focused primarily on pictures, while the most prevalent signs in consumer research are words, numbers, and other textual symbols. Thus, in this section, I will embark on a theoretical path from iconic pictures to iconic texts. This path can be made arduous by a tradition of debate over whether texts or pictures have superior representative power (Goodman 1976; Gombrich 1959; Mitchell 1986). Alternatively, it can be shortened considerably by the observation that pictures are "texts" (e.g. Messaris 1997; Scott 1994b), and that some texts (such as Chinese writing) are essentially pictographic. However, rather than arguing about the potential differences (or lack thereof) between texts and pictures, my aim in this section is to show only that what Westerners generally consider to be texts can be iconic.

When Peirce writes that anything can be an icon of anything, he explicitly includes words as potential icons (Peirce 1940: 105). A relatively straightforward example of an iconic word is that representing a non-human sound, such as that of a grandfather clock ("tick-tock") or a cow ("moo"). More subtle examples of verbal icons come from the field of mimology, where scholars draw connections between objects in the world and the shapes and sounds of the words that represent them (for an extensive review, see Genette 1995). For example, the "rough" sound made by the consonants "gr" is said to be iconically appropriate for rough-meaning words such as "grate" and "grind."

Literary critics have also examined the iconic quality of literature and poetry. The visual shape of poetry can be iconic, as with George Herbert's "The Altar," whose words are arranged in the shape of an altar (Morgan 1995: xlv; see Bollobás 1986 for other examples). Alternatively, the sounds and rhythms of literary works can also produce iconic experiences. For example, the "complex and teeming" vocabulary of Charles Dickens is said to resemble iconically the unstructured richness of the modern metropolis that was his object (Nänny 1986: 200–1). As another example, consider the following lines from Robert Frost's "The Span of Life:"

> The old dog barks backward without getting up.
> I can remember when he was a pup.

Bernhart (1986: 216) observes that the halting rhythm of the first line iconically represents the slowness of the old dog, whereas the flowing rhythm of the second represents the liveliness of the young dog. Those unschooled in literary conventions may not see an iconic metropolis in Dickens's prose or an iconic dog in Frost's poetry. But neither will those unschooled in the German language perceive a rooster's crow in "kikeriki," and this is just the point. One must be familiar with conventions – be they pictoral or textual – before one can experience icons. However, this requirement does not diminish the unique impact of an iconic experience.

In discussing verbal icons, I have expanded Ransdell's definition of an iconic experience from seeing the object in the sign to "perceiving" the object in the sign. Unlike seeing a pedestal in Figure 1.4, we do not visually see a dog in the words of Frost's poetry. But thanks to the rhythm of the words and assuming our training as readers of poetry, we may nonetheless perceive the dog in the sign. A more everyday example of a textual icon is a friend's letter which reflects the friend's manner of speaking so well that we can actually "hear" him or her talking as we read it. It is almost as if the friend is talking to us from the page. The experience of perceiving the friend in the text would not be felt by someone unfamiliar with the conventions of our friend's manner of speech. But when it is felt, it is not dissimilar from Peirce's painting experience, where for a moment he forgets the distinction between what is in front of him and what is being represented.

Let us now turn to the textual signs used in consumer research and explore the conditions under which these signs might produce iconic experiences. Under what conditions might we perceive a consumer experience in a consumer-research text? To explore an answer to this question, consider the representations in Figures 1.5, 1.6, and 1.7:

- Figure 1.5 represents via contrasting quotations the difference between the self-images of homeless consumers with previously happy home experiences and the self-images of those with previously unhappy home experiences (Hill 1991).

- Figure 1.6 represents via a multinomial logit formulation the probability that a particular household will buy a specific product on a particular purchase occasion (adapted from Fader and Hardie 1996).
- Figure 1.7 represents via contrasting numerical columns the way that consumers of different ages are differentially sensitive to underlying category structure versus surface cues (John and Sujan 1990).

Each of these figures is a sign chosen by consumer researchers to represent the experience and behavior of the consumer. If you have been trained as a consumer researcher, it is likely that at least one of the figures will catch your eye, and you

---

"I miss many of my possessions, especially my teddy bear that keeps me company, and my stuffed dogs that are so real people pet them! Also, my pictures of clowns and bears – my tablecloth even has bears on it! And a picture of the space shuttle given to me by my brother."

"My godson – he's my second cousin. He's one year old and a couple of months. I watch him, change his diaper, bathe him, feed him. I was the first person to turn him onto baby food! I feel good about myself doing that! He usually sleeps with me on the floor and the couch."

Figure 1.5 A representation of consumer self image
Source: Hill (1991)

$$P_{it} = \frac{\exp\left(\sum_{n=1}^{N} m_{in}\alpha_{nh} + \beta_h x_{it}\right)}{\sum_{j=1}^{J} \exp\left(\sum_{n=1}^{N} m_{jn}\alpha_{nh} + \beta_h x_{jt}\right)}$$

Figure 1.6 A representation of consumer purchase behavior
Source: Adapted from Fader and Hardie (1966)

	Number of underlying cues			Number of perceptual cues		
	Very young children	Younger children	Older children	Very young children	Younger children	Older children
Free sort	2.8	3.6	5.7	4.2	3.2	1.4
	(1.8)	(1.6)	(1.7)	(2.0)	(2.2)	(1.8)
Cued underlying sort	3.5	5.4	5.7	2.3	0.7	0.6
	(1.4)	(1.7)	(2.5)	(1.3)	(1.3)	(1.7)

Figure 1.7 A representation of consumer categorization
Source:: John and Sujan (1990)

will begin immediately to perceive the consumer experience "in the sign." It is also likely that one or both of the remaining representations will seem more distant from the consumer experience, perhaps considerably so.

When we feel that a sign in consumer research is distant from the consumer experience, we must on occasion be in the same position as Gombrich's Aborigine wondering why on earth someone would paint a two-legged animal as if it has only one leg. There are a number of related factors that put us in this position, but one of the most influential is academic specialization. In our work as consumer researchers, we are generally encouraged – by our own personal predilections and by the practicalities of our profession – to focus on a defined subset of theories, methodologies, and applications. By reading and re-reading the works of researchers with a similar expertise, we gain a literacy – or what Potter (1996: 116) calls an "interpretive repertoire" – in understanding their signs and in producing signs like theirs. At the same time, we do not gain a comparable literacy in the signs of other researchers. Our specialized literacy is further encouraged by the fact that it is often accompanied by a rationale: after careful consideration, reading, and discussion, many of us come to believe that certain signs are better representations of the consumer experiences that interest us, and that other signs are a bit too general, too specific, or too artificial.

This is not to say that the work of researchers using other interpretive repertoires will be entirely opaque to us. The Aborigine understands that the Westerner has intended to represent a bird, and the poetry novice understands that Frost has intended to represent a dog. However, our interpretive repertoires do dramatically influence our perception of consumer-research signs as icons, indices or symbols. For example, to a reader who is not quantitatively literate, Figure 1.6 may at best seem like a symbol. The consumer experience will appear to be separate from the sign and the relationship between sign and experience will seem more theoretical than actual. However, a reader truly literate with quantitative modeling techniques will also immediately see the consumer experience in the sign. There on the page, this reader will perceive how product attributes, consumer preferences, marketing activity, and competitive offerings all interact in a real consumer's mind to produce a real purchase decision on a given shopping trip.

Conclusion: signification and deception revisited

I began this chapter by suggesting that signification often involves at least a little deception. One of Peirce's (1982: 79–80) earliest assertions is that signification always offers only a partial truth because if it offered the complete truth it would destroy itself by becoming identical with its object. Similar thoughts from Socrates and Burke launched this chapter's examination of how we might create the most truthful signs, which make a clear connection between sign and object. My central conclusion from this line of reasoning is that the perceived link between sign and object is dependent on the semiotic context in which the sign is presented, and on the facility that a sign reader has in understanding signs in this context (see also Crosman 1980).

However, we cannot conclude from this that researchers who share interpretive repertoires are least likely to deceive one another. Such researchers may be more able to create iconic experiences for one another, but throughout this chapter we have seen that iconic experiences can be the most deceptive of all. Thus, the signs of researchers working with different interpretive repertoires than our own may be least likely to deceive us, because we will approach these signs with a skepticism that naturally precedes familiarity, and we may never experience their signs as icons.

It is not very disturbing to think that unfamiliar signs are likely to make us more critical and therefore less susceptible to deception or misrepresentation. More unsettling is the conclusion that the signs of those who share our interpretive repertoires may be most likely to deceive us. This kind of deception comes not because icons offer explicitly false information, but because they leave us with the impression that we have seen the object in the sign and have therefore come closer to the truth. Instead of drawing our attention to the gaps that always exist in representation, iconic experiences encourage us subconsciously to fill in these gaps and then to believe that there were no gaps in the first place. Of course, as consumer researchers, we have been trained to approach research with a skeptical attitude, and this makes us more vigilant readers of all types of research. But we must not forget to be most vigilant just at the moment when we think we are seeing the consumer experience in the sign. This is the paradox of representation: it may deceive most when we think it works best.

Acknowledgments

The author thanks Dawn Iacobucci, Barbara Stern, Bruce Hardie, and Lysa Miller for their helpful comments on previous drafts of this chapter.

References

Baron, N.S. (1984), "Iconicity in Language and Art," *Semiotica*, 52: 187–211.

Belk, R.W., Sherry, J.F., Jr., and Wallendorf, M. (1988), "A Naturalistic Inquiry into Buyer and Seller Behavior at a Swap Meet," *Journal of Consumer Research*, 14 (March), 449–70.

Bernhart, W. (1986) "The Iconic Quality of Poetic Rhythm," *Word & Image*, 2 (July–September): 209–27.

Bierman, A.K. (1962), "That There Are No Iconic Signs," *Philosophy and Phenomenological Research*, 23: 243–9.

Bollobás, E. (1986), "Poetry of Visual Enactment: The Concrete Poem," *Word & Image*, 2 (July–September): 279–85.

Burke, K. (1945) *A Grammar of Motives*, Los Angeles, CA: University of California Press.

Cook, T.D. and Campbell, D.T. (1979), *Quasi-Experimentation: Design & Analysis Issues for Field Settings*, Boston, MA: Houghton-Mifflin.

Crosman, R. (1980), "Do Readers Make Meaning?" in S.R. Suleiman and I. Crosman (eds), *The Reader in the Text*, Princeton, NJ: Princeton University Press.

Deely, J. (1986), "Idolum: Archeology and the Ontology of the Iconic Sign," in P. Bouissac, M. Herzfeld, and R. Posner (eds) *Iconicity: Essays on the Nature of Culture*, Germany: Stauffenburg Verlag, 29–49.

Derrida, J. (1976), *Of Grammatology*, trans. G.C. Spivak, Baltimore, MD: Johns Hopkins University Press.

Eco, U. (1979), *A Theory of Semiotics*, Bloomington, IN: University of Indiana Press.

Fader, P.S. and Hardie, B.G.S. (1996), "Modeling Consumer Choice among SKUs," *Journal of Marketing Research*, 33 (November): 442–52.

Gadamer, H.-G. (1996), *Truth and Method*, 2nd edn, London: Sheed & Ward.

Genette, G. (1995), *Mimologics*, trans. T.E. Morgan, Lincoln, NE: University of Nebrasca Press.

Gombrich, E.H. (1959), *Art & Illusion*, Hong Kong: Phaidon.

Goodman, N. (1976) *Languages of Art*, Indianapolis, IN: Hackett.

Hasenmuller, A.C. (1981), "The Function of Art as 'Iconic Text' An Alternative Strategy for a Semiotic of Art," *Semiotica*, 36: 135–52.

Hill, R.P. (1991), "Homeless Women, Special Possessions, and the Meaning of 'Home': An Ethnographic Case Study," *Journal of Consumer Research*, 18 (December), 298–310.

Hoopes, J. (ed.) (1991), *Peirce on Signs*, Chapel Hill, NC: University of North Carolina Press.

Hudson, L.A. and Ozanne, J.L. (1988), "Alternative Ways of Seeking Knowledge in Consumer Research," *Journal of Consumer Research*, 14 (March): 508–21.

John, D. R. and Sujan. M. (1990), "Age Differences in Product Categorization," *Journal of Consumer Research*, 16 (March): 452–60.

Kleine, R.E., III, and Kernan, J.B. (1991), "Contextual Influences on the Meanings Ascribed to Ordinary Consumption Objects," *Journal of Consumer Research*, 18 (December): 311–24.

Loken, B. and Ward, J. (1990), "Alternative Approaches to Understanding the Determinants of Typicality," *Journal of Consumer Research*, 17 (September): 111–26.

Merrell, F. (1997), *Peirce, Signs, and Meaning*, Toronto, Canada: University of Toronto Press.

Messaris, P. (1997), *Visual Persuasion: The Role of Images in Advertising*, Thousand Oaks, CA: Sage.

Mitchell, W.J.T. (1986), *Iconology: Image, Text, Ideology*, Chicago: University of Chicago Press.

Morgan, T.E. (1995), "Invitation to a Voyage in Cratylusland," intr. to *Mimologics*, G. Genette, Lincoln, NE: University of Nebraska Press, xxi-lxvi.

Nänny, M. (1986), "Iconicity in Literature," *Word & Image*, 2 (July–September): 199–208.

Nöth. W. (1995) *Handbook of Semiotics*, Bloomington, IN: University of Indiana Press.

Ogden, C.K. and Richards, I.A. (1923 [1985]), *The Meaning of Meaning*, London: Ark.

Peirce, C.S. (1940), *Philosophical Writings of Peirce*, J. Buchler (ed.) New York, NY: Dover Publications.

—— (1982), *The Collected Papers of Charles Sanders Peirce, Volume One (1857–1866)*, M.H. Fisch (ed.), Bloomington, IN: Indiana University Press.

—— (1991), *Peirce on Signs*, J. Hoopes (ed.), Chapel Hill, NC: University of North Carolina Press.

Pelc, J. (1986), "Iconic Signs or Iconic Uses of Signs?" in P. Bouissac, M. Herzfeld, and R. Posner (eds), *Iconicity: Essays on the Nature of Culture*, Germany: Stauffenburg Verlag, 7–15.

Plato (1989), "Republic," trans. P. Shorey in E. Hamilton and H. Cairns (eds) *The Collected Dialogues of Plato*, Princeton, NJ: Princeton University Press, 575–844.

Potter, J. (1996), *Representing Reality*, Thousand Oaks, CA: Sage.

Ransdell, J. (1986), "On Peirce's Conception of the Iconic Sign," in P. Bouissac, M. Herzfeld, and R. Posner (eds), *Iconicity: Essays on the Nature of Culture*, Germany: Stauffenburg Verlag, 51–74.

Rosch, E., Mervis, C.B., Gray, W.D., Johnson, D.M., and Boyes-Braem, P. (1976), "Basic Objects in Natural Categories," *Cognitive Psychology*, 8: 382–439.

Saussure, F.D. (1959), *Course in General Linguistics*, C. Bally and A. Sechehaye (eds), trans. W. Baskin, New York, NY: McGraw-Hill.

Scott, L. (1994a), "Images in Advertising: The Need for a Theory of Visual Rhetoric," *Journal of Consumer Research*, 21 (September): 252–73.

—— (1994b), "The Bridge from Text to Mind: Adapting Reader-Response Theory to Consumer Research," *Journal of Consumer Research*, (December): 461–80.

Sheriff, J.K. (1989), *The Fate of Meaning*, Princeton, NJ: Princeton University Press.

Shulman, D. (1994), "Dirty Data and Investigative Methods: Some Lessons from Private Detective Work," *Journal of Contemporary Ethnography*, 23 (July): 214–53.

Silverman, K. (1983), *The Subject of Semiotics*, Oxford: Oxford University Press.

Singer, M. (1984), *Man's Glassy Essence*, Ann Arbor, MI: UMI Books on Demand.

Stern, B. (1994), "Authenticity and Textual Persona: Postmodern Paradoxes in Advertising Narrative," *International Journal of Research in Marketing*, 11 (September): 387–400.

Stierle, K. (1980), "The Reading of Fictional Texts," in S.R. Suleiman and I. Crosman (eds), trans. I. Crosman and T. Zachrau *The Reader in the Text*, Princeton, NJ: Princeton University Press, 83–105.

Tallis, R. (1995), *Not Saussure*, 2nd edn, New York, NY: St. Martin's Press.

2

QUANTITATIVE TOOLS AND REPRESENTATION

Dawn Iacobucci

Researchers who rely upon quantitative methods have representational issues like their qualitative colleagues. Most of the chapters in this book focus on issues for the qualitative researcher. This chapter focuses on representational issues faced by the quantitative researcher.

Many representational issues regarding quantitative techniques are implicit, having been examined explicitly only as each new quantitative tool is created, or being re-examined anew only when some sort of fresh controversy sparks. No major debates are currently "hot" in quantitative representation, and so to read the literature, an outsider might form the impression that there are no such issues, or if there are, they are of little concern. This impression is misleading – the very nature of quantitative methods requires that observed phenomena become represented as numbers, which may then be manipulated to varying degrees of torture and enlightenment.

A consumer behavior researcher uses theories and interests to choose a topic of study. Focal phenomena are further selected and rules are used to assign numbers to subsequent observations. The numbers themselves are simplifications, signs or symbols of the recorded behavior. The issue of representation for the quantitative researcher is to map the observed phenomenon onto numbers that somehow capture the essence of that which is observed. The question of representation then is how that mapping occurs, what appropriate manipulations may be made on the numerical symbols to yield greater insights, and how one captures phenomenal essence. These issues correspond to the three primary quantitative tools that are useful in representation: measurement, statistics, and modeling. This chapter considers each.

In measurement, we map numbers onto characteristics we wish to represent so that the numbers behave roughly like the phenomenon being measured. We look for convergence across multiple measures or raters, and we use techniques such as factor analysis and scaling to assist in the measurement mapping.

Statistics are used in the social sciences to establish laws of predictable and replicable behaviors. In particular, in this chapter we examine the scientific logic of Aristotle's syllogisms to understand validation versus falsification and relate this logic to research versus statistical null hypotheses.

The very intention of modeling is the representation of interesting phenomena, albeit in a simplified version. Unfortunately, in that simplification, models can be capricious in their assumptions. Let us examine each of these three primary tools in turn.

Measurement

As social scientists, we are often interested in observing and understanding the behavior of individuals or corporations in the marketplace. We may observe two consumers, one who makes a purchase using a coupon, and one who does not, and we may label the former "price sensitive." We may observe two firms and seek to understand whether the apparently greater employee satisfaction in one firm contributes to that firm's higher customer satisfaction indices. When comparisons yield obvious, literally qualitatively different results, such as the behavioral use of a coupon or not, we do not need numbers except to demonstrate how much more of a quality one consumer has than another or to finesse our understanding of that behavior by relating it to other observations made on those same respondents. Numbers help mostly in distinguishing subtle patterns: for example, the point along a pricing continuum at which the consumer becomes sensitive; the ratings of satisfaction that predict whether the consumer will repeat or withdraw purchase, and so forth. When patterns are apparent, numbers serve as summary indices but are redundant in identifying the phenomenon.

For many social scientists, measurement has come to mean the hierarchy of scales commonly attributed to Stevens (1951). In this hierarchy, a data point is classified as nominal, ordinal, interval, or ratio.[1] Let us quickly review these labels. Nominal variables are those that represent qualities that differ categorically on observations such as brand choice among consumers. Given that brand choice is only nominally different, we can claim no higher properties for the numbers representing the brands. For example, Nestle may be assigned a "1" and Hershey a "2," or vice versa.

Ordered variables are those whose numbers express more or less of the quality being measured, such as rankings among brands. For example, a consumer may prefer Hershey to Nestle, and the ranks would be 1 and 2 respectively. Alternatively, we could score these preferences as 1 and 27 because we do not know the strength of the consumer's preference.

Nominal and ordinal data are best analyzed using statistics like frequencies or percentages and log linear or logit models. Means and correlations cannot be computed or interpreted in a meaningful manner because the numbers have such weak measurement properties that they only reflect categorical or ordered differences.

Interval scales are those variables for which differences between numbers are meaningful. Strictly speaking, ratings scales like Likert (strongly agree to strongly disagree) or semantic differential scales (good to bad, intense to weak) are only ordinal and not interval because the difference between a 6 and 7 may not be psychologically equivalent to the difference between a 3 and 4 on the scale. Nevertheless, such ratings scales are frequently assumed to be interval in property to enable the computation of somewhat more sophisticated statistics, including means, standard deviations, and correlation coefficients.

Finally, ratio scales are those with meaningful zeros such as the number of Cubs' wins by the end of April of any given year, the likelihood of attending a Demi Moore movie this weekend, and so forth. Scales higher on the hierarchy subsume properties of the less sophisticated scales, so ratio variables are those with numbers that reflect a meaningful zero, intervals, order, and categorical distinctions.

This simple four-level hierarchy is most of what is meant by measurement. We wish to assign numbers to the phenomena we observe because manipulating numbers (in statistics or modeling) further instructs our scientific pursuit in terms of being able to describe and predict phenomena. However, we wish to be strict in the application of numbers – they are not arbitrary. Thus, we create these simple rules of mapping numbers onto the focal characteristics so that the numbers behave roughly like the phenomenon being measured, and, subsequently, we manipulate the measurements with statistical tools theorized to be appropriate.

There are a few additional measurement tools that have yielded helpful results in our pursuit of labeling phenomena with numbers. First, we acknowledge that even with the aforementioned guidelines, our assigned numbers may be errorful. We assume that any given indicator variable is a function of a deterministic true reflection that is somewhat contaminated by measurement error. When consumers complete questionnaires by circling numbers on a 9–point scale, we mindlessly key-code their responses into a data set as if the selected number from the 9–point scale were carved in stone. We know enough about psychological responding to consider that there may be limitations in terms of the reliability and validity of the respondents' answers: various response biases, fatigue, mood, and so forth. Thus, as with any scientific tool, we seek convergence.

Convergence is desirable because it is considered to be a means of obtaining a unified perspective on the truth of the phenomenon. Divergence can be interesting and useful in generating subsequent theoretical propositions, but in the examination of a given hypothesis, we seek convergence upon one message, obtained from multiple questionnaire items, raters, time points, research methodologies, and so forth.

Convergence can be achieved in a number of ways. Most commonly, we develop multiple items to measure the focal construct and make assumptions that while the responses to each item may be somewhat errorful, presumably the response to the entire pattern of items will be less so. The items should covary if they measure anything, and determining patterns of covariance is what we call factor analysis (Kim and Mueller 1978).

We can also seek convergence by having more than one respondent make judgments, as when multiple informants report on the relational properties of their firms' joint alliances or when multiple graduate students use a common behavioral coding scheme to record consumer behavior in the marketplace. Covariation in this paradigm is termed "multirater agreement". We would hope that if a phenomenon were "real" then two or more observers would produce similar constructions about its character. When multiple raters present divergent observations, we usually seek to reconcile the discrepancies, perhaps learning something about their perceptual differences in the process, but almost always seeking an aggregate, consensual view.

A final methodological tool that has been useful in the pursuit of good measurement is scaling. Most scaling conducted these days is multidimensional in character (Kruskal and Wish 1978), but its origins were unidimensional in that researchers were seeking methods to create clean scales tapping a single construct. Techniques such as Thurstone's pairwise comparisons are sophisticated in their very simplicity. Few assumptions are made about the respondent; he or she may be asked a binary question, such as, "Do you prefer *ER* or *Chicago Hope*?," "Is Pepsi or Coke sweeter?," "Would you vote for Greeneggs or Ham?" We may be suspicious as to whether consumers can truly make 7–point or 9–point distinctions with any inherent meaning, but the simplicity of a binary choice is such that we may grant that a consumer can report on such preferences with relatively little error.

If the binary questioning format were the only machinery that scaling offers, then presumably we would not have progressed beyond the nominal level in our measurement hierarchy. Instead, with a few relatively benign assumptions (for example, that preferences are normally distributed), we can assign scale values to the stimuli being considered with precision that increases roughly as the number of stimuli increases. The reason is that the addition of each new brand, say, adds data points for which that new brand is compared to all previous brands, and the model must fit the brand along the (uni-dimensional or multidimensional) scale in such a way as to be consistent with as many of the binary judgments as possible.

For example, if twice as many people prefer Coke to Pepsi, and people prefer Pepsi to 7up by odds of two to one, and people prefer Coke to 7up by four to one, then scale values of 25, 50, and 100 for 7up, Pepsi, and Coke respectively would fit the pattern of preference data. In general, the scaled values do not perfectly predict the actual judgment data, and the question becomes one of how well the model fits, an issue of statistics that we consider next. At this point, however, we note that from binary (nominal) judgments, various scaling methods can yield interval-level or even ratio-level scales that reflect the extent to which one brand is preferred to another.

At the very least we see that social scientists are very much concerned with the appropriate use of measurement. Assigning numbers to observations is intentional, and there are tools to try to strengthen this conceptual mapping (Coombs 1964). The representation issue is that the researcher's intention is to represent the phenomenon as faithfully as possible, without introducing inaccuracies by assigning numbers with fewer or greater properties than the phenomenon warrants.

We might note that all sciences in which observations are taken struggle with measurement issues. We often look longingly to the "hard" sciences as if they have a simpler situation because they tend not to take measures on unpredictable, flighty, fickle humans, and we seem to hold a collective belief that gravity is more consistent than household shopping behavior. However, in a delightful little paperback called *The Game of Science*, McCain and Segal (1988: 69) note that measurement issues are pervasive. They give an example of Avogadro's number (the number of molecules in one "mole," a large unit useful in their discussions), 6.02486×10^{23} which impresses one as terribly precise. They note that this is an estimate with 0.0027 percent error, not quite 6-sigma, if you will, but certainly more precise than we could claim on a 9-point rating scale. Nevertheless, this percentage translates to the estimate being off by roughly some 1.6×10^{19} (that is, 16,267,000,000,000,000,000) molecules. Try selling that level of imprecision to the journals!

Statistics

Let us similarly consider the pursuit of statistics in a non-technical, conceptual manner. Why do we make such computations, contorting our little data points into some hopefully powerful index? Statistics are simply quantitative tools to help us identify whether the phenomenon we just observed is "real" or not in the sense of whether it is replicable, and is it related to and perhaps explainable by another phenomenon, etc. There are many fine introductory statistics books (for example, Hays 1988), but the issue at present is the logic underlying the statistics.

Take a timely example of the concern for the relationship between employee empowerment and customer service. A researcher may want to believe and argue conceptually for the following general principle:

   i   All empowered employees will provide good customer service.

In a particular firm, then, the researcher may wish to demonstrate that:

   ii   Firm XYZ's employees are empowered.

The researcher deduces and wishes to test and verify the implication that:

   iii   Therefore, Firm A's employees will provide good customer service.

If we label the component pieces of this argument, A = "firms with empowered employees" and B = "providers of good customer service," then we may use symbolic logic shorthand notation. This notation is in itself a representational convention, and it allows us to see the structure of the underlying Aristotelian syllogism:

   i   All As are Bs.

   ii Firm XYZ is an A.

   iii Therefore, Firm XYZ is a B.

One question that statistics can help address is the problem of non-universalism. A general conceptual statement might be true that most As are Bs. However, insofar as i states that all As must be Bs for the statement to be true, the empirical discovery of a single A that is not a B negates the major premise. The relationship might be softened to hold that generally most As are Bs. The few As that were not Bs would be presumably attributed to measurement or experimenter error, for example. Then statistics can provide quantitative thresholds to define most in contrast to the unforgiving all.

Most frequently, statistics are used to study these associations in a logically equivalent form that takes on a slightly different appearance. The same logical argument may be presented alternatively in an if–then statement:

   i′   *If* employees are empowered, *then* they will deliver good customer service.

   ii′ *And* Firm XYZ's employees are empowered.

   iii′ *Therefore*, Firm XYZ (should) provide good customer service.

And the argument in shorthand appears as:

   i′   If A then B.

   ii′ And A.

   iii′ Therefore B.

In the literature, these if–then relationships are commonly presented in the form of causal linkages from A to B, frequently drawn as arrows in diagrammatic form (as per path diagrams, structural equations modeling, or even simpler "boxologies" or frameworks that relate some concepts to other concepts).

Statistics are tools that allow us to test these arguments. The question is how to define A and B. If we began with the statement:

   i″ If my hypothesis is true, then I will observe phenomenon X

then A would be "hypothesis is true." According to this reasoning, the second premise must be "And A," or "yes, my hypothesis is true." But we cannot simply validate the premise with no empiricism, or why call ourselves scientists? Empirical observations are means of testing our conceived representation of reality. One may be tempted to say that the second premise becomes:

   ii″ I observed phenomenon X,

thereby concluding that:

iii″ The hypothesis is true.

However, doing this commits the fallacy of affirming the consequent (the "if" part of i″ is the antecedent, the "then" part is the consequent, and we may speak of either being affirmed and supported or negated and rejected, though only some combinations are logically sound; Beardsley 1975; Dauer 1989; Slife and Williams 1995). Phenomenon X may arise for reasons other than our favorite hypothesis. Thus, the conclusion iii″ is invalid.

If we were to begin with the first major premise i″, it would comprise valid reasoning in support of the hypothesis if we were to negate the phenomenon X. That is, it is valid to argue:

    i″ If my hypothesis is true, then I will observe phenomenon X

    ii″ I did not observe phenomenon X, so

    iii″ My hypothesis is not true.

Thus, these structures of reasoning and empirical verification allow us only to falsify, not to validate. That is, we may deduce that a hypothesis is *not* likely, but we may not prove that a hypothesis *is* true.

Notice though, that the argument form requires us not to observe the focal phenomenon. However, we are uneasy about arguing from the null voice, since we know that there are many plausible explanations for not validating an empirical finding (for example, poor power resulting from small samples). Thus, while we become enthusiastic about relationships between A and B and present research hypotheses (or propositions) in our articles, logically we are merely testing statistical null hypotheses of the following sort:

    i‴ If the null H_0 is true, then in our data we shall see $\mu_1 = \mu_2$.

    ii‴ In our data, we (hope to) see that $\mu_1 \neq \mu_2$; i.e. not $\mu_1 = \mu_2$.

    iii‴ Thus we conclude that the null hypothesis is not true.

By implication then, since the null and the alternative (research) hypotheses are mutually exclusive, we thereby conclude that the alternative hypothesis is plausible or at least better supported than the null.[2]

Step i in these arguments is created by the researcher, drawing from the literature and derivations from previous research, and writing a statement of expected implication: if . . . then. This selection in itself is the beginning of a representational issue, given that the researcher is determining where to focus the conceptual effort. Step ii is tested empirically by the researcher using statistics to see whether the phenomenon is demonstrably existent in data to a significant degree, implying substantial effect size and likely reproduceability. Step iii is a simple deduction resulting from i and ii. When the result in iii is counter to the researcher's desires, steps i and ii are often reconsidered for error. Thus, while non-positivists are explicit in their interest in representation, scientists working from within a positivist paradigm must acknowledge the implicit representation issues.

Most assuredly there is potential for error in these steps – the conceptualization and clear thinking required in i are not always present, and formal errors often occur in step ii. In particular, in step ii, statistics are used with conventionally agreed upon, but yes, somewhat arbitrary rules (e.g., alpha = 0.05). Users of statistics realize that they might fall into Type I or Type II errors, finding or not finding phenomena when they should not have or should have, respectively. Statistics are further affected by the previous topic of measurement – inaccurate scaling adds noise to a quantitative system designed to detect signals and thereby impedes its power and performance. However, we proceed because adding noise to the quantitative system only makes the system more conservative and less likely to represent phenomena clearly. While this bias can kill careers, it presumably adds minimal junk to our collective science. Evidently the system screens out researchers who are poor at representation.

There are certainly many types of statistics, some better suited for nominal and ordinal data (categorical methods, frequencies, percentages) and others that make better use of the additional information contained in interval and ratio data (linear methods, means, variances, correlations, and so forth). All other statistics are simply footnotes to these, finessing a more encompassing analysis of the data or a more intricate consideration of the data pattern's subtleties. So the reader who has always been intimidated or confused by statistics is best-off taking another course by someone who can communicate the material better. The researcher armed with the basic logic of statistics will provide more enlightenment than the researcher steeped in the statistical trees without a clue about the research forest.

Let us now turn to the last of the three major quantitative tools, modeling. There are certainly relationships among measurement, statistics, and modeling. For example, we have seen that measurement impacts statistics. Statistics are also often used as indicators of a model's fit (such as how much of the variance observed in one phenomenon is explained by what we know about another). It is not always clear where the statistics of data analysis leave off and where modeling begins, but I believe that it has to do with how seriously one takes one's assumptions. For example, in fitting regressions, we assume that the relationships are linear; as one effect goes up, so does the other in some specifiable proportion. However, our theories rarely posit particular shapes of functions (the omnipresent inverted-U may be an exception), because we know these linear shapes are simple and often describe our data suitably well. The modeler, on the other hand, wishes to understand precisely whether the functional relationship is linear or quadratic or logarithmic or whatever in character.

Modeling

There are good introductory texts on modeling (Lilien and Kotler 1983), and since much of what the field of marketing refers to as modeling is really econometrics, those sources should also be consulted. Consumer behavior seeks universal laws, the equivalent of $E = mc^2$ or rules regarding gravity, for consumer and firm behavior. The model then would be the expression, $E = mc^2$, and a statistical fit on that model would be $E = mc^2 + \epsilon$, where we would hope that ϵ, the error term, were small. In theories, we describe circumstances for which ϵ would not be small, because under those conditions the model that should hold is $E = k/mc^2$ or some such thing. That is, the initial hypothesis is too simple to hold in all complex situations.

Modeling is a close relative of measurement (no empirical progress can be made without being able to attach numbers to the phenomenon being modeled) and statistics (examination of model fit and improvement of model), and it is another powerful quantitative analytical tool. However, some legitimate complaints may be registered against some modeling work.

It is of course true that since models are simplifications of the world, their assumptions may not appear entirely descriptive of the world the modeler seeks to represent. However, sometimes the very first assumptions make the resulting modeling work so trivial as to have no apparent contribution except to show the modeler's technical skills. For example, when I hear talks that begin with the words, "Let us assume that we have no competition," I stop listening. There is nothing interesting in consumer or firm behavior in a marketplace that is wholly uncompetitive (and, thus, difficult to find empirically). The modelers inevitably promise to relax the assumption later in the talk, and sometimes they do and sometimes they do not, but even if they do, the intervening insights were a waste of time. A related critique is the uselessness of results obtained by modelers who are apparently unaware of assumptions being made that restrict the meaning or applicability of their subsequent analytical work.

There are also examples of models that make no sense. I have written critically (e.g. Iacobucci *et al.* 1994) about a model proposed in which X was a function of A and B, where A was defined at the outset to be C-D:

$$X \ = \ \text{fn (A and B)} \ = \ \text{fn (C-D and B)},$$

and subsequently, B was defined to be C-D, resulting in:

$$X \ = \ \text{fn (C-D and C-D)},$$

a result from the redundancy department of redundancy. This sort of error is thankfully rare.

More often a poor model is one that is simply confusing. If we return to our logic of "If A, then B," we note that for some models, the conceptualized structure of A can be very complicated. As a result, when the deduced finding B does not occur, and the researcher concludes, "not A," the researcher can be left with little new knowledge, because there are so many components within the complicated A that could have yielded the misfit prediction. That is, we would be left with no understanding as to why B did not occur.

Summary

We have explored measurement, statistics, and modeling in this chapter. Each of these quantitative tools bears on representational issues in science. Measurement issues are fundamental to representation: how we translate the observed phenomena of interest into codes and numbers that may be manipulated. Statistics offer rules of thumb as to how the numerical symbols may be manipulated: what sort of hypotheses may be examined and what logic underlies the testing. Modeling is also fundamental to representation: how we might create a mathematical representation that is parsimonious yet captures the primary nature of the phenomenon.

The philosophies and issues of representation in quantitative work are not that different from those in qualitative research. It is simply the case that our primary metaphor is numbers. We strive to understand which numbers are to be selected and what should be done with those select values.

To sum up, it is clear that each of these quantitative tools must be used with some knowledge, caution, and facility. However, they are simply tools to track the scientific logic of comparing cases and drawing general conclusions. Scientific logic, contribution and progress can (of course) also be conducted using qualitative techniques; it is simply the case that sometimes quantitative tools are useful. Thus, in conclusion, for those qualitative researchers who have experienced p-value envy, know that:

$$Q_u \, A \mathcal{N}^t = he^{L\Pi} \, (\phi_u \, L),$$

$$\beta_u T \neq \int u^{\Pi} \, (\epsilon R) \, I^{or}$$

Notes

[1] The first letters form the acronym, "noir," the French word for black. On marketing research midterms, I give MBA students a "bonus point" if they can tell me the French word for black. It is evidently not a particularly useful acronym, because usually they have forgotten it – students counter by giving me the word for black in Spanish, Hebrew, or Japanese.

[2] See Cohen (1994) and Cortina and Dunlap (1997) for discussions of the complexities of probabilistic reasoning.

Acknowledgments

I wish to thank Kent Grayson, who instigated my involvement in this project, and to Barbara Stern, who encouraged and tolerated it. I am also grateful for their comments and those of Jonathan Schroeder on a previous draft of this chapter.

References

Beardsley, M.C. (1975) *Thinking Straight: Principles of Reasoning for Readers and Writers*, 4th edn, Englewood Cliffs, NJ: Prentice Hall.

Cohen, J. (1994) "The Earth is Round (p.<.05)," *American Psychologist*, 49: 997–1003.

Coombs, C.H. (1964) *A Theory of Data*, New York: Wiley.

Cortina, J.M. and Dunlap, W.P. (1997) "On the Logic and Purpose of Significance Testing," *Psychological Methods*, 2: 161–72.

Dauer, F.W. (1989) *Critical Thinking: An Introduction to Reasoning*, New York: Oxford University Press.

Hays, W.L. (1988) *Statistics*, 4th edn, New York: Holt, Rinehart and Winston.

Iacobucci, D., Grayson, K.A., and Ostrom, A.L. (1994) "The Calculus of Service Quality and Customer Satisfaction: Theoretical and Empirical Differentiation and Integration', in T.A, Swartz, D. Bowen, and S.W. Brown (eds) *Advances in Services Marketing and Management*, vol. 3, Greenwich, Ct: JAI Press, 1–67.

Kim, J. and Mueller, C.W. (1978) *Introduction to Factor Analysis: What it is and How to do it*, Beverly Hills, CA: Sage.

Kruskal, J.B. and Wish, M. (1978) *Multidimensional Scaling*, Beverly Hills, CA: Sage.

Lilien, G.L. and Kotler, P. (1983) *Marketing Decision Making: A Model-Building Approach*, New York: Harper and Row.

McCain, G. and Segal, E.M. (1988) *The Game of Science*, 5th edn, Pacific Grove, CA: Brooks/Cole.

Slife, B.D., and Williams, R.N. (1995) *What's Behind the Research? Discovering Hidden Assumptions in the Behavioral Sciences*, Thousand Oaks, CA: Sage.

Stevens, S.S. (1951) "Mathematics, Measurement, and Psychophysics," in S.S. Stevens (ed.) *Handbook of Experimental Psychology*, New York: Wiley.

3

NARRATOLOGICAL ANALYSIS OF CONSUMER VOICES IN POSTMODERN RESEARCH ACCOUNTS

Barbara B. Stern

> . . . under this almost infinite diversity of forms, narrative is present in every age, in every place, in every society; it begins with the very history of mankind and there nowhere is nor has been a people without narrative.
>
> (Barthes 1966: 79)

Narratives representing the "voice" of the consumer – prose passages in which the consumers' own words are reported – first appeared in the *Journal of Consumer Research* less than a decade ago and are in large part responsible for the changed look of the journal. The new look is signaled by articles in which indented passages of consumer-generated prose are interspersed with blocks of researcher-generated prose. Indentation is a printing convention signifying poly-vocality, for it separates the researcher's narrative voice from those of consumers. Articles with indents exemplify the postmodern spirit of eclecticism, drawing from traditions of ethnographic, existential-phenomenological, and introspective research. Verbal rather than numerical data are the raw material, and researchers engage in the collection, analysis, and presentation of individual "narratives" or "stories." Their mission is to identify, describe, and comment on consumption themes in the data set (see White 1973, 1987; Gossman 1978). Several alternative methods of collecting and analyzing verbal data have been set forth (see Belk *et al.* 1988; Heisley and Levy 1991; Thompson *et al.* 1989), and disciplinary debate centers on those processes (see Gould 1991, 1995; Wallendorf and Brucks 1993).

However, the debate has not extended to the problematics of writing and reading consumer culture (but see Joy 1991; Stern 1990). Thus, the influence of Hayden White's analysis of historical narratives (1973, 1987) and of W.B. Gallie's analysis of philosophical narratives (1968; see Danto 1985) has not yet spread to our field. In consequence, the narrative aspects of representation considered in anthropology (Van Maanen 1988), sociology (Richardson 1990, 1995), psychology (Halasz 1988), and organizational theory (Gephart 1996) still await examination in consumer research. We lack a critique of writing and reading consumer narratives from the perspective of literary criticism, "an influential source of new ideas about theory and method" (Marcus and Fisher 1986: 5) that has already invigorated other disciplines.

The purpose of this chapter is to begin this critique by problematizing consumption narratives much as Van Maanen (1988) and Marcus and Fisher (1986) did ethnographic tales. However, instead of following their adaptation of literary theory to develop narrative typologies (Van Maanen's realist, confessional, impressionist tales; Marcus and Fisher's realist, psychodynamic, modernist tales), I propose a return to literary theory to identify the building blocks of narratives and the problems therein. This requires accessing a specific body of criticism known as "narratology" (Todorov [1968] 1981), whose business is "the identification of structural elements and their diverse modes of combination, with recurrent narrative devices, and with the analysis of the kinds of discourse by which a narrative gets told" (Abrams 1993: 123).

My rationale for this decision is twofold. First, insofar as consumption narratives draw from traditions other than ethnography, analysis requires a back-to-basics theoretical framework. Second, by revisiting the basics, the study of general literary dimensions such as plot, character, and language (cf. White 1973) can be made more relevant to specific structural elements determined by the way that researchers and consumers tell their stories. The narratological approach enables closer scrutiny of the polyvocal relationships said to underlie postmodern research by bringing "to light some often overlooked narrative conventions . . . so that different modes of cultural portraiture can be identified, appreciated, compared, and perhaps improved" (Van Maanen 1988: 1). In this way, a new approach that challenges entrenched habits of writing and reading can contribute to improvement of "the representational style selected to join the observer and observed (the 'tale')" (Van Maanen 1988: xi).

To begin identifying areas where the juncture is weak, the chapter opens with an overview of general political and rhetorical problems that beset postmodern consumption narratives using verbal data. Their source is in the authorial dominance that characterizes researcher/consumer relationships, which is examined in detail. The chapter then moves to specific problems of voice in introspective, ethnographic, and existential-phenomenological articles in the *Journal of Consumer Research*, here used as the data set. It concludes with suggestions for remedying the problems and improving representation in three ways: clarification of narrative conventions, inclusion of silenced "others," and encouragement of narrative experiments.

Problematic narratives: politics, rhetoric, characterization

> . . . *why* is it that narration is so universal, present in all human
> beings everywhere? The fact that narrative is so universal, so
> "natural," may hide what is strange and problematic about it.
>
> (Miller 1990: 66)

Whereas modernist criticism takes narrative language for granted as a universal conduit linking a mental or material phenomenon to its verbal symbol, postmodern criticism focuses on the problematic network of meanings coproduced by authors, informants, and readers. These meanings are formally structured in accordance with rhetorical conventions (cf. McQuarrie and Mick 1996), here defined as narrative devices that writers use to stimulate reader responses (see Booth [1961] 1983). Conventions are often so internalized as "natural" by the interpretive community that neither readers nor writers question them (Fish 1980). However, articulation is essential to expose the unacknowledged political and ideological relationships.

Articles in the *Journal of Consumer Research* comprise the data set (see Table 3.1) used to provide examples. Table 3.1 lists the thirty-four articles in the *Journal of Consumer Research* (1987–95, volumes 14–22) in which consumer voices are represented in indented passages. No such articles pre-date 1987. The sample frame includes only those articles in which consumer prose was generated as part of a primary research project. The reason is that researcher shaping of primary data is the domain of interest and, hence, articles using quotations from historical sources (Belk 1992), court transcripts (Deighton and Grayson 1995), and previously published books/articles (e.g. Hirschman 1990) are excluded. This criterion reflects a distinction (Chatman 1978) between primary shaping of consumer text versus quoting secondary text, already shaped by another hand.

This data set was selected because its frame is the "journal of record" for the discipline, a status that conveys the interpretive community's stamp of approval (Fish 1980). Note that the accolade implies acceptance of coproduction as the norm, for reviewers and editors as much as researchers and informants influence the published account – what we read in the journal is a negotiated product. I want to emphasize this, lest anything in this chapter be mistakenly read as a trashing of a specific researcher's work. My comments are not aimed at any one researcher in particular but, rather, are intended as a critique of practices accepted by the entire discipline. To demonstrate this point, let me begin with an overview of general problems shared by consumption narratives.

Politics

The most evident problem in the negotiated product that we label "research" is that it is determined by the politics of exclusion. The consumer research canon,

Table 3.1 Consumption narratives 1987–95

Date	Authors	Subject	Raw data	Goal
9/87	Rook	Impulse buying	Three open-ended survey questions, self-completed or via interview	"Thicker description" using consumer verbatims
3/88	Belk, Sherry, Wallendorf	Swap meet	On-site interviews, fieldnotes, journals, memos, video/audio tapes	Ethnographic, naturalistic, emic/etic perspectives
9/88	Belk	Extended self	Depth interviews, fieldnotes	Conceptual overview
6/89	Belk, Wallendorf, Sherry	Odyssey: sacred/ profane	Interviews, fieldnotes, journals, videotapes	Ethnographic, researcher's use of revelatory incidents
9/89	Thompson, Locander, Pollio	E-P method	Audiotaped interviews	Phenomenological
	O'Guinn, Faber	Compulsive buying	Depth interviews, mailed survey	Phenomenological
	O'Guinn, Belk	Heritage village	On-site interviews, fieldnotes, video/audiotapes	Ethnographic, emic/etic perspectives
6/90	Sherry	Midwest flea market	On-site interviews, fieldnotes	Ethnographic case study of flea market
12/90	Hill, Stamey	Homeless	On-site interviews, fieldnotes photos, journals, audiotapes	Ethnographic "thick description"
	Mick, Demoss	Self gifts	Survey, unstructured questions, written responses	Phenomenological, content analysis, data analysis
	Fischer, Arnold	Gender and Xmas gifts	In-home interviews, structured questions	Field study, data analysis
	Thompson, Locander, Pollio	Married women's consumption	Unstructured interviews, audiotaped	Phenomenological
3/91	Mehta, Belk	Indian immigration	Depth interviews, inventory of rooms, photos	Ethnography of "favorite things"
	Schouten	Plastic surgery	Ethnographic interview with consumer and family, consumer journals	Phenomenological account
6/91	Wallendorf, Arnould	Thanks-giving	Depth interview, fieldnotes, photos	Ethnographic

Table 3.1 Consumption narratives 1987–95 (continued)

Date	Authors	Subject	Raw data	Goal
9/91	Gould	Self energy	Self-observation, memory	Introspective "thick description"
12/91	Heisley, Levy	Auto-driving (dinner)	Consumer tells story about picture, interview follows	Ethnographic, projective stimulus
	Hill	Homeless women	Observation, interviews, fieldnotes	Ethnographic
9/92	Hirschman	Addictive consumption	Interviews, group participation/ observer, audiotaped staff notes	Phenomenological case histories
	McQuarrie, Mick	Advertising, resonance	Interviews, semiotic analysis of ads	Phenomenological account of ad meanings
12/92	Mick, Buhl	Advertising and "life themes"	Two constructed interviews: experience of ad life experience, researchers' journals	Phenomenological account of ad meanings
6/93	Celsi, Rose, Leigh	Sky-diving	Depth interviews, photos, videotapes	Ethnographic account of phenomological experience
	Arnould, Price	River rafting	Focus groups, depth interviews, written protocols, fieldnotes, surveys	Multimethod account, tabular summary of methods
9/93	Otnes, Lowrey, Kim	Gift recipients	Depth interviews, notes on shopping trips, fieldnotes	"Thick description"
12/93	Belk, Coon	Gifts dating	Depth interviews, consumers' journals (on computers), Audiotaped interview, fieldnotes	Data analysis with coding by ZyIndex and WordCruncher
3/94	Tepper	Elderly and age cues	Audiotaped interviews with scripted questions.	Identify themes, experiment, develop model
	Hirschman	Pets	Audiotaped interviews, "begin at beginning," nondirective, nonjudgmental	Phenomenological account of relationship with pets
	Baben, Darden, Griffin	Shopping work/fun	Focus group transcripts	Analysis of focus group, scale development

Table 3.1 Consumption narratives 1987–95 (continued)

Date	Authors	Subject	Raw data	Goal
6/94	Penaloza	Mexican immigration	Interviews, fieldnotes, researcher's journal photos	Critical ethnography
12/94	Thompson, Pollio, Locander	Cultural views	Audiotaped interviews, verbatim transcripts	Phenomenological account of "unspoken" meanings
3/95	Kover	Copywriters	Audiotaped interviews, semi-structured	Discover "implicit" theories
	Patterson, Hill, Maloy	Abortion	Audiotaped interviews, "tell-us-your-story"	Phenomological approach to abortion decision
6/95	Holt	Baseball spectators	Observation at games	Ethnographic etic perspective, develop typology
	Schouten, McAlexander	New bikers	Interviews, fieldnotes, photos	Ethnographic account of subculture

Notes: Total of thirty-four articles, volumes 14–22.

like all others, is a political domain: some voices are more equal than others. Some are over-represented and others omitted; some are dominant and others are subordinate. The political status quo is enforced by negotiation in three stages: researchers/informants, researchers/reviewers/ editor(s), and researchers/read-ers. The problematics flow from the multistage process of producing research: going into the field, returning home to write (Marcus and Fisher 1986), and getting the work published.

In the first stage, exchange occurs between "experience-near" participants (informants) and "experience-far" ones (researchers) (Geertz's terms, 1973) who engage in the negotiated dialogues of fieldwork. Here, informants appear to have the upper hand, if only because they can sabotage the process: they can lie, distort experiences to impress or satisfy researchers, withdraw from contact, and so forth. However, once informants provide verbal data, they forfeit control.

In the second stage, researcher dominance is enforced when informants are reconstructed by researchers in the writing of an ethnographic account (Marcus and Fisher 1986). Power belongs to the "transmitters" of language (Shohat and Stam 1987), not to its originators; evidence that the convention of control over numerical data has been adopted by users of verbal data. Interestingly, the second stage does show polyvocality, but the extra voices are the "experience-far-far" ones – translators, friendly readers, reviewers, editors, and so forth. In the third stage, readers respond to the voices that make it onto the printed page. Reader response is acquiescent insofar as representational practices go unchallenged.

Yet a challenge should be mounted, especially in regard to the many segments of consumers who remain unrepresented. The most glaring absence is that of African-American consumers, not represented in any accounts of non-deviant consumption (Hill and Stamey 1990; Hirschman 1992). In this regard, the *Journal of Consumer Research* could fairly be retitled the *Journal of White Consumer Research*. Note that even though this exclusion is probably not deliberate, continued absence suggests implicit acceptance. So, too, does the absence of gay and lesbian voices and those of Asian-Americans and the under-representation of Hispanics (but see Peñaloza 1994). The claim to polyvocality does not possess face validity, for the politics of exclusion reduces the kinds of voices that are heard.

Rhetoric

Political exclusion works in tandem with rhetorical inclusion, for researchers are empowered to represent informant voices in whatever way they please. A pot-pourri of narrative conventions adds up to so arbitrary a research code that the consumer voices we do hear are dominated by the researcher's "positional super-iority" (Said 1979: 7). As Said pointed out in his attack on Western researchers' representation of non-Western cultures, rhetorical devices are used to empower writers and subordinate informants. His argument applies to our own discipline as well. Here, only one representational convention is universally respected – the prohibition against revealing an informant's real name in full. Other than that, both the "naming" of informants and the choice of formats for presenting their words vary from author to author. This sends the message that researchers are free to manipulate – or in Tyler's phrasing, "steal" – the only thing that informants possess – their voices (1987: 205).

In this regard, random conventions of naming sustain researcher power – naming is the means by which the giver bestows identity upon the recipient. The process in consumer research is mystifying – it is an aspect of control so well-accepted that it is never mentioned. That is, even though the labels given to informants are idiosyn-cratic, the reasons for one or another choice are unstated. Sometimes first names are used, sometimes nicknames or initials; sometimes no naming devices are used, merely gender/race/age abbreviations. The lack of uniformity implies both researcher imperialism and communal disinterest in what is perceived as a non-issue.

The same applies to variant formats for representing verbal data. The data set reveals numerous and disparate ways of presenting passages of consumer prose. In addition to indents, we also find tables (McQuarrie and Mick 1992; Tepper 1994) and quoted passages embedded throughout the account (Hirsch-man 1992). This is a broad spectrum, for tables are conceptually similar to those used in scientific presentations, whereas indented dialogues and monologues are similar to those used in fiction. Further, quotation styles include direct quotation (informant's words in quotes) and indirect quotation (informant's words para-phrased), and quotation length can be as short as a phrase or as long as a full column. When passages generated by non-English speakers are quoted, they are either represented via original verbatims with translations or via translations alone. Finally, non-verbal accompaniments (smiles, sighs, vocal tone) may or may not be included.

The significance of peer acceptance of variant usage can be seen as an exercise of arbitrary power by imagining a parallel situation in formats for numerical data. What if researchers decided to use roman numerals? What if they decided not to use tables at all, but instead to present the data in sentence form? What if they chose to arrange numbers in a variety of interesting shapes (perhaps circles or zig-zags)? At the very least, they would have to justify these decisions, for norms of numerical representation are an important enough issue to warrant discussion. In contrast, anything-goes verbal conventions imply that the informants' words are as unimportant as their names.

Characterization

This is the term I use to refer to the representation of consumers as if they were literary characters. It is borrowed from an ancient genre (see p. 14) that has reappeared in consumer research, and is used to identify the problem of unex-amined borders between social science and literature. Postmodern critics applaud the borrowing of techniques honed in literature to represent real-world events (White 1987). What Van Maanen calls "literary tales" show evidence of "the author's explicit borrowing of fiction-writing techniques to tell the story" (1988: 132). The assumption is that researchers may freely dip into the literary grab-bag. However, neither the purpose nor the possible value of borders between social science and literature have been discussed in consumer research. There is no sense of communal consensus as to whether blurring is imaginative, unwarranted, or perhaps even accidental.

A more specific problem surfaces when tension exists between the literary form and the scientific matter. Even though researchers do treat informants as char-acters, no debate about the rights of each party in the transaction has come forth. Let us look at an example of characterization that derives from the genre itself known as "the character" – a short prose sketch of an imaginary individual (Abrams 1993; Aldington 1924). After peaking in popularity three centuries ago, it returns in consumer research, where informants such as "Sam Lane" (Sherry 1990), the "Diversity of Sellers" and "Diversity of Buyers" (Belk *et al.* 1988), and "Three Lives" and "Two More Lives" (Hirschman 1992) are repre-sented as if they were characters in a story.

These are direct descendants of the page-or-less description of a typical person, occupation, range of activities, age, and so forth (Boyce 1947) that ultimately dates back to the Hebrew Proverbs and the Greek *Characters* (Theophrastus, second century BC). In our discipline, the genre fulfills its original purpose of compressing details so that vivid descriptions take up minimum space, as Sir Thomas Over-bury's definition (1616, in Brinkley 1951; see Paylor 1977) indicates: a character is "an impress or short emblem; in little, comprehending much." These sketches are meant to convey an emotional jolt, for as Van Maanen points out, "intense, well-crafted sketches crowd the literary tales" (1988: 132).

However, there has been no justification for the use of this borrowed genre. In consequence, neither the problem of ethicality nor the processing implications have been discussed. Some questions that need airing are:

- To what extent are researchers justified in representing consumers as characters?
- What literary devices are appropriate for enlivening research accounts?
- How does the interpretive community read social science in literary form?

It is important to acknowledge the characterization of informants so that the problem of whether and how literariness serves our brand of social science becomes a part of debate, not a *fait accompli*. We do not know whether there are any alternatives to this kind of representation because we have not openly acknowledged its status as a problem.

In sum, political exclusivity, rhetorical inclusivity, and characterization problematize representation by blocking out some consumer voices, shaping many by literary devices, and orchestrating all as the researcher sees fit.

Matters of voice: authorial dominance

> How social reality is conveyed through writing involves, among other things, authorial voice. The author's perspective exhibited through voice marks particular ethnographic styles and genres. But, reader beware . . . Matters of voice can quickly grow complicated.
>
> (Van Maanen 1988: ix)

The heart of the complication is that the authorial voice is so dominant that the claim to polyvocality must be revisited. Tyler's comment about ethnography – "the voice of the text is primarily that of the narrator" (1987: 77) – fits equally well in consumer research, where the researcher's voice controls the consumer's in a published account. Narrative control is indebted to nineteenth-century realist fiction in which univocal authors "claim to represent a world as only one who has known it firsthand can" (Marcus and Fisher 1986: 23). The researcher's interpretive omnipotence is generally acknowledged to be a feature of the realist tale (Marcus and Fisher 1986; Van Maanen 1988), which offers a single reading of an event and marshals facts to support this reading.

In contrast, polyvocal authorship is more characteristic of twentieth-century fiction, the locus of narrative experimentation. A popular metaphor for polyvocality is "dialogue," referring to "practical efforts to present multiple voices within a text, and to encourage readings from diverse perspectives" (Marcus and Fisher

1986: 68). The hallmark is the introduction of many voices – those of consumer narrators and of researcher narrators – as opposed to the univocal narrating researcher(s).

Nonetheless, researchers control the writing of verbal data as surely as they do the writing of numerical data. As Van Maanen points out, even when jointly told tales are negotiated, the researcher holds the editorial and publishing keys, not the informant: "informants speak, ethnographers write" (1988: 137). Tyler challenges the dialogic metaphor even more directly: "since ultimately the ethnographer holds the pen, true dialogue is not represented in recent modernist experiments, and cannot be in any fundamentally authentic way" (1987: 68). He castigates the postmodern dialogue as "a text masquerading as a dialogue, a mere monologue about a dialogue since the informant's appearances in the dialogue are at best mediated through the ethnographer's dominant authorial role" (Tyler 1987: 66). Recall that joint construction is not the same as polyvocality, for the researcher can eliminate any conflicting voices – the research community empowers authorial dominance as a necessary condition of writing research.

But is this automatically bad? In order to address the claim to polyvocality more knowledgeably, we need to look more closely at the nature, function, and structure of each narrative voice. This will permit identification of each narrator's "specific manner of using language, with distinct rules and contextual constraints" (Lanser 1981: 54) to discern the laws guiding the research culture's assumptions about the status of the participants in narrative accounts (Miller 1990).

To do so, we must sort out the voices of researchers and consumers. This can be done by analyzing the consumers' prose (indented) and the researchers' prose (full column width) separately. Note that the printing convention is a physical representation of the power map, for the consumer narratives are shown as parts of a whole. When the part/whole gestalt is analyzed in terms of narrative voices, the research relationships (Miller 1990) that underlie the typographical norm can be examined. Table 3.2 specifies the differences between researcher and consumer voices across typical narratological dimensions.

Ideology

The hierarchical placement of the researcher/consumer reflects a fundamental power difference that applies in most social science disciplines – researchers are the ones responsible for theory building. They generalize from individual experience to universal human truths and conceptualize abstract meaning. In contrast, consumers are controlled subjects – each is an individual expert on his/her own experience, but one whose representation in print is constructed by the supravening expert in the total experiential domain. That is, the consumer's voice is heard through the researcher's, who has the final choice of how the consumer's story is to be told (in snippets of quoted matter versus extended quotations; in direct speech versus indirect; in dialogue with the researcher, and so forth). This power relationship has been carried over into postmodern consumer research from the modernist

Table 3.2 Researchers' and consumers' voices

	Researcher	*Consumer*
Ideology	Controlling Belief in generalizability Thematic convergence	Controlled Belief in individuality Particular experience
Strategy	Global Responsible for entire narrative Motivated selection criteria	Local Responsible for his/her portion Indeterminate selection criteria
Time	Summary Tendency toward abridgment Produces finished product	Scene Tendency toward recapitulation Supplies raw materials

Structure	Plot
	Beginning: "Closed"
	  Narrative preliminaries
	  Explicit introduction
	  Exposition oriented toward reader
		Story
		"Open"
		  Abrupt, random beginning
		  Presupposition (reader
		  must deduce exposition)

	Ending: "Closed"
	  Constructs gestalt meaning
	  Orderly meaning
	  Complete, coherent account
		"Open"
		  Conveys "moment of perception"
		  Problematical meaning of "moment"
		  Incomplete, fragmentary bits

Role	Analyst, interviewer, observer Disembodied/partially embodied	Participant, observer Fully embodied
Position	Mobile Mediates between self/other Central to research experience	Fixed Self is central Central to consumption experience
Focalization	External "Of action" Objective	Internal "In action" Subjective

paradigms, although without the debate characteristic of other fields (see Marcus and Fisher 1986; Tyler 1987; Van Maanen 1988, 1995).

Strategy

The researcher's dominance flows from the power to determine the totalizing strategy. Researchers are responsible for crafting the entire narrative and are obligated to select the form in which to display the data, and the contributor to the final account who drops out of sight earliest is the informant. That is, the discursive process of inquiry differs from the discursive process of representation. The selection of material to include and the shape it takes are dictated by the researcher and the publication establishment, for they comprise a collective that determines which consumer voices are selected and how they are written into the totalizing entity.

Consumers, on the other hand, make strategic decisions only on the local level,

within their own stories. Their motivation for selection of details may be indeterminate or incomprehensible. In these cases, researchers can clarify, ignore, or
discard the individual bits, depending on the selection process invoked to attain the
goal. This process is problematized when the authors do not discuss the choice
criteria, leaving readers unenlightened as to why some material is in the account and
some is omitted, how the material has been compressed to fit limited journal space,
what determines presentation in dialogue or monologue, and so forth.

Time

The need to make presentational choices is an authorial obligation in all writing,
for authors must find some way to ensure communication across temporal and
spatial distances. Economical time-management techniques exemplify the modernist "attempt to overcome time . . . by mastering space and reducing time to the
ordered array of intersecting lines" (Tyler 1987: 3). Mastery of time distinguishes
the researcher's voice from the consumer's, for each tends to treat time distinctively. The consumer's oral speech is "rambling, repetitious, [and] redundant"
(Tyler 1987: 75), whereas the researcher's written word is closed, finished and
presumed to be reliable (Johnson 1990).

The terms "summary" versus "scene" (Lanser 1981) reflect the obligations of
each voice: "summary" condenses the passage of past time in indirect discourse,
and "scene" replicates the moment-by-moment unfolding of present time in dialogue. This opposition (Stanzel [1979] 1984) is one of the oldest in narrative theory,
contrasting "telling" with "showing."

Researchers commonly use summary to speed up time representation by abrid-
ging detail so that long temporal periods can be compressed in short passages. In so
doing, they provide a service to the audience by "foregrounding" their understandings so that the audience can comprehend the most important points quickly (Stanzel
[1979] 1984). In contrast, consumers are more likely to use scenes to recapitulate the
fullness of details and to recount lived experiences. The researchers' decision to
represent "a particular scene or setting . . . either in great detail or in a brief sketch"
(Stanzel 1978: 117) is based on an evaluation of what the audience needs to know.

Although the degree of narrative guidance reflects literary decision-making (see
Wells 1989), political strategy ought not be overlooked as an influence on the choice of
summary rather than scene. That is, articles using verbal data tend to be long, which
not only delays the review process but also uses up scarce journal space. Looked at this
way, the researcher's decision to summarize reinforces modernist top-down research
production rather than postmodern co-construction. Consumers contribute bits of
themselves – their identities in time – that researchers then compress.

Structure

The summary/scene distinction is fundamental to the difference between the
researchers' responsibility for devising a single "plot" and the consumers' respon-

sibility for providing a number of "stories" (see Forster [1927] 1954; Stern 1994). "Plot" is defined as an ordered sequence of events made coherent by causality, linear structure, and purpose, while "story" is defined as a chain of events randomly set forth. A consumer research account of a homeless woman reveals the difference:

> I had my ideal home! It was in 1954 and it was beautiful! It was a split level. The outside, the grounds were beautiful. Maybe half an acre of grass. We had a garden with flowers and we planted trees. We finished off the inside ourselves and that was beautiful – I even put down a tile floor! I learned how to wallpaper and paint, insulate, and hang wallboard. A little bit of everything!
>
> (Hill 1991: 307)

This is a story, for the temporal chronology is random (wallpapering, painting, insulating walls, and hanging wallboard are placed in juxtaposition rather than in chronological sequence), the spatial progress is jagged (inside the home to outside to inside again), and the causality is not made explicit (why is she saying this?). The researcher turns it into a plot by prefacing the quoted matter in the indented passage as follows: "Linda told me that she once lived in her 'dream' home. This was a time when her young family was together and happy. She told me that: 'I had my ideal home! . . . '" The quote is preceded by an unindented prefatory introduction that explains the rationale for including the quotes: " . . . the women who came from troubled backgrounds that also featured periods of stability and happiness were more apt to fantasize about homes that contained elements of previous happy residences." The researcher thus imposes a plot by making explicit the story's meaning, chronology, and causality.

Explicitness requires different *beginnings* and *endings* in plots and stories. Research beginnings are expected to provide exposition – the preliminary information that the audience needs to understand what follows – and justification for the researcher's position as a reliable narrator who will not lead readers astray (Stanzel [1979] 1984). Note that the value placed on an orderly expository beginning and attentiveness to the readers' needs is socially constructed by the discipline, not a universal norm. Other options are beginning in the middle of events (as Homer and Virgil do), beginning at the end (as James Joyce does), or totally forgoing linearity (Jacques Derrida).

However, these options pertain only to consumers' narratives, for they are given more leeway as narrators "whose perception, interpretation, and evaluation of the matters he or she narrates" do not necessarily coincide with those of the authors and the audience (Abrams 1993: 168). The consumer-narrator can begin a story wherever he or she pleases, plunging into the middle, beginning, end, or discarding all linearity. One reason for representing "open" beginnings is that they convey "a sense of immediacy or involvement [and give] a story verisimilitude" (Stanzel [1979] 1984: 163). The lack of preliminaries thrusts the audience directly into the consumption scene.

"Open"/"closed" beginnings are linked to "open"/"closed" endings. Researchers are expected to use "closed endings", in which assignation of meaning rounds out the work. Consumers, on the other hand, are free to use "open" endings (ambiguous, indeterminate) in telling stories that stop suddenly rather than achieve definitive closure. One consumer informant comments on role expectations, saying, "Well, I guess I'm sounding coherent [laughter]. Seems odd to me listening to yourself talk . . . " (Heisley and Levy 1991: 268). However, her shift in pronouns ("I" and "yourself") suggests tension in the researcher/informant transaction. The shift indicates that whereas the consumer is aware of the researcher's role in establishing coherence, she is uncomfortable in her own role in the process ("seems odd to me listening to yourself talk"). This is a rare instance of the consumer's voice breaking through to express less than wholehearted acceptance of the subject role.

Role

Unlike consumers, researchers control the strategy and structure, taking on the analyst's role to provide necessary explanations. Role is expressed by degree of embodiment – the separation or distance between the researcher-teller and the consumer's tale. The analytical role is ultimately disembodied or separated, removed from the action in time and space. Even when researchers are participant/observers and present in the action, they must separate at some point to function as analysts. An early example of the researcher as analyst only (Rook 1987) demonstrates a high degree of disembodiment, for in this study the researcher analyzed consumers' written answers to open-ended questions in a mailed survey.

For consumers, the necessary and sufficient role is that of embodied participant. They are presumed to be part of the story, not separate from it. Consumers are "encaged" (Henry James's term) in their own consumption world, where an existential connection links the narrating and experiencing self. Embodiment limits their perspective within self-oriented boundaries, for they are more engaged in living consumption than analyzing it.

Position (self/other)

The source of information for consumers is primarily self-experience, whereas for researchers it is primarily the experience of others (see Marcus and Fisher 1986). Note that when researchers refer to themselves as "I" (see page 71), they may be expressing involvement in the consumption event with others (ethnographic participant-observation), involvement in the process of data collection from others (existential-phenomenological interview), or involvement in self-analysis (introspection). In the former two, the researcher aims at constructing explanations of the consumer self. In the latter (see Gould 1991), the researcher aims at achieving penetration of the mysteries of the self to construct explanations of his/ her own consumer behavior.

In contrast, consumers dwell almost exclusively on information about the self, for they regard themselves as central to the experiences they relate. However, their concept of the self may be different from that of the researcher, for personhood and individuality are "culturally variable" (Marcus and Fisher 1986). Hence (see Hill 1991), when consumers speak from within a personal frame of reference, their "categories, metaphors, and rhetorics" may not be those of the research community (Marcus and Fisher 1986: 47; cf. Geertz 1973). When researchers represent others with different notions of the self, they move back and forth between cultures. The researchers' position is mobile, in that collecting data about the consumer involves them in otherness, whereas writing about it returns them to the self. Consumers, on the other hand, are fixed within their notion of the self, an instance of immobilization that reinforces the researchers' positional dominance (Said 1979).

Point of view

Representation of the perspective of researchers and of consumers (Stanzel's "focalization," [1979] 1984) also refers to the narrator's point of view in terms of the action: is the narrator an observer (external), a participant (internal), or somewhere in-between? Perspective – the narrator's stance or attitude toward characters and events – is a dimension called by an abundance of names (see Cohn 1981; Genette [1972] 1980; Lanser 1981; Stanzel [1979] 1984). In our field, the linguistic terms "emic" and "etic" (see Stanzel [1979] 1984; Wallendorf and Brucks 1993) have been adopted, with "emic" referring to the researcher's interpretation of behaviors and "etic" to the reported or observed behaviors without researcher interpretation (Wallendorf and Brucks 1993). In other words, the "emic" researcher is a participant in the action (internal perspective), whereas the "etic" researcher is an observer (external). The representational aspects of perspective are actualized via narrative "point of view" – the way that a tale gets told (Stanzel [1979] 1984; Stern 1991; Cohn 1981). The narrative focus determines whether the point of view is primarily that of the narrator or of the characters, which can be discerned by examining the distance between the narrator, the characters, and the events (Todorov [1968] 1981; Genette [1972] 1980). Objectivity is considered a narrative quality possessed by a narrator removed from the action, and subjectivity a quality possessed by a narrator in the midst of it.

In this regard, consumers usually demonstrate the subjective point of view. They report intimate details reminiscent of spiritual revelations but associated with consumption events such as conversions from one product to another and discovery of identity in material things (Belk *et al.* 1989). These experiences are articulated as personal occurrences, and the version of events that consumers relate is determined by what they see, feel, and report. Researchers, on the other

Table 3.3 Grammatical person

First person
Gould (1991)

First/third person

Belk/Sherry/Wallendorf (1988)
Belk/Wallendorf/Sherry (1989)
Sherry (1989)
Hill/Stamey (1990)
Hill (1991)
Arnould (1991)
Hirschman (1992)
Arnould/Price (1993)
Otnes/Lowrey/Kim (1993)
Belk/Coon (1993)
Celsi/Rose/Leigh (1993)
Tepper (1994)
Peñaloza (1994)
Schouten/McAlexander (1995)

Third person

Rook (1987)
Belk (1988)
Thompson/Locander/Pollio (1989)
O'Guinn/Faber (1989)
O'Guinn/Belk (1989)
Mick/DeMoss (1990)
Fischer/Arnold (1990)
Thompson/Locander/Pollio (1990)
Mehta/Belk (1991)
Schouten (1991)
Heisley/Levy (1991)
McQuarrie/Mick (1992)
Mick/Buhl (1992)
Hirschman (1994)
Thompson/Pollio/Locander (1994)
Patterson/Hill/Maloy (1994)
Babin/Darden/Griffin (1994)
Holt (1995)
Kover (1995)

---

hand, are expected to embody an external perspective, for even when they enter the consumption experience, they do so to mediate between consumers and readers. That is, the external narrative voice tells the audience what is going on (Abrams 1993), guiding reader perceptions of the experience.

In sum, researchers are the dominant partners in the relationship with consumers. They have the power to shape consumer stories, no matter the thematic content or means of collection. To continue the examination of problems related to the power of representation, let us now turn to the domains of introspection, ethnography, and existential-phenomenology.

Person and representation

These domains have been "most often conceived as a clash of theoretical paradigms" (White 1973). However, the claimed differences can be identified more precisely by translating them "into the writer's problem of representation" (ibid.). This opens the door to examination of the oppositional pronoun usage – "third-person" (he, she, they) versus "first-person" (I) – which is the most generally accepted differentiating factor in narratology (see Cohn 1978, 1981; Genette [1983] 1988; Lanser 1981; Stanzel [1979] 1984). Its logic is rooted in form and function (Hamburger [1957] 1973), for "person" distinguishes between first-person narrators limited to what the "I" knows, and third-person narrators able to know what is in others' minds (Lanser 1981).

Table 3.3 sorts the accounts in the data set by the person that the researcher uses (note that consumers use the first person most frequently in their stories). Ethnographic accounts most often use first and third-person narration, reflecting the researchers' use of the first person for themselves and the use of the third person in references to consumers. In contrast, existential-phenomenological accounts most often use third-person narration, reflecting the researchers' distance from the actual consumption experience. Introspective accounts are limited to the first person, for the only voice represented is the researchers'.

Notice that no narrative form is necessarily better than any other, for differences are a matter of trade-offs. That is, like novelists, researchers look for a good deal, one that will minimize the disadvantages and maximize the advantages of the grammatical person they select (Martin 1986). In order to determine whether researchers have dealt well, we must weigh the advantages and disadvantages of each form. In so doing, problems in representation are exposed. Let us begin with those in the introspective account.

Introspection: first person

Gould's article (1991) is the only one in the data set that uses a researcher-narrator restricted to the first person. Introspective accounts center on the self, a "filter of worldly happenings," and readers have no doubt that "a single, creative, and wilful voice is shaping the work" (Van Maanen 1988: 134). Here, the researcher *is* the sole consumer, one who views him/herself from the inside and remains on a wholly interior plane. Of necessity, it is a confessional tale (Van Maanen 1988), one whose literary heritage is illuminating. Its ancestor is the spiritual autobiography (Olney 1972, Pascal 1960) in which a first-person narrator reveals intimate aspects of him/herself. St Augustine's *Confessions* (fourth century AD) is the model for later secular works characterized by self-presentation of an individual (Holden

Caulfield in *The Catcher in the Rye*). The rationale for autobiography is that the narrator is the best source of information about him/herself.

The advantage of introspection is that it permits an inside look at the narrator's own mind (McHale 1981) which reveals personal experience unknowable to anyone else. The dramatic device of recollected dialogue quoted at length conveys intimate material to the audience. Self-revelation permits the "I" to establish direct contact with readers in an "I–you" relationship mimetic of personal communication. The immediacy of the first-person revelation of psychological detail to an audience is thought to inspire audiences to relive the experiences vicariously, as if what they are told is happening to them.

The disadvantage is that although introspective first-person accounts are long on intimacy, they are short on any information other than what the "I" can conceivably know. Critics point out that readers have no way of knowing if the author got it right (Van Maanen 1988). The intimacy of the narrative stance – an individual who remains within his/her own head – may not strike an audience as credible for researchers because it is too encaged. Gould's introspective, self-revelatory account (1991) has already been problematized in terms of methodology and topical appropriateness (see Wallendorf and Brucks 1993).

Let me add that the article is also problematical on representational grounds. It plays to the form's weaknesses rather than to its strengths, for there are *no* direct quotes at all (only indirect speech). Hence, the author forgoes the opportunity to reveal the contents of his mind in his own words (Stanzel [1979] 1984), which casts doubt on the value of using the form. Admittedly, introspective research is limited by total immersion in one's own being – the inevitable "ontological basis of the position of the first-person narrator in the world of the narrative" (Stanzel [1979] 1984: 89). Yet insofar as the form's advantage – direct quotation to reveal one's inner voice – is not demonstrated in Gould's article, the limitation is more evident than it might otherwise be.

If introspective narrators do not reinforce the form/content synergy of mental experience, they set up a double bind by simultaneously distancing readers and pulling them closer. According to Chatman (1978), embodiment and self-revelation ordinarily are expressed by direct quotations so that the narrator can convey the illusion of intimacy to the audience. When direct quotation is absent, the implication is that some tension exists between the subjective point of view and the objective representation of it. The tension is unresolved in this article, which may explain why it is one-of-a-kind.

Existential–phenomenology: third person

At the opposite end of the narrative spectrum from the introspective narrator is the omniscient narrator, who is all-seeing and free to comment on the events at will, most often in the third person. Existential–phenomenological accounts feature narrators who most consistently speak in the third person, referring to those described or quoted as "he," "she," "they," "it," or by name. Here, an authoritative relationship to the audience replaces an intimate one (Stanzel [1979] 1984). The convention of omniscience supports the readers' acceptance of narrators with unlimited knowledge as authoritative (Abrams 1993), for readers in Western culture have been conditioned to accept this point of view as truthful.

As Van Maanen (1995) points out, the advantage of freedom from personal bias enhances narrative authority. The disadvantage is obtrusiveness, in that the narrator is perceived as an outside voice, telling readers what to think (Wells 1989). Unlike first-person narration, which aims at persuading readers to buy into the illusion of experiencing events as they evolve, third-person narration interposes a mediating voice between the events and the readers.

To overcome the disadvantage of narrator-as-busybody, the self-effacing third-person narrator was devised by experimental novelists such as James Joyce and Virginia Woolf. The God-like narrator (Banfield 1982; Benveniste 1971; Lubbock 1957) appears most convincingly in Molly Bloom's soliloquy in *Ulysses*, where he recedes so far into the background that readers experience the illusion of hearing Molly directly without any mediation at all.

Nonetheless, the logic of narratorless narration is still hotly debated. Recall that a basic premise in narratology is that every narrative has a narrator, and there is no such thing as a story that tells itself (Genette [1983] 1988). As Genette points out, even "in the most unobtrusive narrative, someone is speaking to me, is telling me a story, is inviting me to listen to it as he tells it, and this invitation . . . constitutes an undeniable stance of narrating, and therefore of a narrator . . . " (ibid.: 101). Tyler (1987) emphasizes that in research accounts (Barthes 1966; Todorov [1968] 1981), the claim that the researcher-narrator is so self-effacing that the readers are able to gain an unmediated view of the informant's mental processes cannot be substantiated.

Nonetheless, the existential–phenomenological accounts in the data-set aim at conveying absentee narration. The purpose is to do away with an intrusive narrator by letting the researcher recede so far away in his/her own right that the audience experiences events as the participants did. Eliminating mediation is said to be the way to highlight the consumer's "first-person description of the phenomenon as lived" (Thompson *et al.* 1989: 139), allowing it to unfold in front of the readers' eyes. That is, the representation is aimed at gaining the advantage of first-person intimacy (the "I" is the consumer's) without paying the price of its restricted point of view.

Researchers in this tradition emphasize their departure from the realist ethnographic use of descriptive third-person narration (Marcus and Cushman 1982). They claim that in that type of narration, "a researcher adopts a detached third-person perspective and views some phenomenon in an objective (object-like) sense" (Thompson *et al.* 1989: 139). In contrast, their own accounts are said to differ by including "what is missing" – the first-person "experience." Emphasis on the consumer's first-person voice is expected to keep the researcher's third-person voice in the background and allow readers to get closer to the consumer's lived experience.

Counter-claim: the problem

Yet the existential–phenomenological accounts in our data-set are problematical in that the representational form actually in use works against the research claim of a self-effacing narrator. Indeed, the accounts do the opposite of making researchers disappear from view, instead highlighting their presence. Because the indents are often dialogues, the researchers are situated right up front with the consumers (see Thompson *et al.* 1989, 1990). A short excerpt from an example in which the consumer is "S" and the interviewer is "I" follows:

> I: How do you feel about those times you are with someone and they say buy this item?
> S: I love it. I like that.
> I: What is it like when you shop for your home alone?
>
> (Thompson *et al.* 1990: 350)

Notice that the researcher's presence in the dialogue is the opposite of self-effacement. That is, the researcher is as much in evidence as a narrative guide as he or she is in descriptive ethnographic representations from which existential–phenomenological accounts claim to differ. The claim is not supported, for the paradigmatic difference has not yet overcome the "problem of representation" (White 1973, 1987).

The ethnographic blend: first and third person

The participant–observation ethnographic tradition accepts the researcher in the first person (see Stanzel [1979] 1984) as well as in the third person. Here, the researcher is both a player in and a witness to the events (Friedman 1955; also see Genette [1972] 1980), but is not the central character. When researchers enter the consumption experience and indicate their presence by using "I," they are situated on the periphery of experience (Abrams 1993). Even though they are involved in it, they are not the most important or the only consumers. Representation flows from the assumption that researcher understanding is constructed and verified *in situ* (Belk *et al.* 1989) by means of interaction with consumers. The goal is to express a relationship in which the researcher (Belk *et al.* 1989) achieves intimacy with consumers by experiencing revelatory incidents with them.

The blend of first and third person found in the data-set resembles what Van Maanen calls the "impressionist tale" (Van Maanen 1988). One advantage of blending is that the first person can draw readers into an unfamiliar world and allow them to see, hear, and feel what the researcher saw, heard, and felt. An increase in evocative power is said to occur when readers are "asked to relive the tale with the fieldworker, not interpret or analyze it" (Van Maanen 1988: 103). When this is coupled with the advantage of third-person objectivity, the researcher's ability to enter and leave the account openly may increase verisimilitude by eliminating the pretense of an absentee third-person narrator hidden in the bushes.

However, in order to distinguish between first-person and third-person commentary, the researcher's point of view must shift from his/her own personal perspective to that of others. The great disadvantage of the blended form is that the audience will be discomfited by the narrative shifts. Notwithstanding the precedent of the self-reflexive novel's "doubled mirror" – "a novel about a novelist writing a novel . . . including his novelist's journal" (Levin 1966: 289) – a research account in this form can be confusing. Not every author of research can handle the intricacies of the form successfully, and even masterful novels such as Gide's *The Counterfeiters* and Nabokov's *Pale Fire* are rare exceptions.

Problem

The ethnographic accounts in the data set are problematical on this dimension, for the multiple voices are occasionally too confusing for readers to follow. Unexplained ambiguity (McHale 1981) surfaces when both first-person and third-person narrators appear in the same verbal passage, leading to unclear "relationships between author, narrator(s), characters, and audience" (Lanser 1981). Let us look at an example of shifting narrators to see this in action:

> After lunch, after cleanup, Mel organized a little hike up the cliff behind us to a site where there were model fossils of rock. I sort of got started early, as I wanted to. The others came along in a bit – single file. Mel talked a little about the geology. We showed off the fossils, talked a little about the fossil crals, rim rock and further up, krinoid stems. As she talked about those, people looked on appreciatively.
>
> (Arnould and Price 1993: 34)

There are several possible narrators, signified by singular pronouns ("I," "she"), plural pronouns ("we," "us'), a proper noun (the name "Mel"), and common nouns ("others," "people"). The verb "talked" is first preceded by the third-person "Mel" and then by the plural "we." Clarification does not occur until the last sentence, when readers realize that Mel is "she" and that Mel and the researcher-narrator ("I") together are referred to as "we," in contrast to the others, referred to as "people." The abundance of pronouns, the narrative shift from "I" (narrator as participant) to "people" (narrator as observer), and the use of a unisex name ("Mel") complicate the passage.

Playing the devil's advocate, let us argue that the ambiguity is intentionally designed to reinforce the metaphor of the trip as an orchestra. The introduction to the excerpt tells us that it is "from participant–observation field notes," which signals the reader to expect doubled narrative. This becomes multiplicative in the sentence immediately after, which describes the trip as one that "orchestrates" different opportunities for different participants. It may be that the shifts in person replicate the complexity of orchestral harmonies to sustain the metaphorical association. However, the problem is whether or not readers will expend the effort necessary to disentangle the pronominal shifts to "get" the metaphor. In sum, the unintended confusion in ethnographic accounts, the unwarranted intrusion in existential–phenomenological ones, and the uneasy articulation in introspective ones make the representations borrowed from other fields problematical in consumer research.

Toward improving representation

Representation can be improved by clarification of narrative conventions, inclusion of silenced "others," and encouragement of experimental modes of narrative expression.

Clarification and increased self-awareness

More attention to textualization – the process "by which unwritten behavior, beliefs, values, rituals, oral traditions, and so forth become fixed, atomized, and classified as data of a certain sort" (Ricoeur [1973] 1981: 95) – is a prerequisite to increased researcher self-awareness. The benefit is greater understanding of the relationship between the ideology of representation and attitudes to the consumer, and communication of new understandings to the reader.

The choice of naming conventions is especially in need of ideological justification, for it relates to consumer "subjectification" (Todorov [1968] 1981; Genette [1972] 1980). Insofar as researchers have the power to assign names to consumers, they have the obligation to justify the choice, especially in situations where usage seems arbitrary. To take but one example, in Holt's article (1995), two boys are given names ("Billy," "Tommy"), but their fathers are simply called "Father"; similarly spectators at baseball games are sometimes identified generically ("A young woman seated next to me") and sometimes by name ("Jim," "Craig"). In the absence of authorial comment, the reader is left with the impression that the names simply do not matter a great deal. The unpleasant concomitant is that consumers themselves do not matter a great deal – "subject" is a term of subordination.

Researchers need to become more sensitive to the power of representation, lest they commodify consumption by "dealing with it, by making statements about it, authorizing views of it, describing it, by teaching it, settling it, ruling over it" (Said 1979: 3). One way to heighten awareness is by performing inside-out readings to identify the narrative conventions invoked. Just as those who use numerical data attend to representational conventions, so too should users of verbal data. The point is not necessarily to generate a set of generally accepted rules, but to shine a spotlight on the hidden ideology that supports researcher-choice scenarios.

Exclusion and affirmative action

The prospect of a spotlight on excluded voices is embarrassing, and continued debate is no longer adequate. The more pro-active step of affirmative action must be taken so that these voices can enter consumer research as soon as possible. Note that the *Journal of Consumer Research*, like *Psychology and Marketing*, and the *Journal of Consumer Psychology* lag behind the American Psychological Association journals in having an "abysmally low" number of articles with a racial/ethnic minority focus (Graham 1992; Williams 1995). To move forward, journals in marketing and consumer research should consider setting aside a special section in an issue or devoting an entire issue to culturally diverse consumers. That is, instead of waiting until articles come over the transom, we have to seek them out and, if necessary, help grow them.

Experimental expression

Clarification of the conventions and inclusion of the unrepresented voices is likely to improve representation, a matter of some urgency since our field is in catch-up mode. Consumer researchers need to enter the discussion of experimental textual strategies in the social sciences that has been going on since at least the 1930s, when Bateson declared that "the writing of this book has been an experiment" ([1936] 1958: 257). The reason for a pressing need to begin the debate is that there is some danger of cutting off experimentation before it has properly gotten under way. That is, some experiments may be "mistaken for models" (Marcus and Fisher 1986: 42) rather than tentative efforts. This may already be happening in introspective research, where the sole example – one that does not even fairly represent the entire category – seems to have discouraged further efforts.

However, Tyler points out that the main issue may be "not how to make a better representation, but how to avoid representation" altogether (1987: 105). He suggests that the goal should be evocation rather than representation, and his proposals for achieving evocative polyvocal accounts include presentations of "just the dialogue itself, or possibly a series of juxtaposed paratactic tellings of a shared circumstance . . . or perhaps only a sequence of separate tellings in search of a common theme" (1987: 203). Marcus and Fisher (1986) offer similar proposals with a bit more guidance for implementation, and Rose (1993) suggests an even more radical reconfiguration. Let us consider three experimental proposals that take a different approach to narrative, and in this way, challenge researcher dominance.

1: *Open narratives* are close in spirit to "dialogic interchange" (Marcus and Fisher 1986), which aims at presenting the raw material of researcher field notes to expose the evolutionary process of knowledge development. The focus is on creating a bond between researcher and reader, who work together to discover meaning. The rough field notes illustrate the "fieldworker's imperfect, shaky control of material," and instead of a closed ending, the researcher asks the reader to "judge what can be done" with the material (ibid.: 70). The use of open texts to engage the reader in interpretive work (Marcus and Fisher 1986) is characteristic of twentieth-century literary experiments in which "unreliable" narrators (not derogatory) often supersede the omniscient ones of earlier novels.

If researchers were to begin as unreliable narrators, ones who do not fully understand the material they relate, the change in their interpretations as they narrate would become the reader's center of interest (Abrams 1993). One benefit is that when readers buy into the discovery process, they become active partici- pants in meaning construction. As such, they are less likely to feel manipulated by a bossy narrator who denies alternative interpretations that might differ from the one he or she has stamped "final." The act of moving representation away from a finished product and toward the raw materials and manufacturing process encourages readers to pitch in, making their own inferences and coming to their own conclusions.

2: *Dramatic scripts* actualize what Marcus and Fisher call "polyphonic text" (1986), in that their goal is to present the activeness of oral discourse. The difficulty in rendering polyvocality textually – that is, the representation of "different points of view in multiple voices" (Marcus and Fisher 1986: 71) – has garnered much commentary. However, if we look to drama rather than the novel as a model of representation, we can find new ways of handling a variety of voices. One way is to present the voices sequentially, as if each one were a speaker in a script. That is, the representation would look more like a drama in print than like a novel. Another way is to present overlapping voices polyphonically, as one would do in a musical composition. The simplest means of so doing is to represent different speakers' passages side-by-side in columns or on facing pages. More complex means can be found in the works of Derrida, whose use of footnotes, typographical variations, marginalia, and unequal columns of text from different sources comprise a primer of polyphony on the printed page.

3: *Interactive constructions* are the most radical form of experimentation, adapted from Rose's "multigenre ethnography" (1993: 219). Rose suggests that a single work can include mini-essays, conversations, and poetry as well as pictures, drawings, and photographs, all cohabiting together. However, we can go further, neither stopping at static representations nor adhering to the tradition of finite authorship. The capabilities of interactive media vastly exceed those of print in providing opportunities for active representation such as videotapes that can incorporate music, dance, and spectacle as well as split-screen dramatic devices more flexible than pages.

Perhaps more important, interactive media allow authorship to be reconcep- tualized such that consumers, researchers, readers, and any other interested parties can engage in joint on-line construction in real time. Advocates of experi- mentalism yearn to give readers the opportunity to reconstruct imaginatively the "doing" of experience instead of passively witnessing the "doer or the done" (Marcus and Fisher 1986). Rose's call for "polyphonic, heteroglossic, multigenre construction" (1993: 218) may best be answered in consumer research by turning away from even the most avant-garde literary models and, instead, looking toward the futuristic narrative possibilities of the web.

References

Abrams, M.H. (1993) *A Glossary of Literary Terms*, 6th edn., New York: Holt, Rinehart and Winston.

Aldington, R. (ed.) (1924) *A Book of "Characters" from Theophrastus*, London: G. Routledge & Sons.

Arnould, E.J. and Price, L.L. (1993) "River Magic: Extraordinary Experience and the Extended Service Encounter," *Journal of Consumer Research*, 20,1: 24–45.

Banfield, A. (1982) *Unspeakable Sentences: Narration and Representation in the Language of Fiction*, Boston: Routledge & Kegan Paul.

Barthes, R. (1966) "Introduction to the Structural Analysis of Narratives," in S. Heath (trans.) (1977) *Image – Music – Text*, New York: Hill & Wang, 1977: 79–124.

Bateson, G. ([1936] 1958) *NAVEN: A Survey of the Problems Suggested by a Composite Picture of the Cultures of New Guinea Drawn from Three Points of View*, 2nd edn., Stanford: Stanford University Press.

Belk, R.W. (1992) "Moving Possessions: An Analysis Based on Personal Documents from the 1847–1869 Mormon Migration," *Journal of Consumer Research*, 19,3: 339–61.

Belk, R.W, Sherry, J.F., Jr., and Wallendorf, M. (1988) "A Naturalistic Inquiry into Buyer and Seller Behavior at a Swap Meet," *Journal of Consumer Research*, 14,4: 449–70.

Belk, R.W, Wallendorf M., and Sherry, J.F., Jr. (1989) "The Sacred and the Profane in Consumer Behavior: Theodicy on the Odyssey," *Journal of Consumer Research*, 16,1: 1–38.

Benveniste, E. (1971) *Problems in General Linguistics*, trans. M.E. Meek, Coral Gables: University of Miami Press.

Booth, W.C. ([1961] 1983) *The Rhetoric of Fiction*, 2nd edn, Chicago: University of Chicago Press.

Boyce, B. (1947) *The Theophrastan Character in England to 1642*, Cambridge: Harvard University Press.

Brinkley, R.F. (ed.) (1951) *English Prose of the XVII Century*, New York: W.W. Norton.

Chatman, S. (1978) *Story and Discourse: Narrative Structure in Fiction and Film*, Ithaca: Cornell University Press.

—— (1981) "What Novels Can Do That Films Can't (and Vice Versa)," in W.J.T. Mitchell (ed.) *On Narrative*, Chicago: The University of Chicago Press: 117–36.

Cohn, D. (1978) *Transparent Minds: Narrative Modes for Presenting Consciousness in Fiction*, Princeton: Princeton University Press.

—— (1981) "The Encirclement of Narrative: On Franz Stanzel's *Theorie des Erzahlens*," *Poetics Today*, 2,2: 157–82.

Crapanzano, V. (1980) *Tuitami: Portrait of a Moroccan*, Chicago: University of Chicago Press.

Danto, A.C. (1985) *Narration and Knowledge*, New York: Columbia University Press.

Deighton, J. and Grayson, K. (1995) "Marketing and Seduction: Building Exchange Relationships by Managing Social Consensus," *Journal of Consumer Research*, 21,4: 660–76.

Fish, S. (1980) *Is There a Text in This Class? The Authority of Interpretive Communities*, Cambridge: Harvard University Press.

Forster, E.M. ([1927] 1954) *Aspects of the Novel*, New York: Harcourt, Brace, & World.

Friedman, N. (1955) *Stream of Consciousness: A Study in Literary Method*, New Haven: Yale University Press.

Gallie, W.B. (1968) *Philosophy and the Historical Understanding*, 2nd edn, New York: Basic Books.

Geertz, C. (1973) *The Interpretation of Cultures*, New York: Basic Books.

—— (1988) *Works and Lives: The Anthropologist as Author*, Stanford: Stanford University Press.

Genette, G. ([1972] 1980) *Narrative Discourse*, trans. J.E. Lewin, Ithaca: Cornell University Press.

—— ([1983] 1988) *Narrative Discourse Revisited*, trans. J.E. Lewin, Ithaca: Cornell University Press.

Gephart, R.P., Jr. (1996) "Management, Social Issues, and the Postmodern Era," in D.M. Boje, R.P. Gephart, Jr., and T.J. Thatchenkery (eds) *Postmodern Management and Organization Theory*, Thousand Oaks: Sage, 21–44.

Gossman, L. (1978) "History and Literature: Reproduction or Signification," in R.H. Canary and H. Kozicki (eds) *The Writing of History: Literary Form and Historical Understanding*, Madison: University of Wisconsin Press, 3–39.

Gould, S.J. (1991) "The Self-Manipulation of My Pervasive, Perceived Vital Energy through Product Use: An Introspective-Praxis Perspective," *Journal of Consumer Research*, 18,2: 194–207.

—— (1995) "Researcher Introspection as a Method in Consumer Research: Application, Issues, and Implications," *Journal of Consumer Research*, 21,4: 719–22.

Graham, S. (1992) "Most of the Subjects Were White and Middle Class: Trends in Published Research on African Americans in Selected APA Journals, 1970–1989," *American Psychologist*, 47,5: 629–39.

Halasz, L. (1988) "Cognitive and Social Psychological Approaches to Literary Discourse. An Overview," in L. Halasz (ed.) *Literary Discourse: Aspects of Cognitive and Social Psychological Approaches*, Berlin: Walter de Gruyter, 1–37.

Hamburger, K. ([1957] 1973) *The Logic of Literature*, trans. M.J. Rose, Bloomington: Indiana University Press.

Heisley, D.D. and Levy, S.J. (1991) "Autodriving: A Photoelicitation Technique," *Journal of Consumer Research*, 18,3: 257–72.

Hill, R.P. (1991) "Homeless Women: Special Possessions, and the Meaning of 'Home': An Ethnographic Case Study," *Journal of Consumer Research*, 18,3: 298–310.

—— and Stamey, M. (1990) "The Homeless in America: An Examination of Possessions and Consumption Behaviors," *Journal of Consumer Research*, 17,3: 303–21.

Hirschman, E.C. (1990) "Secular Immortality and the American Ideology of Affluence," *Journal of Consumer Research*, 17,1: 31–42.

—— (1992) "The Consciousness of Addiction: Toward a General Theory of Compulsive Consumption, *Journal of Consumer Research*, 19,2: 155–79.

—— (1994) "Consumers and their Animal Companions," *Journal of Consumer Research*, 20, 4: 616–32.

Holt, D.B. (1995) "How Consumers Consume: A Typology of Consumption Practices," *Journal of Consumer Research*, 22,1: 1–16.

Johnson, B. (1990) "Writing," in F. Lentricchia and T. McLaughlin (eds) *Critical Terms for Literary Study*, Chicago: The University of Chicago Press, 39–49.

Joy, A. (1991) "Beyond the Odyssey: Interpretations of Ethnographic Writing in Consumer Behavior," in R.W. Belk (ed.) *Highways and Buyways: Naturalistic Research from the Consumer Behavior Odyssey*, Provo: Association for Consumer Research, 216–33.

Joyce, J. ([1916] 1957) *A Portrait of the Artist as a Young Man*, New York: The Viking Press.

Lanser, S.S. (1981) *The Narrative Act: Point of View in Prose Fiction*, Princeton: Princeton University Press.

Levin, H. (1966) *Refractions: Essays in Comparative Literature*, New York: Oxford University Press.

Lubbock, P. (1957) *The Craft of Fiction*, New York: Viking Press.

Lyotard, J.F. ([1979] 1984) *The Postmodern Condition: A Report on Knowledge*, trans. G. Bennington and B. Massouri, Minneapolis: University of Minnesota Press.

Marcus, G.E. and Cushman, D. (1982) "Ethnographies as Text," *Annual Review of Anthropology*, vol. 11, 25–69.

Marcus, G.E. and Fischer, M.M.J. (1986) *Anthropology as Cultural Critique: An Experimental Moment in the Social Sciences*, Chicago: The University of Chicago Press.

McHale, B. (1981) "Islands in the Stream of Consciousness: Dorrit Cohn's *Transparent Minds*," *Poetics Today*, 2,1: 183–91.

McQuarrie, E.F. and Mick, D.G. (1992) "On Resonance: A Critical Pluralistic Inquiry into Advertising Rhetoric," *Journal of Consumer Research*, 19,2: 180–97.

—— (1996) "Figures of Rhetoric in Advertising Language," *Journal of Consumer Research*, 22,4: 424–38.

Martin, W. (1986) *Recent Theories of Narrative*, Ithaca: Cornell University Press.

Miller, J.H. (1990) "Narrative," in F. Lentricchia and T. McLaughlin (eds) *Critical Terms for Literary Study*, Chicago: The University of Chicago Press, 66–79.

Olney, J. (1972) *Metaphors of Self; The Meaning of Autobiography*, Princeton: Princeton University Press.

Pascal, R. (1960) *Design and Truth in Autobiography*, Cambridge: Harvard University Press.

Paylor, W.J. (ed.) (1977) *The Overburian Characters: to which is added, A Wife/by Sir Thomas Overbury*, New York: AMS Press.

Peñaloza, L. (1994) "Atravesando Fronteras/Border Crossings: A Critical Ethnographic Exploration of the Consumer Acculturation of Mexican Immigrants," *Journal of Consumer Research*, 21,1: 32–54.

Richardson, L. (1990) *Writing Matters*, Newbury Park: Sage.

—— (1995) "Narrative and Sociology," in J. Van Maanen (ed.) *Representation in Ethnography*, Thousand Oaks: Sage, 198–221.

Ricoeur, P. ([1973] 1981) *Hermeneutics and the Human Sciences: Essays on Language, Action, and Interpretation*, ed. J.B. Thompson, Cambridge: Cambridge University Press.

Rook, D.W. (1987) "The Buying Impulse," *Journal of Consumer Research*, 14,2: 189–99.

Rose, D. (1993) "Ethnography as a Form of Life: The Written Word and the Work of the World," in P. Benson (ed.) *Anthropology and Literature*, Urbana: University of Illinois Press, 192–224.

Said, E.W. (1979) *Orientalism*, New York: Pantheon Books.

Sherry, J.F., Jr. (1990) "A Sociocultural Analysis of a Midwestern American Flea Market," *Journal of Consumer Research*, 17,1: 13–30.

Shohat, E. and Stam, R. (1987) "The Cinema after Babel: Language, Difference, Power," in S.F. Staton (ed.) *Literary Theories in Praxis*, Philadelphia: University of Pennsylvania Press, 234–47.

Stanzel, F.K. (1978) *Narrative Situations in the Novel*, trans. J.P. Pusack, Bloomington: Indiana University Press.

—— ([1979] 1984) *A Theory of Narrative*, trans. C. Goedsche, Cambridge: Cambridge University Press.

Stern, B.B. (1990) "Literary Criticism and the History of Marketing Thought: A New Perspective on 'Reading' Marketing Theory," *Journal of the Academy of Marketing Science*, 18,4: 329–36.

—— (1991) "Who Talks Advertising? Literary Theory and Narrative 'Point of View'," *Journal of Advertising*, 20,3: 9–22.

—— (1994) "Classical and Vignette Television Advertising Dramas: Structural Models, Formal Analysis, and Consumer Effects," *Journal of Consumer Research*, 19,4: 601–15.

Tepper, K. (1994) "The Role of Labeling Processes in Elderly Consumers' Responses to Age Segmentation Cues," *Journal of Consumer Research*, 20,4: 503–19.

Thompson, C. J., Locander, W.B. and Pollio, H.R. (1989) "Putting Consumer Experience Back into Consumer Research: The Philosophy and Method of Existential–Phenomenology," *Journal of Consumer Research*, 16,2: 133–46.

—— (1990) "The Lived Meaning of Free Choice: An Existential–Phenomenological Description of Everyday Consumer Experiences of Contemporary Married Women," *Journal of Consumer Research*, 17,3: 346–61.

Todorov, T. ([1968] 1981) *Introduction to Poetics*, trans. R. Howard, Minneapolis: University of Minnesota Press.

Tyler, S.A. (1987) *The Unspeakable: Discourse, Dialogue, and Rhetoric in the Postmodern World*, Madison: The University of Wisconsin Press.

Van Maanen, J. (1988) *Tales of the Field: On Writing Ethnography*, Chicago: The University of Chicago Press.

—— (1995) "An End to Innocence: The Ethnography of Ethnography," in J. Van Maanen (ed.) *Representation in Ethnography*, Thousand Oaks: Sage, 1–35.

Wallendorf, M. and Brucks, M. (1993) "Introspection in Consumer Research: Implementation and Implications," *Journal of Consumer Research*, 20,3: 339–59.

Wells, W.D. (1989) "Lectures and Dramas," in P. Cafferata and A.M. Tybout (eds) *Cognitive and Affective Responses to Advertising*, Lexington, MA: Lexington Books, 13–20.

White, H. (1973) *Metahistory: The Historical Imagination in Nineteenth Century Europe*, Baltimore: Johns Hopkins University Press.

—— (1987) *The Content of the Form: Narrative Discourse and Historical Representation*, Baltimore: Johns Hopkins University Press.

Williams, J.D. (1995) "Review: John H. Stanfield II and Rutledge M. Dennis, eds., *Race and Ethnicity in Research Methods*," *Journal of Marketing Research*, 32,2: 239–43.

Part II

REPRESENTATION AND
VERBAL DATA

4

DARING CONSUMER-ORIENTED ETHNOGRAPHY

Eric J. Arnould

with the participation of Linda L. Price, Barbara B. Stern,
Craig J. Thompson, and Melanie Wallendorf

The general question I address in this chapter is: "How can ethnography be used to formulate theoretically useful representations of consumer-related phenomena?" The term *consumer-oriented ethnography* indicates my substantive focus: applying ethnographic methods to the study of consumer behaviors. The chapter builds on ethnographic and interpretive work conducted with several collaborators. The significance of these "interpretive communities" in informing my understanding is reflected in the co-authorship with Price, Stern, Thompson, and Wallendorf. (This chapter draws heavily on Arnould and Wallendorf (1994).)

The chapter has multiple objectives, corresponding to its main sections. In the first section, I discuss the goals of ethnography and then review the types, their particular contributions to representation, and the limitations of several techniques of data collection. In the second section, I discuss questions of ethnographic representation. In the third section, I articulate a model of interpretation–construction that situates ethnographic data in a multi-layered representation of consumption phenomena. In the discussion, I review points of similarity and difference with related representational strategies and types of research issues for which ethnographic methods are appropriate. I conclude by indicating that ethnographic methods are appropriate for apprehending four main kinds of consumption and use situations. Throughout, examples are drawn from two ethnographic projects, one concerning U.S. Thanksgiving Day, and the other, commercial white water river rafting (Wallendorf and Arnould 1991; Arnould and Price 1993; Price *et al.* 1995; Arnould *et al.* 1997).

Goals of ethnography

First, ethnography aims to clarify systematically the ways that culture (or sub-culture) simultaneously constructs and is constructed by the behaviors and experiences of members. This, of course, is something that individual members (and individual ethnographers!) only partially grasp themselves. Thus, ethnography attempts to explicate structured patterns of action that are cultural and/or social rather than merely cognitive, behavioral, or affective. Ethnographers achieve their goals by adopting four major strategies. As James Fernandez points out:

> the first requirement for such study is detail in ethnographic description . . . This method gives us, as none other, an awareness of the many different domains of experience in a culture to which expressive events may, in their predications, be making a linkage.
>
> (Fernandez 1986: 61)

In other words, ethnographers rely on systematic data collection and recording in natural settings during the first moment of ethnography (Belk, *et al.* 1988) for the subsequent construction of interpretive representations. In this way, ethnography is rooted in empiricist social science tradition. Indeed, the methods I discuss here sit squarely in the modernist tradition of interpretive social science associated with Durkheim, Weber, and Simmel (Giddens 1971; Miller 1987). Furthermore, ethnography has been conjoined to applied social research since its inception, demonstrating ethnography's deep connection to the projects of modernist scientific philosophy, such as the capacity of social science to predict and affect causally linked variables (Rabinow 1991; Wulff and Fiske 1987). Thus, the gap between traditional ethnography and positivist social science has sometimes been exaggerated in marketing research by critics who focus on a limited set of ethnographic practices (Hirschman 1986; Sherry 1990b).

Second, ethnographic research involves extended, experiential participation of the researcher in a specific cultural context. Ethnographers "tend to explain relationships or attitudes or social events by looking for their connections to other-things-happening in a defined analytic whole" (Wallman 1997: 250). Since it is also necessary to decide which context is most relevant to making sense of the matter in hand, in contrast to most market research, ethnography is intentionally less focused, less purposeful, and longer term – a point I shall return to below. Fernandez captures some key purposes of long-term field work:

> [ethnography] begins with those "revelatory incidents" which we have mentioned . . . those especially charged moments in human relationship which are pregnant with meaning. As a consequence of long-term participant observation, of "being there," an anthropologist is likely to be present at a number of these very real events . . . It is only such participation that enables us to give these moments of a sudden

constellation of significances an adequate reading. I regard these moments as a prime source of insight in fieldwork . . . an opportunity to relate events to the structures we otherwise spend much of our time studying in the field.

(Fernandez 1986: xi)

Participant observation thus aims to discern cultural patterns that structure human behavior. Long-term immersion in context improves the likelihood of experiencing the "revelatory incidents" that give meaning to cultural patterns. Long-term field work disquiets. The disquiet is engendered by the simultaneous experience of long-term embodied participation in a novel cultural context and the disengagement from that context provoked by persistent, detailed data collection. Tacking between engagement and disengagement motivates the scientific reflection that leads to ethnographic representation (Lederman 1990).

Figure 4.1 suggests a two-dimensional space onto which the ethnographic data collection might be inscribed. Data-collection tactics vary in terms of the degree of researcher intrusion and the degree to which natural behaviors are the locus of research activity rather than by the type of data collected.

Third, ethnography tends to be particularistic rather than generalizing in orientation. The ethnographic method is primarily concerned with the "ability to contextualize elements of culture and to make systematic connections among them" in a way that natives find credible in light of their own experience (Marcus and Fischer 1986: 23). Ethnographers prefer to mark and naturalize cultural differences and generally espouse pluralistic accounts of consumption and exchange behaviors.

Ethnographic data-collection techniques range from surveys and observations collecting quantitative data, to unstructured interviews and observations collecting qualitative data, and still and moving photos taken either by ethnographers or their "native" collaborators. Recordings of speech-in-action, informant conversations, and transcriptions of informant texts are other important data sources (Bernard 1988). Data-collection methods are combined to obtain access to disjunctures in consumers' behavior or praxis (established practice and associated norms). These divergent elements of praxis include manifest behaviors in all their

	Setting	
Member	Natural	Non-natural
participant	ongoing events	researcher-initiated instruction/initiation
non-participant	ongoing events	researcher-initiated demonstration/explanation

Figure 4.1 Effects of setting and membership roles on ethnographic data collection

rich complexity as opposed to articulated norms or ideals, in turn opposed to informants' value-laden accounts of their behavior (such as marginal, extraordinary, non-occurring, ordinary, personal choice, traditional, unique, and so forth).

Fourth, ethnography's distinctive potential results from directing multiple data-collection methods at a single phenomenon, a social science research strategy long advocated (Campbell and Fiske 1959). We combine data-collection methods in ethnographic research to achieve representations consistent with informant experience rather than merely to triangulate or achieve cross-sample reliability (Denzin 1970; Sanjek 1990b; Wallendorf and Belk 1989).

In accomplishing their disparate purposes, ethnographers employ numerous data-gathering techniques. However, *multiple* data-gathering strategies are almost always employed (and sometimes paradigmatic frames as well). Some researchers improperly refer to ethnography as qualitative research. In this way, they mix up ethnography with "humanistic inquiry" (Hirschman 1986; Hirschman and Holbrook 1992) defined by qualitative, often introspective data collection. To ethnographers the adjectives *qualitative* or *quantitative* identify the form of particular data sets rather than the set of procedures and assumptions that comprise a research program (Anderson 1986).

Fifth, the distinctive characteristic of ethnographic strategy concerns tactics for representing research findings. The modes of representation that ethnographers employ depend upon the representational purposes at hand. A kind of ongoing "reciprocal criticism" (to paraphrase Merleau-Ponty), whereby the cultural context of research informs and is in turn informed by the ethnographer's cultural experience, gives authenticity to classical ethnographic accounts (Josephides 1997: 25) that privilege representational consistency with informant experience. Recent political and epistemological critiques have led to heightened concern with representational strategies in ethnography, a point returned to later in the chapter (Clifford and Marcus 1986; Clifford 1990; Fernandez 1986; Geertz 1988).

In sum, by relying on extended participation in cultural context and employing data collected using multiple methods in the second moment of ethnography, ethnographers construct particularistic representations of meaningful cultural phenomena. These representations aim to penetrate divergent elements of praxis and, in so doing, to unravel the layered and contending meanings that marketing mixes – and acquisition, use, and disposition situations – have for consumers. This method can then ground theory-building in a variety of descriptive rhetorics. Nevertheless, contemporary ethnography eschews objectivist claims with regard to individual data sets, since data collection always already represents a theoretically and socially situated practice. Subsequent interpretations will always be partial, and always reflect the theoretical and personal biases of the individual ethnographer.

One might argue that consumer-oriented ethnography in marketing is fundamentally oxymoronic. As Murray and Ozanne (1991) point out, most consumer research is dominated by objective-order scientific positions. Extreme objectivist

positions assume that social reality exists as a concrete objective entity independent of human perception. Objectivist positions assume a status quo; things are
the way they appear to be. Order-based positions focus on the way that society
holds together and/or on behavioral management, control, and regulation.
Explanation and prediction of existing social behavior is firmly ensconced in
marketing practice. Fischer and Bristor (1994, Bristor and Fischer 1993), following
other feminist critiques of scientific practice (Keller 1985), show that these objective-order positions in marketing are bolstered by profound gender biases.
Attempts to unsettle dominant positions by advancing alternative interpretive
approaches are mostly ignored in marketing and consumer research. If acknowledged, they are routinely coopted or rejected in scholarly and practitioner
oriented articles (e.g., Calder and Tybout 1989; Hunt 1989, 1991). In addition,
such approaches and their champions are sometimes treated with derision in
intra-departmental scuttlebutt and in political struggles over hiring, promotion,
tenure, and resource allocation. Further, given the paucity of ethnographic studies
in marketing and consumer research, one might conclude that consumer-oriented
ethnography is at best a quixotic enterprise. Nevertheless, the interest of young
researchers in this method, the growing use of ethnographic techniques in for-
profit market research, and the successful elucidation of consumer phenomena by
ethnography outside of marketing research (Miller 1995) justifies the methods
here advocated.

Ethnographic representation

In the second moment of ethnography, namely data analysis and representation-
building, ethnographic practice shifts away from simultaneous engagement with
participants in the field and disengagement from them through data collection
and recording. Here, ethnography moves to engagement with informant voices
inscribed in field notes and recordings, and various traditions of representation.
Particular ethnographies, then, issue from a dialogue, argument, and confrontation between strategies of representation and the local voices of informants.

The use of multiple methods

Ethnographic research goes beyond a mere search for repetition of themes
summarizing common emic understandings (see Prus 1989a, 1989b). It demands
sufficient data from a variety of data-collection methods (1) to identify the themes
that summarize informants' emic experience and understandings, and (2) to
substantiate an etic representation that provides theoretical accounts of informants' representations and behaviors and culturally significant disjunctures
between them. Venkatesh (1995) has called for the use of alternative ethnoconsumerist conceptual categories in consumer research. But his claim that ethno-
consumers represent a conceptual innovation suggests a misunderstanding of the
nature of emic and etic constructs. Emic constructs are built up of native cultural

categories as he proposes ethnoconsumerist categories should be. Etic constructs are synthetic, theorized constructs. Well-developed etic constructs like "ritual," "marriage," or "household" express accumulated knowledge about the dimensions of cross-cultural continuity and variation associated with particular empirical instances. But etic constructs are not universalized reductionist categories as most constructs in economics and psychology tend to be. Hence, ethnoconsumerism collapses a useful distinction between emic–etic constructs without adding a new conceptual dimension.

In positivist scientific practice, multiple methods are considered useful in establishing convergent validity (Campbell and Fiske 1959) and are typically deployed with the goal of refining research instruments that provide internal consistency, test–retest reliability, and reliability across cases (Bearden, et al. 1993). By contrast, multiple methods of data collection are considered useful in ethnographic practice because they access different realms of experience that may diverge from one another. The term *disjunctures* refers to the differences between the data provided by various methods. This difference between the positivist concern for reliability and the ethnographic concern with incorporating disjunctures stems from the ethnographers' view of culture. Cultures are not taken to be singular unitary phenomena that are somehow "out there" in contrast to the views of positivist inquirers (Hofstede 1981, 1991). Rather, as Clifford says, "cultures are not like coherent languages or texts but are composed of conflicting discourses" (1990: 58).

Bearden, et al. (1993) point out that response set bias, the tendency for subjects to respond to attitude statements for reasons other than the content of the statements, constrains reliability in survey research. The two most common forms of response set bias they cite are acquiescence bias and social desirability bias, and they confirm that there are no easy ways to eliminate these biases in surveys. These problems of external validity are precisely the ones that ethnographic research addresses directly through long-term researcher immersion in context and non-intrusive procedures of data collection. Instead of asking which type of data provides greater external validity or reliability, however, ethnographers consider the way each type gives voice to a particular view or *perspective* on behavior.

Data collected through multiple methods challenge the skilled ethnographer to provide a representation that takes account of the variance in multiple perspectives. Wolf explains her techniques of analyzing ethnographic data as follows:

> The presence of unfocused, wide-ranging, all-inclusive fieldnotes was essential to the success of this unplanned [writing] project, but so were the purposefully subjective "data" recorded in my journal and the so-called objective data recorded under the stopwatch in the child observations. From parts of each of them I pieced the puzzle together . . . [this is] the value of using a variety of methods to record details and conversations that may or may not seem to make sense at the time.
>
> (Wolf 1990: 347)

In the next two sections of the chapter, I discuss the separate contributions that ethnographic observational and textual data make to interpretation. I then discuss the special benefits that result from combining data-collection methods in consumer-oriented ethnographic research. I present these benefits by discussing disjunctures between observed behavior and verbal articulations that are particularly important in understanding market behavior.

Observation's contribution to representation

Observation of human action provides the ethnographer with data about market behaviors as they are enacted within a culturally constructed constellation of behaviors (Baudrillard 1968; Boyd and Levy 1963; Douglas and Isherwood 1979; McCracken 1988b; Solomon and Assael 1987). For example, observation of an evening meal in the U.S. permits us to see its actual performance, complete with discussions of menu, displays of branded products served in their containers, dishes served, television playing a situation comedy, and teenagers talking on the telephone with friends while eating left-over pizza (Nichter and Moore 1992).

Observation documents specific actions of informants as they occur rather than as they are later remembered, recounted, and generalized by participants themselves. Primary reliance on observation reflects ethnography's acknowledgment of informants' inability to report fully on their behaviors. Certainly, there are some behaviors about which informants are willing and able to provide accurate, detailed accounts. But as unobtrusive observation reveals most acutely in "garbology," even the most articulate informants do not formulate accurate statements about some clear-cut behavioral regularities (Harrison, et al. 1974; Schiffer, et al. 1981; Whiting and Whiting 1970). For instance, the frequent inclusion of marshmallows, after dinner walks, and viewing photo albums in U.S. Thanksgiving feasts illustrates the capacity of observation to identify actions that informants rarely articulate despite participating in them. Similarly, observation reveals the absence of dessert and table linens, and the serving of branded foods in their original packaging as part of the taken-for-granted behaviors at many evening meals in the U.S. Thus ethnography can provide a technique for systematic recording of product-use contexts.

By analyzing fieldnotes from numerous observations of action in context, ethnographers construct interpretations that point to the prevalence of particular actions and raise questions about the recurrence of meanings enacted by different types of action. From observation, the ethnographer can also generate information about what informants actually do when a desired outcome does not occur or when an attempt to attain a valued outcome is frustrated (for example, when the Thanksgiving meal is spoiled by lack of ingredients, over-cooking, forgotten ingredients, failure to provide left-overs, or the extended family falling into dispute (Bagozzi and Warshaw 1990; Wallendorf and Arnould 1991)). Systematic analysis of such instances across sets of fieldnotes elucidates the constituting role of subsequent attempts at rectification (such as repeated trips to the supermarket, disappointment, laughter, and changes in feast group membership, respectively). For example, an informant notes both a common Thanksgiving dilemma and its resolution through the medium of a commercial purchase:

> 1.45p.m. Suzanne and I were sent on a very important errand. Angela had noticed that the munchie tray did not include their traditional [*sic*] Polish sausage. We went to the nearby ABCO [a supermarket] to purchase this along with another package of pretzels. 2.00p.m. We returned with the fulfillment of a Thanksgiving tradition. (swf20s.[1])

Another informant reports a case of consumers resolving a dilemma with a commercial purchase:

> 9.40a.m. I start making the jello salad so that it will gel in time for dinner. We usually have this particular salad as well as all the other dishes that we are preparing. The salad is made with lime jello, whipped cream, and crushed pineapple. As I start to open the pineapple, I notice that it is chunk pineapple and not crushed. We need crushed.
>
> Dad and I debate whether to put the pineapple in the blender to crush it or whether to go and get some from the Shumway's Storeroom Market about three-quarters of a mile down the road.
>
> Dad wins. "We'll use the [Dole] chunk pineapple for the fruit salad and I'll go to the Shumway's for crushed pineapple. I need to get a few other things too." (shf20s.)

Still and moving pictures taken in a natural setting increase ethnographers' ability to represent four types of observed behavior phenomena. First, ethnographic photographers and filmmakers balance the pressure to capture dramatic moments as framed by cultural expectations (Chalfen 1987; Sontag 1977) by photographing moments that do not "feel right" to photograph, such as backstage preparations and moments when participants maintain "nothing is going on." In this way, pictures provide evidence of the cultural scripts that underlie behavioral sequences. In the Thanksgiving research, for example, photos of pre-feast "down time" feature males more than females. Photos also are more efficient than written fieldnotes in documenting the proxemics (spatial relationships) among participants and between participants and products, thereby providing clues to the recurring nature of their emotional significance (Collier and Collier 1986; Heisley, *et al.* 1991).

Second, when participants guide the researcher's photographic choices or take pictures themselves, they gain the opportunity to mark moments that encode common and divergent understandings of events (Worth and Adair 1972). When participants take a series of photos or a film, the action sequences shown conform to the event's unarticulated, but nonetheless enacted, cultural script.

Particular moments that participants routinely choose to mark by a photograph provide an index of emotional intensity and unarticulated meaningfulness. Taking photos "feels right" at particular moments that encode the shared emotions, meanings, and values that informants experience at those times. The persuasive potential of such moments is evident. Thanksgiving photos of basting, seating, carving, and display confirm interpretations associated with the themes of abundance and wholeness developed from participant observation and verbal data (Wallendorf and Arnould 1991).

A third behavioral phenomenon that photographs record efficiently are the performative dramaturgical aspects of social and human-object interaction (Deighton 1992; Turner 1988). This includes the aesthetics of display and behavioral expressions of social division or integration that may be taken for granted both by informants and participant observers long-familiar with a subgroup or cultural context. In the Thanksgiving research, photos documented the social distance that members of families blended together for the holiday felt towards one another. In a different project, informant photos taken at the end of a commercial white water rafting trip dramatize the journey's pilgrimage-like qualities: the transformation of a group of strangers (including both customers and guides) into triumphant friends. In one shot, they huddle together laughing, all standing inside their waterproof gear bags (Arnould and Price 1993).

Fourth, photographs are efficient at providing documentation of the varying behavioral referents (the signified) that are glossed in verbal descriptions. For example, photographs reveal what behaviors informants are glossing when they speak of "dressing up" for New Year's parties, or say that Thanksgiving Day requires "nice clothes" or "lots of food." Photographs record specific actions; they disclose that "homemade" Thanksgiving cooking refers to (but does not mean merely) a time-consuming transmutation of an assemblage of branded ingredients. Similarly, a photo of physicians and lawyers cavorting with river guides in a freezing waterfall indicates what white water river guides mean when they say customers "open up" emotionally.

In summary, observation provides data about actual behavior in specific situations that may differ from accounts obtained through verbal data. By documenting specific behaviors, observation and especially participant observation overcomes biases of acquiescence, self-censorship, and social desirability inherent in methodologies that rely on self-report data (Bearden, et al. 1993; Josephides 1997). As discussed below, photographic observation is particularly useful in constructing "thick transcriptions," multi-vocalic ethnographies that convey emic experience such as those of ethnographic film makers (Ruby 1993; Stoller 1992). Observational data are particularly valuable in marketing research on consumption of products subject to strong social-desirability norms such as drugs, pornography, alcohol, and some luxury goods. In addition, observational data enrich interpretations when informants provide verbal data that are evocative rather than informational in character (Crapanzano 1980; Stoller 1989). The evocative use of language is typical in preliterate communities, embedded subcultures, cults, and remote, homogeneous groups of all sorts. In summary, if the goal of etic interpretation in ethnography is the elucidation of linkages between both overlapping and discrepant meanings of different consumption behaviors in action settings, observational data are essential.

Verbal data's contribution to representation

Ethnographic textual data provide informant statements about 1) ideal behavioral patterns, 2) informants' representations of the meaning of instances of behavior, and 3) stories about behaviors that informants interpret as unique.

Ideal behavior

Ethnographic textual data often describe informants' desires regarding consumption experiences. Even interview material that reportedly describes actual experience reflects the informant's experience potentially distorted by what the informant would ideally like to experience.

Many excellent examples of idealized statements occur in the Thanksgiving Day data, as the following exchange shows:

INTERVIEWER: I just wanted to ask you a few questions about Thanksgiving. Who you spend your holiday with, where, and what you usually eat?

RESPONDENT: We *always* had Thanksgiving at our house. *All* the kids would come and bring their husbands and children. Sometimes we would have up to 24 people over for dinner. The kids would *usually* sit in the foyer for dinner because the floor was marble and they could spill and nobody would care. You could mop the floor with a special chemical that they recommended. The parents would sometimes sit on the stairs that overlooked the foyer and watch their children eat. My husband was *always* the initiator in family gatherings. They called him "leader", he *always* made sure *everyone* came home for Thanksgiving. It was a lot of work; sometimes it took over two days to do the preparations for the dinner. My daughters would bring salads *usually*. I *always* cooked the turkey. The turkey was the center of attention. *Always* the main focus of the meal.

The description takes the form of a conventionalized narrative. It is a story filled with word play – "the leader", "center of attention" – that requires interpretation. In spite of the narrative framing, the declarative tone and the words "always," "usually", "all," "everyone," are cues to the ethnographer that the informant is describing idealized goals masked as accurate reports of actual behavior. Critical scrutiny indicates that it is unlikely that all (or even any) of her statements are categorically true. Instead, her statement uses symbolic devices – over-generalization, signs, and iconic relationships (Mick 1986) – that gloss the variety of the past as the informant constructs meaning from her experience. Communicative conventions facilitate communication between members of a speech community but make it difficult for ethnographers to grasp the underlying ideals, norms, rules, and relationships they encode. Because of the complex trophic relations in which informant reports are embedded, ethnographers steer informants to report particular instances, such as what happened yesterday, rather than to describe what they "generally" or "often" do. This approach resembles the critical incident technique (Bitner, *et al.* 1990). However, ethnographers are just as interested in typical incidents as in the memorable ones analyzed in critical incident methodology.

Informant's statements about behavioral regularities

Ethnographic interviews allow informants to describe aspects of their behavior of which they are aware. However, because informants have not done systematic research, their comparative statements can only articulate what they believe to be true about themselves and those like them. For example, Exhibit 1 provides excerpts from interviews with river guides reporting on the emotional sequence of events on multi-day river trips. The sequences they report make sense in the aggregate, although each guide usually tells just part of the story.

EXHIBIT 1

Notes from interviews with river guides reporting on the emotional sequence of river trips

Day 1: Confusion, uncertainty, fear, anticipation

Lots of anticipation . . . They're nervous . . . Unsure . . . They don't know what to expect so I'm sure a lot of them are pretty sacred when you get to a rapids or something. First day. (swm20s.)

Very confused, they're confused they're kinda standing on the bank at the launch point and there is always a few bugs flying around, they tend to look at the boats and say "Oh! We are riding in those? Oh, sure there is got to be a trail out down here where we can just hike out and go to a motel if we don't like this", and they realize once you get into a canyon, no. (mwm30s.)

Day 2: Calming down, relaxing, fun

So the next day they woke up realized that there were no grizzly bears that were going to invade their tents, they realized that snakes weren't in their sleeping bags, and the sun was shining, it was nice and cool out, breakfast is going, coffee is going, this type of thing and all of a sudden their attitudes were completely different. (mwm30s.)

Day 2 you get these great waves and people get wet, and it's tons of fun. (mwm30s.)

Day 3: Flow, letting go, excitement

And you notice, at least I notice, that somewhere around the third day everyone has gotten into the flow of the river. (swm30s.)

. . . 3 days later it's not there, they're kicking back, like "whatever you want, whatever you want to do, no big deal." The first day's hard work and orientation and day 2 is like big waves and everybody kinds of gets this big feel of the waves. Then on day 3 you're off on beautiful, beautiful canyons, and the canyons are just winding through. Really tune down a couple of notches into a slower mode. (swm20s.)

You can just tell. You can . . . from when you see them get off the plane, you see some businessman who's all uptight and what not and by day 3, he's *running around naked* or something, you know. (mwm40s.)

Day 3 it's incredibly beautiful, but sort of the *big excitement* at the end is Warm Springs, at the end of the day. But I just notice that people are, everybody knows each other, the anxiety is gone for the most part, except at Warm Springs gives you that *excitement*. (mwm30s.)

Day 4: Authenticity, aesthetic pleasure, confidence

And I mean . . . the moon rise and the sunset at the same time. It happens but *it's always just . . . takes you.* But to happen on that trip was really a neat surprise I thought. And on the last night, it was like . . . it was like, I don't know, *whoever* just gave a gift to us, you know, for our last night on such an *awesome* trip. (swf20s.)

Day 5: Storing feelings, emotion and meaning transfer

I think . . . I remember somebody on my last trip saying, uh, you know, I'm gonna go back to work and all those things seemed like they were, you know, things that were stressing me out aren't gonna be stressing me out anymore. You kinda . . . you *keep that feeling with you.* Keep that feeling of . . . it just kinda keeps things in perspective a little bit. Things that we let disturb us so much in our lives that really aren't that . . . problems. (swf20s.)

You know, in The Grand Canyon, where I started working, you'd do like 14 to 20 day trips, and by the end of the trip you knew these people inside out, you know? You *knew what made them tick*, you knew what pleased them, *you knew their buttons*, – their hot buttons, you know? (swm20s.)

. . . the person coming away from the river kind of feeling a little bit of *transcending force* or changing force through their river trip. I think a lot of that *comes from a kind of instructor's attitude* towards it. (wm30s.)

In the Thanksgiving Day research, unstructured interviews contain substantial amounts of material in which informants report or imply that they are similar to others in the way they celebrate the holiday. As shown in Exhibit 2, despite numerous differences in what they actually do, informants often report that they serve "the traditional meal." Yet by "rummaging" across fieldnotes (McCracken 1988a), one discovers the many varieties of household consumption tradition encompassed in the U.S. Thanksgiving tradition gestalt.

EXHIBIT 2

Fieldnote excerpts concerning tradition

Last year I brought a friend of mine because he had nowhere else to go for Thanksgiving. He said it was the best Thanksgiving he had ever had because his family is casual and they don't have a *traditional*-type Thanksgiving.

Basically, my parents and his parents have *traditional* . . . turkey and all the trimmings. Occasionally his mom will have ham and turkey too, sort of a thing.

Another *traditional* activity in Tricia's family is that each member of the family has to make one dish for the Thanksgiving feast and everyone helps make the turkeys.

Second most important holiday of the year, at first it was *traditional* but now it's more special and family orientated.

We always have a *traditional* dinner. I remember one time when we had a little program before dinner. Our daughter Quinn recited the 100th Psalm, and everyone did a little thing.

My great grandma makes homemade bread every year. It's so good! She always so sweet. She does shoulder rubs after dinner for all of her grandsons. Well . . . , *traditional* food. We eat all of those *traditional* Thanksgiving dishes. We have turkeys, dressing, sweet potatoes, cranberry sauce, homemade bread, relish tray, mashed potato, and pumpkin pies and pecan pies . . .

Since I have lived in Tucson, I haven't gone home to spend Thanksgiving with my mother once. So I would say it has been about four years. I have spent my Thanksgiving dinners with friends, but it has not been a *traditional* experience since my grandmother died.

INTERVIEWER: Today I would like to ask you various questions about Thanksgiving. What do you usually eat?
RESPONDENT: The *traditional* fare, turkey, stuffing, mashed potatoes, vege-tables – corn and other various vegetables – cranberry sauce, pies: lemon meringue, cherry, pecan, pumpkin more than any other, twice as many.

INTERVIEWER: Do you use paper plates or cups at all for this occasion?

RESPONDENT: No, I don't recall using these ever. My family is pretty *traditional*, and I guess I can say well-off too, so we never use paper plates or cups.

It's probably one of, if not the best, meals of the year, only better dinner may be Christmas. I think it is just the *traditional* Thanksgiving dinner. A big turkey, stuffing, potatoes, you know, the works. What a meal.

Well, we eat pretty much the *traditional* thing. We have turkey, potatoes, cranberry sauce, vegetables, and pumpkin pie. Stuffing too. I don't even remember. We have salad and breads too. That's about it.

Reejeenies (stuffed cheese balls that are breaded) that grandma makes that are best. Turkey, which dad and uncle slice. Mostly all that *traditional* stuff.

Oh yeah. Now that the kids are getting bigger I feel it's more important to emphasize the *traditional* values that the holidays are meant to . . . uhm symbolize. It's different today though. I mean, I can go out to a restaurant and have a very nice meal with my family and feel very thankful about what I've got and still go to work.

RESPONDENT: . . . cornbread stuffing, what else? . . . oh yeah, good old cranberry orange relish. That's really about it.

INTERVIEWER: Sounds pretty *traditional* to me.

RESPONDENT: Yeah. But I guess I forgot my additional *traditional* element . . . frozen margaritas!!!

INTERVIEWER: What will you do on Thanksgiving?

RESPONDENT: I'll cook a *traditional* Thanksgiving dinner.

INTERVIEWER: One last question would you eat the *traditional* food if you were a guest at a dinner since your diet is health orientated?

RESPONDENT: Oh yeah. I do a lot of concessions in that area. I'm not a vegetarian . . .

INTERVIEWER: What did the dinner consist of?

RESPONDENT: Usually turkey would be the meat, we would have. *Traditional*, I would say. A *traditional* Thanksgiving dinner.

Thanksgiving dinner is very *traditional* at our house, that is, there is hardly any deviation from the original menu. Always turkey with gravy, stuffing, green beans with French fried onions, mashed potatoes, yams, *pistachio fluff*, homemade bread, butter, cranberry sauce, soft drinks, water and wine. The turkey was baked and basted in an oven in a large covered pan. We generally do not have any ethnic specialties at dinner, except when my father's relatives are visiting. The cranberry sauce served was Ocean Spray

> from a can. The most *traditional* dish would have to be the turkey. Desserts consist of apple crisp, chocolate chip cookies, pecan pie, and nut bars.

In analyzing ethnographic interviews, the ethnographer critically analyzes informants' comparative statements about themselves, asking what sample of experiences these inferences are drawn from and what function they serve. What the ethnographer regards as "traditional" here is a contextually specific belief in common experience that suppresses perceptions of temporal, regional, race, historical, and class differences permeating American life.

Representations of the meaning of particular actions

Verbal data include informants' descriptions of action entangled with statements about what these behaviors mean. Ethnography proceeds on the assumption that the behavioral referents may differ across people, even though the guiding value or meanings remain the same. For example, unstructured interviews about Thanksgiving Day include rich and detailed informant descriptions of the behaviors that transform bulk commodities and branded products into culturally appropriate holiday menus. Informants' reports of making things "from scratch" conveyed a key value connected with holiday satisfaction. This value is exemplified in the following exchange:

INTERVIEWER: What types of food do you eat at Thanksgiving dinner?
RESPONDENT: Well, *everything was homemade*, because my grandmother made *everything from scratch*. She made stuffing, mashed potatoes, cranberry sauce, rolls, and turkey. My uncle would carve the turkey *every* year no matter what [emphasis added].

Foods transformed in emic reports differ, but the particulars are less significant than the guiding theme of making from scratch. We interpret multiple emic reports such as this as metaphorically related to the holiday celebration's guiding values rather than as a factual recounting of food preparation details. Instead of seeing the foods as assemblages constructed from branded products, informants uncritically describe their preparations as "homemade." Repeated reports such as these point the consumer oriented ethnographer to the strategic import of the underlying values, (in this case decommodification and family continuity (Wallendorf and Arnould 1991)). What is important, then, in interpreting interviews is to focus on the emic importance and meaning of the behaviors that informants report.

Stories about behaviors that informants interpret as unique

Verbal reports often produce informants' commentary about the uniqueness of some of their experiences. This is particularly common among U.S. informants who pride themselves on individuality and a strong sense of self (Triandis 1989). Across cases, many seemingly unique personal anecdotes prove from an etic perspective to enunciate common themes. Lacking the researcher's contact with a substantial sample of accounts, informants often depict general patterns of action as unique. As experienced, they seem unique but, as observed, they represent cultural regularities. By themselves unremarkable, the anecdotes assume greater significance in the context of other data in which informants imply that many components of the meal are "unique," "special" or "novel" (see Exhibit 3).

EXHIBIT 3

Fieldnote excerpts concerning special qualities

Everyone who was seated at the table – in this instance the men – watched Mr Orsini carve the bird with a knife and *special* fork.

We also had mom's bean and mushroom soup hot dish which is delicious [authors: and presumably unique], mashed potatoes, rutabaga, squash, mom's own *special* dressing.

Sometimes she cooks them from scratch. They're a *real novelty* around the dinner table. Because you always have turkey and the vegetable and stuff, but for some reason you don't get *the good rolls* any other time of the year.

Mrs Miller then went on to tell me this was *special* prickly pear cactus jam that she and several of her lady friends had been making for some time now. They started making it with a lady named Mary who got the recipe from another lady that lived there in the home with them.

INTERVIEWER: What else happened?
RESPONDENT: My dad would always watch the games on TV and the kids would help clean up. My grandma would always try to serve the food while everyone else was eating. We would tell her to sit down, but she never seemed to listen. Our Thanksgivings were *not very conventional*. My grandma is Polish and she always made *spaetzla* which is noodles and gravy and it is really good. We never had stuffing or pies or anything like that.
INTERVIEWER: Do you eat turkey at least?
RESPONDENT: Yes, we have turkey, but we also have roast beef and all kinds of other foods like cream of spinach which I love. It's like a big feast.
INTERVIEWER: What is you personal favorite?
RESPONDENT: The spaetzla my grandmother used to make was the best. My mother makes it now, but it's not the same. I even make it sometimes, but it never seems to be as good as when grandma made it.
INTERVIEWER: So she had that special touch?

RESPONDENT: Yes, she also made sauerkraut which I loved. We would always take home so much food that there would be enough to last our whole family for at least a couple of days. I remember I would have *peas and sauerkraut for breakfast* and it would remind me of the good time I had the day before.

INTERVIEWER: What are some other foods that you like a lot?

RESPONDENT: Well my parents liked the more traditional foods like cranberry sauce and things like that, but I liked things like pickles and these cookies my grandfather used to make. He owned a bakery and he used to have these *special* cookies made up for Thanksgiving. They were in the shape of a turkey and they had a really good frosting on them that I really can't describe. But since my grandma died he is really sad and doesn't make them anymore.

INTERVIEWER: Do you always have turkey?

RESPONDENT: Always! There is always left-over for a couple of days. They only make *special* dishes that day that they don't really eat during the rest of the year (i.e. yams, fruit salad).

INTERVIEWER: Tell me about Thanksgiving without your family.

RESPONDENT: . . . When I got older, I got to partake in the family tradition of drinking the wine, Cold Duck. Before I was old enough, I had to drink the Kool Aid in a *special* glass.

INTERVIEWER: . . . We eat dinner with *turkey plates*.

RESPONDENT: What is the turkey plate?

INTERVIEWER: Those are china with turkey's picture in the middle. My grandma has a set. My mom and aunt have each set, also.

RESPONDENT: . . . I usually make a lemon pie that everyone really enjoys. It goes so quick that I usually make two of them. One of my aunts makes a delicious peach cobbler, and my mom is known for her *sweet potato soufflé*.

INTERVIEWER: Is it [lemon pie with graham cracker crust] a family recipe?

RESPONDENT: Yes, it is.

When placed in context, "special potatoes" are seen not as an accidental appellation, but one that fits with a cross-case experience of the holiday as "special" and with consumers' expenditure of imagistic-emotional energy to create that experience (Hirschman and Holbrook 1982) using a variety of consumption goods (a fork, sweet potatoes, spaetzla, rolls, salad, stuffing, or cactus jam, all mentioned in Exhibit 3).

As the ethnographer moves across a large number of interviews, unique traditions are seen etically as reflecting common recurrent values or patterns. Consider a tale about a recipe:

> . . . and mom would bring the mashed potatoes. Made the same way. Take the potatoes, peel them, oil them, mash them, um, and add butter and junk and a little salt and pepper. And that's it and mash them and leave real little lumps in them, real little lumps. And we call them homemade lumpy mashed potatoes. And grandma started making them and my brother and I fell in love with them when we were real little kids, and *so it is tradition to make homemade lumpy potatoes*, and homemade gravy . . . I watch my grandmother every year and I still don't know how to make it.

The informant reinforces the unique qualities of these potatoes by identifying their origin ("grandma") and the mysteries of their making ("I still don't know how").

In another tale, an informant describes what was regarded as an unusual form ("special occasion") of consumer behavior associated with the turkey:

RESPONDENT: Yeah, it's [the food] really good. My mother is an excellent cook and we really have a lot of fun. (Giggle) I remember when I was a little kid I always wanted to shift gears. *This sounds really funny, but it is true.* When I was little my mom would get up in the morning and start making dinner. And I would always get up with her; my mom would usually wake me up, because this has been going on for about six years now, and after a few years *my mom would wake me up for this special occasion*. She would clean the turkey and then wake me up. I would run out into the kitchen, I was so excited! I would stand in front of the turkey, put both of my hands on the legs and start shifting the gears as if I'm driving a car, and it was just so funny. My family would get a total kick out of it. Everyone would come in and start laughing.

INTERVIEWER: (Laughing) That sounds like fun.

RESPONDENT: Yeah, it was a lot of fun.

INTERVIEWER: Do you still do that now?

RESPONDENT: To tell you the truth, last Thanksgiving when I went home, my mom came in and woke me up and said, "Janice, just for *old time's sake*, come out and shift the gears on the turkey." I jumped out of bed, ran to the kitchen just like I used to and I shifted those gears. My mom and dad laughed so hard there were tears in our eyes. It was funny, it was really neat, you know, doing that *after all these years*. This was maybe ten years ago now since I have done this. It was just really neat.

INTERVIEWER: So you just had to do it one more time.

RESPONDENT: Yeah, I did. And it was really fun. It was worth it, seeing a smile on my parents face.

Informants naively represent such special occasions and traditions as unique to their families. Yet by "rummaging" across unstructured interviews, we discover many cases in which imperfect (lumpy mashed potatoes) or innovative (shifting gears) consumption behaviors are given meaning by the not-so-unique themes of nostalgia for family traditions ("for old time's sake"), affect associated with temporary family togetherness ("tears in our eyes;" "really fun"), and situational consensus about familial authority ("my mom came in and woke me up," young *adult* female speaking). A consumer-oriented ethnographic interpretation of these meanings is that they represent consumers' efforts to exclude the impacts of mass marketing – commodification and homogenization of experience (Wallendorf and Arnould 1991).[2] Although certainly not everyone pretends to "shift gears" on a turkey or takes pride in lumpy mashed potatoes, etically they are interpreted as enacting a common theme through a culturally constructed rite of integration (Trice and Bayer 1984).

Other examples are available in other ethnographic projects I have conducted among Americans. Participants in commercial river rafting experiences often credit the trip with personal transformation or with bringing members of their family closer together. Participants experience this within the unique narrative of their personal and family histories. Etically, however, the ethnographer is challenged to account for those features of commercial river trips that recurrently produce the unexpected experience.

In summary, emic accounts of every type are used to construct ethnographic representations of culturally constituted behavioral constellations.[3] But rather than merely summarizing emic statements, ethnography accounts for them. "Rummaging" (McCracken 1988a: 33) through many quotations in the interview transcripts allows the researcher to develop working hypotheses about the common guiding values, such as notions of singular and enduring family tradition enshrining images of household stability (Wallendorf and Arnould 1991), or belief in the curative emotional power of river rafting (Arnould and Price 1993; Arnould, *et al.* 1997). Unstructured interviews should reveal prevalent values expressed in different ways by different informants. Repetition of themes across informants' verbal texts such as unprompted speech-in-action and conversation assures the ethnographer that the underlying values that lead to such idealizations are cultural guides for informants rather than merely responses to a priori categories. Textual ethnographic data provide material concerning ideals for behavior, patterns that informants are able to articulate, general meanings of particular actions, and events that informants regard as unique in their cultural experience.

Multiple methods' contribution to ethnographic representation

The special benefit of using multiple data-collection methods in ethnographic market research derives from the access they provide to disjunctures in consumer praxis. In this section, I specify the way that different combinations of methods provide ethnographers with the opportunity to construct a representation of human action that accounts for disjunctures as well as seamless meanings. I organize this material according to four disjunctures: 1) behavior in contrast to ideals; 2) observed behavior in contrast to articulated episodes; 3) recurrent patterns of action in contrast to informants' representations; and 4) recurrent patterns of action in contrast to informants' representations of them as unique.

Behavior in contrast to ideals

People being observed may feel compelled to provide commentary about the difference between what they regard as ideal behavior and what is unfolding as actual behavior. Additionally, people's commentary in interviews superimposes their ideals on reports of what happens in a way that differs from observable behavior. In such cases, the task of etic interpretation is to explain why people view their behavior ideally but behave in a different way. Rather than regarding either perspective as erroneous or as evidence of intentional misrepresentation, ethnographers analyze the coexistence of divergent perspectives to understand the way that both are used in constituting a behavioral constellation.

In some cases, the ideal behavior is desired so strongly that it prevents informants from self-critical consideration of their own reports. In identifying such disjunctures, the ethnographer attempts to account for the functions served by the idealized images of behavior in terms of potential conflicts averted by the reported consumer practices. For instance, we sought to explain the disjuncture between Thanksgiving Day informants' explanations that they "always" do the same thing each year and our observation of them negotiating with one another about what should be done as the ritual unfolds. The belief that the same thing is done each year serves the function of supporting an ideal of stability, whereas the negotiation of arrangements for a particular feast serves the function of providing flexibility to accommodate evolving preferences and changing roles. Both are necessary in this consumption context to protect an image of long-term family stability.

Observed behavior in contrast to what informants articulate

Culture pervades the experiences of individuals. Nonetheless, much of culture is verbally inaccessible to informants and, thus, to interviewers. Photos and participant observation, however, provide access to phenomena that informants do not or cannot verbalize.

For instance, in the river rafting research, consumers have limited ability to articulate the pattern of emotional experiences that unfolds across participants over the course of a multi-day trip. Guides articulate these emotional sequences in interviews, but participant observation is necessary to link lived experience to scientific concepts such as "communitas," "flow," and "magic." Similarly, in Thanksgiving Day research, choices about serving the butter or margarine reflect unarticulated class differences also evident in choices about type of napkins (paper or cloth), extent of color and pattern complementarity for table service, and degree of formality of place settings. Most people imply that they do what "everyone" does at Thanksgiving. This indicates not only that contrasts are unavailable to participants who only celebrate within class boundaries of their social network but also that potential differences are not apprehended. The ethnographer is challenged to interpret the ways that observations diverge from reported emic meanings. In so doing, ethnographic representation articulates the way that culture organizes daily life.

Recurrent patterns of action that contrast with informants' representations

Ethnographic combinations of observation and interviews also direct ethnographers to disjunctures between the way that people regard their own behavior (emic perspective) and the interpretation of that behavior by the ethnographer (etic perspective). For instance, we observed numerous households consuming foods on Thanksgiving Day that they refer to in interviews as "homemade." Observation reveals that the actions behind this preparation consist of assembling branded products such as pie shell, canned pie filling, and frozen whipped topping. The challenge of etic explanation is to provide an account of the action itself as well as an account of the function served by its emic meaning. Neither is regarded as more accurate than the other, for both are elements of consumers' understanding of products and use situations, and both must be included in an explanation.

Recurrent patterns of action that informants represent as unique

Observations combined with informant representations from participant observation and from unstructured interviews are useful in identifying disjunctures between emic and etic perspectives in terms of uniqueness versus general patterns. For example, some individuals experience transformative episodes on rafting trips. Observation across trips reveals the recurrence of such transformations, indicating that they are a patterned performative response to interaction in "wilderness" environments (Arnould, *et al.* 1998).

Similarly, in the midst of observation and in interviews on Thanksgiving Day, several kinds of dishes served were described by participants as if these dishes are unique to their own Thanksgiving Day celebrations. However, as we compared across multiple sets of observation notes and interviews, we came to see the inclusion of dishes regarded as unique as typical of many family Thanksgiving Day celebrations. Through special recipes, families dramatize the decommodification of food to symbolize the persistence of familial tradition. Ethnography uncovers cultural similarity in the importance attached to the household's or individual's claim to uniqueness. From an etic perspective, what these families value as unique or special to their celebration is comparable.

Developing ethnographic representations

In this section, I describe the process of building multilayered and multivocal ethnographic interpretations of consumer behavior constellations from field data. I also discuss in general terms the processes of interpreting disjunctures between different data sets. (This section of the chapter draws heavily from Arnould and Wallendorf (1994).) The potential of wide-ranging data sets under theoretical control to generate ethnographic description is well established (Sanjek 1990a, 1990b). Readers are referred to classic methodological texts for more technical details (Strauss and Corbin 1990; Miles and Huberman 1994; Silverman 1993).

Ethnographic interpretation differs in focus from the individual product, brand, or service emphasis of most consumer research. It is rooted in the idea that behaviors are given meaning as specific enactments within clusters of culturally scripted behavioral expectations (Fernandez 1986). This applies to contexts including consumption sets, styles, and usage situations (Baudrillard 1968; Holt 1995, 1997; Douglas and Isherwood 1979; McCracken 1988b; Solomon and Assael 1987; Srivasteva *et al.* 1984). Thus, cutting up sweet potatoes *per se* is not meaningful; it takes on specific syntagmatic meanings as part of a sequence of Thanksgiving Day meal preparation behaviors and paradigmatic ones as part of the objects and activities central to the female holiday experience.

Ethnographers resist interpreting discrete consumer behaviors in isolation because doing so produces atomistic and mechanistic portraits that preclude a vision of cultural gestalts. Instead, ethnographers view consumer behaviors as integrally connected by the cultural contexts in which they are embedded. For example, traditional market research might well uncover consumer segments of heavy partiers versus non-partiers on New Year's Eve and a set of product preferences for each of these segments. But holistic ethnographic inquiry uncovers the meanings attached to the sets of behaviors of these segments and links them with pervasive macro themes in American culture. Partiers may be associated with youthful, romantic, and hedonistic values; non-partiers may be associated with maturity, Calvinist, and ascetic values. Both poles of activity are associated with the Protestant ethic and the play of nostalgia in American cultural experience (Arnould and Wallendorf 1991; Campbell 1987; Davis 1979).

Ethnographic representation articulates the layers of meaning underlying a behavioral constellation such as cooking Thanksgiving dinner rather than cutting potatoes, or grooming for the office rather than merely using deodorant. As our discussion of disjunctures indicates, ethnography does not search for a one-to-one relationship between behaviors and underlying meanings. Rather, it articulates some of the many layers of meaning that are shared, resonant, or discrepant across behaviors comprising a constellation. Ethnography attempts to uncover the layers of meaning based in individual consciousness, group structure, culture, and economic forms. These simultaneously operating layers of meaning are regarded as complementary rather than as mutually exclusive.

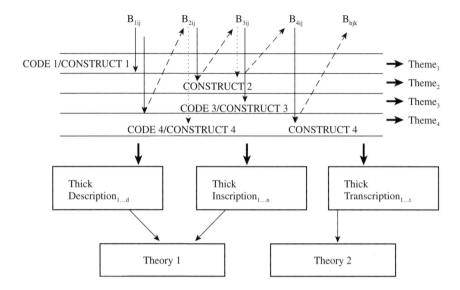

Figure 4.2 Coding, troping, and representation in consumer-oriented ethnography

To summarize the complex, untidy, and iterative process of interpretive coding and data analysis, Figure 4.2 provides a simplified visual model.

As Figure 4.2 shows, consumer-oriented ethnography gathers data about behaviors (B) that occur in a context. Rather than studying only one behavior (purchase and use of a particular product), consumer-oriented ethnography studies a set of behaviors that co-occur (B_h). Emic understanding of the "goes together" nature or co-constituting meanings of behaviors is termed the "quality space" (Fernandez 1986: 40); etic representation of co-occurring behaviors (whether or not their co-occurrence is recognized by participants) and their emergent meanings is called a behavioral constellation.

Data about the behaviors in a behavioral constellation (B_h, h = 1 . . . m, where m = the number of behaviors the ethnographer identifies as part of the constellation) are gathered from purchase or consuming units in the sample (i = 1 . . . n) using various data collection methods (j = 1 . . . x, where x = the number of ethnographic data collection methods employed). Effective ethnographic interpretation begins during data collection by attending simultaneously to three aspects of sampling: across purchase or consuming units (denoted by subscript i), across several interrelated behaviors of those units or individuals (subscript h), and across forms of data collection (subscript j). As the examples in this chapter illustrate, rather than studying product or service use in isolation, the ethnographer studies the meaningful behavioral constellation in which product or service use is embedded. To summarize, the data set (B_{hij}) spans the several behaviors in a constellation for numerous purchasing or consuming units collected using multiple data-collection methods.

All efforts at interpretation begin with deep familiarity with their data achieved through frequent reading and re-reading (Agar 1980). Ethnographers then organize their data through codes that represent similar behaviors in the constellation. Such data organization may be accomplished by hand by means of margin notes (Miles and Huberman 1994) or may be aided by (not substituted for) text coding and retrieval computer programs such as AskSam, Ethnograph, GoFer, Notebook, NUD*IST, Tally, WordCruncher, or ZyIndex (Miles and Huberman 1994). Although either approach can produce credible and insightful interpretations, computer programs overcome human information-processing deficits. The process of organizing data about particular behaviors (B_{hij}) into codes ($Code_h$) is shown in the solid arrows in Figure 4.2. Codings are developed initially by noting fieldnote recurrences of a particular behavior across the sample ($i = 1 \ldots n$) (for one data-collection method). At this stage, the ethnographer examines the entire sample from one data-collection method with respect to a particular behavior in the constellation.

Initially, each behavior is coded with as many emergent codes as needed to record the ethnographer's developing understanding of recurrences. Rather than being developed a priori, as in content analysis (Kassarjian 1977; Spiggle 1986), codes are developed as the ethnographer reads the data and notes recurring word usage, phrases, complex behavioral sequences, or meanings. Codes are simply a way to mark recurrences, but they go beyond merely marking recurrences in emic language. For example, "Day 1" is a code used for more than just each emic mention of the words "day one" or "first day" of a rafting trip; it potentially includes not only all elements associated with the day but also any objects, behaviors, or relationships regarded as noteworthy by the informant. Some behaviors have only one code, whereas others may be coded in multiple ways. Consider the following verbatim:

> I think, river magic . . . I see it all the time . . . I saw it when I guided. Just the spell that the river environment can cast on people, and just bring them – pulling away from that urban 9 to 5 lifestyle that most people live – and, you know, just bring them back to the basics . . . The moon rise, listening to the water, sitting on a sandy beach and a warm breeze blowing through the cottonwoods, seeing wildlife. That, to me, is river magic.
>
> (interview, river guide, swm40s.)

This statement might be coded to exemplify the codes "river magic," "nature," or "ordinary life" depending upon the emic and theoretical orientations used to organize the data. Some codes may apply to only one behavior, whereas others may mark similarity across several different behaviors (HOMEMADE describes the preparation of a variety of foods, including rolls, pies, potatoes, and cranberry sauce).

But ethnographic interpretation must go beyond codes that mark recurrences in emic understandings and practice by discovering additional connections in the data. To do so, the consumer-oriented ethnographer works with the codes and attempts to identify convergences and disjunctures by moving across data about a behavior gathered through different data-collection methods (across B_j, 1 . . . p). Codes for data about a behavior from one method are compared with data about the same behavior collected using a different method. For example, river guides' statements about what happens on day three are compared with participant observation notes from day three of a river trip:

> Another thing about Day 3 is that, Day 1 everyone walks way upstream, or walks way downstream to pee, by Day 3, people are just peeing right there. Sorta, that's what I think, when I think of Day 3, people are just sorta *given up* anything that happened on Day 1.
> (river guide, mwm30s)

> When I went down to the river bank just a few minutes ago, I said, "Hey, is this a public bath house? Can anyone come?" And, Sinead said, "Oh, you're very welcome." . . . So, I noticed there is this kind of *emotional opening up* that goes on. [But] not everyone participates . . . But, I think some have hung back from doing things, some have also hung back emotionally – it's interesting.
> (Participant observation notes, 6/96)

These comparisons indicate convergences (a definite loosening of behavior strictures) as well as disjuncture (giving up stress as described by the guide is not identical to the experience of emotional openness captured in the field note). The interpretive meanings of codes are refined in light of tacking between additional data points. The key point is that codes maintain their contextualized meaning rather than being decontextualized as in content analysis. And rather than just noting the presence of disjunctures or forcing them into one convergent interpretation, the consumer-oriented ethnographer at this point asks why the disjunctures between methods occur.

Figure 4.2 shows the way that the consumer-oriented ethnographer proceeds with interpretation building, further refining the codes into constructs by moving across the behaviors themselves (B_h). Since ethnography presumes that important cultural values or meanings are expressed by several behaviors in a constellation, data interpretation next attempts to identify these resonances. Iterative tacking between data sets enables codes for behaviors to be compared with other behaviors and verbal data that initially appear only loosely connected (Belk and Coon 1993: 395). In developing interpretations, a variety of systematic relations of contrast and association between behaviors and verbal data are considered (Durham and Fernandez 1991: 192):

1 *Paradigmatic*, that is, one of a possible set of similar behaviors such as the various kinds of HOMEMADE dishes. Paradigmatic constructs developed from the interview excerpts on river magic include "communion with nature" and "mediation between visible and invisible worlds."

2 *Syntagmatic*, that is, part of a culturally prescribed temporal sequence such as interrupting the river trip to kiss Tiger Wall in order to propitiate the river gods or telling Thanksgiving Day stories about bad times overcome.

3 *Metaphoric*, that is, a relationship of similarity, such as consumers' acting as if Thanksgiving turkeys, pies, houses, and people should all be "stuffed."

4 *Metonymic*, that is, a causal or hierarchical relation of contiguity or part–whole within the same domain. Through metonymy, running a particular rapid, or preparing the core dishes in a Thanksgiving Day feast, may provide summary symbols for the entire cultural constellation of behaviors.

Thus, the ethnographer builds an interpretation by constructing *tropes*, which are the meaningful symbolic linkages between constructs (Fernandez 1986, 1991). Comparing different contructs to identify symbolic linkages is known as "troping". Rather than merely assessing whether codes can be directly applied to additional behaviors, the ethnographer constructs tropes by assessing the symbolic applicability of the meanings represented by codes across behaviors.

Troping across behaviors and methods is shown in Figure 4.2 as upward dashed lines moving from codes to data about other behaviors and then as downward dashed lines returning to refine the codes into constructs. Troping refines the codings so that they can be referred to as constructs that then form identifiable themes (horizontal layers in Figure 4.2) in the interpretation (see Strauss and Corbin 1990 for a similar argument). Interpretive layers or themes connected to several behaviors in the constellation are taken to represent important cultural constructs and, therefore, are accorded broader etic significance in the final ethnographic interpretation. Thus in the river rafting research, themes like communitas, magical transcendence, and social constructions of nature inform the final interpretation (Arnould, *et al.* 1998).

Ethnographic interpretation is composed of constructs that form complementary themes shared, resonant, or discrepant across the behavioral constellation. This multilayered and cultural nature of ethnographic interpretation is referenced in Geertz's (1973) oft-cited term *thick description* (see Figure 4.2), which is the desired outcome of traditional ethnography. Thick descriptions are realistic ethnographies (Van Maanen 1988). As such, they have been criticized for failing to recognize power relationships and other implicit factors that structure them (Clifford and Marcus 1986; Gubrium and Holstein 1997). But the phenomenologically distanced, monologic, and non-participant stance implied by the term (see Figure 4.3) is not the only ethnographic representation possible in marketing, although it has dominated consumer research. An alternative is the presentation of customer stories, transcribed observations and unstructured interviews, or focus groups as *thick transcription*. In this mode of representation, the ethnographic subjects are natives; that is, they are customers or prospective customers who speak of and for themselves. The ethnographer's role becomes one of compilation, editing, and juxtaposition of texts based on his/her expertise. Here the presentation is polyphonic, and the voices of participants come through clearly as they recount their experiences. Nevertheless, authorial responsibility ultimately resides with the ethnographer, and the representation is somewhat phenomenologically distant. Thick transcription is practiced by ethnographic filmmakers (e.g., Stoller 1992) and found in some experimental ethnographies (Josephides, 1997; Tsing 1994). Colgate-Palmolive made use of this technique to segment the fragmented Mexican market for cleaning products and to develop improved positionings and new market offerings (Evans and Berman 1992, Video 3, 21).

In addition, consumer researchers have begun to make use of a third mode of representation pioneered by ethnographers (Seremetakis 1991; Stoller and Olkes 1987). This is *thick inscription*: a mode of representation that privileges the experiences of researchers who immerse themselves in an acquisition or consumption use context. They are participants if not natives, and the presentation reflects lived experience in the phenomenological sense. Introspective, confessional modes of inquiry move in the direction of thick inscription (Van Maanen 1988; Wallendorf and Brucks 1993). Recent examples include accounts of high-risk commercial recreations such as sky-diving and martial arts (Celsi *et al.* 1993; Donohue 1991), addictive consumption (Hirschman 1992), expatriate Indians' homes and possessions (Joy and Dholakia 1991), and Harley-Davidson subcultures (Schouten and McAlexander 1992a, 1992b, 1993, 1995. These examples of thick inscription suggest promising directions for the improvement of consumer diaries and the study of experiential consumption products and services.

The result of the sifting and resifting of data is a representation of the constellation of consumer behaviors included in an American Thanksgiving dinner, a river rafting trip, a New Year's party, a "homey" house (McCracken 1989), a swap meet (Sherry 1990a), a gift or toy store (McGrath 1989; Sherry and McGrath 1989; Wallendorf *et al.* 1998), or a biker rally (Schouten and McAlexander 1995), and the culturally constituted quality space from which individual enactments are generated and which render them meaningful to participants. Note that the representations in Figure 4.2 are contained in frames and that arrows are shown between them and theories. This indicates that a given representation is always a finite, partial, historically contingent account designed to achieve some theoretical purpose. Given the generativity and transitory nature of culture, multiple accounts are always possible and indeed desirable since they voice other themes and other experiences. Multiple ethnographic accounts, including those presented in different ways, contribute to new theory-building efforts as in Arnould and Price (1993), Price *et al.* (1995), and Arnould *et al.* (1998), all of which are based on river rafting.

The various dimensions of the three modes of ethnographic representation are summarized in Figure 4.3. Modes of ethnographic representation and the theoretical purposes to which ethnography may be put vary in terms of three elements: the membership roles assumed by the ethnographer; the locus of authority within an ethnographic representation; and the phenomenological stance adopted by the ethnographer. All ethnography is participatory in the first moment of data collection. However, only thick inscription foregrounds participation in the third representational moment of ethnography. Both thick description and transcription are phenomenologically more distant modes of representation than thick inscription. In both thick description and inscription, representational authority lies with the researcher, while in thick transcription it lies more with the participants. Some authors view the latter mode of ethnographic representation as more ethical, since the ethnographer relinquishes some authority to represent participants to the participants themselves (Clifford and Marcus 1986; Josephides 1997).

Most consumer researchers interested in ethnography (Hirschman 1986; Hill 1991; Hill and Stamey 1990; McGrath 1989; O'Guinn and Belk 1989; Sherry 1990a; Sherry and McGrath 1989) have drawn on the single rhetorical strategy of "thick description" and have claimed a singular phenomenological stance. However, some work (Hirschman 1986), including some reports about the Consumer Behavior Odyssey, corresponds more closely to thick inscription than to thick description, and some even aspires to a dialogic mode of writing like that associated with thick transcription (Holbrook 1991; Jaworski and MacInnis 1991; Rook 1991). In fact many representational strategies are available to consumer-oriented ethnographers (Joy 1991). Further, although some authors have assimilated all ethnography to postmodern social science (Hirschman 1986; Hirschman and Holbrook 1992; Sherry 1990b), only thick inscription should be so character-

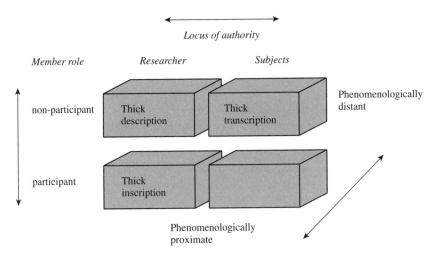

Figure 4.3 Modes of ethnographic representation

ized. Thick description, as Geertz's critics have observed, is not inconsistent with the project of modernist science. Consistent with postmodern social science, only thick transcription and inscription decenter subject–object relations and repudiate naturalistic modes of representation, and only thick transcription subverts the authority of the author. However, the three representational strategies countenance multiple readings of a social phenomenon, hence when combined they constitute a clear attack on modernist scientific objectivity (Rosenau 1992).

Discussion

To round out the chapter, the following discussion makes explicit some of the fruitful methodological relationships now developing between three divergent approaches for interpreting consumer behavior. Here, I wish to emphasize the benefits of methodological pluralism in representation. The discussion is phrased in terms of the mutual benefits that ethnography, literary criticism, and existential phenomenology derive from their mutual interpenetration. The discussion thus links emerging ethnographic practice to two of the most important representational genres discussed in this book.

Ethnography and literary criticism

From literary criticism, contemporary ethnography gets a concern for narrative voice missing in classical ethnography. Third-world critics like Edward Said (1978) have, in fact, demanded that ethnographers pay heed to the question of voice. They ask: "Who is speaking, and for whom are they speaking in ethnographic writing?"

> Edward Said's (1978) *Orientalism* is an attack on the genres of writing developed in the West to represent non-Western societies . . . He attacks particularly the rhetorical devices which make Western authors active, while leaving subjects passive. These subjects who must be spoken for, are generally located in a world dominated by Western colonialism or neocolonialism; thus, the rhetoric both exemplifies and reinforces Western domination.
>
> (Marcus and Fisher 1986: 1)

From literary criticism contemporary ethnography also gets a concern for person and gender. A flood of modern feminist ethnography was unleashed by Rosaldo and Lamphere's *Women, Culture and Society* (1974) and Reiter's *Towards an Anthropology of Women* (1975). Rosaldo was especially influenced by literary theory (Fernandez 1991). These anthropologists' work sought both to critique androcentricism in anthropological writing and to insist on the difference in men's and women's voices in non-western contexts. A vigorous stream of ethnographies now foreground the gendered voice. Stern's critique of Arnould's narrative style illustrates the pervasive androcentric bias in ethnographic writing (Arnould 1989; Thompson, Stern, and Arnould 1998).

In addition, literary criticism provides ways of reading consumers' and researchers' stories by exposing the hitherto unnoticed narrative conventions in their prose that shape meaning. Information can be extracted from the narrative structure when consumption experiences are read as if they were fictional stories (Stern 1994).

Finally, both ethnography and existential-phenomenology can improve their concern for representation by developing the technical, poetic, and political skills that make narratives evocative and effective. Recordings made by existential phenomenologists or ethnographic fieldnotes are forms of culturally embedded text and must be treated as such, even though they differ from the texts used by literary critics. Clifford points this out:

> We begin not with participant-observation or with cultural texts (suitable for interpretation), but with writing the making of texts. No longer a marginal, or occulted dimension, writing has emerged as central to what ethnographers do both in the field and thereafter . . . [Ethnographers now] see culture as composed of seriously contested codes and representations; they assume that the poetic and the political are inseparable, that science is in, not above, historical and linguistic processes.
>
> (Clifford 1990: 2)

> To a growing number [of ethnographers] . . . the "literariness" of anthropology – metaphor, figurations, narrative – affect the ways cultural phenomena are registered, from the first jotted "observations", to the completed book . . .
>
> (Clifford 1990: 5)

What ethnography gives to literary criticism is a sense of limitations to the scope and methods revealed by non-Western narrative conventions in many oral literatures. For example, Paul Stoller (1989) discusses praise-naming, an extremely common and widespread West African oral tradition:

> Irvine's study of the rhetoric of praise-naming among the Wolof of Senegal provides a significant hypothesis. Praise-naming, she suggests, has a far-reaching "rhetorical effect". People who are named during a bard's performance "are thought to be morally, socially, and even physically transformed by the words that are said" (Irvine 1980). During a praise-naming ceremony among the Wolof, a stratified caste society, the praise-naming increases the addressee's moral standing, augments his rank in a rank conscious society, and precipitates some kind of physiological transformation. It is believed that these transformations occur because the praise-naming ceremony arouses emotion in

the addressee which, in turn, alters the balance of his bodily fluids. According to Wolof theories, these bodily fluids are the biological determinants of social position. The physiological (magical) transformation in the addressee is also influenced by the physical sound of words.

(Stoller 1989: 111)

Clearly, Wolof praise-naming is a textual genre and narrative convention foreign to western literature, but one like haiku in the Japanese literary tradition that merits more study by consumer researchers interested in global consumer behavior (Sherry and Camargo 1987; Stanlaw 1992).

Ethnography also provides literary criticism with evidence for the existence of culturally universal narrative elements. Thus, James Fernandez (1991) argues that ethnographers have long contributed to an ethnology of narrative forms. Sir James Frazer's (1922) theory of magic makes uses of metaphor and metonymy in arguing that principles of similarity and contiguity are magic's constituent elements. Franz Boaz, Bronislaw Malinowski, and Paul Radin, three of the founders of modern ethnography, also wrote on the universalism of certain narrative elements in myth and magic. And Claude Levi Strauss's *The Savage Mind* (1966) almost argues for a universal tropic structure in the non-scientific mind.

Ethnography also offers literary criticism an appreciation of non-narrative modes of rhetorical communication. Paul Stoller's *The Taste of Ethnographic Things* discusses these forms:

Anthropological writers have long discussed the meaning of words in cultural life. From Malinowski to Tambiah, anthropologists have attempted to explain the magical power of incantations from a variety of perspectives. Rarely, however, have these analysts focused on the importance of the sound of words. Rarer still are analyses of the importance of the sound of musical instruments . . . The sound of the *godji*, or monochord violin . . . is a tangible link between the Songhay present and past, for this wailing sound revivifies deep-seated cultural themes about the nature of life and death, the origin of Songhay, the juxtaposition of social and spiritual worlds.

(Stoller 1989: 108–9).

These non-narrative themes, in turn, reinforce Songhay cultural identity, not entirely unlike the way advertisements and "soap" operas replay narrative themes in North American culture (Stern 1991a, 1991b).

Finally, ethnography gives literary criticism a more self-critical approach to narrative structures. Fernandez (1991: 9) argues that the contribution of ethnography to literary theory is twofold: first, the insistence upon the role of culture in the formation of metaphoric models with which various peoples reason, and second, the view of literary tropes in dynamic relationship within specific cultural contexts.

Clifford (1990) makes a still larger claim that ethnographic texts help release scientific discourse from the limited repertoire of signifying practices that have long characterized it:

> But if they [the essays] are post-anthropological, they are also post-literary. Michel Foucault (1973), Michel de Certeau (1983), and Terry Eagleton (1983) have recently argued that "literature" itself is a transient category. Since the seventeenth century, they suggest, Western science has excluded certain expressive modes from its legitimate repertoire; rhetoric (in the name of "plain", transparent signification), fiction (in the name of fact), and subjectivity (in the name of objectivity). The qualities excluded from science were localized in the category of "literature" . . . The essays that follow do not, in fact, appeal to a literary practice marked off in an aesthetic, creative, or humanizing domain. They struggle, in their different ways, against the received definitions of art, literature, science, and history. And if they sometimes suggest that ethnography is an "Art", they return the word to an older usage – before it had become associated with a higher or rebellious sensibility – to the eighteenth-century meaning Williams recalls: art as the skillful fashioning of useful artifact. The making of ethnography is artisanal, tied to the worldly work of writing.
>
> (Clifford 1990: 4, 6)

Ethnography and existential phenomenology

What ethnography gets from existential phenomenology is above all an appreciation for building the "knower" into the "known". Marcus and Fisher (1986) argue:

> In ethnography, phenomenology has became a label for the detailed attention paid to the way natives see their world while bracketing as much as possible the enthnographer's point of view. Some ethnographers have seen this as a fulfillment of Weber's call for a *verstehen Soziologie*, a sociology which gives a central role to the "understanding" of the actors . . . Hermeneutics similarly became a label for close reflection on the way natives decipher and decode their own complex "texts" be they literally texts or other forms of cultural communication, such as rituals . . .
>
> (Marcus and Fisher 1986: 30)

What ethnography gives to existential phenomenology is empirical, cross-cultural support for the idea that human realities are multiple and contextually embedded. For example, Stoller (1989: 56ff.) shows that the apparently unplanned layout of Songhay residences in a town in western Niger is actually invested with mystical cosmological significance, embodying both enduring caste hierarchy, based on descent and magical power, and challenges to it, based on money and secular authority. In a related article, Stoller (1989: 69ff.) shows that both the behavior and seating arrangements of passengers, driver, and helpers on a Songhay bush taxi dramatize Songhay caste hierarchy to participants but not to outsiders.

In addition, ethnography incorporates the existential–phenomenological goal of building arguments about behavior that use the "other" in the examination of the "self." Thus, Joy (1991) points out that Arnould (1989) uses the composite cases of preference formation in Niger (the other) to critique the ethnocentric assumptions on which ordinary models of preference formation are based, as well as to reconfigure standard models of preference formation and diffusion of innovations (the self). Further, ethnography provides a systematic defamiliarization of reality that reinforces the phenomenological agenda:

> The other promise of anthropology, one less fully distinguished and attended to than the first, has been to serve as a form of cultural critique for ourselves. In using portraits of other cultural patterns to reflect self-critically on our own ways, anthropology disrupts common sense and makes us re-examine our taken for granted assumptions.
>
> (Marcus and Fisher 1986: 1)

Finally, ethnography also offers phenomenology examples of the way that researchers become altered by their research. A popular culture example is provided by the story of ethnographer Carlos Castenada. His feeble efforts to collect data for a doctoral dissertation result in an epic (if apocryphal?) quest for self-knowledge and mystical power, as reported in *The Teachings of Don Yuan* and six subsequent books. In consumer research, examples of the phenomenological transformation of the ethnographer are provided by Hill's research among the homeless (Hill 1991; Hill and Stamey 1990), Schouten and McAlexander's (1992a, 1992b, 1993, 1995) on Harley-Davidson owners, and Alwitt's (1995) on poor consumers.

Benefits of methodological pluralism in interpretive research

It is a truism that practitioners of varying methods can benefit from the critical reflection of others, particularly at the research frontier. At the same time, this confrontation exposes the limitations and biases inherent in the adoption of a particular disciplinary or methodological stance. It is difficult to do literary criticism without assuming the existence of a narrative corpus with a certain set of linguistic, generic and structural conventions. But how is a literary critic to approach the timeless dream-time myths of the Australian? It is difficult to do existential phenomenological analysis without assuming something about the context in which informants construct their experiential world. But how is the existential phenomenologist to make sense of a Songhay sorcerer's experience in a world populated by demons, giant snakes, pixies, sprites, and djinns visible only to those who have learned how to see (Stoller 1989)? It is difficult to do ethnography without assuming an authorial voice that speaks of and for others. But how can the multiple, far-away voices of Hausa-speaking peasant women be orchestrated to tell a consumption story that Westerner consumer researchers can understand?

Bias and limitation do not characterize these three particular disciplinary choices alone. Similar arguments can be made for information processing, behaviorism, or decision-modeling approaches to consumer behavior. Recognition of bias and limitation should lead us away from the temptation to construct hierarchical ordering of scientific practices based on criteria such as assumed convergence, body of proven propositions, and logical consistency. Empirical evaluations across the sciences show that cognitive dissensus and disagreement about the value of contributions are the rule rather than the exception (Cole 1983). Further, Kuhnian history shows that even the most secure scientific paradigms (bodies of theory *and* method) are destined for obsolescence.

However, to expose our disciplinary biases and inclinations is not to propose that they be abandoned. On the contrary, minimum levels of consensus, including pre-theoretical taken-for-granted narrative conventions, are necessary in order to communicate within a discipline, to maintain disciplinary credibility, and to serve as a condition for the accumulation of knowledge. To admit that these standards are based primarily on meta-theoretical considerations is simply to recognize that science is first and foremost a social process in which consensus is maintained by the evaluation and reward systems (Cole 1983).

Conclusion

In this chapter, at the risk of perpetuating a quixotic quest within the epistemic landscape of modern marketing, I try to demonstrate the value of multimethod ethnographic investigation for developing representations of consumption phenomena. I discuss ethnographic goals, analysis, and interpretation. At the risk of presenting a model of ethnography that marginalizes postmodernist critiques and innovations, I describe the methodological foundations of consumer-oriented ethnographic research. I show that ethnographic techniques of data collection require researcher immersion in the context of interest. While time-consuming, these techniques incorporate divergent rather than merely convergent data into the data corpus and provide systematic access to recurrent disjunctures between perspectives of and perspectives in action. I discuss the strengths and limitations of verbal and observational data in building thick representations of behavior and meaning in cultural context. Interpretation aims at building an understanding that incorporates both concordant and discordant notes, a multilayered representation of a consumer behavior constellation that maps a particular culturally constituted quality space. Finally, I point out that ethnographic representation complements the representational strategies provided by literary criticism and existential–phenomenology.

Ethnographic methods are appropriate for apprehending a wide variety of consumer behavior phenomena (Miller 1995). First, ethnographic techniques are suitable for investigating the consumption dimensions of phenomena long-studied by anthropologists such as ritual, myth, magic, gift exchange, and kinship. They are particularly strong in elaborating models of material culture: that is, consumption sets, structures, use systems, and life styles (Holt 1997). Second, ethnography is appropriate for analysis of service encounters (Arnould and Price 1993; Fine 1990; Hochschild 1983; Mars and Nicod 1984; Kunda 1989) and other marketing research problems concerned with human interactions observable in everyday life (Jorgensen 1989). Thus, ethnographic representations may be used to penetrate the meanings that corporate culture has for employees, the way in which corporate culture shapes strategy formulation, organizational self-understanding, and the meanings that channels relations have for channels members (Dannhaeuser 1983; Prus 1989a, 1989b; Morgan 1997; Rafaeli and Sutton 1987; Sutton and Rafaeli 1988). Third, ethnography is useful in uncovering dynamics of interaction hidden by a script of "mindlessness" or "mindless reactive behavior" such as mundane shopping behavior and "ordinary" consumption (Langer 1983; Langer and Imba 1980). Finally, ethnography is especially appropriate for eliciting the dimensions of meaning and value embedded in unfamiliar market cultures and subcultures throughout the world and now incorporated into the global consumer economy (e.g., Applbaum and Jordt 1996; Appadurai 1986; Friedman 1994; Howes 1996; Rutz and Orlove 1989; Tobin 1992). All four types of analysis have significant potential for the development of culturally sophisticated theories of consumption and consumer behavior.

Notes

1 All Thanksgiving Day fieldnotes excerpted from fieldnote records of Melanie Wallendorf and Eric J. Arnould. All river rafting fieldnotes excerpted from fieldnote records of Eric J. Arnould and Linda L. Price. Abbreviations conform to the usual conventions, for example "swf20s" means a single white female in her twenties and "mhm40s" means a married Hispanic male in his forties.

2 Decommodification is a term adopted from Appadurai (1986), and especially Kopytoff's (1986) notion of singularization. It refer's to a "special kind of transvaluation, in which objects are placed beyond the culturally demarcated zone of commoditization. This type of transvaluation can take different forms in different societies, but it is typical that objects which represent aesthetic elaboration and objects that serve as sacra are, in many societies, not permitted to occupy the commodity state (either temporally, socially or definitionally) for very long" (Appadurai 1986: 23). An alternative term might be Miller's concept of appropriation which refers to creative recontextualization or the restructuration and reinvention of market resources according to domestic situations and expectations as part of more general strategies of social positioning and living

through the contradictions in society (1987: 174–5). See Levy's (1996) critique of Wallendorf and Arnould's (1991) claims about decommodification.

3 The notion of behavioural constellations is more complex than this "portmanteau" phrase suggests, making it both theoretically appealing and operationally challenging. Any one product may be used as part of several behavioral constellations: eating ready-to-eat cereal may be placed in the constellation of behaviors that comprise breakfast consumption as well as those that constitute snacking. Using toothpaste may be placed in the constellation of behaviors that comprise morning grooming or those that constitute preparing for a romantic encounter. Further complexity is introduced by the fact that any one geographic site or temporal event may contain several kinds of consumer enacting different behavioral constellations: different kinds of baseball spectator enact very different behavioral constellations, despite being present at the same game (Holt 1995). Swap-meet consumers at the same site include those engaging in a form of family recreation (who may view a collective break for a meal or a snack as essential), while others at the same site may be encting their version of economic rationality searching for "deals" (and may therefore resist purchasing the somewhat costly prepared foods). A commercial white water river rafting trip may include people searching for a predictable, guide-controlled ride such as they might have at a water sports theme park, as well as people intent on athletic adventure and unexpected challenges. Because of the complexity of this concept, ethnography looks to observation of the individual in context to determine the composition of behavioral constellations rather than their identification through use of a single product or location at a particular site.

References

Agar, M.H. (1980) *The Professional Stranger: An Informal Introduction to Ethnography*, New York: Academic Press.

Alwitt, L. (1995) "Marketing and the Poor," *American Behavioral Scientist* 38, 4: 564–77.

Anderson, P.F. (1986) "On Method in Consumer Research: A Critical Relativist Perspective," *Journal of Consumer Research* 13, 2: 155–71.

Appadurai, A. (ed.) (1986) *The Social Life of Things*, Cambridge: Cambridge University Press.

Applbaum, K. and Jordt, I. (1996) "Notes toward an Application of McCracken's 'Cultural Categories' for Cross-Cultural Consumer Research," *Journal of Consumer Research* 23, 4: 204–18.

Arnould, E.J. (1989) "Toward a Broadened Theory of Preference Formation and the Diffusion of Innovations: Cases from Zinder, Niger Republic," *Journal of Consumer Research* 16, 2: 239–67.

Arnould, E.J. and Price, L.L. (1993) "River Magic: Hedonic Consumption and the Extended Service Encounter," *Journal of Consumer Research* 20, 1: 24–45.

Arnould, E.J. and Price, L.L. and Tierney P. (1998) "The Wilderness Servicescape," in J.F. Sherry, Jr. (ed.) *Encountering Servicescapes: Built Environment and Lived Experience in Contemporary Marketplaces*, Lincolnwood, IL: NTC Publications.

Arnould, E.J. and Wallendorf, M. (1991) "Nostalgia and Holidays: Ritual Forms of Celebrating the Past," paper presented at the Annual Meeting of the Association for Consumer Research, Chicago, IL, 18 October.

—— (1994) "Consumer-oriented Ethnography: Interpretation Building and Marketing Strategy Formulation," *Journal of Marketing Research* 31 (November): 484–504.

Bagozzi, R.P. and Warshaw, P.R. (1990) "Trying To Consume," *Journal of Consumer Research* 17, 2: 127–40.

Baudrillard, J. (1968) *Le Système des Objets*, Paris: Gallimard.

Bearden, W.O., Netemeyer, R.G. and Mobley, M.F. (1993) *Handbook of Marketing Scales*, Newbury Park, CA: Sage.

Belk, R.W. and Coon, G.W. (1993) "Gift Giving as Agapic Love: An Alternative to the Exchange Paradigm Based on Dating Experiences," *Journal of Consumer Research* 20, 3: 393–417.

Belk, R.W. Sherry, J.F. Jr., and Wallendorf, M. (1988) "A Naturalistic Inquiry into Buyer and Seller Behavior at a Swap Meet," *Journal of Consumer Research* 14, 4: 449–70.

Bernard, H.R. (1988) *Research Methods in Cultural Anthropology*, Newbury Park, CA: Sage.

Biggart, N.W. (1989) *Charismatic Capitalism: Direct Selling Organizations in America*, Chicago: University of Chicago Press.

Bitner, M.J., Booms, B.H. and Tetrault, M.S. (1990) "The Service Encounter: Diagnosing Favorable and Unfavorable Incidents," *Journal of Marketing* 54, 1: 71–84.

Boyd, H.W. and Levy, S.J. (1963) "New Dimension in Consumer Analysis," *Harvard Business Review*, November/December: 129–40.

Bristor, J.M. and Fischer, E. (1993) "Feminist Thought: Implications for Consumer Research," *Journal of Consumer Research* 19, 4: 518–36.

Calder, B.J. and Tybout, A.M. (1989) "Interpretive, Qualitative, and Traditional Scientific Empirical Consumer Behavior Research," in E.C. Hirschman (ed.) *Interpretive Consumer Research*, Provo, UT: Association for Consumer Research.

Campbell, C. (1987) *The Romantic Ethic and the Spirit of Modern Consumerism*, Oxford: Basil Blackwell.

Campbell, D.T. and Fiske, D.W. (1959) "Convergent and Discriminant Validation by the Multitrait-Multimethod Matrix," *Psychological Bulletin* 30: 81–105.

Celsi, R., Rose, R.L. and Leigh, T.W. (1993) "An Exploration of High-Risk Leisure Consumption through Skydiving," *Journal of Consumer Research* 20, 1: 1–23.

Chalfen, R. (1987) *Snapshot Versions of Life*, Bowling Green, Ohio: Bowling Green State University Popular Press.

Clifford, J. (1990) "Notes on (Field)notes," in R. Sanjek (ed.) *Fieldnotes*, Ithaca, NY: Cornell University Press.

Clifford, J. and Marcus, G.E. (eds.) (1986) *Writing Culture*, Berkeley, CA: University of California Press.

Cole, S. (1983) "The Hierarchy of the Sciences?", *American Journal of Sociology* 89, July: 111–39.

Collier, J., Jr., and Collier, M. (1986), *Visual Anthropology* (revised and expanded), Albuquerque: University of New Mexico Press.

Crapanzano, V. (1980) *Tuhami: Portrait of a Moroccan*, Chicago: University of Chicago Press.

Dannhaeuser, N. (1983) *Contemporary Trade Strategies in the Philippines*, New Brunswick, NJ: Rutgers University Press.

Davis, F. (1979) *Yearning for Yesteryear: A Sociology of Nostalgia*, New York: The Free Press.

Deighton, J. (1992) "The Consumption of Performance," *Journal of Consumer Research* 19, 3: 362–72.

Denzin, N.K. (1970) *The Research Act*, Chicago: Aldine.

Donohue, J. (1991) "Dancing in the Danger Zone: The Martial Arts in America," paper presented at the Annual Meeting of the Association for Consumer Research, 18 October, Chicago, IL.

Douglas, M. and Isherwood, B. (1979) *The World of Goods*, New York: Norton.

Durham, D.J. and Fernandez, J.W. (1991) "Tropical Dominions: The Figurative Struggle over Domains of Belonging and Apartness in Africa," in J.W. Fernandez (ed.) *Beyond Metaphor: The Theory of Tropes in Anthropology*, Stanford: Stanford University Press.

Evans, J.R. and Berman, B. (1992) *Marketing*, 5th ed, NY: Macmillan.

Fernandez, J.W. (1986) *Persuasions and Performances: The Play of Tropes in Culture*, Bloomington: University of Indiana.

Fernandez, J.W. (ed.) (1991) *Beyond Metaphor: The Theory of Tropes in Anthropology*, Stanford: Stanford University Press.

Fine, G.A. (1990) "Organizational Time: Temporal Demands and the Experience of Work in Restaurant Kitchens," *Social Forces* 69, 1: 95–114.

Fischer, E. and Bristor, J.M. (1994) "A Feminist Poststructuralist Analysis of the Rhetoric of Marketing Relationships," *International Journal of Research in Marketing* 11: 317–31.

Frazer, J.G. (1992) *The Golden Bough*, New York: Macmillan Publishing.

Friedman, J. (1994) *Consumption and Identity*, Chur, Switzerland: Harwood Academic Publishers.

Geertz, C. (1973) *The Interpretation of Cultures*, New York: Basic Books.

—— (1988) *Works and Lives: The Anthropologist as Author*, Stanford, CA: Stanford University Press.

Giddens, A. (1971) *Capitalism and Modern Social Theory: An Analysis of the Writings of Marx, Durkheim, and Max Weber*, Cambridge: Cambridge University Press.

Gubrium, J.F. and Holstein, J.A. (1997) *The New Language of Qualitative Method*, New York: Oxford University Press.

Harrison, G., Rathje, W.L. and Hughes, W.W. (1974) "Socioeconomic Correlates of Food Consumption and Waste Behavior: The Garbage Project", paper presented at the American Public Health Association Meetings.

Heisley, D.D., McGrath, M.A. and Sherry, J.J. Jr. (1991), "To Everything There is A Season: A Photoessay of a Farmer's Market," in R.W. Belk (ed.) *Highways and Buyways: Naturalistic Research from the Consumer Behavior Odyssey*, Provo, UT: Association for Consumer Research.

Hill, R.P. (1991) "Homeless Women, Special Possessions, and the Meaning of 'Home': An Ethnographic Case Study," *Journal of Consumer Research* 18, 3: 298–310.

Hill, R.P. and Stamey, M. (1990), "The Homeless in America: An Examination of Possession and Consumption Behaviors," *Journal of Consumer Research* 17, 3: 303–22.

Hirschman, E.C. (1986) "Humanistic Inquiry in Marketing Research: Philosophy, Method, and Criteria," *Journal of Marketing Research* 23, 3: 237–49.

—— (1992) "The Consciousness of Addiction: Toward a General Theory of Compulsive Consumption," *Journal of Consumer Research* 19, 2: 155–79.

Hirschman, E.C. and Holbrook, M.B. (1982) "Hedonic Consumption: Emerging Concepts, Methods, and Propositions," *Journal of Marketing* 46, 3: 92–101.

—— and Holbrook, M.B. (1992) *Postmodern Consumer Research*, Newbury Park, CA: Sage.

Hochschild, A. (1983) *The Managed Heart*, Berkeley: University of California Press.

Hofstede, G. (1981) *Culture's Consequences*, abridged edn, Beverly Hills, CA: Sage Publications.

—— (1991) *Cultures and Organizations*, London: HarperCollins.

Holbrook, M. (1991) "From the Log of a Consumer Researcher: Reflections on the Odyssey," in R.W. Belk (ed.) *Highways and Buyways: Naturalistic Research from the Consumer Behavior Odyssey*, Provo, UT: Association for Consumer Research.

Holt, D.B. (1995) "How Consumers Consume: A Typology of Consumption Practices," *Journal of Consumer Research* 22, 1: 1–16.

—— (1997) "Poststructuralist Lifestyle Analysis: Conceptualizing the Social Patterning of Consumer in Postmodernity," *Journal of Consumer Research* 23, 4: 326–50.

Howes, D. (ed.) (1996) *Cross-Cultural Consumption*, New York: Routledge.

Hunt, S. (1989) "Naturalistic, Humanistic, and Interpretive Inquiry: Challenges and Ultimate Potential," in E.C. Hirschman (ed.), *Interpretive Consumer Research*, Provo, UT: Association for Consumer Research.

—— (1991) "Positivism and Paradigm Dominance in Consumer Research: Toward Critical Pluralism and Rapprochement," *Journal of Consumer Research* 18, 1: 32–44.

James, A., Hockey, J. and Dawson, A. (eds.) (1997) *After Writing Culture*, London: Routledge.

Jaworski, B.J. and MacInnis, D.J. (1991) "On Being an Informant on the Consumer Behavior Odyssey," in R.W. Belk (ed.) *Highways and Buyways: Naturalistic Research from the Consumer Behavior Odyssey*, Provo, UT: Association for Consumer Research.

Jorgensen, D.L. (1989) *Participant Observation: A Methodology for Human Studies*, vol. 15, Applied Research Methods Series, Newbury Park, CA: Sage.

Josephides, L. (1997) "Representing the Anthropologist's Predicament," in A. James, J. Hockey, and A. Dawson (eds) *After Writing Culture*, London: Routledge.

Joy, A. (1991) "Beyond the Odyssey: Interpretations of Ethnographic Writing in Consumer Behavior," in R.W. Belk (ed.) *Highways and Buyways: Naturalistic Research from the Consumer Behavior Odyssey*, Provo, UT: Association for Consumer Research.

Joy, A. and Dholakia, R.R. (1991) "Remembrances of Things Past: The Meaning of Home and Possessions of Indian Professionals in Canada," in F.W. Rudmin (ed.) *To Have Possessions*, Corte Madera, CA: Select Press.

Kassarjian, H.H. (1977) "Content Analysis in Consumer Research," *Journal of Consumer Research* 4, 1: 8–18.

Keller, E.F. (1985) *Reflections on Gender and Science*, New Haven: Yale University Press.

Kopytoff, I. (1986) "The Cultural Biography of Things: Commoditization as Process," in A. Appadurai (ed.) *The Social Life of Things*, Cambridge: Cambridge University Press.

Kunda, G. (1992) *Engineering Cultures: Control and Commitment in a High-Tech Corporation*, Philadelphia: Temple University Press.

Langer, E. (1983) *The Psychology of Control*, Beverly Hills, CA: Sage Publications.

Langer, E. and Imba, L. (1980) "The Role of Mindlessness in the Perception of Deviance," *Journal of Personality and Social Psychology* 38, September: 260–7.

Lederman, R. (1990), "Pretexts for Ethnography: On Reading Fieldnotes," in R. Sanjek (ed.) *Fieldnotes*, Ithaca: Cornell University Press.

Levi-Strauss, C. (1974/1962), *Le pensé sauvage*, Paris: Plon.

Levy, S. (1996) "Stalking the Amphisbaena," *Journal of Consumer Research* 23, 3: 163–77.

Marcus, G.E. and Fischer, M.M.J. (1986) *Anthropology as Culture Critique*, Chicago: University of Chicago.

Mars, G. and Nicod, M. (1984) *The World of Waiters*, London: George Allen & Unwin.

McCracken, G. (1988a) *The Long Interview*, Newbury Park, CA: Sage.

—— (1988b) *Culture and Consumption*, Bloomington: Indiana University Press.

—— (1989) "'Homeyness': A Cultural Account of One Constellation of Consumer Goods and Meanings," in E.C. Hirschman (ed.) *Interpretive Consumer Research*, Provo, UT: Association for Consumer Research.

McGrath, M.A. (1989) "An Ethnography of a Gift Store: Wrappings, Trappings, and Rapture," *Journal of Retailing* 65, 4: 421–49.

Mick, D.G. (1986) "Consumer Research and Semiotics: Exploring the Morphology of Signs, Symbols, and Significance," *Journal of Consumer Research* 13, 2: 155–73.

Miles, M.B. and Huberman, A.M. (1994) *Qualitative Data Analysis*, 2nd edition, Thousand Oaks, CA: Sage Publications.

Miller, D. (1987) *Material Culture and Mass Consumption*, Oxford: Basil Blackwell.

—— (1995) *Acknowledging Consumption*, London: Routledge.

Morgan, G. (1997), *Images of Organization*, 2nd edn, Thousand Oaks, CA: Sage Publications.

Murray, J.B. and Ozanne, J.L. (1991) "The Critical Imagination: Emancipatory Interests in Consumer Research," *Journal of Consumer Research* 18, 2: 29–144.

Nichter, M. and Moore, N. (1992) "Fat Talk: Body Image Among Adolescent Girls," Working Paper, Tucson, AZ: University of Arizona

O'Guinn, T.C. and Belk, R.W. (1989), "Heaven on Earth: Consumption at Heritage Village, USA," *Journal of Consumer Research* 16, 2: 227–38.

Price, L.L., Arnould, E.J. and Tierney, P. (1995) "Going to Extremes: Managing Service Encounters and Assessing Provider Performance," *Journal of Marketing* 59, 2: 83–97.

Prus, R. (1989a) *Making Sales*, Newbury Park, CA: Sage.

—— (1989b) *Pursuing Customers*, Newbury Park, CA: Sage.

Rabinow, P. (1991) "For Hire: Resolutely Late Modern," in R.G. Fox (ed.) *Recapturing Anthropology*, Santa Fe: School of American Research Press.

Rafaeli, A. and Sutton, R.I. (1987) "Expression of Emotion as Part of the Work Role," *Academy of Management Review* 12, 1: 23–37.

Reiter, R.R. (ed.) (1975), *Towards an Anthropology of Women*, New York: Monthly Review Press.

Rook, D. (1991) "I Was Observed (*In Absentia*) and Autodriven by the Consumer Behavior Odyssey," in R.W. Belk (ed.) *Highways and Buyways: Naturalistic Research from the Consumer Behavior Odyssey*, Provo, UT: Association for Consumer Research.

Rosaldo, M.Z. and Lamphere, L. (eds) (1974) *Women, Culture and Society*, Stanford, CA: Stanford University Press.

Rosenau, P.M. (1992) *Post-Modernism and the Social Sciences*, Princeton: Princeton University Press.

Ruby, J. (ed.), (1993) *The Cinema of John Marshall*, Philadelphia: Harwood Academic Publishers.

Rutz, H. J. and Orlove, B.S. (eds) (1989) *The Social Economy of Consumption*, Lanham, MD: University Press of America.

Said, E. (1978) *Orientalism*, London: Penguin Books.

Sanjek, R. (1990a) "A Vocabulary for Fieldnotes," in R. Sanjek (ed.) *Fieldnotes*, Ithaca, NY: Cornell University Press.

———— (1990b) "On Ethnographic Validity," in R. Sanjek (ed.) *Fieldnotes*, Ithaca, NY: Cornell University Press.

Schiffer, M.B., Downing, T.E. and McCarthy, M. (1981) "Waste Not, Want Not: An Ethnoarchaeological Study of Reuse in Tucson, Arizona," in M.B. Schiffer (ed.) *Modern Material Culture: The Archaeology of Us*, New York: Academic Press.

Schouten, J.W. and McAlexander, J.H. (1992a) "Market Impact of a Consumption Subculture: The Harley-Davidson Mystique," in G. Bamossey and F. van Raaij (eds) *European Advances in Consumer Research*, Provo, UT: Association for Consumer Research.

—— (1992b) "The Harley-Davidson Consumption Subculture," presentation made to Marketing Operations Group, Harley-Davidson Co., Milwaukee, August.

—— (1993) "Harley-Davidson Research Summit," presentation made to personnel from Marketing Operations Group of Harley-Davidson Co. and from contract research firm, Chicago, August.

—— (1995) "Subcultures of Consumption: An Ethnography of the New Bikers," *Journal of Consumer Research* 22, 4: 43–61.

Serematakis, C.N (1991) *The Last Word: Women, Death and Divination in Inner Mani*, Chicago: University of Chicago Press.

Sherry, J.F., Jr. (1990a) "A Sociocultural Analysis of a Midwestern American Flea Market," *Journal of Consumer Research* 17, 1: 13–30.

—— (1990b) "Post-modern Alternatives: The Interpretive Turn in Consumer Research," in T. Robertson and H.H. Kassarjian (eds) *Handbook of Consumer Behavior*, Englewood Cliffs, NJ: Prentice-Hall.

Sherry, J.F., Jr. and Camargo, E.G. (1987) "'May Your Life Be Marvelous:' English Language Labeling and the Semiotics of Japanese Promotion," *Journal of Consumer Research* 14, 2: 174–88.

Sherry, J.F., Jr. and McGrath, M.A. (1989) "Unpacking the Holiday Presence: A Comparative Ethnography of Two Gift Stores," in E.C. Hirschman (ed.) *Interpretive Consumer Research*, Provo, UT: Association for Consumer Research.

Silverman, D. (1993) *Interpreting Qualitative Data*, London: Sage Publications.

Solomon, M.R. and Assael, H. (1987) "The Forest or the Trees?: A Gestalt Approach to Symbolic Consumption," in J. Umiker-Sebeok (ed.) *Marketing and Semiotics: New Directions in the Study of Signs for Sale*, Berlin: Mouton de Gruyer.

Sontag, S. (1977) *On Photography*, New York: Farrar, Straus, Giroux.

Spiggle, S. (1986) "Measuring Social Values: A Content Analysis of Sunday Comics and Underground Comix," *Journal of Consumer Research* 13, 1: 100–13.

Srivasteva, R., Alpert, M.I. and Shocker, A.D. (1984) "A Customer-oriented Approach for Determining Market Structures," *Journal of Marketing* 48, 2: 32–45.

Stanlaw, J. (1992), "'For Beautiful Human Life:' The Use of English in Japan," in J.J. Tobin (ed.) *Re-Made in Japan*, New Haven: Yale University Press.

Stern, B.B. (1991a) "Literary Analysis of an Advertisement: The Commercial as 'Soap Opera'" in R.H. Holman and M.R. Solomon (eds) *Advances in Consumer Research*, vol. 18, Provo, UT: Association for Consumer Research.

—— (1991b) "Who Talks Advertising?: Literary Theory and Narrative 'Point of View,'" *Journal of Advertising* 20, September: 9–22.

—— (1994) "Classical and Vignette Television Advertising Dramas: Structural Models Formal Analysis and Consumer Effects," *Journal of Consumer Research* 20, 4: 601–15.

Stoller, P. (1989) *The Taste of Ethnographic Things*, Philadelphia: University of Pennsylvania Press.

—— (1992) *The Cinematic Griot*, Chicago: University of Chicago Press.

Stoller, P. and Olkes, C. (1987) *In Sorcery's Shadow*, Chicago: University of Chicago.

Strauss, A. and Corbin, J. (1990) *Basics of Qualitative Research*, Newbury Park, CA: Sage.

Sutton, R. and Rafaeli, A. (1988) "Untangling the Relationship between Displayed Emotions and Organizational Sales: The Case of Convenience Stores," *Academy of Management Journal* 31, 3: 461–87.

Thompson, C.T., Stern, B.B. and Arnould, E.J. (1998), "Writing the Differences: Postmodern Pluralism, Retextualization, and the Construction of Reflexive Ethnographic Narratives in Consumer Research," *Culture, Markets, and Consumption* 3 (1, June).

Tobin, J.J. (ed.) (1992) *Re-Made in Japan*, New Haven: Yale University Press.

Triandis, H.C. (1989) "The Self and Social Behavior in Differing Cultural Contexts," *Psychological Review* 96, 3: 506–20.

Trice, H.M. and Bayer, J.M. (1984) "Studying Organizational Cultures Through Rites and Ceremonials," *Academy of Management Review* 9, 4: 653–69.

Tsing, A. L. (1994), "From the Margins," *Cultural Anthropology* 9, 3: 279–97.

Turner, V. (1988) *The Anthropology of Performance*, New York: PAJ Publications.

Van Maanen, J. (1988) *Tales of the Field: On Writing Ethnography*, Chicago: University of Chicago Press.

Venkatesh, A. (1995), "Ethnoconsumerism: A New Paradigm to Study Cultural and Cross-Cultural Consumer Behavior," in J.A. Costa and G.J. Bamossy (eds) *Marketing in a Multicultural World*, Thousand Oaks: Sage Publications.

Wallendorf, M. and Arnould, E.J. (1991) "'We Gather Together': The Consumption Rituals of Thanksgiving Day," *Journal of Consumer Research* 19, 1: 13–31.

Wallendorf, M. and Belk, R.W. (1989) "Assessing Trustworthiness in Naturalistic Consumer Research," in E.C. Hirschman (ed.) *Interpretive Consumer Research*, Provo: UT: Association for Consumer Research.

Wallendorf, M. and Brucks, M. (1993) "Introspection in Consumer Research," *Journal of Consumer Research* 20, 3: 339–59.

Wallendorf, M. Lindsey-Mullikin, J. and Pimentel, R. (1998) "Gorilla Marketing: Shifts in Customer Animation and Regional Embeddedness during the Relocation of a Toy Store," in J.F. Sherry, Jr. (ed.) *Encountering Servicescapes: Built Environment and Lived Experience in Contemporary Marketplaces*, Lincolnwood, IL: NTC Publications.

Wallman, S. (1997) "Appropriate Anthropology and the Risky Inspiration of 'Capability' Brown," in A. James, J. Hockey, and A. Dawson (eds) *After Writing Culture*, London: Routledge.

Whiting, B. and Whiting, J. (1970) "Methods for Observing and Recording Behavior," in R.N. and R. Cohen (eds) *A Handbook of Method in Cultural Anthropology*, Garden City, NY: The Natural History Press.

Wolf, M. (1990) "Chinanotes: Engendering Anthropology," in R. Sanjek (ed.) *Fieldnotes*, Ithaca, NY: Cornell University Press.

Worth, S. and Adair, J. (1972) *Through Navajo Eyes: An Exploration in Film Communication and Anthropology*, Bloomington: Indiana University Press.

Wulff, R.M. and Fiske, S.J. (eds) (1987) *Anthropological Praxis: Translating Knowledge into Action*, Boulder, CO: Westview Press.

5

LIVING THE TEXTS OF EVERYDAY LIFE

A hermeneutic perspective on the relationships between consumer stories and life-world structures

Craig J. Thompson

Science, metaphor, and the tragic tale

Kuhn's (1970) classic work on the dynamics of scientific revolutions and paradigm shifts can easily be read as a tale about the recurrent conflict among new and conventionalized metaphoric models of reality. Metaphoric models that once inspired creative theoretical innovations and engendered radically new ways of thinking about a given domain have a disconcerting tendency to become vehicles of conformity and congealed conventions. During such transformations, the practitioners of the established metaphor seldom recognize the implicit constraints placed on their creative horizons. The very qualities that allow the metaphor to captivate a scientific community eventually sow the seeds of the metaphor's own demise. Once the revolutionary metaphoric model becomes institutionalized as a system of "normal" scientific practices, the stage is set for a new, seemingly more innovative and productive metaphor to gain advocates and to inspire the inevitable challenge to the disciplinary status quo.

In consumer research, "the linguistic turn," which metaphorically models human experiences as text-like phenomena, has enjoyed a decade-long run as the revolutionary paradigm of the moment (Hirschman and Holbrook 1992; Sherry 1991; Gergen and Gergen 1986; Maines 1993). The narratological metaphor is now ascending to new heights of trans-disciplinary influence and is even displacing the computer metaphor in many recent cognitive theories (Crites 1986; Hermans 1996). For consumer researchers who have embraced this world-view, the time may be at hand to consider seriously the likelihood of this narratological paradigm taking its tragic turn.

The old adage about those who do not learn from the past being condemned to repeat it seems quite apropos. Recall that the shift in psychological research and theory toward the computer metaphor (i.e. the person as an information-processing system) was initially hailed as a liberating and humanizing transformation in psychological theory (Miller *et al.* 1960). During the fifty-year dominance of the behaviorist paradigm in American psychology, human beings were viewed as merely more complex versions of laboratory animals whose actions could be explained (and controlled) by a system of mechanistic laws and principles (e.g., Bower and Hilgard 1956). Whereas behaviorist models had no place for concepts such as intentions, beliefs, goals, thoughts, or mental images, the information-processing paradigm (based on the "mind is a computer" metaphor) placed these marginalized constructs on center stage and, in so doing, posited a profound qualitative difference between human and animal psychology.

As a revolutionary alternative to the dominant behaviorist paradigm, the information-processing paradigm appeared to be more closely connected to the experiences of everyday life. However, as the information-processing tradition gained prominence, its representation of human experience as an essentially disembodied, rationalized, and analytic phenomenon became increasingly problematic to theorists interested in the embodied, emotional, holistic, and social qualities of perceptions, action, and thought (Gergen 1985; Neisser 1976; Wertz 1987). In consumer research, these critiques led to calls for an experiential paradigm (Hirshman and Holbrook 1982; Thompson *et al.* 1989) that would place greater emphasis on the symbolic and social qualities of consumption behaviors (Arnould 1989; Belk *et al.* 1988; McCracken 1988a; Mick 1986; Solomon 1983). The theoretical and methodological confluences among the hermeneutic, anthropological, literary, and semiotic traditions provided the impetus for consumer research's "linguistic turn" (see Arnold and Fischer 1994; and Hirschman and Holbrook 1992; Sherry 1991).

In other social sciences, the person-as-text metaphor is at a later stage in its paradigmatic lifecycle and, not surprisingly, signs of the predictable Kuhnian dynamic – such as theorists emphasizing phenomena that pose anomalies – are beginning to appear. One prominent challenge calls attention to disjunctures between the text metaphor and the conditions of human experience (Gergen 1991; Hermans 1996). A number of these critiques emanate from a genre of postmodern theory that emphasizes the deconstructive implications of text metaphor (see Firat and Venkatesh 1995). The postmodern accounts are deconstructive in the sense that the modernist view of the "self" as an organizing principle of human experience is dismissed as an outmoded and nostalgic image of authenticity.

From a modernist view, the self is the inner core of something which lies "deep" within our psyches (and spirits). Freudian analyses, which Ricoeur (1981) aptly dubbed as the hermeneutics of suspicion, exemplified this modernist view by treating every action or verbalization as a text that could be deciphered for a deeper meaning. In contrast, the postmodernist view eschews any notion of a hidden "deep" self. Rather, self-identity equates to a malleable juxtaposition of commodified symbols that are fragmented across an array of disparate consumption contexts (Baudrillard 1988; Cushman 1990; Firat and Venkatesh 1995).

Whereas modernists assume that consumption is a symbolically laden activity that must be deciphered to understand its "deep meaning," postmodernists argue that consumption is a "depthless text" (Jameson 1991) that does not reflect any underlying reality. In this postmodern world of free floating "signs," the modernist-self dissolves into an almost schizophrenic amalgam of fragmented, emotionally intensified, consumption experiences (see Featherstone 1991). The self, like consumption, becomes a "depthless text."

However, this postmodern conception of consumers – like some of the more mechanistic versions of information-processing theory – seems to be referring to a very different form of life (Wittgenstein 1958) than anyone might recognize in his or her everyday life. Hannerz (1992) makes this point in the following way:

> On the other hand, the depictions of the postmodern age deserve some of their own incredulity. When it is claimed, for example, that identities become nothing but assemblages from whatever imagery is for the moment marketed through the media, then I wonder what kind of people commentators on the postmodern know. I myself know hardly anybody of whom this would seem true.
>
> (Hannerz 1992: 35)

The "linguistic turn" has sensitized consumer researchers to the theoretical utility offered by concepts and analytic tools originating in the field of literary criticism (McQuarrie and Mick 1992; Scott 1990, 1994; Stern 1988, 1989, 1995; Thompson *et al.* 1994). However, the comments by Hannerz highlight the excesses of abstraction that can arise when the text metaphor is taken too literally. One qualifying response to this dilemma is to make it clear that human existence has some text-like qualities but it is not a text *per se*:

> In literature and history, the narrator has control of the story and decides what events to include or exclude. In the life narrative, the self is the narrator of its own story. Unlike the authors of fiction and history, the self has to integrate materials that are at hand. Authors of fictional and historical narratives describe events that have already ended but the self is in the middle of its story and has to revise its plot constantly without knowing how the story will end.
>
> (Polkinghorne 1988: 69)

This chapter follows in the spirit of Polkinghorne's commentary by advocating a non-reductionistic, narratological model of consumer experience. Although consumer experiences are structured by narratives and stories (see Arnould and Price 1993; Stern 1995; Thompson and Haytko 1997), these textual aspects are embedded in a larger field (or system) of relationships constituted by psychological and socio-cultural processes. This view of narrative as one aspect of a broader existential constellation is characteristic of Heidegger's hermeneutic ontology

([1927] 1960), the latter works of Wittgenstein (1958), and the phenomenological psychology of Merleau-Ponty (1962, 1968). While these works played pivotal roles in the emergence of the linguistic turn (Gier 1981; Dreyfus and Rabinow 1983; Rabinow and Sullivan 1979), their proposal that language has meaning only within a broader life-world context has been marginalized by the dominance of the text metaphor (see Packer 1985, 1989; Pollio *et al.* 1997a, for some exceptions).

My argument is that consumer researchers have borrowed liberally from literary concepts to gain new insights into consumer experience but that this interdisciplinary conversation has simply become too one-sided. The relevant implication of the life-world is that the consumer-as-text metaphor needs to be reflexively adapted and enriched. Here, I am talking about a circular (or dialogical) process that offers a mean for keeping the text metaphor alive and theoretically productive rather than allowing it to follow the Kuhnian path toward sedimentation and eventual irrelevance. The theoretical dialogue I am proposing is one between the textual paradigm as it now stands in consumer research and the phenomenological tradition that highlights aspects of human experience not reducible to the mere play of narrative conventions.

In this chapter, I will first describe the Husserlian concept of the life-world and its reformulation in the "hermeneutic turn." The general discussion will highlight the importance of *existentials* (i.e. the prereflective structures of the life-world) that have been frequently overlooked in recent accounts of hermeneutic thought for consumer research (for example Arnold and Fischer 1994; Holbrook and O'Shaughnessy 1988; Thompson *et al.* 1994). Incorporating consideration of these existential structures into interpretations of consumer narratives offers one means to modify the consumer-is-a-text metaphor in a way that can preclude its deconstructive and dehumanizing implications and, thereby, avoid (or at least delay) the tragic Kuhnian fate.

After providing this overview, I will show how this hermeneutic model can be used to understand the existential significance conveyed in the consumption stories of consumers who are situated in a common set of life-world circumstances. The participants in this study are professional working women of the baby-boom generation who see themselves as leading a "juggling" lifestyle reflecting the often competing demands of career and family. The analysis will show how their narratives of personal identity frame their consumption stories which are all, in turn, grounded in their relationships to the key existential facets of the life-world such as habituated patterns of action and interpersonal dynamics, emotional ties to others, and the limitations posed by embodiment.

A hermeneutical model of the life-world

The Husserlian legacy

One would be hard-pressed to find a discussion of the phenomenological tradition that does not pay heed to the works of the German philosopher Edmund Husserl (1859–1938). Over the course of his influential career, Husserl's proposals gravitated from the "transcendental" position that sought to describe the essential structures of consciousness to one that sought to analyze the relationships between everyday meanings and the structure of the *lebenswelt* or *life-world*: that is, the world as lived by a human subject. In his later works, Husserl drew heavily from the works of his contemporaries, particularly the humanist philosopher Wilhelm Dilthey and the cultural anthropologist Levy-Bruhl, who argued for a historically grounded and culturally relative account of human understanding.

Husserl's ([1936] 1970) revised philosophy retained his transcendentalist orientation by positing a common foundation for all human understanding. For Husserl, an underlying field of prereflective experiences, such as emotional experiences, practical knowledge, and the intuitive understanding of one's cultural way of life, served as the ultimate foundation of human understanding. The logocentric rules of consciousness central to his earlier works were now seen to emerge from this "background" of prereflective experience (Merleau-Ponty 1962).[1]

Husserl's account of the life-world remained a precursory one that offered an intriguing thesis rather than a fully developed theoretical system (Gadamer 1993; Merleau-Ponty 1962). However, post-Husserlian scholars such as Heidegger, Merleau-Ponty, and Schutz and Luckmann (1973, 1983) further developed the Husserlian thesis that the life-world functioned as a kind of meta-structure in which human consciousness unfolds. They argued that the life-world is a system or network of fundamental relationships that structure a person's everyday experiences and that shape the personal meanings he or she ascribes to them (Merleau-Ponty 1962; Schutz and Luckmann 1973, 1983). From my hermeneutical perspective, the life-world is an *interpretive construct* exhibiting an ambiguous ontological status. In other words, the life-world highlights important aspects of human existence, but this interpretive frame is itself situated within the same field of historical and hence narratological conditions that it seeks to describe. Thus, the life-world does not describe human existence as seen from an omnipotent view, but rather it offers a situated perspective from which to generate reflexive insights into the human condition.

As a hermeneutical construct, the life-world functions as a multidimensional interpretive framework whose analytic categories highlight specific kinds of relationships between consumption-oriented meanings and the lives of consumers. These life-world categories provide an interpretive basis for organizing the different circumstances of consumers along a common set of thematic dimensions. More importantly, these life-world categories ground the interpretation of consumer "texts" – the stories they tell about consumption experiences – in a series of existential considerations.

For purposes of clarity, the core analytic categories of the life-world framework will be described separately. However, the process of interpreting consumer meanings by means of the life-world categories is an iterative one in which the goal is to arrive at a sense of the whole: that is, the interrelationships among the various facets of the life-world (Giorgi 1986). Holistic understanding arises from the interpretive interaction between these core life-world categories and the developing understanding of consumers' life narratives.

The existential aspects of the life-world

Perceptions of the cultural setting

A basic premise of the life-world is that the meanings of specific experiences emerge in relation to the socio-cultural setting in which a person lives (Merleau-Ponty 1962). Although the background of cultural factors has a broad scope and encompasses social influences of which individuals may not be explicitly aware, life-world analysis is most concerned with the way that individuals understand their social surroundings. To use classic phenomenological terms, the emphasis is placed on understanding how one's social and material surroundings become incorporated into the *eigenwelt*, the personally meaningful world of experience (Keen 1975).

Although the relatively small samples typical of in-depth qualitative studies cannot be considered statistically representative, they can demonstrate that the identified meanings and life issues are based in a common set of life-world conditions rather than in the idiosyncrasies of specific individuals (Levy 1981; McCracken 1988b). Accordingly, an important step in conducting a life-world analysis of a consumer segment is establishing that the consumer meanings expressed by a set of participants are grounded in shared perceptions about the salient features of their everyday lives.

In pursuing this logic, a useful first step is to ascertain the socio-cultural factors likely to be salient to a consumer's perception of her or his life situation. This initial step need not be a "shot in the dark," for a variety of secondary information sources ranging from mass media reports to academic studies are available to assist marketers in the task of reading the cultural scene. For example, anyone seeking to market products and services to the consumer group commonly referred to as "working mothers" should be well-aware that the phenomenon of the "second shift" (see Hochschild 1989) is quite likely to be relevant to their perceived consumption needs (also Berg 1986; Crosby 1991; Shreve 1987).

The life-world concept also implies that the expected meanings identified by these secondary analyses may not always correspond to the perceptions of those who actually live out these cultural conditions (Thompson *et al.* 1989). Hence, an iterative process of interpretation is needed to specify the meaning relationships between consumers and their social settings. In this process, researchers' background knowledge of potentially relevant socio-cultural factors can inform their understanding of consumer perceptions and, reciprocally, their acquired knowledge of consumer perceptions can modify this developing sense of the pertinent cultural issues. Iterative analysis, for example, may reveal that a presumably salient factor is less significant than anticipated. Conversely, it may identify an unexpected factor that consumers do perceive as being important. Moreover, the primary goal of life-world analysis is to understand the personal meanings that emerge for consumers in these social circumstances: meanings that could not be ascertained through a generic knowledge of the social setting.

Emotional relationships to others

This facet of the life-world encompasses two key dimensions. The first concerns the face-to-face interactions that comprise the social fabric of everyday life and that are central to a person's sense of connection to a social network or community (Giddens 1991). Routine social interactions with family members and co-workers, as well as more transient encounters with salespersons and service providers, comprise a continuous stream of meaning-laden interpersonal encounters, each marked by differing degrees of emotional involvement (Bellah *et al.* 1985).

In consumer research, interpersonal relationships have often been conceptualized in terms of a rationalistic *exchange paradigm* (see Bristor and Fischer 1993). The exchange paradigm represents consumers as relatively autonomous agents who choose to enter and exit relationships based on calculations of their perceived utility. In contrast, the life-world concept proposes that interpersonal relationships are emotionally charged with symbolic significance that transcends rational assessments of their benefits and costs (also see Belk and Coon 1993). Feelings of care, trust, obligation, love, guilt, jealousy, power, acquiescence, fulfillment, anger, and disappointment animate social relationships, including those orchestrated in the public domain of the service industries (Hochschild 1983). These emotionally charged interpersonal relationships are an essential facet of human existence. Reciprocally, a person's sense of self-identity and life satisfaction are heavily vested in these enduring interpersonal relationships (Van den Berg 1970).

The lived body

The life-world concept of the *lived body* derives from a longstanding phenomenological interest in the ways in which the embodied nature of human existence structures experience (Dillon 1988; Merleau-Ponty 1962; Pollio *et al.* 1997b; Valle *et al.* 1989). The phenomenological argument is that the body is *the* fundamental ground of human experience (Merleau-Ponty 1962). In his later works, Merleau-Ponty (1968) pushed this thesis further by positing an embodied theory of speech: that is, speaking is the means by which our bodies "sing the world."

The influential works of Lakoff and Johnson (1980), Johnson (1987) and Lakoff (1987) provide a contemporary formulation of this thesis by positing embodied experiences as the foundation of higher-order conceptual constructs. Through imaginative projection, embodied relationships to the world are metaphorically extended so that the individual can understand more abstract conceptual and symbolic domains. In this way, the metaphysics of Cartesian dualism are transformed such that mind–body dualism becomes a dialectic relation characterized as the body-in-the-mind view (Johnson 1987).

The lived body also exemplifies the inherent ambiguity of human existence that so captivated the imaginations of phenomenologists. In one sense, the body is an object in the world subject to all of the forces that impact on material objects. The body can also be readily objectified as an entity to be monitored and controlled (Thompson and Hirschman 1995). Conversely, the body is a unique facet of each person's identity and the subjective center of the perceived world. To alter one's body is to transform the way in which one relates to all other aspects of the life-world. Whereas we can conceive of our bodies in objectified terms, and indeed view the bodies of others as objects, this stance seldom resonates with our own sense of embodied subjectivity. In the words of Marcel (1960), "my body is mine insofar as for me my body is not an object but, rather, I am my body" (in Pollio, *et al.* 1997b: 67).

A number of consumer research issues that have been conventionally classified as "experiential" and/or hedonic phenomena are relevant to the lived body concept (e.g., Hirschman and Holbrook 1982; Holbrook and Hirschman 1982; Thompson *et al.* 1989). These phenomena include visceral and emotional responses to the consumption of products and services, "non-rational" motivations for consumer behavior such as the desire for play, fantasy, or hedonic pleasure (see Hirschman and Holbrook 1982), and the kinesthetic and sensual dimensions of consumption experiences. In addressing these experiential phenomena, however, consumer researchers have for the most part been more inclined to identify them than to analyze their phenomenological qualities systematically.

The consumer research study that perhaps comes closest to articulating a phenomenologically attuned understanding of the "lived body" is Gould's (1991) introspective analysis of manipulating his vital energy through consumption. In this paper, Gould offers a vividly detailed recounting of the shifts in bodily experiences that arise in the course of consuming products and engaging in a number of broadly defined consumption activities such as fasting and sex. Gould's analysis became one of the more controversial pieces published in the *Journal of Consumer Research* (see Gould 1995; Wallendorf and Brucks 1993). The primary points of contention were the use of the researcher as the only informant and the questionable veridicality of recalled introspective assessments (particularly when consciousness-altering substances were employed). Some of this controversy also quite likely ensued from the taboo nature of Gould's reported consumption experiences. However, a number of the critiques aimed at this introspective (or more accurately, retrospectively reflective) analysis could have been circumvented had Gould explicitly taken into account the ways in which culturally given meanings and narratological formats necessarily shaped his experiences of energy manipulation and the consumption stories he could subsequently tell.

Thompson and Hirschman (1995) provide an account that moves in this direction by analyzing consumers' stories about their body image. This analysis highlights the cultural meanings through which consumers interpret their bodies in objectified terms and the ways in which their perceptions of self and others are negotiated through these body-centered meanings. Thompson and Hirschman interject a phenomenological motif into their poststructural perspective by arguing that a consumer's historicized self is marked by perceptions of "disconcerting physical changes that could not be chosen away." Consumers interpreted their bodies as a kind of material text that could not be abandoned or easily rewritten and that stood as living records of their personal histories and consumption habits (Thompson and Hirschman 1995).

In sum, the lived body is the material from which and through which we construct our narratives of self, and it is not reducible to the narrative structures that we employ to make sense of our embodied relationships to the life-world.

Historicity and the historicized self

These closely related terms speak most directly to the hermeneutical reformulation of Husserl's proposals for the life-world. *Historicity* refers to the living legacy of cultural practices, beliefs, and meanings that provide the transcendent or intersubjective ground of human existence. Thus, human existence is a process that unfolds within historically established cultural traditions of meaning (Faulconer and Williams 1985; Gadamer 1993; Heidegger 1960). One significant means by which history becomes a meaningful human event is through stories and narratives. To become socialized in a culture is to become fluent in the stories and the ways of narrating that express the cultural-way-of-life (Geertz 1983; Shweder 1989; Wittgenstein 1958). From a hermeneutic perspective, consumers appropriate this system of cultural meanings to make sense of their life-world circumstances, and these personalized stories express a dialectic between textual and life-world structures.

The *historicized self* emphasizes that self-identity is not a collection of traits possessed by an individual. Rather, it is "the self as reflexively understood by the person in terms of his or her biography" (Giddens 1991: 53). In this theoretical spirit, the life-world category of the historicized self refers to self-identity as a network of meanings that are situated in a continuously evolving narrative of personal history (Widdershoven 1993). This term also implies that a person's understanding of his or her past is continuously constructed in the present and that this present-centered perspective is in turn shaped by future-directed expectations, desires, and life goals (Van den Berg 1970).

Individuals' consumption stories express a history of cultural meanings that have been appropriated into their specific life-world contexts. In direct contrast to postmodern accounts suggesting that consumption stories are fragmented and decontextualized, the hermeneutic concept of historicity proposes that a coherent sense of personal history inscribes individuals' consumption stories in a network of biographical connections, which are in turn constituted by an organized set of enduring personal meanings, values, and epiphanic life stories. This network functions as a personalized cultural frame-of-reference from which context-specific meanings are ascribed to a given experience.

The concept of historicity relates to a construct that is often characterized as the *life-project*: a nexus of higher-order goals and personal meanings that endow an individual's life with a sense of purpose and that provide an existential foundation to his or her self-identity (Sartre 1956; Van den Berg 1970). As Frankl (1984) observes, the life-project is often based upon a desire to make a meaningful difference in the world that will endure beyond one's lifetime and a wish to play an essential role in the lives of others.

In consumer research, constructs such as "the deep meaning of possessions" (Belk *et al.* 1989) or "life themes" that are manifested in consumer perceptions (Mick and Buhl 1992), have been assumed to bear a systematic relationship to higher-order personal meanings. Whereas life-world analysis shares this assumption, it posits an existential relationship between the life-project and its symbolic manifestations in everyday consumer behaviors. In these terms, the life-project is not regarded as a conscious plan from which everyday consumer meanings flow. Rather, it is a predisposition toward certain patterns of everyday meanings and actions whose specific contours are comprehended by reflecting upon one's life experiences (Sartre 1956; Van den Berg 1970).

From a research standpoint, the reflective dimension of the life-project harbors an important implication: the motivational influences of the life-project are often latent in the explicit meanings that consumers ascribe to their possessions and consumer experiences. These latent motivations are revealed by analyzing the pattern of everyday meanings in which these consumer actions and goods are embedded (see Holbrook 1988).

An illustrative application

Research context

In the following section, this hermeneutic framework will be used to interpret the consumption stories of professional working mothers living in two-income households. An extensive body of research has documented that experiences of time-scarcity are pervasive among this market segment (Bielby and Bielby 1988; Crosby 1991; Gerson 1985; Hochschild 1989). From a hermeneutic standpoint, these experiences should be analyzed as a dialectical structure. That is, time-scarcity is a narrative construction in which various elements of the life-world are organized around a metatheme of "having no time." Reciprocally, these narrative constructions are grounded in a specific configuration of existentials, such as relations to others, embodiment, and historicity, that render time-scarcity a salient and resonant aspect of the life-world. In other words, time-scarcity is neither a subjective choice nor an objective condition; rather, it is a narrative form that coheres with the existential structure of professional working mothers' life-worlds.

In applying a hermeneutic framework to this configuration of narrative and existential forms, the goal is to provide a systematic and in-depth understanding of the personal meanings, symbolic values, and broader life-issues that animate these consumption stories. Verbatim texts of audiotaped depth interviews with volunteer participants provide the qualitative data for the present analysis (see Kvale 1983; McCracken 1988b; Thompson *et al.* 1989). In this study, interviews were conducted with seven women who fit the aforementioned demographic profile (see Thompson 1996 for further descriptions of the participants and data collection procedures).

Perceptions of the cultural setting

A number of socio-cultural factors have been implicated in working women's experiences of time-scarcity. First, it appears that working women have in large part retained the majority of the domestic responsibilities traditionally associated with the maternal role or, stated conversely, an egalitarian sharing of domestic responsibility has remained an elusive ideal in the majority of America's two-income households (Coverman 1989; Schwartz 1994). Second, on the public policy front, the provision of institutional-level family supports, such as easily accessible and affordable childcare, has been impeded by a nexus of historical barriers and societal conflicts (Crosby 1991). Third, historical evidence suggests that standards of household maintenance have steadily risen throughout the twentieth century and, paradoxically, that the diffusion of "labor saving" domestic appliances has been correlated with an increase in the number of hours women spend on housework (Cowan 1983; Jackson 1992; Stern 1989; Strasser 1982; Schor 1992).

The life issues and daily experiences described by these participants bore a number of similarities that were grounded in this set of cultural conditions. They consistently characterized themselves as almost always feeling pressed for time and as having to be continuously "on the go" to squeeze all that had to be done into their time-pressed routines. They also were very aware of being far more involved in domestic activities than their spouses. Although the participants noted many personal benefits that accrued from their lifestyles, they also described recurrent feelings of being frustrated and occasionally overwhelmed by this wide array of responsibilities. The overall tenor of their descriptions was consistent with general patterns identified by sociological research on working women (Bielby and Bielby 1988; Berg 1986; Crosby 1991; Gerson 1985; Hochschild 1989; Shreve 1987). This ground of shared general experiences sets the context for several prominent meanings that highlight the participants' meaning-based relationships to this cultural setting.

Although the metaphor of "juggling" has become the conventional way to characterize this time-pressed lifestyle (Crosby 1991), the central image in these participants' consumption stories was that of balancing. The subtle difference in connotations is that "balancing" directly invokes personally relevant images of undertaking compensatory adjustments, the fear of losing one's stability, and ultimately, a broader life-project of leading a balanced life.

Such acts of symbolic balancing are consistent with Hochschild's (1989) proposal that family myths enable a pattern of inequities in regard to domestic involvement to be rationalized and/or symbolically equalized. Other participants also described similar symbolic acts such as insisting that their spouse cook dinner one night a week, take responsibility for the children on a particular evening, or take charge of a specific routine domestic task, as illustrated in the following passage:

SUE: Basically I told my husband, "Let's have a rule in our house, whoever cooks doesn't have to clean up." So I'll hear him moan and groan about the fact that, you know, I dirty every single dish in the kitchen while I'm doing it. So I'm like, "OK, if you don't want that, you cook and I'll clean up after you." Well, he doesn't like to cook at all. So, over the years, that's how we"ve worked it out.

In this life-world context, these family myths express the participants' ongoing effort to balance their perceived family responsibilities with their own personal interests and, a pervasive sense that tilting this balance towards their needs was exceedingly difficult:

ELSA: I'm kind of embarrassed to say this, but I really don't have time to do things for me. If I had the time I would take classes. Sometimes I get upset, and my husband says, "Well, we'll do something this year. You can do your 'Jazzercise,' and we'll just juggle the schedules so that you can go." But it gets hard, and if we have to pick between your priorities and the kids', they come first because you want something better for them in their life. So you put the kids first. If there's any time left, then you might use it. But most of the time you're too tired to use it (Laugh).

AMY: Well, I had gone to the doctor, already, two years ago, and I was having these dizzy spells. They did CAT scans and all this other stuff and decided it was a combination of stress and also allergies. I think a lot of it was stress though. One of the important things they told me was, "Be sure and find time for yourself, even if it's an hour a day," and to do some kind of physical activity. I took water aerobics for a while, and when I did that, I did feel better but then I had to stop because it interfered with my son's basketball practice and stuff. It just seems like now I can't fit exercise in, any place.

INTERVIEWER: How did you feel about that, having to stop?

AMY: Well, it's frustrating because that was something for me, and it made me feel better. At the same time, when you're a parent your kids come first and they need these things too. I always seem to put them first. Sometimes I think we're not going to do basketball and Cub Scouts because that's like three nights a week. But I know he [son] needs it and I end up doing it. I guess it is balancing different things. There is just a lot to balance.

As these passages demonstrate, the life-world theme of leading a balanced life magnified the significance of those discrepant times when things seemed to be out of balance. Although the balance theme lent itself to recurrent feelings of frustration, it primarily functioned as a *displaced meaning* (McCracken 1988a) that assuaged the sense of self-sacrifice that also pervaded their life-worlds. By rendering balance as a long-term life-project in which the rewards of motherhood and career achievement can both be attained eventually, the participants could construct a life narrative that had a comedic structure – a point of crisis resolved through a happy ending – rather than a tragic one (see Gergen and Gergen 1986; Stern 1995):

SUE: You have only got one life and the kids only have one childhood. I mean my career is going to last probably forty years and if for ten years I am on a slower "mommy track" or whatever they call it, then that is just the way it is. I am not going to make them suffer because I want a promotion or something. Like I said it is not a big martyrdom. I am not giving everything up. I am slowing things down but that is not the same thing to me as giving them up. I am still going to be doing what I want to do when they are in college. And my view of aging is changing as I get older. I start seeing the things people can do at different stages and you know that people used to seem ancient at fifty, I am beginning to realize that you still have a lot of freedom. My parents just now have the youngest one in college and they are doing a lot of things that they have not been able to do before, which is really nice. Or I look at my husband's parents, they have done a lot of traveling and they built their dream home. So I don't think I have to be in a great rush to have everything right now. Just one thing at a time. I wanted children and that is a part of my life.

Because of the alignment among relatively uncontrollable cultural forces such as entrenched gender roles, attitudes in the workplace, contemporary theories of child-rearing, shortages in affordable quality day-care, the participants constantly found themselves compromising their own career goals and personal interests. Although they noted moments of taking time for themselves, they primarily described their everyday experiences and interpersonal orientations in terms consistent with the traditional ideal of the supportive, nurturing, and rather selfless mother (e.g. Shreve 1987). The lingering specter of traditional gender roles can also be seen in the participants' expressed view that their professional careers provided a way of claiming personal time. In this narrative framing of their careers as "something I do for me," professional work assumes a meaning similar to a self-gift (Mick and DeMoss 1990) and reflects a dramatic reversal of conventional (and masculine-oriented) conceptions of work time and leisure time.

One interpretive strategy for coping with the nexus of concessions posed by their juggling lifestyle was to extend the time frame in which things would balance out. In this narrative construction, "being a mom" represented an important aspect of their identity which they understood as necessitating a number of personal compromises. At some point in the future, however, their personal goals outside the role of being a good mother could be pursued. In accordance with this narrative framing, the participants described revising their views on "aging" and their own expectations about the pace of their life accomplishments.

This revised view of their historical horizons was especially significant to the participants who felt that they had forgone opportunities for career advancement, travel, and other valued dimensions of life and marriage. From this extended perspective, their many lifestyle trade-offs could be understood as having been deferred rather than abandoned. This shift in perspective also offered a way of coping with the immediate pressures of their time-pressed lifestyles. That is, to accept a sense of having no time in the present, the participants redefined the trajectory of their life narratives in a way that fostered a sense of having more time in a much broader sense of their life course. Their reinterpretation of the meaning of aging also offered a logic of self-identity that runs counter to the cultural idealization of youthfulness that has historically structured women's social identities (see Friedan 1993).

Emotional relationships to others

In their consumption stories, these participants characterized themselves as routinely engaging in a "second shift" of tasks and interpersonal responsibilities that began at the conclusion of their professional workday and extended throughout the entire evening. Through this narrative frame, the participants' understood themselves as being the connective force that held the household together. Moreover, their consumption stories reflected an intertwining of domestic and professional schedules such that professional demands sometimes encroached upon private time. For example, a common consumption story told by these participants described the necesssity of incorporating household responsibilities into their workday schedules:

SARAH: Well, to tell how I fit things in. Yesterday morning, [son] was sick and I had to take him to the doctor. The doctor's appointment was at eleven o'clock and I had to be at work at one because I was doing a flex-time evening. So I got everybody up and going and took [Son] to Stern's Youth World. Now he's sick, he's running a fever, but the appointment wasn't until eleven and it was in that end of town. So I dragged him off to Stern's to buy school pants, before I took him to the doctor, and then took him to the doctor, and then went to the grocery store, to buy things that we needed, and went home. I certainly wouldn't have wanted to do those things if I was not feeling well. But those were things that I truly had to do. He was down to one pair of pants.

At face value, this narrative coheres with the concept of *polychronic time use* in which consumers, by means of planning and activity bundling, "enrich their time budgets, producing the output of more than twenty-four hours of single monochronic activities" (Kaufman *et al.* 1991: 394). Although their descriptions seem consistent with a utility-maximizing goal of "producing more output," their consumption stories emphasized that unwanted trade-offs and concessions had to be made in the face of time pressures no matter how efficiently these participants organized their daily routines. Thus, professional working mothers interpreted their bundling of errands and reliance of extensive time scheduling – two key features of polychronic time use – as a necessary response to their life-world conditions rather than as a utility-maximizing choice.

As the following passage illustrates, this common cultural notion of "making more time" offers little solace to these time-pressed consumers, for it fails to acknowledge their daily dilemma of coping with the seemingly immutable limitations of time:

AMY: I love to go shopping, I love to go to the mountains and hike, things like that. I haven't been ice skating in a long time. I used to macrame but you can't do that with kids around. My husband tells me that I need to develop my own hobby.

INTERVIEWER: How do you feel when he says, "develop your own hobby?"

AMY: I tell him, "When do I have time?" "You just need to make time" he says. Well, how do you make time? Get out your hammer and nails? He just doesn't understand.

A sense of immediacy pervaded the participants' consumption stories: for individuals who understand themselves as having no time, there is no time to procrastinate. Under this subtle pressure to stay on schedule and get things done *now*, they became the protagonists in an ongoing family drama who constantly had to push other family members to do specific activities at certain times. These actions, while perceived as necessary, also inspired feelings of ambivalence and occasional pangs of guilt:

LIZ: I'm always rushing everybody around here, because, I get everybody up and get them [children] ready and I take [baby daughter] to the babysitter. So I'm always rushing and telling everybody to "hurry, hurry, hurry we have to leave right now" because I have to get the baby to the babysitter so I can get to work and have thirty minutes to get myself organized, so it's hurry, hurry, hurry. So I'm stressed out a little bit just by trying to rush all the children around. Like this morning, I was rushing [oldest son] to get dressed and get his breakfast eaten. And he turned around, he made some kind of comment to me, and I said, "That's not very respectful and I want you to talk nicer to me." And he said, "Well, then would you please be nice to me?" I realized I had not been very nice to him and I was the bad guy again. But I'm always the one that has to make everything happen here so everything kind of stays on a schedule and works out. So I'm always the bad guy.

For these participants, domestic activities that were tied to images of a traditional lifestyle held particularly strong emotional meanings. These activities, most notably cooking, were seen as significant to the quality of life experienced by their families. In their stories, the "home-cooked" meal represented an important symbol of nurturance and devotion to the family. The widely promoted linkages between nutrition and health, coupled with the participants' own fond childhood memories of "mom's cooking," imbued cooking with an undeniable experiential importance. This veneration of the home-cooked meal also set the stage for feelings of "guilt" when the participants' daily lives routinely deviated substantially from this valued image of traditional family life:

ELSA: It's the burden and the guilt kind of thing. You say, "well, we should have a family meal where we should sit down at this round table and have our decent meal." Then, you're fast fooding it or I call it fast food. You're tired and it's easy to grab the fish sticks and whip up some instant potatoes and get some corn that's already canned, and all this kind of stuff than preparing a full fledged meal. I guess a lot of women may do that, more credit to them but I just don't have time. Like if soccer is at quarter to six, that disrupts dinner.

In many of these consumption stories, a seemingly mundane item of household technology, the microwave oven, emerged as a "heroic" figure who assuages this nexus of emotional stress. By expediting meal preparation, the microwave enabled these participants to create a workable balance between their traditional family ideals and the trade-offs necessitated by their time-pressed lifestyles:

BETTY I rely on that microwave. I cannot be a working mother, working outside the home that is, without it. What I do is bake on the weekends. I'll cook main dishes and freeze them in family size portions, freeze everything. When I come home from work, I'll get home a quarter of six, pop something into the microwave, make a side dish to go with it and supper's on the table by six thirty.

JAN: It would have to be the microwave and microwavable products. Speed, that's of the essence when you have a very short time, roughly two hours to feed, bathe, do homework, and interact with your children at night. So you try to manage everything to the point where you have extra time and just that free time with your children. I think that's the most critical time of the day, from work to bedtime. We rarely use the conventional oven now. It's vital.

In the participants' consumption stories, products and services were not only portrayed as "saving the day" by obviating conflicts and trade-offs, but also as villains who created problems, dilemmas, and undesired complications:

ELSA: They [credit card company] get you on this big rigmarole with an answering machine. That's real helpful for the consumer. You get on and you push this if it's this, and you push that if it's that, and by the end of all

142

these buttons that you have to push, you've forgotten the number of the department you needed. You're like "well, was it one or two? I'll have to call back again, and find out." Well, then you've made another phone call for something that was supposedly ease and convenience. I understand having a business, that not everybody's available all at the same time, but, there are some things where they just go too far. It really upsets you because you don't, have time to deal with it. You are just so mad.

The strong aversive emotions inspired by a perceived lack of concern on the part of service providers is further illustrated in the following passage where Jan describes a "stir of anger" that she feels when recalling her experiences with the seller of a malfunctioning heating pump:

JAN: I wasn't really dissatisfied with the heat pump. I was more angry with the individuals who represented themselves as being experts in this. I rely upon outside expertise in a field like that, I don't hold myself to be a heating and air conditioning expert and I paid for their top of the line product.

INTERVIEWER: So you were primarily disappointed with the service people?

JAN: Right because after numerous occasions out to look at the thermostat and heat pump, they could never figure out . . . they kept saying it was an electrical problem with our internal wiring. We went out another expense and hired an electrician to come in see what the problem was and there was no problem. So, it kind of compounded itself there. They would not respond to calls. Days would go by and they would not respond to calls. This was in January with three kids and a forty degree house. They also had a 24-hour weekend call service, so they held themselves out to be something they were not. And we perceived that they weren't making an effort to garner more knowledge about the problem. It was just, "it's broken and we don't know why. And no we are not going to give your money back." They didn't care if we were inconvenienced. The money was in their hand and they were gone. Finally we had to call Carrier corporate headquarters to get the problem fixed.

Experiences of the lived body

These working mothers' consumption stories highlighted the physically demanding nature of their juggling lifestyles. They repeatedly emphasized the hectic pace of their lives, their sense of always having to do multiple things at once, the pervasive feeling of never being able to relax or slow down, and the acute awareness of limits to their energy and patience:

JAN: It [the evening routine] is like Whhhurrrr. It's trying to listen to three different sets of day's experiences of school, problems that have arisen. It's very physically demanding, physically and mentally demanding experience so you got to be in good shape. Gee I never tried to put it into words before, (laughs) I just know I have to do it, get it done, that sort of thing.

AMY: What's it [the daily routine] like? Usually hectic . . . Like I'll leave my car and go walking into the office to get something done, or something, and they'll [coworkers] say, "Whoa, is there a fire behind you, or something?" because I'll be walking real fast, you know, and I don't really consciously think of it. It's just got to hurry up and get there and do this and that. So, I feel like I'm in a rush most of the time, because most of the time I am. As soon as I get off from work, I rush over get the kids, and rush over to do this, and stuff.

Stories of being rushed serve as a structural counterpoint to those that represent the lived body in a relaxed and quiet state. These contrasting consumption stories emphasize the pleasure of dwelling in a tranquil moment where attention did not have to be divided across multiple demands. Such stories often were framed as momentary experiences of escape or "getting away:"

JAN: Right before I go to sleep at night I spend 40 minutes to an hour reading.
INTERVIEWER: What is that time like?
JAN: Oh, it's great. I get to read mysteries. I guess it's something of escapism and it's also challenging to try to figure out, "who did do it and how did I miss this at the end." It is very quiet. The kids are in bed and things are ready for the next day and it is kind of a reward I give to myself. Very quiet, very relaxing. Quiet. That is something I don't get much of.

A number of participants expressed similar feelings about reading and highlighted that its experiential qualities, such as being able to focus their thoughts and attention in a self-directed manner, offered a dramatic change from the usual conditions of their time-pressed lifestyles. Catalogue shopping also assumed a meaning that supplemented its practical benefit of shopping convenience. Catalogues – particularly specialty offerings such as J. Peterman's – afforded an experience of escape by allowing the participants to immerse themselves in an enjoyable private experience and engage in imaginative thinking.

These acts of escape were often characterized as a well-earned reward. The following passage demonstrates that a self-gift narrative (Mick and DeMoss 1990) also provided a needed rationale for managing feelings of guilt evoked by not spending available "leisure" time with one's children:

LIZ: I don't get to get away very often, with the kids and all. I do feel guilty a little bit doing that you know, taking time for myself, because I feel like if there is a couple of hours I ought to be giving it to the kids, so I don't do it very often. I mean, I'll take a little bit of time for myself. Once a month, or once every two months, I'll go off and go shopping for me. Like Talbots, I love that store, Talbots and Laura Ashley. It's very relaxing to shop there and

I like to do that when the spring clothes come out. I like to go out and have an afternoon to myself where I can look at the clothes, and decide what's going to be in for the spring and maybe pick up a couple things. That's nice. It's a real enjoyable experience getting to go out by myself and buying something for me.

The historicized self and life project

The final life-world category manifested itself in a set of higher order life themes that motivate the interpretive orientations of these professional working mothers. Prominent among these life themes is the desire for a particular form of personal accomplishment that the participants felt could not be attained by living in accord with the traditional model of motherhood:

BETTY: I've been able to balance things. A lot of it is self-choice. In terms of needing to be a two-income family, we don't need to be a two-income family. I want to be. I can't imagine sitting at home. I'm not a "homebody" type person, I'm much more comfortable doing the things that I do, in the press, pressure of time and only doing them halfway, than I would be if I could stay at home and clean all the splatter stains off the refrigerator. I mean, I just couldn't do that.

Domestic tasks did not provide participants with a needed feeling of enduring accomplishment or personal development. Whereas careers could be "built" and projects completed, domestic tasks were "thankless" ones that were done only to be later undone:

SUE: Doing laundry is the pits. Cleaning the toilet is the pits. Cleaning the kitchen, it's dirty the next time you serve a meal so it is really hard to feel like you have done much of anything. I know the stuff is important but I just don't like doing it. I like what I do at work. I am doing energy conservation research. I am writing reports, I am analyzing data. You work on a project for a while and you find your answers, you write it up, you present it at meetings, you're going boom, boom, boom and you can see what you have done. I have got a stack of reports over the last 10 years that are the projects I have done and these are the answers that I have found. It's something that is concrete that is not going to get undone the next time somebody takes a bath with dirty feet.

Further, a professional identity is significant not only to the participants' self-concepts but also to the interpersonal meanings that are incorporated into tacit understandings of their marriages:

LIZ: There's a sense of security that I enjoy because even all our money goes into the same bank account, I feel like if I just want some spending money, some fun money, I don't feel guilty about taking it out and having it available to me. I remember when we were first married after [first child] was born and we were living overseas, and I wasn't working that year, and Christmas was coming up and I had no money of my own. And I wanted to buy my husband a Christmas present, so he said I'll give you some money. And that was kind of his attitude too; "I'll give you some money." What I ended up doing was earning it by doing things that he normally would pay someone else to do. So, that I could feel that it was from me. I don't know if he would still feel that way now like "if you want something, I'll give you some money." I don't think he would anymore, but then his attitude was that he earned the money and it was his. I'm afraid that might be his attitude again. I don't think I want to take the chance to find out. I'll keep working and having money.

When reflecting on any given day or any given week, they acknowledged that the daily frustrations were probably more numerous than the emotional rewards. Nonetheless, each was quite clear that in a more global sense their personal rewards loomed larger than their daily tribulations:

SARAH: I choose to work. It is self-fulfilling to me. It is something I choose to do. Even though there are a lot of demands on my time, they are roles that I adopted and not roles that were thrust upon me. I guess that sounds like a contradiction from before, but working is something that I do for me. It gives me a sense of fulfillment that I am not sure I could get out of being home all the time. Maybe I could, but I have never tried. I have never not been in school or working. I'm not a traditional mom. I love my children and I love my family but I think that they would drive me crazy if I had to be with them 24 hours a day.

This broader historical perspective also rendered the hectic pace and time constraints of their life-worlds acceptable and enabled them to envision deferred personal interests as attainable in the future:

LIZ: My husband and I don't really have a chance to listen to each other because he's so busy and I'm so busy, and we're tired. We do go out occasionally but in a normal routine, we're both so busy there's hardly time to listen to each other either. It used to bother me and as each child came along I realized it wasn't getting any better and I came to accept that this is the way things are going to be for a while. So, it's not sad. We think that each other is important. It's just that I have other priorities on other things. It's more the children. I keep looking and saying, the children, enjoy them now, and don't worry about it because there's going to be a time when there will be time for the two of us, there was before and will be again. If we can survive this we'll be fine and we have been for a long time. We'll get there.

Discussion

Who is the postmodern consumer?

As Brown (1995) notes, the marketing literature frequently uses "postmodern" as a broad categorical term encompassing a diverse array of research traditions, many of which are grounded in a thoroughly modernist, intellectual tradition. A more specific usage of "postmodern," and one less idiosyncratic to the field of marketing, refers to a particular conceptualization of consumer culture and the nature of consumers who exist within this socio-cultural matrix (Featherstone 1991; Firat and Venkatesh 1995). This latter feature of postmodern thought is most relevant to the present discussion. Specifically, the life-world model of consumer meaning stands in direct opposition to "postmodern" consumption theories arguing that the activities and interests of contemporary consumers are inherently depthless and decontextualized (Jameson 1991), fragmented across disparate consumption contexts (Firat and Venkatesh 1995), and symbolic replacements for the psychologically fulfilling "conditions of community, tradition, and shared meaning" that are seen as missing in post-industrial societies (Cushman 1990: 600).

This genre of postmodernist theorizing tends to be based on a general cultural critique of consumer society rather than on specific analyses of the stories consumers tell about their life experiences. Although these "etic" analyses highlight some important structural features of consumer culture, their status as adequate descriptions of "consumer lives" can be challenged on a number of grounds (see Featherstone 1991 and Jenkins 1992 for further discussion of this issue).

First, these readings of consumer culture harbor a nostalgic view of the past as a mythic time when communities were closely knit and individual actions were "authentically" meaningful. The nostalgic reading is needed to support the rather dystopian view of contemporary consumer culture typically offered in these accounts (see Scott 1993 for an alternative view) and, furthermore, express an elitist conception that devalues popular culture and the lives of actual consumers. That is, such readings tacitly privilege the position of the postmodern theorist while relegating consumers to the position of a marginalized "other" who is schizoid, driven by the pursuit of immediate emotional gratification, in need of liberation and enlightenment, hopelessly entangled in superficial pursuits, and unable to forge a sense of purpose and self-directed meaning in his or her life. The description bears a marked resemblance to misogynist cultural portrayals of women in turn-of-the-century American and European discourses on women's "place" (Ehrenreich and English 1979; Sparke 1995). Not surprisingly, a number of feminist researchers have critiqued postmodern theory for reproducing the conventions of patriarchal authority and privilege in their narratives (see Lutz 1993).

A final counterargument to the postmodern thesis that consumers' lives are fragmented and lacking in meaningful connection to a shared community is that it

147

simply does not mesh with a vast body of research on the nature of consumer experiences. This research consistently shows that consumers actively strive to forge a sense of connectedness, and interpret their lives in terms of communally shared values, such as beliefs about religion, health, individual rights, social solidarity, and family togetherness, despite socio-cultural transformations that pose barriers to the formation of enduring community ties (see Bellah *et al.* 1985). In this spirit, consumer research has repeatedly shown that consumers' life stories are grounded in communal and family relationships (Hirschman 1994; Mick and Buhl 1992; Thompson *et al.* 1990, 1994) and that consumers often build a sense of community through consumption behaviors and the use of consumption symbolism (Arnould and Price 1993; Holt 1995; McCracken 1988a; Peñaloza 1994; Schouten and McAlexander 1995).

A hermeneutic approach to interpreting consumer stories reaffirms this body of literature. Specific consumption experiences and consumption sites are organized in terms of narratives that forge meaningful connections and symbolic linkages among life-world structures. To borrow a phrase from Foucault (1972), human actions are *dispersed* across a range of social settings and socio-linguistic frames, such as speaking as a parent, speaking as a professional, or speaking as a sports fan, that have their own cultural logic, social history, and conditions of intelligibility. However, for a given consumer, these dispersed modalities of experience/social meaning are personalized ones that are inscribed in terms of a coherent narrative of personal history and life values and grounded by the concrete conditions of the life-world (see Lifton 1993; Romanyshyn 1982; Pollio *et al.* 1997b; Thompson *et al.* 1994).

Conclusion: interpreting consumers

The phrase "interpreting consumers" has an instructively ambiguous denotative quality. It can refer to consumers who interpret their experiences, or to the actions of consumer researchers who interpret consumers' narratives or, finally, to a dynamic combination of both. This chapter has argued for the last alternative in conceptualizing the relationship between consumer researchers and consumers. As Fish (1979) writes:

> . . . we are never not in a situation. Because we are never not in a situation, we are never not in the act of interpretation . . . But in every situation some meaning or another will appear to us as uninterpreted because it is isomorphic with the interpretive structure (and therefore our perception) the situation already has.
>
> (Fish 1979: 251)

Here, the situated nature of Fish's *we* is equally transferable to the "we" of consumer researchers.

In sum, life-world analysis ensues from a theoretical view of consumers as active, meaning-imputing agents. Accordingly, it aspires to a hermeneutical understanding of the meanings by which consumers interpret the marketing activities directed at them. While the consumer-as-text metaphor is a useful way to conceptualize the active story-telling quality of consumer meanings, it can result in an overly abstract account of consumers' lives. By incorporating the phenomenological construct of the life-world into this textual metaphor, consumer research can become sensitized to consumer stories as *existentially grounded texts*. Unlike actual literary narratives, consumer stories are structured by a network of trans-linguistic relations that fundamentally shape their "plots." Moreover, the stories of everyday life are not the mere play of literary conventions (see Arnould in Chapter 4 of this book for an ethnographic analogue to this phenomenological claim) but, rather, the efforts of active social agents to ascribe a meaningful form on the life-world dynamics. Consumer stories then exist in the ambiguous onto-logical space that can neither be characterized as a mirror of an extant subjective reality or an autonomous semiotic system. For consumer researchers to prevent the consumer-as-text metaphor from succumbing to the tragic Kuhnian fate of displaced paradigms, I suggest we develop the genius for ambiguity needed to convey this dialectic relation in the stories we tell about the stories consumers tell.

Note

1 This conception of a prereflective foundation of consciousness (sometimes referred to as commonsense understanding) has many analogues in contemporary psychological the-ories of human understanding (see Packer 1985; Winograd and Flores 1987). One prominent consumer research example is Zajonic and Marcus's (1982) review of research on the "somatic" basis of consumption preferences. These studies suggest that many types of consumer preference emanate from non-cognitive, emotional, and neuro-muscular processes. Furhtermore, cognitive capacities may often be placed in a secondary role of generating rationalizations for these somatically driven preferences.

References

Arnold, S. and Fischer, E. (1994) "Hermeneutics and Consumer Research," *Journal of Consumer Research*, 21,1: 55–70.

Arnould, E.J. (1989) "Toward a Broadened Theory of Preference Formation and the Diffusion of Innovations: Cases from Zinder Province, Niger Republic," *Journal of Consumer Research*, 16,2: 239–67.

Arnould E.J and Price, L.L. (1993) "River Magic: Extraordinary Experience and the Service Encounter," *Journal of Consumer Research*, 20,1: 24–46.

Bartos, R. (1989) *Marketing to Women Around the World*, Boston; Harvard Business School Press.

Baudrillard, J. (1988) *Selected Writings*, ed. M. Poster, Stanford, CA: Stanford University Press.

Bielby, D.D. and Bielby, W.T. (1988) "She Works Hard for the Money: Household Responsibilities and the Allocation of Work," *American Journal of Sociology*, 93,5: 1031–59.

Belk, R.W. and Coon, G.S. (1993) "Gift Giving as Agapic Love: An Alternative to the Exchange Based Paradigm Based on Dating Experiences," *Journal of Consumer Research*, 20,3: 393–417.

Belk, R.W, Sherry, J.F., and Wallendorf, M. (1988) "A Naturalistic Inquiry Into Buyer and Seller Behavior at a Swap Meet," *Journal of Consumer Research*, 14,4: 449–70.

Belk, R.W., Wallendorf, M., and Sherry, J.F. (1989) "The Sacred and the Profane in Consumer Behavior: Theodicy on the Odyssey," *Journal of Consumer Research*, 16,1: 1–38.

Bellah, R.N., Madsen, R., Sullivan, W.M., Swidler, A., and Tipton, S.M. (1985) *Habits of the Heart*, Berkely, CA: University of California Press.

Berg, B.J. (1986) *The Crisis of the Working Mother: Resolving the Conflict Between Family and Work*, New York: Summit Books.

Berger, P.L. and Luckmann, T. (1967) *The Social Construction of Reality*, Garden City, NY: Anchor Books.

Bower, G.H. and Hilgard, E. (1956) *Theories of Learning*, 3rd edn, Englewood Cliffs, NJ: Prentice-Hall.

Bristor, J.M. and Fischer, E. (1993) "Feminist Thought: Implications for Consumer Research," *Journal of Consumer Research*, 19,4: 518–36.

Brown, S. (1995) *Postmodern Marketing*, London: Routledge.

Bryant, K.W. (1988) "Durables and Wives' Employment – Yet Again," *Journal of Consumer Research*, 15,1: 37–47.

Coverman, S. (1989) "Women's Work is Never Done: The Division of Domestic Labor," in J. Freeman (ed.) *Women: A Feminist Perspective*, Mountain View, CA: Mayfield Publishing Company.

Cowan, R.S. (1983) *More Work for Mother: The Ironies of Household Technology from the Open Hearth to the Microwave*, New York: Basic Books.

Crites, S. (1986) "Storytime: Recollecting the Past and Projecting the Future," in T.R. Sarbin (ed.) *Narrative Psychology: The Storied Nature of Human Conduct*, New York: Praeger, 152–73.

Crosby, F.J. (1991) *Juggling: The Unexpected Advantages of Balancing Career and Home for Women and their Families*, New York: The Free Press.

Cushman, P. (1990) "Why the Self Is Empty: Toward a Historically Situated Psychology," *American Psychologist*, 45,5: 599–611.

Deshpande, R. (1983) "Paradigms Lost: On Theory and Method in Marketing Research," *Journal of Marketing*, 47,4: 101–10.

Dholakia, R.R. (1987) "Feminism and the New Home Economics: What Do They Mean for Marketing?" in A.F. Firat, N. Dholakia, and R.P. Bagozzi (eds) *Philosophical and Radical Thought in Marketing*, Lexington, MA: Lexington Books, 341–9.

Dillon, M.C. (1988) *Merleu-Ponty's Ontology*, Bloomington, IN: University of Indiana Press.

Douglas, S. (1994) *Where the Girls Are: Growing Up Female With the Mass Media*, New York: Times Books.

Dreyfus, H.L. (1982) *Husserl, Intentionality, and Cognitive Science*, Cambridge, MA: MIT Press.

Dreyfus, H.L. and Rabinow, P. (1983) *Michel Foucault: Beyond Structuralism and Hermeneutics*, Chicago, Ill: University of Chicago Press.

Ehrenreich, B. and English, D. (1979) *For Her Own Good: 150 Years of Experts' Advice to Women*, Garden City, NY: Anchor Books.

Faulconer, J.E. and Williams, R.N. (1985) "Temporality in Human Action: An Alternative to Historicism and Positivism," *American Psychologist*, 40,11: 1179–88.

Featherstone, M. (1991) *Consumer Culture and Postmodernism*, London: Sage.

Firat, F.A. and Venkatesh, A. (1995) "Liberatory Postmodernism and the Reenchantment of Consumption," *Journal of Consumer Research*, 22,3: 239–67.

Fish, S. (1979) "Normal Circumstances, Literal Language, Direct Speech Acts, the Ordinary, the Everyday, the Obvious, What Goes Without Saying, and Other Special Cases," in P. Rabinow and W. Sullivan (eds) *Interpretive Social Sciences*, Berkely, CA: University of California Press, 243–65.

Foucault, M. (1972) *The Archaeology of Knowledge*, New York: Pantheon Books.

Frankl, V. (1984) *Man's Search for Meaning*, 3rd edn, New York: Simon & Schuster.

Friedan, B. (1993) *The Fountain of Age*, New York: Simon & Schuster.

Gadamer, H.G. (1993) *Truth and Method* 2nd edn, New York: Continuum.

Geertz, C. (1983) *Local Knowledge*, New York: Basic Books.

Gergen, K.J. (1985) "The Social Constructionist Movement in Modern Psychology," *American Psychologist*, 40,3: 266–75.

—— (1991) *The Saturated Self*, New York: Basic Books.

Gergen, K.Y. and Gergen, M.M. (1986) "Narrative Form and the Construction of Psychological Science," in T.R. Sarbin (ed.) *Narrative Psychology: The Storied Nature of Human Conduct*, New York: Praeger, 22–44.

Gerson, K. (1985) *Hard Choices: How Women Decide about Work, Career, and Motherhood*, Berkeley, CA: University of California Press.

Giddens, A. (1991) *Modernity and Self-Identity*, Stanford, CA: Stanford University Press.

Gier, N. (1981) *Wittgenstein and Phenomenology*, Albany, NY: State University of New York.

Giorgi, A. (1986) "Theoretical Justification for the Use of Descriptions in Psychological Research," in P.D. Ashworth, A. Giorgi and A. de Koning (eds) *Qualitative Research in Psychology*, Pittsburgh, PA: Duquesne University Press, 3–22.

Gould, S.J. (1991) "The Self-Manipulation of My Pervasive, Perceived Vital Energy Through Product Use: An Introspective-Praxis Perspective," *Journal of Consumer Research*, 18,2: 194–207.

—— (1995) "Researcher Introspection as a Method in Consumer Research: Applications, Issues, and Implications," *Journal of Consumer Research*, 21,4: 719–23.

Hannerz, U. (1992) *Cultural Complexity*, New York: Columbia University Press.

Heidegger, M. ([1927] 1960) *Being and Time*, New York: Harper & Row.

Hermans, H.J. (1996) "Voicing the Self: From Information Processing to Dialogical Interchange," *Psychological Bulletin*, 119,1: 31–50.

Hirschman, E.C. (1993) "Ideology in Consumer Research, 1980 to 1990: A Marxist and Feminist Critique," *Journal of Consumer Research*, 19,4: 537–55.

Hirschman, E.C. (1994) "Consumers and their Animal Companions," *Journal of Consumer Research*, 20,4: 616–32.

Hirschman, E.C. and Holbrook, M.B. (1982) "Hedonic Consumption: Emerging Concepts, Methods, and Propositions," *Journal of Marketing*, 46,3: 92–101.

Hirshchman, E.C. and Holbrook, M.B. (1992) *Postmodern Consumer Research: The Study of Consumption as Text*, Newbury Park, CA: Sage.

Hochschild, A.R. (1983) *The Managed Heart: Commercialization of Human Feeling*, Berkeley, CA: University of California Press.

—— (1989) *The Second Shift: Working Parents and the Revolution at Home*, New York: Viking Press.

Holbrook, M.B. (1988) "The Psychoanalytic Interpretation of Consumer Behavior: I Am an Animal," in E. Hirschman and J. Sheth (eds) *Research in Consumer Behavior, Vol. 3*, Greenwich, CT: JAI Press, 149–78.

Holbrook, M. and Hirschman, E. (1982) "The Experiential Aspects of Consumption: Consumer Fantasies, Feelings, and Fun," *Journal of Consumer Research*, 20,4: 616–32.

Holbrook, M. and O'Shaughnessy, J. (1988) "On the Scientific Status of Consumer Research and the Need for an Interpretive Approach in Studying Consumer Behavior," *Journal of Consumer Research*, 15,3: 398–402.

Holt, D.B. (1995) "How Consumers Consume: A Typology of Consumption Practices," *Journal of Consumer Research*, 22,1: 1–16.

Husserl, E. ([1936] 1970) *The Crisis of European Sciences and Transcendental Phenomenology: An Introduction to Phenomenological Philosophy*, English translation D. Carr, Evanston, IL: Northwestern University Press.

Jackson, S. (1992) "Towards a Historical Sociology of Housework: A Material Feminist Analysis," *Women's Studies International Forum*, 15,2: 153–72.

Jameson, F. (1991) *Postmodernism or the Cultural Logic of Late Capitalism*, Durham, NC: Durham University Press.

Jenkins, H. (1992) *Textual Poachers: Television Fans & Participatory Culture*, New York: Routledge.

Johnson, M. (1987) *The Body in the Mind: The Bodily Basis of Meaning, Imagination, and Reason*, Chicago, Ill: University of Chicago Press.

Kaufman C.F., Lane, P.M., and Lindquist, J.D. (1991) "Exploring More than 24 Hours A Day: A Preliminary Investigation of Polychronic Time Use," *Journal of Consumer Research*, 18,3: 392–401.

Keen, E. (1975) *A Primer in Phenomenological Psychology*, New York: Holt, Rinehart and Winston.

Kuhn, T. (1970) *The Structure of Scientific Revolutions*, Chicago: University of Chicago Press.

Kvale, S. (1983) "The Qualitative Research Interview: A Phenomenological and Hermeneutical Mode of Understanding," *Journal of Phenomenological Psychology*, 14,2: 171–96.

Lakoff, G. (1987) *Women, Fire, and Dangerous Things: What Categories Reveal about the Mind*, Chicago, Ill: University of Chicago Press.

Lakoff, G. and Johnson, M. (1980), *Metaphors We Live By*, Chicago, Ill: University of Chicago Press.

Levy, S.J. (1981) "Interpreting Consumer Mythology: A Structural Approach to Consumer Behavior," *Journal of Marketing*, 45,3: 49–62.

Lifton, R.J. (1993) *The Protean Self: Human Resilience in an Age of Fragmentation*, New York: Basic Books.

Lutz, C. (1993) "Social Contexts of Postmodern Cultural Analysis," in J.P. Jones, W. Natter, and T.R. Schatzki (eds) *Postmodern Contentions: Epochs, Politics and Space*, New York: The Guilford Press, 137–63.

Maines, D.R. (1993) "Narrative's Moment and Sociology's Phenomena: Toward a Narrative Sociology," *The Sociological Quarterly*, 34,1: 17–38.

Marcel, G. (1960) *The Mystery of Being*, Chicago, Ill: Gateway.

Matthews, G. (1987) *Just A Housewife*, New York: Oxford.

McCracken, G. (1988a) *Culture and Consumption*, Bloomington, IN: Indiana University Press.

—— (1988b) *The Long Interview*, Newbury Park, CA: Sage.

McQuarrie, E.F. and Mick, D.G. (1992) "On Resonance: A Critical Pluralistic Inquiry in Advertising Rhetoric," *Journal of Consumer Research*, 19,2: 180–97.

Merleau-Ponty, M. (1962) *The Phenomenology of Perception*, London: Routledge & Kegan Paul.

—— (1968) *The Visible and the Invisible*, Evanston, Ill: Northwestern University Press.

Mick, D.G. (1986) "Consumer Research and Semiotics; Exploring the Morphology of Signs, Symbols, and Significance," *Journal of Consumer Research*, 13,2: 196–213.

—— (1991) "Giving Gifts to Ourselves: A Greimassian Analysis Leading to Testable Propositions," in H.H. Larsen, D.G. Mick, and C. Alsted (eds) *Marketing and Semiotics*, Copenhagen: Handelshojskolens Forlag, 143–59.

Mick, D.G. and Buhl, C. (1992) "A Meaning Based Model of Advertising Experiences," *Journal of Consumer Research*, 19,4: 317–38.

Mick, D.G. and DeMoss, M. (1990) "Self Gifts: Phenomenological Insights From Across Four Contexts," *Journal of Consumer Research*, 17,4: 322–32.

Miller, G.A., Galanter, E., and Pribram, K. (1960) *Plans and Structure of Behavior*, New York: Holt, Rinehart and Winston.

Murray, J.B. and Ozanne, J.L. (1991) "The Critical Imagination: Emancipatory Interests in Consumer Research, *Journal of Consumer Research*, 18,3: 129–44.

Neisser, U. (1976) *Cognition and Reality*, New York: W.H. Freeman.

Orpesa, R.S. (1993) "Female Labor Force Participation and Time-Saving Household Technology: A Case Study of the Microwave from 1978 to 1989," *Journal of Consumer Research*, 19,4: 567–79.

Packer, M.J. (1985) "Hermeneutic Inquiry in the Study of Human Conduct," *American Psychologists*, 40,10: 1081–93.

—— (1989) "Tracing the Hermeneutic Circle: Articulating an Ontical Study of Moral Conflicts," in M. Packer and R.B. Addison (eds) *Entering the Circle: Hermeneutic Investigation in Psychology*, New York: State University of New York Press, 95–119.

Peñaloza, L. (1994) "Atravasando Fronteras/Border Crossings: A Critical Ethnographic Examination of the Consumer Acculturation of Mexican Immigrants," *Journal of Consumer Research*, 20,1: 32–54.

Polkinghorne, D.E. (1988) *Narrative Knowing and the Human Sciences*, Albany, NY: SUNY Press.

Pollio, H.R., Henley, T.B., and Thompson, C.J. (1997a) *The Phenomenology of Everyday Life*, New York: Cambridge University Press.

Pollio, H.R. Henley, T.B., Thompson, C.J., with MacGillivary, W. (1997b) "The Body as Lived," in *The Phenomenology of Everyday Life*, New York: Cambridge University Press, 61–92.

Rabinow, P. and Sullivan, W. (1979) "The Interpretive Turn: Emergence of an Approach," in P. Rabinow and W. Sullivan (eds) *Interpretive Social Science: A Reader*, Berkeley, CA: University of California Press, 1–21.

Ricoeur, P. (1981) *Hermeneutics and the Social Sciences*, Cambridge: Cambridge University Press.

Romanyshyn, R.D. (1982) *Psychological Life: From Science to Metaphor*, Austin, TX: University of Texas Press.

Sarbin, T.R. (1986) "The Narrative as a Root Metaphor for Psychology," in T.R. Sarbin (ed.) *Narrative Psychology: The Storied Nature of Human Conduct*, New York: Praeger, 3–21.

Sartre, J.P. (1956) *Being and Nothingness*, New York: Washington Square.

Schor, J.B. (1992) *The Overworked American: The Unexpected Decline of Leisure*, New York: Harper-Collins.

Schouten, J. and McAlexander, J. (1995) "Subcultures of Consumption: An Ethnography of New Bikers," *Journal of Consumer Research*, 22,1: 43–61.

Schutz, A. and Luckmann, T. (1973) *The Structures of the Life-World, Vol. 1*, Evanston, Ill: Northwestern University Press.

Schutz, A. and Luckmann, T. (1983) *The Structures of the Life-World, Vol. 2*, Evanston, Ill: Northwestern University Press.

Schwartz, P. (1994) *Peer Marriage*, New York: The Free Press.

Scott, L. (1990) "Understanding Jingles and Needledrop: A Rhetorical Approach to Music in Advertising," *Journal of Consumer Research*, 17,2: 223–36.

—— (1993) "Spectacular Vernacular: Literacy and Commercial Culture in the Postmodern Age," *International Journal of Research in Marketing*, 10,3: 251–76.

—— (1994) "The Bridge from Text to Mind: Adapting Reader–Response Theory to Consumer Research," *Journal of Consumer Research*, 21,3: 461–80.

Sherry, J. (1991) "Postmodern Alternatives: The Interpretive Turn in Consumer Research," in T.S. Robertson and H.H. Kassarjian (eds) *Handbook of Consumer Behavior*, Englewood Cliffs, NJ: Prentice-Hall, 548–91.

Shreve, A. (1987) *Remaking Motherhood*, New York: Viking.

Shweder, R.A. (1989) *Thinking Through Cultures: Expeditions in Cultural Psychology*, Cambridge, MA: Harvard University Press.

Solomon, M.R. (1983) "The Role of Products as Social Stimuli: A Symbolic Unteractionism Perspective," *Journal of Consumer Research*, 10,3: 319–29.

Sparke, P. (1995) *As Long As It's Pink: The Sexual Politics of Taste*, San Francisco, CA: Pandora.

Stern, B.B. (1988) "Medieval Allegory: Roots of Advertising Strategy for the Mass Market," *Journal of Marketing*, 52,3: 84–94.

—— (1989) "Literary Criticism and Consumer Research: Overview and Illustrative Analysis," *Journal of Consumer Research*, 16,3: 322–34.

—— (1993) "Feminist Literary Criticism and the Deconstruction of Ads: A Postmodern View of Advertising and Consumer Responses," *Journal of Consumer Research*, 19,4: 556–66.

—— (1995) "Consumer Myths: Frye's Taxonomy and the Structural Analysis of Consumption Text," *Journal of Consumer Research*, 22,2: 165–85.

Strasser, S. (1982) *Never Done: A History of American Housework*, New York: Pantheon.

Thompson, C.J. (1996) "Caring Consumers: Gendered Consumption Meanings and the Juggling Lifestyle," *Journal of Consumer Research*, 22,4: 388–407.

Thompson, C.J. and Haytko, D. (1997) "Speaking of Fashion: Consumers' Use of Fashion Discourse and the Appropriation of Countervailing Cultural Meanings," *Journal of Consumer Research*, 24,1: 15–42.

Thompson, C.J. and Hirschman, E.C. (1995) "Understanding the Socialized Body: A Poststructuralist Analysis of Consumers' Self-Conceptions, Body Images, and Self-Care Practices," *Journal of Consumer Research*, 22,2: 139–54.

Thompson, C.J., Locander, W.B., and Pollio, H.R. (1989) "Putting Consumer Experience Back into Consumer Research: The Philosophy and Method of Existential-Phenomenology," *Journal of Consumer Research*, 16,2: 133–47.

Thompson, C.J., Locander, W.B., and Pollio, H.R. (1990) "The Lived Meaning of Free Choice: An Existential-Phenomenological Description of Everyday Consumer Experiences of Contemporary Married Women," *Journal of Consumer Research*, 17,3: 346–61.

Thompson, C.J. Pollio, H.R., and Locander, W.B. (1994) "The Spoken and the Unspoken: A Hermeneutic Approach to Understanding the Cultural Viewpoints that Underlie Consumers' Expressed Meanings," *Journal of Consumer Research*, 21,3: 432–52.

Valle, R.S., King, M., and Halling, S. (1989) "An Introduction to Existential-Phenomenological Thought in Psychology," in R.S. Valle and S. Halling (eds) *Existential-Phenomenological Perspectives in Psychology*, New York: Plenum Press, 3–16.

Van den Berg, J.H. (1970) *A Different Kind of Existence: Principles of a Phenomenological Psychotherapy*, Pittsburgh, PA: Dusquesne University Press.

Wallendorf, M. and Brucks, M. (1993): "Introspection in Consumer Research: Implementation and Implications," *Journal of Consumer Research*, 20, 3: 339–59.

Wertz, F. (1987) "Cognitive Psychology and the Understanding of Perception," *Journal of Phenomenological Psychology*, 18,2: 103–42.

Widdershoven, G. (1993) "The Story of Life: Hermeneutic Perspectives on the Relationship Between Narrative and Life History," in R. Josselson and A. Lieblich (eds) *The Narrative Study of Lives*, Newbury Park, CA: Sage, 1–20.

Wilke, R. (1995) "Learning to be Local in Belize: Global Systems of Common Difference," in D. Miller (ed.) *Worlds Apart: Modernity Through the Prism of the Local*, New York: Routledge, 111–33.

Winograd, T. and Flores, F. (1987) *Understanding Computers and Cognition*, New York: Addison-Wesley.

Wittgenstein, L. (1958) *Logical Investigations*, 3rd edn, trans. G.E.M. Anscombe, New York: Macmillan.

Zajonc, R.B. and Markus, H. (1982) "Affective and Cognitive Factors in Preference," *Journal of Consumer Research*, 9,2: 123–31.

6

CREATING THE FRAME AND THE NARRATIVE

From text to hypertext

Susan Spiggle

Researchers represent consumers by transforming data into a research narrative. Initially the researcher transforms an observed *reality* into a *data set* by selecting and arranging observations. The researcher then transforms the data set through analysis and interpretation, constructing a conceptual *frame* or theoretical perspective. In the third transformation the researcher "re-presents" the consumer in a research *narrative*. We can view the observed reality, the data set, the frame, and the narrative as "texts" (see Geertz 1973; Hirschman and Holbrook 1992; Manning 1987) created by progressive transformations. As Atkinson points out in reference to ethnographic research, the further along in the process of transforming data into a written report, the thinner becomes the methodological and practical advice that is available (1992: 4).

This chapter presents methodological and practical advice further along in the research process. I focus on the second and third phases of transformation – the construction of the conceptual frame and its transformation into a narrative. I offer this perspective for interpretive consumer research, a diverse body of work – ethnography, structuralism, deconstruction, phenomenology, semiotics and hermeneutics, for example – that uses qualitative analysis and typically focuses upon meanings. I use the term "qualitative analysis" to refer to performing operations on data in which the data are not reduced to numerical symbols. Rather, the data remain in verbal, graphical, or other visual form throughout the research transformations. In contrast, in "quantitative analysis" the data are captured, coded, or otherwise represented as numbers (cf. Wallendorf and Brucks 1993).

The *re-presentation* of consumers in research narratives has particular relevance for interpretive researchers who explicitly incorporate, address, and represent consumers' perspectives and points of view. Additionally, relative to quantitative research, interpretive research lacks codification for constructing a frame and

156

transforming it into a narrative, and it lacks a narrative template (cf. Lofland's (1974)) comments on qualitative sociological research).

I discuss four topics relevant to representing consumers:

1 the interrelations between analytic strategy, interpretive stance, and narrative strategy;
2 a typological analysis of analytic and narrative strategies in consumer research;
3 a framework for the representation of consumers in crafting the narrative;
4 the issues and possibilities in moving from text to hypertext in constructing the narrative.

An example of a hypertext research document accompanies this chapter.

Analytic and interpretive strategies

Analysis and interpretation form the foundation from which the researcher constructs the narrative. Arnould and Wallendorf (1994) and Spiggle (1994) have recently provided parallel descriptions of strategies for analyzing and interpreting qualitative data – specifically data from field research and semi-structured interviews. They both distinguish analysis from interpretation. In *analysis* the researcher sorts, reduces, manipulates, and reconstitutes the data in searching for patterns and co-occurring phenomenon. Through *interpretation* the researcher applies insights, imagination, or illuminations in making sense of, accounting for, and understanding the identified patterns. While we can distinguish these two activities, they occur not in a distinct sequence but as iterative and interpenetrating phases.

Wolcott's (1994) definitions of analysis and interpretation parallel those of Arnould and Wallendorf (1994) and Spiggle (1994). He argues that they both represent processes related to data: analysis *transforms* data, while interpretation *transcends* data. However, he primarily uses these terms to characterize the relative emphasis that a text or account allots to analysis: the more data-constrained, "objective," "confirmable" presentation of elements and their properties, patterns and relationships – versus interpretation – the more speculative, data-distant, intuitive presentation of the researcher's insights about what the analysis means.

Wallendorf and Brucks (1993), Arnould and Wallendorf (1994), and Spiggle (1994) argue for researchers to move beyond the identification of patterns, redundancies, or themes in the data. They encourage researchers to take interpretive leaps that account for, explain, and illuminate these patterns. In similar spirit, Wolcott (1994) proposes that the relative emphasis upon description – the reporting of observations and data – analysis, and interpretation in research accounts, reflects researcher maturity: novices limit themselves more to description, and seasoned researchers engage in more interpretation. He also suggests that the quality and richness of data shape the manner and the extent to which the researcher can transform data through analysis and transcend them through interpretation. Using a cuisine metaphor, Wolcott points out that researchers "cook" data. Even a simple description does not present the "raw" data, but employs them selectivity. Studies weighted heavily on analysis are more cooked than descriptive ones, and those that emphasize interpretation of data are even more cooked.

In discussing strategies for analysis, interpretation and narrative construction – that is, cooking a data set – I rely on a traditional distinction between opposing principles of representation. These opposing principles provide us with abstract guidelines for enhancing our ability to represent consumers because they suggest the way we can make connections in developing conceptual frames and representing consumers in research narratives. I compare interpretive consumer researchers' conceptual frames and narrative strategies using the distinction between these opposing principles.

Connections based on two opposing principles

Textual transformations and representation depend on identifying *connections* among elements such as objects, symbols, episodes, words, patterns, indices, and behaviors. Scholars from a wide range of academic fields concerned with meaning have distinguished *two contrasting principles* for making connections. I draw here from three extensive bodies of writing:

1   the semiotic (Saussurean) distinction between paradigmatic and syntagmatic relations (Mick 1986);
2   Jakobson's (1956) contrast between connections based on similarity and those based on contiguity;
3   the literary classification of metaphor and metonymy (Atkinson 1990; Fernandez 1986, 1991; Lakoff and Johnson 1980; Lakoff and Turner 1989; Lodge 1977; Manning 1979).

Semiotics

As Mick (1986) notes, people use signs (anything that stands for something else) to communicate to others. Signs include gestures, words, and artifacts that carry meaning when combined into sign systems governed by rules. Following Barthes, to illustrate the paradigmatic and syntagmatic distinction, Lodge (1977) describes an example of meaning construction with artifacts that function as signs – in this case a clothing ensemble (cf. Holman's analysis ((1980a, 1980b)) of clothing ensembles as messages).

He refers to a girl dressed in tee-shirt, jeans, and sandals. This ensemble sends a message about what type of person she is, or what mood she is in, depending on the context. Each of these three items of dress serves as a sign. The girl creates this clothing ensemble and corresponding message through *two processes*:

1   She selects signs from three *paradigms* (i.e., sets of possible signs – upper body garments, lower body garments, and footwear). Each paradigm contains a possible *set* of pieces from which she can choose only one. From the upper-body-garment paradigm (including blouses, tee-shirts, tunics, sweaters), she selects one. These items share a *similar* structure, function, and/or other attribute with others in the set: they are related to one another on the basis of similarity. She further selects items related by similarity from the lower-body-garment and footwear paradigms. A socially defined, shared classification system or code shapes her selections.

2   She *combines* the selected signs through rules (i.e., tee-shirts go with sandals, not high heels), sending a *message* through the ensemble – the *syntagm*. Selection requires her to perceive similarity and opposition among signs within the set (the paradigm), classifying them as items having the same function or structure, only one of which she needs. She can *substitute*, or select, a blouse for the tee-shirt – conveying a different message. The combination, tee-shirt–jeans–sandals, requires her to know the "rules by which garments are acceptably combined. . . . The combination . . . is, in short, a kind of sentence" (Lodge 1977: 74). The tee-shirt–jeans–sandals syntagm conveys a different meaning (sends a different message) at the beach than at a formal occasion.

Jakobson's contrast

Jakobson (1956), also drawing upon the structural linguistics of Saussure, proposed that language, as any other system of signs, has a "two-fold character" – the dimension anchored by *selection* and *combination*. Jakobson provided evidence of this distinction by describing two opposing forms of language disturbance, depending on whether the impairment exhibits a selection (*similarity*) deficiency or a combination (*contiguity*) deficiency. In the similarity disorder, the victim fails to understand and create connections based on similarity and remains very dependent upon context or contiguous relations to communicate. For example, unable to utter "knife", the victim may say "plate". These objects are not similar in function and cannot substitute for one another, but are found together (co-occur or associated through contiguity) in a context – the table setting. In the opposite problem, contiguity disorder, the victim is unable to form coherent sentences and resorts to one or few word utterances. Because the ability to make connections based on similarity is not impaired, the victim may use inappropriate substitutions, confusing "spyglass" for "microscope", for example.

Following through on the two-fold character of language, Jakobson argues that "The development of a discourse may take place along two different semantic lines: one topic may lead to another either through their similarity or through their contiguity (1956: 76). Jakobson further argues that similarity and contiguity anchor opposite poles of a dimension critical to understanding culture. He then classifies the literary tropes, metaphor and metonymy, as well as a number of other cultural phenomena in accordance with the contiguity/similarity distinction.

Metaphor and metonymy

The rhetorical devices, metaphor and metonymy, provide a foundation for much of our understanding and communication of meaning in everyday life (Lakoff and Johnson 1980). They function figuratively: in both one object or item stands for or represents, another. These representations operate on one of the two opposing principles for making connections. (See McQuarrie's and Mick (1996) ingenious alternative scheme for classifying rhetorical devices.)

Metaphor

Metaphor operates through the principle of similarity. To think or speak metaphorically involves connecting two objects that share some similarity but represent two different domains. In product lifecycle, for example, "product" belongs to the domain of economics/marketing and "life cycle" to that of biology. The phrase "product life cycle" creates a connection between them based on the similarity of developmental stages. To map life cycle development onto product stages implies conception, birth, growth, maturity, and death. The power of metaphor derives from the juxtaposition of two domains that share a similar feature but are obviously different.

One generates a metaphor by *selecting* a source domain (life cycle) to represent a target domain (product development) (Lakoff and Turner 1989). Potential source domains share a similarity in function, structure, property, or sensory impression along any of the five senses. We create a metaphor when we link one of these source domains to the target domain based on their perceived similarities. Rooted in relations of similarity, metaphoric connections are iconic (Mick 1986). Metaphors enhance understanding and meaning by permitting one to see or to convey an unfamiliar, distant, or abstract domain in terms of one that is familiar, near, or concrete (Spiggle 1994).

Metonymy

Metonymy operates through the principle of contiguity. To think or speak metonymically involves representing one object or item by another as in metaphor. However, in metonymy the two objects are connected by virtue of belonging to the same domain: they are contiguous (Stern 1992). The objects may be causally, culturally, temporally, spatially, physically, or structurally contiguous. We find them together.

Common journalistic metonyms include the "Beltway" for the Washington establishment (spatially contiguous), the "White House" for the President (culturally and spatially contiguous), "labor" for blue-collar workers (causally contiguous), and "Wall Street" for the financial community associated with the stock market (spatially contiguous). As Mick (1986) notes, in advertising we frequently see narrow, confined roles and scenes representing broader, extended realities of life (structurally contiguous). Such representations function metonymically in that a part stands for the whole.

In other metonyms the whole may stand for the part – for example the "market" for customers, "GE" for top management of General Electric. Metonyms also include the use of one object to represent another object that is closely associated (culturally contiguous) – for example, "the carriage trade" represents up-scale customer segments, but a part–whole relationship is absent.

One generates metonyms "by deleting one or more items from a natural combination" (Lodge 1977: 76). A "natural" combination is a set of elements linked together (i.e., contiguous) by rules (as in speech), broader cultural codes (as in clothing ensembles), natural or physical structures, cause and effect, time frames, spatial proximity, and other related phenomena. Signs connected by metonymy (based on contiguous associations) are indexical (Mick 1986).

Unlike metaphor, which creates connections across domains, metonymic connections fall within the same domain, field, or sphere. In metonym one object stands for another where the two are conjoined through contiguous association. Metonyms enhance understanding by permitting one to see or convey some aspect of a domain by means of other aspects of it that are more easily identified, more visible, more exemplary, or more salient.

In sum, interpretive research depends upon seeing, pursuing, and constructing connections between objects, domains, items, or elements. Connections are based on one of two opposing principles – one based on selecting items from a set defined by their similarity and the other on combining items into units creating contiguity. Table 6.1 presents a summary of the opposing principles. I employ the distinction between connections based on similarity and those based on contiguity to describe the transformational processes of research and the outputs.

Analysis

Spiggle (1994) and Arnould and Wallendorf (1994) both present analysis as a systematic activity in which researchers manipulate the data set, reducing and reorganizing data to develop an interpretation. While their discussions are *linear*, they argue for an emergent non-programmed but disciplined approach to analytic activities and iterative movement through the data and across data collection, analysis, and interpretation.

Spiggle identified seven basic analytic operations used to manipulate data for building interpretations.

- *Categorization* (coding) involves classifying a unit of data as representing a phenomenon of interest.
- *Abstraction* groups identified categories into higher order conceptual classes – constructs.
- *Comparison* explores similarities and differences across empirical instances,

161

Table 6.1 Two opposing principles for creating connections

	Paradigmatic	Syntagmatic
Basis for connections	Similarity in: function structure sensory impression properties	Contiguity by: culture causality spatiality temporality structure
Principle for creating	Selection and substitution	Combination and deletion
Garment example	Tee-shirt, blouse, shirt	Tee-shirt, jeans, sandals
Speech disorder	Similarity disorder: inappropriate substitution based on contiguities – "fork" for "plate"	Contiguity disorder: inability to form coherent sentences, inappropriate substitutions based on similarity – "spyglass" for "microscope"
Figurative trope	Metaphor Connections across domains	Metonymy Connections within domains
Figurative example	Product life cycle	Wall Street
Connection of sign to signified	Iconic	Indexical

categories, and constructs, enhancing the identification of patterns and co-occurring phenomena.

- *Dimensionalization* identifies and explores variations in the properties of emerging concepts.
- *Integration* builds explicit connections and relationships between concepts.
- *Iteration* involves a back-and-forth movement through data, between data collection and inferences, and between analysis and interpretation, that permit the exploration of emergent categories, constructs, conceptual linkages, and ideas.
- *Refutation* subjects emerging inferences to empirical scrutiny.

Categorization, abstraction, comparison, and dimensionalization exhibit parallels with the two opposing principles for making connections. Categorization is essentially a classification operation. Researchers may code or categorize in one of two ways. They may group units of data (discrete instances of a phenomenon) into a single class based on a perceived *similarity* between them. As empirical referents for the category, each data unit may *substitute* for one another. Categorizing by similarity facilitates the location of patterns in the data.

Alternatively, researchers might categorize a passage of data with a label that links the passage to another based upon *contiguity*. Here the presumed connection between passages categorized with the same label springs from *shared membership in some larger domain or empirical co-occurence.* For example, in organizing the data the researcher may wish to code all passages that represent events, activities, or processes that take place during holidays versus other times. The relationship between the passages categorized with such codes exhibits contiguous connections – co-occurrences based on cultural, structural, temporal, or other intra-domain connections. The researcher is likely to use categorization by contiguity to facilitate retrieval of passages of data rather than to search for common patterns. Abstraction is a specialized higher-order classification operation. In abstraction the researcher collapses categories into higher-order constructs based on similarity, or opposition.

The principle of similarity underlies comparison. When researchers explore commonalities and oppositions *across* theoretically significant units such as informants, actors, situations, processes, activities, or contexts, and particularly across categories and constructs, they use the similarity principle. Comparison enables the researcher to find or confirm patterns and co-occurring phenomena. In contrast, dimensionalization examines the properties – attributes, characteristics, or elements – within categories and constructs, permitting one to explore their empirical variations. Dimensionalization investigates relations *within* empirical domains, categories, and constructs, representing the contiguity principle.

In contrast to Spiggle's general analytic operations, Arnould and Wallendorf (1994) describe specific procedures for building interpretation from ethnographic data. Their analytic strategy begins with identifying *disjunctures* – for example, glosses, overgeneralizations, and claims of idiosyncracies – from ethnographic interviews. These categories represent informant assertions (emic perspectives) that the investigator (etic perspective) views as culturally sanctioned *distortions* of reality. The significance of disjunctures in building interpretation lies in their recurrent nature. The researcher defines the frequently reported overgeneralizations, glosses, and idiosyncratic claims as indicative of shared meanings.

Interpretation

For Arnould and Wallendorf (1994) and Spiggle (1994), interpretation involves *accounting for the patterns* identified through the analysis of data. For research using either qualitative or quantitative analysis, they view interpretation as an iterative process in two senses.

1   The researcher moves back and forth *between data and emerging insights, perspectives, visions, and ideas* that make sense of and account for the patterns uncovered through analysis. These ideas do not automatically unfold from the data as the researcher follows a particular analytic procedure. Rather, interpretive insights spring from the researcher who tests them against data previously or subsequently collected.

2   As such, the researcher cycles back and forth *between analytic and interpretive phases.* Building interpretation involves an alternating immersion in and

distancing from data (Levy 1981; Thompson and Hirschman 1995; Thompson 1996; Wallendorf and Brucks 1993). In the immersion phase the researcher pores over the data, using analysis to locate patterns. In the distancing phase researchers engage their imaginations, the source from which creative ideas spring. These ideas suggest constructs and provide the foundation for developing an inferential structure around which the researcher can organize the patterns in the data and the disparate loosely connected constructs.

Arnould and Wallendorf's ethnographic interpretive strategy (1994; also Wallendorf and Arnould 1991) proceeds as the researcher derives interpretive constructs from the passages categorized as disjunctures. For example, they use the construct *decommodification* to describe informant assertions of Thanksgiving fare as "homemade". Field observations indicated that this label was a gloss. Informants actually transformed pre-processed commodities in ritualized ways. They did not prepare these dishes "from scratch" as they claimed. Arnould and Wallendorf impute significance to this recurrent gloss and the decommodification construct by noting its frequency and locating its co-occurrence with other constructs (cf. Strauss's (1987) description of axial coding).

Arnould and Wallendorf use systematic search for and location of covariation among constructs for building ethnographic interpretation. These covariations provide the keys to uncovering culturally significant themes that indicate underlying cultural values that function to uphold social order. The researcher uncovers them by making systematic comparisons across behaviors, data sets, and informants in search of patterns of meanings.

The researcher develops an etic perspective by defining "behavioral constellations" – co-occurring meaning structures recognized by the researcher but not the informants. The researcher builds an etic perspective by identifying co-occurrences in emic redundancies – informants' shared definitions, meanings, and perspectives. The researcher sees symbolic linkages that are not consciously accessible to informants.

Arnould and Wallendorf suggest literary tropes as tools for identifying the *symbolic linkages* that point to culturally significant themes. They present "troping" as identifying similarities across behaviors through figurative relations. (Compare their tripartite scheme to the metaphoric/metonymic poles.) As such, tropes aid in the abstraction process by suggesting the shared meanings of the behavioral constellations which, in turn, are integrated under broader cultural themes – for example, Thanksgiving as a celebration of simple abundance and domestic stability.

In summary, Arnould and Wallendorf's strategy for building multilayered interpretation includes the following steps: identify disjunctures and other indicators of culturally shared meaning; locate co-occurrences among them to define configurations; use tropes to generate higher level constructs and find linkages between them; and integrate these linked constructs under broader cultural themes. Each of these phases of interpretation building rests on systematic analytic operations.

Paralleling Arnould and Wallendorf, Spiggle (1994) also proposes the use of literary tropes for enhancing the interpretive process (cf. Zaltman and Higie 1993). She suggests that literary tropes, conceptualized as lenses, can provide insights for decoding meaning – grasping the experiences of others, seeing patterns in interpretive data, and unmasking cultural codes. Spiggle argues that understanding the experience of others (emic perspective) and recognizing patterns in their experience (identifying emic redundancies (Arnould and Wallendorf 1994, Wallendorf and Brucks 1993), or creating higher level emic abstractions) involve a translation process. Researchers translate between their own experience (a familiar and experientially based domain) and that of informants (a distant and mediated domain).

Metaphors perform in the same way: they involve viewing one domain in terms of another – seeing or defining one aspect of the world as if it were another, or viewing similarities in the dissimilar. This logic holds as we ask how we can translate the experiences described by informants into our own in order to grasp the "other." Further, seeing the parallels across informants' diverse experiences, which function as separate domains, permits researchers to discover patterns (abstractions of similarities) in diversity. Both of these activities – grasping meaning and pattern recognition – reflect metaphoric logic in forming conceptual bridges *across domains*.

Spiggle argues that in deciphering cultural codes, researchers employ: metaphors (such as viewing a market as if it were a festival (Sherry 1990); metonyms (enlarging understanding by viewing one element as representing another when both elements fall *within a domain*), and irony (seeing commonalities across opposing domains, or opposing dimensions within a domain, such as the religious within the commercial (Belk *et al.* 1989) or the commercial within the religious (O'Guinn and Belk 1989).

Although their descriptions differ, parallels exist between Arnould and Wallendorf's and Spiggle's discussions of the way literary tropes inform interpretation. They both employ the logic of literary tropes to see beyond the ordinary, literal, taken-for-granted view. Further, they view literary tropes as lenses that aid in discovering meaning. Interpretation using literary tropes depends on the creative application of the researcher's unique store of knowledge across domains, and imaginative insights about the way phenomena represent other things.

Assessing analytic strategies

Arnould and Wallendorf

Arnould and Wallendorf present specific procedures for developing ethnographic interpretations of consumption patterns. To the extent that a researcher's purpose is to decode specific culturally defined consumption patterns, Arnould and Wallendorf's work may provide a useful analytic and interpretive strategy.

However, their work rests on several assumptions underlying the disjuncture concept that limit its applicability and generalizability. Their method presumes that informants embrace culturally sanctioned distortions of "reality" – disjunctures – in contrast to the "undistorted" perspective accessible to researchers. This view represents a particular epistemological position – an independent reality that exists apart from the agency of human construction can be known. Ethnographers and other researchers occupy a privileged position in comprehending this "reality". In contrast, Hirschman and Holbrook (1992) and Hudson and Ozanne (1988) contest this assumption of a single, "knowable" reality. These perspectives challenge the assumption that some knowers are in a better position than others to distinguish between that which is real and that which is illusion.

The researcher's ability to infer layers of meaning and see connections not made by informants does not require assuming that informants mistake illusion for reality. The previously discussed recurrent theme of preparing Thanksgiving food "from scratch" may represent informants' correct perception that they undertake extraordinary preparation efforts for special meals relative to ordinary ones, rather than engage in self-delusion.

The key to Arnould and Wallendorf's method rests on identifying disjunctures and their associated meanings and behaviors. Because disjunctures represent inaccurate informant inferences, the centrality of this construct overweights informant inconsistencies and illusions. If researchers focus on disjunctures, they ignore culturally sanctioned but accurate informant perceptions, outlooks, and inferences. We can avoid this problem and still make use of Arnould and Wallendorf's general analytic strategy by identifying repetitive themes, assertions, and understandings across informants, no matter whether the representations are accurate or inaccurate. Then following Arnould and Wallendorf, we can search for meanings and behaviors that frequently co-occur with them to build interpretation and unlock the cultural meaning of consumption patterns.

Spiggle

Spiggle describes analytic operations applicable to a variety of data sources and theoretical perspectives. She defines these as a generic vocabulary for describing different analytical operations in manipulating data for interpretation. She neither defines a specific set of procedures nor limits their application to specific types of categories as do Arnould and Wallendorf.

Spiggle enjoins researchers to go beyond identifying recurring themes in the data and build integrated conceptual frameworks around identified constructs. Her discussion, however, underplays the use of prior theory and research in creating these frameworks, focusing narrowly upon literary tropes as aids to interpretation. Even where interpretive researchers begin with no a priori theories, constructs, or conceptual predispositions, they build on prior theoretical foundations and research findings. A subsequent section on thinking theoretically addresses this issue.

The frame

Whether researchers describe, explain, or interpret data, or assume a univocal or multivocal approach to reality, they must select and represent data in some coherent way. Inferential structures that frame the data provide varying degrees of structure, organization, and integration. Lofland (1974) argues that reviewers of qualitative sociology preferred research framed by a conceptual scheme that exhibits *generic abstraction, novelty, elaboration, interpenetration,* and *eventfulness.* The *frame* incorporates several conceptual elements and connects the conceptual and the empirical levels in a unique way. *Generic* frames exhibit a level of abstraction sufficient to encompass a much wider set of phenomena than the specific individuals, locales, and events studied. Their value lies in their ability to help us understand other domains, phenomena, activities, processes, and actions.

A *novel* frame provides a new conceptual perspective – one not reworked, rehashed, borrowed, or evident to common sense. Lofland notes that reviewers found the use of existing frames novel if researchers refined and extended them by defining variations in, subtypes of, or dimensions of the concepts that form the frame. They did not find novelty in the mechanical application of existing frames to new domains, phenomena, or circumstances, however exotic. An *elaborated* frame exhibits conceptual density. It supersedes the abstraction of redundant themes found in the data, incorporating several major conceptual elements, each with subelements that specify the properties, dimensions, and categories of the major elements. In Wolcott's (1994) terms, it is more cooked. An *eventful* frame incorporates descriptions of *specific* actors, events, activities, and settings that provide concrete empirical referents for grounding the abstract. The interweaving of quotes, fieldnotes, and descriptive passages with interpretive ones produces an *interpenetrated* frame. Eventfulness and interpenetration represent attributes of the narrative exclusively, whereas the conceptual frame is characterized by novelty, generic abstraction, and elaboration.

The frame arises from inferential efforts as the researcher moves back and forth between analyzing data and constructing interpretation. The researcher's analytical procedures – how and what the researcher categorizes, abstracts, compares, dimensionalizes, and integrates – and the conceptual predispositions that the researcher brings to and/or derives from the analysis, shape the frame. The following illustrates variations in the way that different interpretive researchers use frames to organize and present their analysis. Included are Wallendorf and Arnould's (1991) and Stern's (1995) research on Thanksgiving, which highlight the role of different frames in transforming the same data set.

Illustrative variations in frames and analysis

Below I describe seven frames and analytical strategies chosen for their novelty, generic abstraction, and elaboration. They exhibit different numbers of layers of interpretation and use various mechanisms for integrating and connecting layers of meaning. They also use the similarity and contiguity principles differently. Following a description of each illustrative frame, I present a generic analytic procedure derived from it to suggest its potential applicability across a range of purposes, domains, and research questions. The linear presentation of generic analytic strategies understates their actual iterative and hermeneutic reality.

The building blocks of frames and texts are *elements* such as structures, objects, individuals, processes and their relationships. Interpretive researchers define these elements from *a priori* notions or generate them from the analysis or both. I designate the elements of frames by letters (such as X, Y, Z) to indicate abstract representations. I place their more concrete referents next to them to ground the discussion.

Food symbolism

Levy (1981) created a multidimensional frame for integrating his analysis of the symbolic distinctions of food and food practices in the U.S. His method is metaphoric: he compares the "little tales or bits of family lore" that people tell to cultural myths, drawing parallels in their structure and function. Following Levi-Strauss's interpretation of myths, he interprets consumers' stories about food through a structural analysis of binary oppositions.

Levy illustrates the resulting integrative frame "to resemble a three-dimensional urban scene" – an explicit metaphor. The basic *elements* include objects – food (X), people (Y) and settings (Z) where people (Y) act on (consume) food (X). He represents these elements as *building* blocks, stacked in three layers. Blocks in the top layer represent *types* of people (Y) – e.g. infant/teen, lower/upper class, boy/girl and *types* of settings for eating (Z) – e.g. in home dining/executive lunch. Those in the middle layer represent *qualities* or *attributes* of people (Y) – e.g. helpless/mature and *attributes* of settings (Z) – e.g. primitive/ sophisticated. The bottom-layer blocks represent *types* of objects – food (X) e.g. burgers/carrot and *attributes* of objects – food (X) e.g. sweet/bitter.

Levy indicates connections between X, Y, and Z through spatial arrangements. Spatial proximity of elements *within* layers reflects relations of opposition and *similarity* within categories of objects (X), people (Y), and settings (Z). Within each layer the blocks symbolizing elements share membership in a class of objects that can substitute for one another.

Vertical alignment *between* layers reflects cultural *contiguities* – for example, alcohol is associated with sophisticated people eating an executive lunch, whereas warm milk evokes different associations. Thus, the relations between the blocks and the layers represent the connections between people and food, visually reinforcing the larger point: food symbolizes or represents types of people along major binary distinctions and, therefore, carries meaning through connotations.

In sum, Levy began with the structural analysis of binary oppositions as the basis for building interpretations, and he used induction to arrive at specific meanings of food objects and practices. He created a multiconstruct, multidimensional frame illustrated by an architectural form. He proposed explicit linkages between its components with implicit connections based on similarity or contiguity.

Levy's analytic strategy follows: *categorize* basic elements – X,Y,Z – by type (binary oppositions); identify *dimensions* (or binary attributes) of the elements – X,Y,Z; using *comparison* define connections between the dimensions and attributes of elements – X,Y,Z; *integrate* the emerging constructs by linking dimensions of each element with those of the other two elements.

Advertising experiences

Mick and Buhl (1992) defined their meaning-based model of advertising experiences prior to data collection. The model incorporates several conceptual elements, explicitly linked in a circular diagram representing it. It proposes *life themes* (Y) and *life projects* (Z) as key shapers of consumers' *interpretations* (X) of ads – particularly of the higher order, or connotative, meanings.

The label, life *themes* – recurring existential concerns – connects it to artistic, literary, and musical domains in which one can identify a dominant, repetitive pattern among elements. Mick and Buhl cite the melody metaphor to concretize the concept. Grounding their discussion of life themes in literary interpretation, they note that life themes exhibit a dialectical tension between polar anchors such as being free versus not being free.

Mick and Buhl emphasize that the construct life *project* – meanings associated with actions, relationships, and statuses significant to personal identity (national, community/occupational, familial, private) – highlights a voluntaristic assumption. While we use the term project in many domains, it is an implied metaphor that connotes an active constructive pursuit of a set of activities directed at some goal.

Their empirical inquiry utilizing the life histories and interpretations of ads by three brothers corroborated the meaning-based model. Using life-story phenomenological interviews, Mick and Buhl identified the brothers' life themes (one unique primary theme for each and one shared secondary theme for all, constructed as binary oppositions). Connections through *similarity* informed the identification of themes: Mick and Buhl located common issues, concerns and meaning patterns across different domains, situations, spheres, and time frames for each brother singly and all collectively.

Mick and Buhl demonstrate that the life projects (Z) of each brother conjoined with each one's life themes (Y) shape the meanings (X) that are actualized when they viewed ads. Descriptions of the brothers' interpretations of ads indicate that they make frequent *contiguous* associations between the product, brand, or executional elements with images they retrieve from memory. These images are generally charged with meanings and evaluations based on associations, especially cultural *contiguities*. For one brother a Lezard suit represents a business career and *undesirable* behaviors; for another it symbolizes an international, jet-set, high-class and *desirable* image; for the third, the mannequinesque model in the ad, unnaturally photographed in the desert, evokes insincerity and its *inappropriateness* for him as a school teacher. Different life themes shape the brothers' contrasting responses to the triggered images.

In sum, Mick and Buhl define a meaning-based model that specifies connections between the major elements. Their interpretation of the brothers' advertising experiences rests on the researchers' identification of parallels in patterns of meaning across domains (connections based on similarity), and their insight into *contiguous* connections between the associated images (in turn retrieved from *contiguous* associations) and the identified life themes.

Mick and Buhl's interpretation includes an additional layer of meaning beyond that of the informants and, thus, that of Levy. Levy points out the symbolic connections understood by ordinary people living in the culture, but does not construct higher order experience-distant constructs. In contrast, Mick and Buhl add a layer of meaning in their abstract concepts, life project and life themes.

Their analytical strategy is as follows: define model and abstract constructs X, Y, and Z; through *categorization* and *abstraction*, identify Z and *dimensions* of Y for each informant; compare X for each informant, linking it for each to Y and Z; *integrate* X, Y, Z through model.

Lived meaning

In their study of the experience of married women, Thompson *et al.* (1990) used phenomenological interview data to create a conceptual frame that exhibits some parallels with that of Mick and Buhl (1992). Thompson *et al.*'s purposes, however, were quite different: they designed their study to illuminate the "life-world" of non-working married women as shoppers, decision makers, and family purchasing agents. Thus, they began with no *a priori* conceptualizations or frame. Similar to Mick and Buhl, they derived themes by seeing commonalities within and across informants' diverse situations – connections of *similarity*.

They illustrate their derived conceptual frame iconically as a circumscribed, trisected triangle, or a circle inscribed by a trisected triangle. The circumference – the life world of contemporary married women – circumscribes their informants' experience. The trisections represent three polar themes of lived experience: being in or out of control, being captivated or deliberate, and being restricted or free from restrictions. Thompson *et al.* demonstrate that these themes exhibit dialectical relations in which the gestalt and complexly experienced meaning of *free choice* (A) accounts for coherence and consistency in the face of seeming contradictions. They employ a figure/ground metaphor to describe the interrelations of the three themes: against the ground of one theme, issues of the other themes appear most figural. The themes exhibit contiguous association connected through the experiential domain of freedom and choice.

Three elements – existential themes X, Y, and Z – comprise the core of Thompson *et al.*'s frame. They derive them as follows: identify the idiographic themes of informants by *comparing* situations and experiences to generate *categories*; abstract these into nomothetic themes – X, Y, Z; *integrate* the X, Y, Z elements under the more *abstract* theme (A) by comparing the interplay of X, Y, and Z across situations and across informants.

High risk leisure consumption

Celsi *et al.* (1993) describe sky diving metaphorically as an example of high-risk leisure consumption by means of a dramatic frame. They impose the frame on their ethnographic data, using the stages of Greek drama (*agon, denouement,* and *catharsis*) to model the sky-diving career and experience. They further use the theatrical elements of set, audience, props, players, roles, performance, stage, and choreography to organize their ethnographic description.

They present their interpretation as an integrated model of high-risk leisure consumption. This is diagrammed as two-way interactions between a dramatic world view (U) identified as a unique Western culture perspective, macroenvironmental factors (Y), three types of motives – (Z) hedonic (Z1), self-efficacy (Z2), normative (Z3) – and high-risk consumption (X). Their general model assumes the form of a recursive, causal system; *contiguous* connections, thus, compose it.

Employing a career metaphor, they further propose a model of the way that motives for engaging in high-risk consumption evolve. They specify a motive trajectory defined by a two-dimensional space – experience (E) and risk acculturation (R) – each from low to high. As experience and risk acculturation increase, the high-risk leisure consumer follows a positively sloping trajectory: the three stages share structural *similarity* to one another. Each stage exhibits a triadic parallel with the other stages; in each stage the *types* of motives across informants (Z1, Z2, Z3) form patterns, that take on different values. The stages are also linked by *contiguous* connections imposed by motive evolution.

Celsi *et al.*'s analytic strategy includes the following: *compare* elements of Western world view (U) to those of Greek drama; compare elements of sky diving to those of the theatre; *categorize* motives by Z1, Z2, Z3 using *abstraction*; *compare* Z1, Z2, Z3 across informants for different levels of E and R; define stages based on patterns; *integrate* these elements through evolutionary model.

Organizational buying

Using semi-structured interviews, Drumwright (1994) generated a grounded theory in her study of socially responsible organizational buying. The resulting conceptual frame includes an identification of two types of key organizational player, a typology of organizational contexts, and a set of emergent propositions linking these.

Drumwright defines the key organizational change agents as *policy* entrepreneurs (P), an obvious metaphor. Her description compares the policy entrepreneur to business entrepreneurs and to zealots. *Converts* (C) are organizational members who initially felt no affinity for socially responsible buying, but whose beliefs, attitudes and behavior underwent conversion. Some of the converts even came to exhibit *evangelical fervor*. Zealous policy entrepreneurs and converts stand in a *contiguous* relation to one another: zealotry and converts occupy the same socio-cultural domain.

Drumwright classified the organizations studied on the basis of the differing types of contexts (Y) in which socially responsible buying arose, primarily that of a deliberate corporate strategy versus motivated by individual commitment. She identified two sub-types within each of these contexts. The resulting typology includes four *types* (Y1, Y2, Y3, Y4) that stand in relations of *similarity* to one another. One can select any one of the four to represent an organizational context for they stand as functional substitutes for one another.

Drumwright further identified themes (propositions) from her data that indicate how organizational context (Y), *attributes* and *strategies* of policy entrepreneurs (P) and converts (C), and other organizational members (O) shape the dynamics (D) and the success (X) of the socially responsible buying process. Her analytic strategy includes the following: *compare* entrepreneurs and zealots to organizational actors (P), and converts to organizational actors (C); *categorize* (and *abstract*) Y by *type*; *compare* D and X across Y; *compare attributes, dimensions* and *strategies* of P, C, O across D and Y; *integrate* elements Y, P, C, O, D, X into implicit model formed by propositions (themes).

Thanksgiving as celebration of simple abundance and domestic stability

Wallendorf and Arnould (1991) "read" Thanksgiving consumption rituals through analytic and interpretive strategies previously described (Arnould and Wallendorf 1994). They develop a multilayered frame in which their etic interpretations spring from comparing participants, participants' perspectives, activities, objects (such as food and clothing), interactions, and social arrangements across Thanksgiving settings. These comparisons employ the *similarity* principle. The frame consists of an implicit proposition. Consumer participants (Y) enact and negotiate broader cultural messages and meanings (X). In the case of Thanksgiving, these messages and meanings are abundance (X1) and social solidarity (X2). These meanings stand in *contiguous association*: they co-occur. Wallendorf and Arnould (1991) organize the frame across five conceptual themes:

1   expressions of abundance (X1); including how Thanksgiving production and consumption activities differ from ordinary and other holiday ones; consequences of X1; type of X1; and epigenetic definition of X1;

2   activities expressing and participants enacting social solidarity (X2);
3   universalistic versus particularistic practices and segregating versus integrat-
     ing activities;
4   expression of values;
5   participants' definitions of, and activities around, consumption objects.

Thanksgiving stories as myths

Using a different frame, Stern (1995) analyzes the same data set, demonstrating that the stories informants tell about Thanksgiving reflect plot structures univer-sally found in Western cultural texts. Stern's reading of Thanksgiving focuses on the form of informant texts, permitting her to grasp these cultural universals. In contrast, Wallendorf and Arnould focus on the content of their texts, permitting them to identify the unique cultural meanings expressed in Thanksgiving celebra-tions relative to other holiday celebrations.

Stern (1995) analyzes the Thanksgiving stories as myths, echoing Levy's (1981) work. In contrast to Levy, Stern imposes a frame derived from Frye's ([1957] 1973) taxonomy of mythic structure to demonstrate the way that informant stories reflect one of four archetypal plot types. The identification of these four plot types rests on the principles of *similarity* and *contiguity*. Plot elements – *characters, struggle/conflict, resolution/outcome*, and *values* achieved, thwarted, or strived for, organized through a *temporal progression* – are common to all myths and Western literary productions. Their universality is recognized in the *similarity* principle. Frye alludes to this principle in noting the parallels between the expression of plot elements in each myth type, such as the four life cycle stages and the four seasons. Within each myth type, the characters, plot, and values exhibit a predictably *contiguous* associa-tion (with potential predictable variations representing subtypes).

Stern employs this frame in her analysis and interpretation of informant "myths." She quotes all of the passages of informant texts used by Wallendorf and Arnould (1991) and one from their unpublished data. She follows with a "reading" that links specific elements of the informant text to the archetypal elements of one of the four plot types (*similarity* principle), focusing particularly on the values revealed. She illustrates how advertisements also reflect each type of plot structure, promising the realization of some values rather than others and implying a particular resolution/outcome, or ending.

In sum, Stern *compares* elements of mythic plot structures to elements of Thanksgiving stories; *categorizes* the stories into one of four plot types (P1, P2, P3, P4) using *abstraction* and *integrates* the elements around the temporal progres-sion and consequent outcomes. She *compares* projected outcomes and values represented by advertisements to those of the four plot types (P1, P2, P3, P4). Stern's alternative reading of Wallendorf and Arnould's text (1991) demonstrates the importance of the frame in the transformation process.

Summary

These studies provide only a glimpse of possible ways researchers locate and account for patterns in data and use a frame to organize them. Through these alternative analytic strategies and frames, researchers create and represent their interpretations of data. The interpretation and the frame are necessarily inter-twined: the frame functions as a vehicle for representing and communicating one's interpretation. Two suggestions that flow from the *similarity* principle for generating or selecting frames and constructing interpretive insights follow.

THINK METAPHORICALLY

Many frames employ an overarching metaphor, using the principle of similarity and the analytic process of *comparison*. The metaphor provides the foundation for integrating the conceptual components, and guidance for understanding data. Becker (1986) argues against the use of tired, trite, scattered metaphors, such as "cutting edge" or "conceptual straitjacket" in social science writing. But he encourages the use of fresh, organizing metaphors, such as Erving Goffman's (1952) use of the con game. Goffman analyzes a variety of concrete and familiar social situations in which an individual "cools out" a victim of social disgrace. Here Goffman employs a framing metaphor and explores its ramifications.

Belk *et al.*'s (1989) use of religion to understand collections, and Celsi *et al.*'s (1993) use of drama and theatre to describe and analyze high-risk leisure consumption, represent overarching metaphors. Hill and Stamey's (1990) description of the homeless as a nomadic society represents a less encompassing but still powerful metaphor to interpret their ethnographic data. Thompson *et al.* (1994) identify organizing metaphors to exemplify individual, but culturally shaped, self-interpretations of three consumers. They point out that by characterizing each informant's interpretations via a dominant metaphor, they were able to capture important distinctions across them. At the same time the metaphor provided a frame that enhanced their ability to see intra-individual similarities in informants' descriptions of specific "concrete events and objects."

THINK THEORETICALLY

Interpreting data through existing constructs and theories parallels metaphoric thinking in which one sees and organizes the elements and interconnections in data through the lens of experience-near, concrete domains. In thinking theoretically, experience-distant abstract constructs form the lens. Both metaphoric and theoretical thinking share the logic of the *similarity* principle through comparison. As illustration, several researchers have formed their interpretations of diverse types of consumption – addiction, plastic surgery, and self-gifts – around theories and constructs of self-identity construction, maintenance, and reconstruction.

Hirschman (1992) interprets addictive consumption as the reaction of an individual with impaired self-identity – an unstable, fragmented, disconnected, and chaotic sense of self – to cope with role and other socially generated stresses. Dysfunctional, addiction and other forms of compulsive consumption represent attempts to gain control and construct authentic and plausible self-identities. Using van Gennep's (1960) model of the process by which *cultural* rites of passage demarcate and reintegrate individuals undergoing role transitions, Schouten (1991) interprets elective plastic surgery as a *personal* rite of passage. Elective plastic surgery represents a symbolic act performed by an individual with a marginal self-identity in an attempt to regain control and restore stability to the self. Describing less troubled selves, Mick and DeMoss (1990) interpret self-gifts through constructs of interpersonal gift giving. Individuals embrace a multiplicity of selves: just as interpersonal gift giving exhibits communication, exchange, and specialness between individuals, self-gifts exhibit the same processes between multiple selves.

Each of these researchers recognizes that episodes in their data represented examples of more abstract structures and processes. All focus on the manner in which identity is maintained, restored, or reconstructed through consumption under conditions that tend to undermine identity. Thus, they link their interpretations to broader analytical issues and conceptual frames. Wolcott (1994) notes that the value of theory rests more on its linking power than on its explanatory power.

Metaphoric and theoretical thinking increase the likelihood that analysis and interpretation relative to description will dominate the data transformation and the consequent textual account. Both involve connecting one's data to other realms, domains, and contexts *during* analysis and interpretation and thus enhance the applicability, or transferability, of the frame. Combined with analytical creativity, metaphoric and theoretical thinking contribute to three of Lofland's (1974) five desirable properties of frames – generic abstraction, novelty, and elaboration. The pursuit of connections and relationships suggested by theories and metaphors particularly enhances elaboration. Loflands' two other desirable properties – eventfulness and interpenetration – result from choices made during the creating of the text to communicate one's research.

Writing: creating the narrative

If analysis *transforms* data and interpretation *transcends* them (Wolcott 1994), creating the narrative *transfers* the data and the frame from the researcher to an audience. Two sociologists, Becker (1986) and Lofland (1971), explicitly distinguish between inference and writing. Becker notes that writing *is* thinking, not merely the reporting of thought. Lofland points out that writing is not a mechanical process of rendering one's analysis and interpretation into written words. Rather, he argues that writing permits one to get new ideas, see new connections, as well as realize the flaws or inconsistencies in thoughts and modify one's perspective. As one "externalizes" one's arguments and insights, they become visible as textual objects, "'things' 'out there' available for scrutiny" (1971:

127). Similarly, Wolcott (1990) points out that writer's block springs from "thinker's block."

Writing further transforms and refines the analysis and interpretation for it is an active process in which the researcher creates a product available to others. Whereas Becker (1986) and Wolcott (1990) focus on the *process* of writing for qualitative researchers, the following emphasizes the *product*.

In interpretative research, the diversity in styles of reporting research noted by Lofland (1974) permits flexibility but provides no template to guide the written product. The researcher may have no clear view of the structure for the final product, which is similar to an architect guiding the construction of a building without a blueprint. In contrast, researchers using the format of physical and experimental sciences work from a template. It generally consists of a linear description of background literature, hypotheses, research design and data collection, results, and discussion of results. Interpretive research does not readily lend itself to this model.

In Van Maanen's (1988: 73) words, writing "is a complex matter, dependent on an uncountable number of strategic choices and active constructions (e.g., what details to include or omit; how to summarize and present data; what voice to select; what quotations to use).' Further, the classic ethnographies in sociology and anthropology are book-length manuscripts. Consumer researchers generally produce article-length manuscripts for journals or consulting reports. Interpretive researchers face particular challenges in article-length manuscripts in presenting data collection, analytic and interpretive procedures, the conceptual frame, interpretations of the data, and vignettes of field observations or quotes from informants as evidence for the interpretation.

The narrative

Anthropologists have recently produced a reflective literature defining ethnography as a narrative or text and addressing the way that ethnographers produce texts (Atkinson 1990; Clifford and Marcus 1986; Geertz 1988; Van Maanen 1988; Wolcott 1990). Joy (1991), also an anthropologist, has employed a textual analysis of ethnographic inquiry in consumer research. These anthropologists variously consider authorial voice (vocality), the organization, unity, and coherence of the manuscript, the use of exemplars (representations of social categories versus individuals), the way that researchers incorporate informant quotes and passages from fieldnotes into the text, and the use of rhetorical devices.

The following discussion addresses two of Van Maanen's "uncountable number of strategic choices" (1988) in constructing a text that describes and interprets qualitative data: (1) the organization of the text and the linking of its elements and (2) the incorporation of data in the text. Atkinson (1992) notes that we can develop models for our work by studying the form and style of others' texts. Examples of different strategies in consumer research for addressing these two issues follow. Here I restrict my discussion to narrative forms in the genre of social science discourse that exhibit author-imposition on text organization. A subsequent section suggests possibilities from other literary genres and from hypertextual organization.

Organizing the narrative

In writing the text, the researcher must decide how to move across informants, sites, and elements of these units (e.g., events, processes, experiences) and how to move back and forth between the interpretation and evidence. The fieldnotes, transcripts of interviews, documents, and other texts that comprise qualitative data are arranged in a *linear sequence* frequently defined by the flow of time or the confluence of space. The researcher breaks up this sequence both in defining topics and placing them in the text and in sorting the data and selecting some, but not all, passages to include in the text.

As Jakobson pointed out (1956), the topics composing a discourse may lead to one another through similarity or contiguity. When one has multiple episodes, informants, or fieldsites, one can develop the descriptions and interpretations in one of two ways. One can proceed by describing themes, issues, or constructs for each informant (or site, or other unit from which data were collected, such as a department within a firm). This organization reflects the contiguity principle for it rests on a naturally occurring arrangement. In contrast, one can describe informants (or sites and units) for each theme, issue, and construct. This organization reflects the similarity principle for it rests on the researcher's definition of commonality.

Mick and Buhl (1992) organize the discussion of themes and constructs by informant. They discuss life themes and life projects individually and sequentially for each of three Danish brothers. The linkage between the parallel discussions of each brother operates via similarity, and each brother can substitute for the other as an illustration of the conceptual discussion.

Hirschman (1992) and Thompson *et al.* (1990) use a different version of this strategy in their texts. In the beginning of their article, Thompson *et al.* rely upon a detailed description of Samantha, one of twelve informants, to demonstrate how they moved from topic to topic in their interviews and began to understand her experiential themes. Just as readers grasp the essence of Carl, Bjorn, or Anders, in reading Mick and Buhl's description of each brother, so too they gain an overall sense of Samantha's life-world as consumer, shopper, and family purchasing agent.

Thompson *et al.* do not provide parallel descriptions of the eleven other informants paralleling that of Samantha. Thus, Samantha's description functions metonymically, representing the analysis and idiographic interpretation of all twelve informants. In the description of Samantha, the flow of topics is guided in some places by contiguous connections (e.g., temporal sequence) and in others by similarity ones (e.g., another situation with parallel issues and dimensions). Following Samantha's description, Thompson *et al.* switch to a different textual organization. They describe three themes and their interrelationships induced from the twelve informants. This discussion proceeds along the similarity princi-ple. The discussion of one theme is linked to the next by their similar conceptual structure (bipolar dimensions) and function (nomothetic abstractions summarizing informant experience).

Hirschman (1992) uses a similar organization in providing "partial case his-tories" of three of thirty-five addict informants. She organizes these histories primarily through contiguity as a temporal sequence. Following the histories, she then moves to a discussion organized around the similarity principle on *a priori* and emergent themes. For purposes of comparing self-labeled addicts with drug users who do not define themselves as addicts, she presents case histories of two of five non-addict, drug-using informants. Paralleling her organization of the text on addicts, she then moves to a discussion of themes, organized on the similarity principle. As does Mick and Buhl's discussion of the three brothers, these case histories function as substitutes for one another with parallel organiza-tion. As with Samantha's description, they also function metonymically as repre-sentations of a larger number of informants.

Drumwright's (1994) discussion of findings provides another variation on tex-tual organization. She begins with a description not of specific individuals but of typifications or exemplars of policy entrepreneurs and converts who represent the primary change agents of socially responsible buying. These constructs stand in contiguous relations, not as substitutes but as complements. In each of these discussions she describes similarities in these exemplars' experiences and tactics. Drumwright then moves to a description of four types of organizational contexts that she differentiates along five conceptual dimensions. Each type is a metonym, an abstraction representing actual organizations, and the types with parallel structure are related through similarity.

Much more typically, authors organize the interpretation around themes or constructs (Celsi *et al.* 1993; Hill 1991; Hill and Stamey 1990; Peñaloza 1994; Schouten 1991). These themes commonly serve as subheadings under *a priori* or emergent "themes" heading. This organization represents the similarity pole comparable to Thompson *et al.*'s (1990) thematic description. The themes gen-erally share a parallel function as a summary abstraction that imposes structure on the data and its interpretation. Within each thematic topic, the discussion may proceed through contiguity or similarity.

Summary

A diversity of textual strategies exists in consumer research. The issue of organiza-tion appears most problematic in the sections communicating the findings and their interpretation. More widely shared conventions dominate the initial sections – defining the research problem, providing background, including an *a priori* model, construct, or themes, and describing methods. Research using this template mirrors the physical and experimental scientific format.

The conceptual frame shapes the textual organization but does not predetermine the way one creates the text. Examination of different textual strategies suggests that no text proceeds entirely by connections of similarity or contiguity. Authors may shift the overall organization (Thompson *et al.* (1990), Hirschman (1992), or employ a consistent overall organization (Mick and Buhl 1992). Within the overall organization, authors shift between the two types of connection. Frequent shifts contribute to conveying the complexity and interwovenness of social and cultural phenomena within the constraints linearity demanded by social science discourse.

Researchers may present abstractions, such as ideal types of informant, sites, processes, or activities (e.g., Drumwright 1994), or very concrete, highly specific descriptions (Mick and Buhl 1992; Thompson *et al.* 1990). The more abstracted the presentation of the data, the more the frame dominates the text, with the researcher's perspective overshadowing that of the informants. Even the more abstracted presentations use quoted or summarized passages from informant interviews to ground the interpretation and provide concrete details. Choices about this issue permit the researcher to interpenetrate the frame with the data (Lofland 1974).

Alternating between the data and the frame

As Lofland noted (1974), reviewers of qualitative sociology valued texts in which the author interweaves the frame and the data. For Lofland this issue included two dimensions: (1) the relative proportion of the text given to data representing concrete events, actors, scenes, and events – versus conceptual discussion and interpretation; and (2) the frequency with which the author moves back and forth from data to frame. Lofland even suggests that reviewers preferred a 60–70 percent to 40–30 percent balance between the concrete and empirical and the abstract and conceptual. He further suggests that frequent alteration between the frame and the data on a micro-level is desirable because either alone is "dull." However, Wolcott (1990) cautions against author intrusiveness in an otherwise interesting passage of data.

Without counting lines, one can note variation in these two dimensions across articles in interpretive consumer research. Within a single manuscript we find considerable difference in Schouten's (1991) interpretation of a priori themes and emergent themes. In the former, the description remains entirely abstract, whereas in the latter considerable and frequent interpenetration of frame and data exists.

On the dimension of high to low penetration, Mick and Buhl (1992) and Thompson *et al.* (1990) exhibit a high percentage of data and frequency of interpenetration. In these texts, the reader can form an image of specific individuals. Bergadaa's (1990) article and Levy's (1981) article exhibit the opposite end of the continuum with a low percentage of data and infrequent interpenetration. Variations on this dimension reflect different research purposes as well as different writing styles.

Summary

Researchers aim to write interesting, coherent, fluid, and informative texts. As they begin to pull their analysis and interpretation together from notebooks, diagrams, outlines, and other fragmented sources, they can profit from considering two decisions of textual organization: (1) how to choose among possible paths that link conceptual and empirical elements together in the necessarily linear structure of social scientific discourse; and (2) how to incorporate data into the presentation of the conceptual frame. As we undertake the task of writing up interpretive research, we can look to Jakobson's (1956) insight that topics can lead to one another through contiguity or similarity as we choose our paths.

Summary

Reviewing the way that other interpretive researchers define elements, employ analysis and interpretation, and organize textual materials expands one's own imaginative possibilities. Interpretive research includes semiotics, ethnography, existential-phenomenology, structuralism, and literary criticism. These diverse perspectives embrace different epistemological and methodological assumptions (Hirschman and Holbrook 1992). However, they share the absence of well-defined procedures and templates for guiding analysis, interpretation, and writing that are available to researchers who follow natural and experimental science models.

I advocate no single procedure or template for all interpretive researchers, as even for any subset. Rather, I advocate the opposite. Researchers can nurture their creativity by identifying others' strategies and using them in novel ways. The generic analytic and interpretive strategies drawn from my review of seven empirical papers provide templates that we could transfer mechanically to other data. However, borrowing would inhibit rather than foster creativity. One can, however, use these strategies and identify others to suggest ways to define elements, compare and contrast them, explore their dimensions, link them to one another, to other domains, and to other constructs, search for patterns, provide an account of the patterns, and *represent* them in a research text.

Alternative textual strategies

Gestalt and nonlinearity problematics and hypertext possibilities

Two issues face interpretive researchers in representing consumers:

1   how to present (or *re-present*) holistic, idiographic portraits of all the units of analysis in formulating the nomothetic, etic interpretation, given space limitations in journal length articles; and

2   how to present (or *re-present*) the complex interwoven non-linear nature of interpretive reality, given the linear constraints of verbal texts.

Holistic idiography

Interpretive research differs from other types of analysis of textual data, such as content analysis, in that it attempts to express holistic systems of related meanings embedded in a context. For example, Thompson *et al.*'s (1990) representation of Samantha (one of twelve informants) and Mick and Buhl's (1992) representations of Anders, Bjorn, and Carl provide the reader with a gestalt sense of these informants in relation to the research goal. The passages in the narratives that present the perspectives of these four informants, and the researchers' consequent interpretations of them, exhibit a high degree of interpenetration and eventfulness (Lofland 1974). With only three informants, Mick and Buhl are able to provide both a textual representation (although not the entire interviews) of the brothers and the researchers' interpretations of their life themes. With twelve informants, Thompson *et al.* present an idiographic interpretation of Samantha alone, leaving a gap in the idiography with the reader responsible for reconstructing the idiographies of the other eleven informants.

When interpretive researchers analyze more than a few informants, episodes, or sites, they face space limitations in representing the gestalt patterns of the individual units that typically provide the basis for a holistic, integrated interpretation. They must *select* illustrative idiographic examples as do Thompson *et al.* (1990). An alternative presentation – a tabular format of summary interpretations for each analytical unit along theoretically relevant dimensions – provides one solution for this problem (Spiggle and File 1997). This solution, however, does not permit interpenetration and eventfulness because there are no passages from the data connected to the interpretations.

Non-linearity

Wallendorf and Arnould (1991: 17) and Mick and Buhl (1992) allude to a second issue complicating the representation of individual informant perspectives and the researcher's interpretations, especially the process by which the researcher arrives at etic insights. The interwoven meaning structures that comprise cultural, psychological, and social systems and the iterative process of interpretation do not lend themselves well to the linear constraints of textual narratives. The reader, of course, may move about a manuscript at will: Mick and Buhl explicitly invite the reader to move to a subsequent part of the article prior to reading a preceding part in order to grasp the way that insights about one part of their data illuminated another part.

Let me suggest hypertext narratives as a medium that frees the narrator and the reader from spatial and linear constraints and that permits reader control over narrative flow (Landow 1992) as well as an interpenetrated and eventful text. In addition, hypertext helps solve a problem of representation in interpretive research – how to summarize data without stripping context and how to link interpretations to the textual passages that illuminate them. Hypertext also allows the reader to assess the extent to which the data ground the interpretation, for the researcher can provide the complete data set and indicate all of the passages that support each interpretive assertion. Readers then may perform the auditing function.

Writing hypertext narratives

We are increasingly familiar with Webpages written in hypertext that invite the viewer to "click" through the document to move other documents and Webpages. The reader may or may not follow the linked paths designated by "hotlink" symbols. Van den Berg and Watt (1991) describe a structured hypertext system that hierarchically organizes material in fields by level of abstraction or difficulty. Each field consists of page-like text exhibiting linear coherence linked to other fields by highlighted words. Readers control the reading sequence by choosing fields indicated by highlighted words:

> The [fields] form a logical tree, with abstract frames near the root and detailed, more concrete, [fields] making up the branches. Conceptually, the explication of any highlighted term consists of all the linked [fields] at a lower level of abstraction and increasingly concrete [fields] can be retrieved by traveling up the branches to the degree of detail needed. A stacking metaphor is used in presenting the [fields], so a user traveling to a less abstract [field] "stacks" it on the current [field]. After reading, the user can choose to "unstack" it and return to the previous, more abstract [field].
>
> (Van den Berg and Watt 1991: 119)

Educators have used such documents as learning aids to deliver material that functions as an alternative or supplement to traditional texts and lectures (ibid.: 1991).

The construction of hypertext documents was quite laborious until recently, for one had to write in HTML code. Claris Homepage™ and Office 97™ both offer much friendlier software versions that make the process of creating hypertext relatively easy. However, the researcher must make many decisions about what constitutes a field and which fields will be linked through which passages.

Text and hypertext narratives

While we can imagine many possibilities for content and structure of hypertext, one plausible format follows the hierarchical structure similar to the one suggested by Van den Berg and Watt (1991). The reader enters the document in the most abstract field which is a presentation of the frame with emphasis on etic and nomothetic constructs. Less abstract fields potentially include discussion of the research question/problem and its importance, a summary of the interpretation of the results/findings and their significance, conclusions, and a discussion of epistemological and axiological assumptions. At higher levels are fields of intermediate abstractness such as idiographic description of informants or other units of analysis, similar to the interpenetrated descriptions of Samantha (Thompson *et al.* 1990), Veronica, Allison, and Joyce (Thompson *et al.* 1994), or Anders, Bjorn, and Carl (Mick and Buhl 1992). Using hypertext, the researcher can provide idiographic descriptions of all of the informants – twelve or more – enabling readers to choose those they want to read. The researcher can also include memos, research journals, and other documents containing emerging ideas, insights, and theoretical musings, as well as descriptions of methods – interviewing strategies or guides, observational techniques, data set(s) and analytical strategies. In the highest and most concrete fields, researchers can include complete transcriptions of interviews, fieldnotes, and other textual and graphical forms of data. By adding hypermedia (see Hoffman and Novak 1996), the researcher can include complete audio recordings of interviews or full motion video data (field observations and video interviews), with the latter representing perhaps the ultimate degree of closeness to informants and the least mediated representation of consumers.

Both text and hypertext contain sections, delineated passages of text, or fields. Hypertext differs from traditional text in the author-constructed linkages that encourage the reader to move in a non-linear manner through the text. These linkages represent paths defined by the researcher that break up the expected linear flow. They allow the reader to move instantaneously back and forth between intra-unit (within informant, episode, site, and so forth) perspectives to cross-unit themes and perspective (cf. Thompson *et al.* 1994: 435–6). For example, the reader following the idiographic interpretation of an informant might "click" upwards through a link to a longer interview passage, thereby gaining a broader context for a short passage illustrating the researcher's etic interpretation. From this passage the reader might then click to others in the interview transcripts that illustrate the same theme. Alternatively, the reader might click to identical, similar, or opposing themes in idiographic interpretations of other informants, or to the more abstract nomothetic interpretation of all the informants, episodes, or sites.

Moving through the data as it is recorded follows a *contiguous* path. Strings of passages in interviews or fieldnotes represent "observations" *as they occur* in an empirical sequence – co-occurring elements arranged in time, space, culture, or structure. Moving through the data across units or idiographic summaries represents analysis, breaking up the empirical sequence and grouping them by conceptual categories, constructs, or themes (Fortes 1970). The researcher or reader connects or arranges observations, units of analysis, or conceptual elements that are not empirically contiguous but that display *similarities*. Thus, narrative flow in text versus hypertext by researcher and reader offers different possibilities.

Postmodern ethnography

Postmodern ethnographers exhibit a self-conscious concern with rhetorical and narrative practice (Clifford and Marcus 1986; Marcus and Cushman 1982; Marcus and Fisher 1986; Van Maanen 1988) and research texts that mirror their concern. Jacobson argues that their claim of engaging in "an experimental moment" ignores the extent to which many ethnographies, including some of the classics, "gave explicit attention to the manner of composing . . . texts and attempted to experiment with . . . argumentation and textual organization" (1991: 2). Thus, it is not experimentation and reflexivity that distinguish the postmodern ethnography. Rather, it is the type of experiment postmodernists conduct. They reject the foundations of modern social science, including the "authority" of the researcher, to construct a representation or interpretation *for* the reader, dominating the voices of "subjects" through authorial commentary or interpretation. They also reject the assumption of an absolute truth against which an account is to be measured. Their work exhibits self-consciousness about textual style, multivocality, dialogic form, fragmentation, and rejection of a superior posture by the researcher *vis-à-vis* informants and readers (Atkinson 1992).

Other genres

Atkinson describes several experimental forms of social science writing that mimic dialogues, plays, journalism, fiction, and combinations of the proceeding. Employing "deliberate transgressions of literary boundaries" (1992: 45), these forms present interesting possibilities that violate the format of scientific genre. Informants speak through a variety of literary devices: texts include conversations between real or imaginary speakers and other contrivances. Incorrigibly postmodern, these playful texts assume ironic and parodic tones. Informants' voices are heard through a variety of literary devices, and readers construct the interpretation.

Atkinson contrasts these accessible engaging accounts with the postmodern style of Tyler (1987), whose work is "a complex, 'writerly' product." Tyler rejects the assumption that researchers *represent* social reality. Rather, he claims that postmodernists evoke "an emergent fantasy" for both the writer and reader. For Tyler, modern science fails because it falsely assumes that language is capable of representation.

The consumer researchers reviewed, even those who have taken the "interpretive turn" (Sherry 1991) and acknowledged that multiple interpretations of texts can coexist, more closely reflect the modern as opposed to the postmodern view. They construct and present unified interpretations of data, exercising their "privileged" position: they neither ask informants to "speak for themselves," nor ask readers to co-construct the interpretation. They expect the critical reader to accept or reject their interpretation based on *evidence*, *reason*, and *logical* arguments that support the interpretations in light of their research purpose (Jacobson 1991).

Their readers are most likely to be research peers capable of evaluating their interpretation and constructing another precisely because they have shared knowledge of research conventions, recognition of the genre, knowledge of other genres, and similar reading strategies (Scott 1994). Thus, while they differ in assumptions, problems studied, research designs, and research goals from "positivists" or empiricists (Hirschman and Holbrook 1992; Hudson and Ozanne 1988), they remain less experimental than postmodern ethnographers and experimental sociologists and more tethered to the fundamental tenets of modernism.

The future of interpretive research

The postmodern ideals of multivocality, author–informant–reader equality, and dialogic form may be attainable only in hypertext and hypermedia. Structured hypertext permits the reader to co-construct as well as to evaluate an interpretation because all of the data are available. Informants can virtually speak for themselves insofar as their complete speech is inscribed or transcribed in the concrete fields. However, Atkinson (1992) argues that the faithful recording and representation of speech in written symbols is always problematic. In hypertext, fragmentation and dialogic form replace the linear authorially controlled narrative.

Can we imagine a future of interpretive research with linked hypermedia documents replacing the individual linear narrative of scientific discourse? Will the product of interpretive consumer research result from surfers' co-constructing interpretations and posting them through a hypermedia/text server on the Internet, inviting others to analyze and interpret large databases of interview transcripts and fieldnotes, video and audio recordings, and reflective journals? Will the distinction between authors, editors, and reviewers disappear in favor of electronic peer co-interpreters? Will the *Journal of Consumer Reaserach* become a "virtual journal" and the Association for Consumer Research a "virtual organization" sponsoring "virtual conferences"?

Three caveats

Is the preceding a nightmare or an utopian vision? It depends upon the diffusion of hypermedia technology and its adoption by interpretive researchers in the service of analysis, interpretation, and writing. Three issues will affect the likelihood and the operation of this scenario.

1 Researcher information overload

The prospects of writing a research report in hypertext may not seem daunting. In fact, constructing the fields and identifying the specific linkages between them may add a useful dimension to analysis and interpretation, and to writing. In viewing analysis as breaking up and rearranging an empirically occurring sequence for the purpose of identifying patterns, categories, constructs, and their relationships, we note the importance of interpretive researchers' definition of linkages and connections among elements. The construction of hypertext with decisions about field content and linkages compels an explicit focus upon linkages at similar and differing levels of abstraction and may enhance analytical and interpretive prowess.

But as hypertext documents proliferate, the sheer amount of data unfiltered by researcher selection might inhibit, rather than promote, cross-study integration. As Wolcott points out:

> The critical task in qualitative research is not to accumulate all the data you can, but to "can" (i.e. get rid of) most of the data you accumulate. This requires constant winnowing. The trick is to discover essences and then to reveal those essences with sufficient context, yet not become mired trying to include everything that might possibly be described . . . computer capabilities entreat us to do just the opposite; . . .because we can accommodate ever-increasing quantities of data – mountains of it – we have to be careful not to get buried . . .
>
> (Wolcott 1990: 35).

The discovery and revelation of essences entail much mental effort. Authors undertake such effort for a variety of intrinsic (curiosity, cognitive mastery, contribution to knowledge) and extrinsic rewards (academic recognition, ego enhancement, attaining for promotion and tenure, and consequent economic rewards). Intrinsic motivators may fall short of propelling and sustaining Internet-hypermedia-scholarship.

2 Getting closure

Atkinson (1992) notes that the experimental social science crossing literary boundaries and borrowing the forms of other genres provides amusing and insightful representations of social worlds. At the same time he argues that the authors fail to bring closure to the material and pull the myriad threads of insights together. The potential for premature interruption of analysis and interpretation would appear magnified in hypermedia. The presentation of the entire data set and all of the lower level abstractions may overwhelm and supplant the drive to integrate and move to higher levels of abstraction. The selection process and strategic choices mentioned by Wolcott (1990) and Van Maanen (1988) require thoughtful integration and careful attention to argumentation and reason. The bounded 40–50 page narrative text places constraints that may encourage more abstraction and integration than hypermedia.

3 Lofland's (1974) five criteria

The novelty of the frame rests upon researcher insight, theoretical grounding, and creativity. These traits do not depend on the textual form in which researchers communicate ideas. Lofland's other criteria might be compromised in hyperme-dia. As the discussion of premature closure suggests, we risk subverting generic abstraction and elaboration in hypermedia. In contrast, we may enhance event-fulness – the incorporation of concrete events and individuals in the text – by inclusion of the entire data set in the most concrete fields. However, if the reader chooses not to move to those fields, the textual experience remains uneventful. Similarly, the interpenetration of the data and frame requires the reader to move up and down the hierarchy of abstraction. Thus, in hypermedia, eventfulness and interpenetration, no longer imposed by the author, depend upon reader strategies and remain problematic.

Conclusion

Hypermedia present interesting possibilities for representing consumers. Their effects are not limited to communication, but are capable of shaping all of the activities of analysis, interpretation, and writing. The anticipation of the way that one can write shapes the way that one thinks. Writing in hypertext alters the strategic choices suggested by Van Maanen (1988). Authors no longer must decide on what material to include and what to omit, which voices to select, and which informant quotations to select. In hypermedia, as in Ragu™ spaghetti sauce, it's all in there. The technology currently exists to create research docu-ments in hypermedia and make them accessible to the community of interpre-tive consumer researchers. Its adoption even as an experimental form depends, as we know, on its visibility, relative advantage, trialability, compatibility, and complexity. In creating a hypertext document for this chapter, I advocate the experiment. The interested reader can access it at the following address: http://mktg.sba.uconn.edu/mkt/faculty/ss/conexp.htm.

In the meantime, this *mostly modern* chapter offers suggestions for the construc-tion of conventional narrative texts whose authors select and arrange data and conceptual elements, impose linear sequence, and indicate the connections and linkages that merit comment through their interpretations. Perhaps the price we pay for delegating these responsibilities is the granting of their authorial privileges.

Acknowledgments

The author thanks Morris Holbrook, Barbara Stern, Sharon Beatty, and Mark Ligas for their helpful comments on a draft of this chapter.

References

Arnould, E. and Wallendorf, M. (1994) "Market-Oriented Ethnography: Interpretation Building and Marketing Strategy Formulation," *Journal of Marketing Research* 31,4: 484–504.

Atkinson, P. (1990) *The Ethnographic Imagination: Textual Constructions of Reality*, London: Routledge & Kegan Paul.

—— (1992) *Understanding Ethnographic Texts*, Newbury Park, CA: Sage.

Becker, H. (1986) *Writing for Social Scientists*, Chicago: The University of Chicago Press.

Belk, R.W., Sherry, J.F. Jr., and Wallendorf, M. (1988) "A Naturalistic Inquiry into Buyer and Seller Behavior at a Swap Meet," *Journal of Consumer Research* 14,4: 449–70.

Belk, R.W., Wallendorf, M., and Sherry, J.F. Jr. (1989) "The Sacred and the Profane in Consumer Behavior: Theodicy on the Odyssey," *Journal of Consumer Research* 16,1: 1–38.

Bergadaa, M.M. (1990) "The Role of Time in the Action of the Consumer," *Journal of Consumer Research* 17,3: 289–302.

Celsi, R.L., Rose, R.L., and Leigh, T.W. (1993), "An Exploration of High-Risk Consumption through Skydiving," *Journal of Consumer Research* 20,1: 1–23.

Clifford, J. and Marcus, G.E. (eds) (1986) *Writing Culture: The Poetics and Politics of Ethnography*, Berkeley: University of California Press.

Drumwright, M.E. (1994) "Socially Responsible Organizational Buying: Environmental Concern as a Noneconomic Buying Criterion," *Journal of Marketing* 58,3: 1–19.

Fernandez, J.W. (1986) *Persuasions and Performances: The Play of Tropes in Anthropology*, Bloomington: University of Indiana Press.

—— (ed.) (1991) *Beyond Metaphor: The Theory of Tropes in Anthropology*, Stanford: Stanford University Press.

Fortes, M. (1970) "Analysis and Description in Social Anthropology," in *Time and Social Structure and Other Essays*, New York: Humanities Press.

Frye, N. ([1957] 1973) *Anatomy of Criticism: Four Essays*, 2nd edn, Princeton NJ: Princeton University Press.

Geertz, C. (1973) *The Interpretation of Cultures*, New York: Basic Books.

—— (1988) *Works and Lives: The Anthropologist as Author*, Stanford: Stanford University Press.

Goffman, E. (1952) "Cooling the Mark Out: Some Aspects of Adaptation to Failure," *Psychiatry* 15,4: 451–63.

Heisley, D.D. and Levy, S.J. 1991) "Autodriving: A Photoelicitation Technique," *Journal of Consumer Research* 18,3: 257–72.

Hill, R.P. (1991) "Homeless Women, Special Possessions, and the Meaning of 'Home': An Ethnographic Case Study," *Journal of Consumer Research* 18,3: 298–310.

Hill, R.P. and Stamey, M. (1990) "The Homeless in America: An Examination of Possessions and Consumption Behaviors," *Journal of Consumer Research* 17,3: 303–21.

Hirschman, E.C. (1986) "Humanistic Inquiry in Marketing Research: Philosophy, Method, and Criteria," *Journal of Marketing Research* 23,3: 237–49.

—— (1988) "The Ideology of Consumption: A Structural-Syntactic Analysis of *Dallas* and *Dynasty*," *Journal of Consumer Research* 15,3: 344–59.

—— (1992) "The Consciousness of Addiction: Toward a General Theory of Compulsive Consumption," *Journal of Consumer Research* 19,2: 155–79.

Hirschman E.C. and Holbrook, M.B. (1992) *Postmodern Consumer Research: The Study of Consumption as Text*, Newbury Park, CA: Sage.

Hoffman, D.L. and Novak, T.P. (1996) "Marketing in Hypermediated Computer-Mediated Environments: Conceptual Foundations," *Journal of Marketing* 60,3: 50–68.

Holman, R.H. (1980a) "Clothing as Communication: An Empirical Investigation," in *Advances in Consumer Research*, vol. 7, ed. J.C. Olson, Ann Arbor, MI: Association for Consumer Research, 372–77.

—— (1980b) "A Transcription and Analysis System for the Study of Women's Clothing Behavior," *Semiotica*, 32,1/2: 11–34.

Hudson, L. and Ozanne, J. (1988) "Alternative Ways of Seeking Knowledge," *Journal of Consumer Research*, 14,4: 508–21.

Jacobson, D. (1991) *Reading Ethnography*, Albany, NY: State University of New York Press.

Jakobson, R. (1956) "Two Aspects of Language and Language Disturbances," in R. Jakobson and M. Halle (eds) *Fundamentals of Language*, The Hague: Mouton.

Joy, A. (1991) "Beyond the Odyssey: Interpretations of Ethnographic Writing in Consumer Behavior," in R.W. Belk (ed.) *Highways and Buyways: Naturalistic Research from the Consumer Behavior Odyssey*, Provo, UT: Association for Consumer Research, 216–33.

Lakoff, G. and Johnson, M. (1980) *Metaphors We Live By*, Chicago: University of Chicago Press.

Lakoff, G. and Turner, M. (1989) *More Than Cool Reason: A Field Guide to Poetic Metaphor*, Chicago: University of Chicago Press.

Landow, G.P. (1992) *Hypertext: The Convergence of Contemporary Critical Theory and Technology*, Baltimore: Johns Hopkins Press.

Levy, S.J. (1981) "Interpreting Consumer Mythology: A Structural Approach to Consumer Behavior," *Journal of Marketing* 45,3: 49–61.

Lodge, D. (1977) *The Modes of Modern Writing: Metaphor, Metonymy, and the Typology of Modern Literature*, Ithaca, NY: Cornell University Press.

Lofland, J. (1971) *Analyzing Social Settings: A Guide to Qualitative Observation and Analysis* Belmont, CA: Wadsworth.

—— (1974) "Styles of Reporting Qualitative Field Research," *The American Sociologist* 9,3: 101–11.

Manning, P.K. (1979) "Metaphors of the Field: Varieties of Organizational Discourse," *Administrative Science Quarterly* 24,6: 660–71.

—— (1987) *Semiotics and Fieldwork*, Beverly Hills: Sage.

Marcus, G. and Cushman, D. (1982) "Ethnographies as Text," *Annual Review of Anthropology*, 11: 25–69.

Marcus, G. and Fisher, M.M. (1986) *Anthropology as Cultural Critique: An Experimental Moment in the Human Sciences* Chicago: University of Chicago Press.

Mick, D.G. (1986) "Consumer Research and Semiotics: Exploring the Morphology of Signs, Symbols, and Significance," *Journal of Consumer Research* 13,2: 196–213.

Mick, D.G. and Buhl, C. (1992) "A Meaning-based Model of Advertising Experiences," *Journal of Consumer Research*, 19,3: 317–38.

Mick, D.G. and DeMoss, M. (1990) "Self-Gifts: Phenomenological Insights from Four Contexts," *Journal of Consumer Research* 17,3: 322–32.

McQuarrie, E.F. and Mick, D.G. (1996) "Figures of Rhetoric in Advertising Language," *Journal of Consumer Research*, 22,4: 424–39.

O'Guinn, T.C. and Belk, R.W. (1989) "Heaven on Earth: Consumption at Heritage Village, USA," *Journal of Consumer Research* 16,2: 227–38.

Peñaloza, L. (1994) "*Atravesando Fronteras*/Border Crossings: A Critical Ethnographic Exploration of the Consumer Acculturation of Mexican Immigrants," *Journal of Consumer Research* 21,1: 32–54.

Schouten, J.W. (1991) "Selves in Transition: Symbolic Consumption in Personal Rites of Passage and Identity Reconstruction," *Journal of Consumer Research* 17,4: 412–25.

Scott, L. (1994) "The Bridge from Text to Mind: Adapting Reader-Response Theory to Consumer Research," *Journal of Consumer Research* 21,3: 461–81.

Sherry, J.F., Jr. (1990) "A Sociocultural Analysis of a Midwestern American Flea Market," *Journal of Consumer Research* 17,1: 13–30.

—— (1990) "Postmodern Alternatives: The Interpretive in Consumer Research" in T.S. Robertson and H.H. Kassarjian (eds) *Handbook of Consumer Research*, Englewood Cliffs, NJ: Prentice Hall, 548–91.

Spiggle, S. (1994) "Analysis and Interpretation of Qualitative Data in Consumer Research," *Journal of Consumer Research* 21,3: 491–503.

Spiggle, S. and File, K.M. (1997) "In My Own Image: A Phenomenological Investigation of Philanthropy," working paper.

Strauss, A. (1987) *Qualitative Analysis for Social Scientists*, Cambridge: Cambridge University Press.

Strauss, A. and Corbin, J. (1990) *Basics of Qualitative Research: Grounded Theory Procedures and Techniques*, Beverly Hills: Sage.

Stern, B. (1992) "Crafty Advertisers: Literary Versus Literal Deceptors," *Journal of Public Policy and Marketing* 11,1: 72–81.

—— (1995) "Consumer Myths: Frye's Taxonomy and the Structural Analysis of Consumption Text," *Journal of Consumer Research* 22,2: 165–85.

Thompson, C.J. (1996) "Caring Consumers: Gendered Consumption Meanings and the Juggling Lifestyle," *Journal of Consumer Research* 22,4: 388–407.

Thompson, C.J. and Hirschman, E.C. (1995) "Understanding the Socialized Body: A Poststructuralist Analysis of Consumers' Self-Conceptions, Body Images, and Self-Care Practices," *Journal of Consumer Research* 22,2: 139–53.

Thompson, C.J., Locander, W.B. and Pollio, H. (1989) "Putting Consumer Experience Back into Consumer Research: The Philosophy and Method of Existential-Phenomenology," *Journal of Consumer Research*, 16,2: 133–46.

Thompson, C.J., Locander, W.B. and Pollio, H. (1990) "The Lived Meaning of Free Choice: An Existential-Phenomenological Description of Everyday Consumer Experiences of Contemporary Married Women," *Journal of Consumer Research* 17,3: 346–61.

Thompson, C.J., Pollio, H. and Locander, W. (1994) "The Spoken and the Unspoken: A Hermeneutic Approach to Understanding the Cultural Viewpoints that Underlie Consumers' Expressed Meanings," *Journal of Consumer Research* 21,4: 432–52.

Tyler, S. (1987) *The Unspeakable Discourse*, Madison, WI: University of Wisconsin Press.

Van den Berg, S. and Watt, J.H. (1991) "Effects of Educational Setting on Student Response to Structured Hypertext," *Journal of Computer-Based Instruction* 18,3: 118–34.

van Gennep, A. (1960) *The Rites of Passage*, trans. M.B. Vizedom and G.L. Caffee, Chicago: University of Chicago Press.

Van Maanen, J. (1988) *Tales of the Field: On Writing Ethnography*, Chicago: University of Chicago Press.

Wallendorf, M. and Arnould, E.J. (1991) "'We Gather Together': Consumption Rituals of Thanksgiving Day," *Journal of Consumer Research*, 18,1: 13–31.

Wallendorf, M. and Brucks, M. (1993) "Introspection in Consumer Research: Implementation and Implications," *Journal of Consumer Research* 20,3: 339–59.

Wolcott, H. F. (1990) *Writing Up Qualitative Research*, Newbury Park, CA: Sage.

—— (1994) *Transforming Qualitative Data: Description, Analysis, and Interpretation*, Thousand Oaks, CA: Sage.

Zaltman, G. and Higie, R.A. (1993), "Seeing the Voice of the Customer: The Zaltman Metaphor Elicitation Technique," working paper no. 93–114, Cambridge: Marketing Science Institute.

Part 3

REPRESENTATION AND PICTORIAL DATA

7

CONSUMING REPRESENTATION

A visual approach to consumer research

Jonathan E. Schroeder

Photography's position in Western Culture is embedded in an ideology of representation that regards it as simultaneously copying and constructing the world that it pictures. Photographic practice, which includes not only the taking of pictures, but also how photographs are looked at, thought about, saved, used, and re-used, illustrates the ways we resolve this apparent paradox.

(Becker 1992: 3)

These free Kodak Hula shows are staged especially for picture takers, in colorful Hawaiian surroundings, framed by the blue Pacific ocean.

(from *Hawaiian Music from the Kodak Hula Show*, 1956, Waikiki Records)

The Kodak Hula Show – event, tourist site, product promotion, record album – serves as an example of the confluence between representation, consumption, photography, and identity. This souvenir album, with a beautiful color photograph of what must be the Kodak Hula Show on the front and specific instructions for performing a hula on the back, recorded in Hawaii according to the liner notes, documents a key component in a Hawaiian vacation – seeing a "hula show." The cover captures the show in full swing, under swaying palm trees framed against a bright blue sky, complete with a few puffy white clouds. On what appears to be an impromptu stage – with a grass shack and a longboat canoe for a backdrop – musicians in bright Hawaiian dress play guitars for the stars of the show. Five women form one line of hula dancers, each wearing a full and flowing bright green "grass" skirt and two yellow flower leis that hang down past their waists.

Consuming representation

The purpose of this chapter is to develop ideas about photography as a consumer behavior and as a researcher practice by examining social science research traditions, photographers, and consumer research that utilizes photography. Photography is one stream of many in representing consumers. Interactions between photography and identity – personal identity, gender identity, ethnic identity – are analyzed to demonstrate the functions of photography as an important site for discussing issues of representation. Through a selective, personal review of photography focused on the production and consumption of photographic representation, I develop a framework for incorporating photography into consumer research that bears on questions of consumption, identity, and representation. The chapter draws on photography writings, consumer research, social science research, and personal narrative to discuss the role photography plays in the construction and representation of identity. Mass media photography – popular magazine photography, art photography, books, and popular film – is analyzed via concepts of the gaze, identity, and representation. Throughout, travel photography will provide illustrative examples. Consumer researchers might be considered "tourists" in these matters, casting the tourist gaze upon other methods, other fields, and research "subjects" in our quest for new scholarly resources and frontiers. This metaphor will be explored through an analysis of travel photography, theories of tourism, and personal reflection. I use this discussion of photography and identity to sketch an outline of a theory of *consuming representation*.

Identity construction is a central motivating force in consumer behavior. Photography is an important representational practice in the lives of consumers, both as a means of representing their own life stories and as a way that information about the world is transmitted. A basic human behavior is to represent oneself through action, word, and image; photography is a powerful technology of representation. The practice of photography can be considered as consumer behavior not simply in terms of buying cameras and film but, more importantly, assigning time to the activities associated with photography such as taking pictures, developing film, sorting and selecting photographs for albums and frames, showing photographs, and looking at others' photographs. "Consuming representation" refers to engaging with, reading, and responding to signs, symbols, and images. In this discussion, consuming representation provides a way of discussing a complex interaction between consuming and producing. For example, an activity such as watching a movie consists of buying a ticket (or renting a video), spending time looking at the screen, eating popcorn, and so forth, as well as making sense of the plot, characters, and meaning. Consuming representation, then, is a perceptual process of integration.

In one sense, of course, one might say that the consumer *produces* representation through photography. Consumers are active producers of their own pictures and videos. Consumer behaviors such as putting together a wardrobe, assembling a library, creating a collection, making a home, all employ production metaphors. In each of these activities, what is being produced is meanings – signs and symbols of identity – through consumption. This apparent paradox – production through consumption – characterizes consumer culture. The concept "consuming representation" is an attempt to capture the complex interactions between consuming and producing representations.

Photography

Photography is a critical medium that consumers use to represent themselves. A model of identity that stresses the life story will be presented as a guide to the use of photography by consumers, for choices that consumers make about how to represent their life story are important for identity formation and maintenance. The practice of photography intersects with personal processes of creating life stories to produce representations of identity that highlight social psychological issues of consumer behavior. This chapter will neither discuss photography as an advertising or television practice (see Coulter and Zaltman 1994; O' Guinn and Shrum 1997; Scott 1994, and Stern and Schroeder 1994), nor as a stimulus in information processing approaches to consumer research. Furthermore, photographic studies of national identity will not be reviewed (e.g., Becker 1992; Chow 1997; Guimond 1991; Rubenstein 1982). What it will do is use an analysis of photographs, photographic practice, and personal narrative to show how photography has captured my own consumer research and has become a frame for future research.

The chapter begins with a Hawaiian excursion to illustrate processes of representation and consumption, to discuss tourism as a site for studying representation, and to introduce tourism as a metaphor for consumer research that draws from disparate fields such as art criticism, literary analysis, and moral philosophy. I consider photographs and the practice of photography to be critical issues in representing consumers. In so doing, I want to tweak the phrase "representing consumers" and discuss the consumption of representations, largely through photography which allows us (ourselves and others) to capture things on film, shoot our subjects, and frame our experience, while removing us from our encounter, placing us behind the lens of the camera, and allowing us to gaze at the scene to capture Kodak moments that we can re-experience at home. Photography adds an additional layer of consumption to our experience of travel, for we buy camera and film and play the role of photographer as well as of tourist. We see through our own eyes as well as through the camera's viewfinder, which frames our experience and lets us gaze at the scene – is it worth photographing or not? Should I pose my companions for a shot or not? Thus we consume by classifying, composing, and clicking (cf. Holt 1995). Photos become consumer artifacts and personal identity markers, representing the vacation, the photographer, the subject, and a vision of the tourist experience that is constructed via consumer choices that photography can help make clear.

Throughout the chapter, personal narrative serves to demonstrate a life-story model of identity, the subject of the second section, "Photography, representation, and identity". Several elements central to reading photographs as texts are discussed: the gaze, denotation, connotation, and interpretation, within a semiotic approach to understanding representation. Photographer Garry Winogrand provides an illustrative example of these issues incorporated into a model of identity. The section concludes by presenting two photographers whose work revolves around identity and representation: Barbara Kruger and Peter Menzel. The next section, "Consuming representations in the construction of identity," reviews several approaches to studying popular photography and film from an identity perspective that invokes cultural, political, and ethical issues in representation. The final section describes some potential problems with photography as a resource. For example, representative practice creates ethical issues, for "some picturing practices representationally 'ensoul' – personify, subjectify – some people for others in morally disturbing or vicious ways" (Walker 1997: 302). The way that subjects are represented in photography – families, children, groups, political events, war – is a critical issue for consumer researchers as well as those interested in ethics and public policy. I invoke an ethics of representation to delineate the ideological power of images and conclude by outlining some questions raised by the practice of representation in photography and in consumer research.

Consuming representation at the Kodak Hula Show

The Kodak Hula Show record album embodies many layers of representation and exemplifies the complexities of consuming representation. The cover photograph is a stunning example of the politics of representation, and it demonstrates a process of consuming representation. The hula dancers on the cover represent Hawaii and the experience of an exotic tropical vacation. Even without the ritualized tropical dress and the red flowers in their hair, the women are clearly represented as native Hawaiians. The photograph, though, only *suggests* a hula show – for photography freezes the image, representing through reproduction what happened years ago and far away, what literary theorist Roland Barthes considers the thing's "having been there" (1981: 76). Moreover, the Kodak Hula Show represents – literally – a stereotyped photo opportunity of a scene that we expect to see, constructed from the vantage point of the tourist consuming the exotic and trivializing the native cultural ritual (MacCannell 1976). If the tourists recognize the staged aspect of the show, they nevertheless have been led to believe that somewhere on the islands, past or present, a similar, but perhaps more authentic show occurs. However, this album cover does not look particularly dated – Hawaiian albums are enjoying a comeback smartly repackaged as "exotica" compact discs – and we might expect a similar spectacle to occur each day at the appointed hours. This photo represents many things – Hawaii and Hawaiian ethnic identity, a vision of cultural practice and power relations, tourism, and nostalgia for the recent past of a vacation or the more distant past of Polynesia before photography. The context of the photograph, however, is critical in apprehending the depth of its import – social, political, colonial, sexist, and racist representations contribute to the power and problems of this image (Lalvani 1995; Little 1991; MacCannell 1976; Urry 1990).

The Kodak Hula Show record album copy offers these pointers for photographers: "If you're looking for natives, you'll find gracious hula girls, Polynesian fishermen sun-drying their nets, and bright-eyed children from a dozen races." The blurb both describes and instructs, echoing an accepted script of the Hawaiian vacation where mainlanders can go to see exotic natives while spending U.S. currency and speaking American English. The Kodak Hula Show, we are told in the blurb, was the creation of the "genial" marketing director of Eastman Kodak in Hawaii, who "saw the need to give visitors a complete picture of the Islands that they were not otherwise able to photograph . . . hula dancers and Polynesian entertainment." The hula became a necessary event on the tourists' to-do list, and the tourist industry provided hula shows as a spectacle of representation. However, seeing the show is not enough, for photos must be taken to capture the vacationer's experience so that it can be brought home and enthusiastically shown to family and friends – the notorious and feared vacation picture show (Belk 1995; Little 1991; Urry 1990). To travel to an exotic locale and not take a camera seems almost unnatural to contemporary consumers – a lost opportunity, incomplete. Taking photographs and, more recently, videotaping the entire trip are essential ways that travelers consume destinations. The photographs help represent the vacation, aid in the construction of the fun and enjoyment of the trip, act as reminders of what the vacationers did and saw, and become somewhat permanent memories placed in photo albums, tucked in letters, posted on refrigerators, and featured in holiday greetings (Belk 1995, 1998; Durgee *et al.* 1991; Nash 1996). Moreover, these photographs become elements in the personal and family life story, a key process of identity formation (McAdams 1985). Thus, photographs constitute both a consumer activity and a consumer artifact, as well as source documents for investigating the way that consumers represent themselves and are themselves represented both in consumer research and in the broader consumer culture.

The Kodak Hula Show is staged specifically for tourists to photograph (using Kodak film for the best results, we assume). In cultural and tourist representations of Hawaii, the hula is a critical element of its allure – the exotic, suggestive "dance" of the natives (or at least a representation of the natives) represents Hawaii as a Polynesian paradise (Borgerson and Schroeder 1997). To visit Hawaii, one must experience a hula show, a luau, and the beach at Waikiki, and take photographs of each to bring back to the folks at home. The Kodak Hula Show provides an essential component of a Hawaiian vacation: the photo opportunity. Vacations represent major expenditures for consumers and are important for their self-image because of the meanings associated with travel, status, exoticism, and adventure (see Lalvani 1995; Torgovnick 1990 and 1997). Where and how we vacation is closely linked to socio-economic status, identity, good or bad taste, and values. Vacation pictures, aside from being a substantial market for the photography industry, are an important family icon; taking vacation pictures is an essential consumption behavior that gives structure and meaning to the tourist experience (see MacCannell 1976). For many vacationers, a camera gives them something to *do*, which facilitates the transition from work to play (see Little 1991). Moreover, photographs document the trip, offering proof that we have been there in the form of substantiation of the sites encountered (Durgee *et al.* 1991).

The Kodak Hula Show record album encapsulates the vacation spectacle in a convenient, portable product. Thus, even if you cannot watch a hula show, you can experience it through the marvel of a hi-fi stereophonic album, complete with a beautiful color photo. What does an event like this mean to consumers? What do vacation photographs represent? It is important to realize that the album pictures represent a real experience, for the representation of Hawaii is as authentic as any other competing representation (cf. Summers 1996). The Hawaii that is represented in tourist brochures, advertising, and Hawaiian record album covers exists in the minds of consumers. This is not meant to obscure the identity of the people who live on the islands of Hawaii or to denigrate their culture and history. However, "Hawaii" has been constructed by economic, social, and political forces to appeal to Western tourists (Torgovnick 1997). Personal identity is constructed through similar processes of representation – the true self is as inaccessible as the true Hawaii. We come to know destinations, social groups, and ourselves through representation.

Photography, representation, and identity

> Polaroid is *not* a camera – it's a social lubricant. So you don't present it as a camera, or take pictures of happy families, or talk about how it's a record of the moment. Pox to all that! What Polaroid is really about is enjoying yourself.
> (John Hegarty, chair of BBH advertising agency, in Heilemann 1997: 175)

Photography is a significant way that consumers create, record, and tell their life story (Belk 1990). From birth, a camera snaps away to capture significant events and rituals in people's lives. Birthdays, bar mitzvahs, graduations, weddings, farewells, vacations – each is associated with photographic opportunities and memories. These events are important in creating a life story, a central idea in biography and psychology. Literary theorist Robert Scholes discusses reading texts (including pictures) as a process of constructing the narrative of one's life (Scholes 1989). We each use stories as a way of creating, maintaining, and refining our identity, the narrative of our life. This process is an important part of identity formation and has been incorporated into a psychological model of identity that provides a link between narrativity in texts and lives. In psychologist Dan McAdams's life-story model of identity, "identity is a life story which individuals begin constructing, consciously and unconsciously, in late adolescence. As such, identities may be understood in terms directly relevant to stories' (McAdams 1985: 57). In the following sections, several approaches to investigating representations of identity are discussed.

Eliciting representations of identity

> Photographs and photographic practice appear as essential ingredients in so many social rituals – from customs checks to wedding ceremonies, from the public committal of judicial evidence to the private receipt of sexual pleasure – that it is difficult to imagine what such rituals were like and how they could be conducted before photographs became widely available.
>
> (Tagg 1989: 164)

Anthropology as a field has developed the most formal role for photography (including film and videotape) in research (Edwards 1994; Taylor 1994). John and Malcolm Collier codify photographic practice as a research tool (1986). They emphasize quantitative, measurable, countable aspects of photographs in their focus on photographs as secondary data in a realist approach to representation. Their overall ethnographic approach to studying culture, with photography as one component, is useful to consumer researchers. The inventory is a collection of photographs taken by the researcher at the site of interest, such as a ritual dance, home, or flea market, and it is the core of the Colliers' method, for "the value of an inventory is based upon the assumption that the 'look' of a home reflects who people are and the way they cope with the problems of life" (ibid.: 45). The Colliers point out that photographs alone are difficult to assess, for they are infused with "independent authority. As we deepen our understanding of the photographic evidence through analysis, its character as primary evidence gives the imagery an independent life. This aspect of photographs as primary experience separates the records from the theoretical procedures of analysis" (ibid.: 165). Photographs, then, transcend the status of illustrations and become documents of identification. Other anthropological approaches depart from the Colliers' realist assumptions and stress photography and film as a process of cultural representation (e.g., Chow 1997; Taylor 1994; Traube 1992). However, consumer researchers have treated photographs primarily as secondary data, rather than as a product resulting from a practice.

In a broad survey of the use of photography in consumer research, Deborah Heisley and Sid Levy (1991) describe the way that photographs serve as data for inquiry into behavioral issues ranging from the consumption of food to the construction of identity. They discuss three research methods related to the use of photography: (1) the creation of cultural inventories; (2) projective techniques, or photoelicitation; and (3) examination of photographs as cultural artifacts. The creation of cultural inventories – photographic collections generated by the research subject, researcher, or secondary source – can be analyzed in several different ways. An inventory can serve as data for research on its own as the main object of attention (e.g., Heisley *et al.* 1991; Holbrook 1998). For example, the photographs kept in albums, books, frames, and on refrigerators can be aggregated and considered an inventory of consumer identity. Although Heisley and Levy concentrate on the creation of inventories by researchers, the research subjects can also participate. Havlena and Holak (1996) used such subject participation in a study of consumer nostalgia that explored nostalgic themes in collages made by consumers out of magazine advertisements and photographs.

Photographs may also serve as a stimulus onto which consumers project their own wishes, desires, identity, and values. Projective techniques, which assume that meaning is projected through photographs, are a rich resource for researchers. Heisley and Levy (1991) employed this approach in an iterative photoelicitation study that investigated consumer behavior during the family dinner. They first photographed and audiotaped three families as they prepared and ate dinner. Then they had a sociology class describe and analyze the photographs in terms of family structure and power. The families were then interviewed about their interactions, using the photographs as stimuli. By means of this rich and multilayered method, Heisley and Levy were able to glimpse the family's gaze – they saw things about themselves of which they were unaware, such as power relations and roles. Looking at themselves in the photographs, the subjects of the research were caught in a public self-reflective matrix not unlike therapy. The photographic element of the project generated narrativity, enabling the subjects to document their behavior in a way that their own family photographs had not. As Susan Sontag claims, "the images that have virtually unlimited authority in a modern society are mainly photographic images" (1977: 153). In providing commentary to the researchers, subjects "corrected" the images, empowered by that fact that "photographs challenge the respondent [to become] projective interpreters of their own actions" (Heisley and Levy 1991: 268).

Family photographs are important repositories of collective memory, self-presentation, and identity. However, they also represent sites of struggle, conflict, and power. For, as icons of family life, they are subject to domination by one ideal over others. For these and other reasons, Belk contends that "our photo albums are in no way representative archives of family life" (1995: 152). What is meant by "representative"? What would a representative archive look like? This is a critical question for research using photography. I contend that family photo albums are certainly representative of family life. However,

> . . . the important point is, *whose* memories are being made of this? It is by and large *parents'* memory that family photos represent, since parents took and selected the pictures. Yet children are offered a "memory" of their own childhoods, made up of images constructed by others.
>
> (Williamson 1986a: 123)

The crucial question for researchers is, "Which representations are of interest?" A family photo album contains a wealth of information about hopes, values, and tastes, in addition to specific evidence of the life story. I cannot think of a better archive for many questions of identity. It is because photographs are specifically selected for photo albums that they are excellent representatives of family life from a particular perspective (mother, grandfather, middle child, survivor, and so forth).

Photographic representation is part of many family's lives, and was an important part of mine. Upon completion of my Ph.D., I received a photograph album filled with pictures of me growing into adulthood. My friends commented that they saw little resemblance between the person in the photographs and the person they knew as "me", not in terms of physical looks but in terms of activities, poses, and settings. My mother had selected photos of me outdoors, hiking, snowskiing, and generally projecting an outdoors lifestyle. In graduate school, this did not mesh with the me that my friends knew. Indeed, the photographs were not my favorites and did not represent my self-concept at that time. However, they did represent my parents' representation of the family as action-oriented, outdoorsy people. Therefore, I do not claim that these photographs were not representative of me, for they did represent my identity as seen through my parents' eyes. The question of accuracy is not crucial to representation within an art-centered approach to consumer research. My representation of myself will never approach truth. What interests me is the role that photographs as consumer objects and photography as consumer behavior plays in representing identity. This is not a trivial example, for the struggle for autonomy and identity between parent and child graphically represented in family photographs is a critical issue in the formation of identity. The issue of *whose* representations is a key one in discovering the way that photography interacts and shapes consumer behavior.

Photographing identity

Social psychologist Robert Ziller presents a method of observing and researching identity through photography in *Photographing the Self* (1990). His approach makes explicit use of the camera by giving research participants a camera to photograph their identity in terms of questions: "Who are you?", "What is your vision of the good life?", "What does college mean to you?". Ziller contends that, when given a chance, individuals display salient aspects of the self via photography, providing an inside-out perspective missing from much research on identity. By demonstrating the close linkage of specific research questions to the generation of photographs, Ziller shows photography to be useful and a unique method for researching identity. In one study, he finds a correlation between shyness and photographs of people in groups, for shy people tend to take photos with fewer people in them than do less shy people. He compares photo analysis with dream analysis by showing that each unit (photo or dream image) can be subjected to many levels of interpretation.

Ziller emphasizes content analytic strategies of sorting, coding, and interpreting photographs, based on the photographs themselves in conjunction with theoretical questions developed from research on identity. Even though consumers take part in their representation, the researcher still is in control of the way they are portrayed, for he or she re-represents the images for the research report. Despite the limitations in Ziller's approach, it does generate unexpected insights into social aspects of identity. For example, Ziller gave five students confined to wheelchairs a camera to record "what the University of Florida campus means to you." Apart from his hypothesized results, Ziller noticed that few people in the photos generated by the wheelchair-bound photographers looked directly at the camera. He understood that "suddenly the viewer glimpses and momentarily experiences the social field of the physically handicapped person . . . There frozen before us is an existential scene of the strained efforts of the crowd of people to avoid eye contact with the handicapped person" (Ziller 1990: 125). The photograph represents not only the self but also the social world that constructs it. However, since there seems to be no researcher–subject dialogue about interpretation, what Ziller's photographers thought of this aspect of representation is unclear. Did they intend to take these photos to document alienation? Were they more random snapshots of momentary scenes? In contrasting these photographs with those of more mobile subjects, viewers gain insight into disturbing social processes. This is a compelling aspect of attempts to photograph identity.

Strengths of Ziller's research tactics include a removal of the laboratory constraints so that researchers can examine an individual's behavior in his or her usual surroundings, engagement of the individual in the production of research materials, and a diversity of approaches to uncover meanings. However, questions remain about what is being represented in an afternoon's worth of snapshots. Does individual talent for photography influence the results? That is, are some people more articulate with a camera than others? What is the role of experience in the process? Might some people know how to take pictures that represent themselves versus others who do not? Motivation does not presuppose skill. Photographs exert a powerful hold on our conception of identity, yet they rely on observable physical characteristics to represent inner states. Only through an analysis of the signifying systems of photography do we gain a deeper knowledge of the role photography plays in representing identity.

Representations, identity, and the life story

> We stuff our houses with photographs . . . the closest most of us ever come to a biography.
>
> (Clarke 1997: 216)

Identity has been conceptualized through the metaphor of a life story, best illustrated by McAdams's (1985) simple yet elegant model, which offers several strengths for this project. First, it ties together several issues in representation: meaning (story); subjective interpretation (narrative); and history (setting). Second, it provides a bridge between empirical and interpretive traditions, for McAdams presents quantitative data in support of his model. Third, it calls attention to the way that life stories are *created* by means of representation. Fourth, it draws on metaphor and narrativity, fundamental humanistic concepts just now entering consumer research discourse.

McAdams proposes that a person's identity or life story is divided into four components: nuclear episodes; imagoes; ideological setting; and generativity script. Thematic lines and narrative complexity constitute second-order variables in the model, which specifies specific links among the four life-story components and the second-order variables. Insofar as this model of identity is useful in organizing my personal response to and engagement with photography, let me describe it and refer to it in my discussion.

Like literary stories, life stories follow different strategies and styles and may or may not take coherent narrative form (Frye 1957; Stern 1995). For example, a person may employ a compensatory strategy to represent a negative view of the present and a positive view of the past (McAdams 1985). In compensatory narratives of one's life story, the past is glorified by means of the important consumer behavior phenomena of nostalgia (Belk 1990; Havlena and Holak 1996). Nuclear episodes "exist as specific autobiographical events which have been reinterpreted over time to assume a privileged status in the story" (McAdams 1985: 63). In the academic world, getting into graduate school, finishing the thesis, and getting tenure are events that are highlighted and serve as nuclear episodes. Thematic lines, or recurring content areas, affect the type and character of an individual's nuclear episodes. McAdams developed his model around central intimacy and power themes, also well-established consumer research concepts (Bearden *et al.* 1989). For example, someone who has a strong power thematic line might emphasize accomplishment by taking or displaying pictures of individual achievement – running a marathon, climbing a mountain, receiving a diploma. In contrast, someone who stresses intimacy might favor pictures of friends and family. Narrative complexity refers to the story's overall organization, plot complications, character development, and structure. Imagoes are characters central to one's life story such as parents, mentors, lovers. Ideological setting is the set of values that serves as backdrop for the life story. Finally, the generativity script contains one's goals and dreams, "a vision of exactly what one hopes to put into life and what one hopes to get out of life" (McAdams 1985: 65). Photographs serve many roles in the life-story and can be incorporated into each of McAdams's identity constructs. Moreover, photography is a metaphor for representing identity, which assimilates well into the life-story metaphor. The next section expands on the life-story metaphor, outlining a semiotic approach to reading photography.

Reading photography

Adequately understanding a photograph, whether taken by a Corsican peasant, a *petit-bourgeois* from Bologna or a Parisian professional means not only recovering the meanings which it proclaims, that is, to a certain extent, the explicit intentions of the photographer; it also means deciphering the surplus of meaning which it betrays by being part of the symbolism of an age, a class or an artistic group.

(Bourdieu 1990: 7)

The field of photography criticism offers consumer researchers an array of tools with which to interpret and understand images. Discourse on art has ancient roots, for visual images preceded written language as a method of representation (Adams 1996; Baxandall 1987; Stokstad 1995). Thus, borrowing from art criticism seems a logical source to analyze consumer behavior within the historical, cultural, and representational contexts of consumption. The ideology of the photograph concerns central issues in representation. For many, cameras offer an easy and convenient way of recording noteworthy events, people, and places such that lived experiences are concretized on film. The domain of photography "constitutes images or representations, consuming the world of sight as its raw material" (Tagg 1989: 165).

Several genres of photography have developed, such as landscape photography, documentary photography, art photography, journalistic photography, and portrait photography. Portraits in particular – from the Sears photo studio, from school, church, the military, and so forth – represent who we were at various stages of our life and are perhaps the most straightforward representations of identity. However, the very artificiality of most portraits – smiling, touched up, well lit, posed – demonstrates the gap between the way we are and the way we would like to appear (Barthes 1981; Clarke 1997). In current practice, we are told to smile in order to represent an inner state that may or may not correspond to our own feelings or our desire at that moment in time (Sontag 1977). The ideology of the portrait suggests that it serves to remind us of what we are expected to be rather than to help remember us the way we were. In my case, the first portrait that I really liked, or at least thought represented me in a satisfying way, is a photo-booth picture taken when I was twenty-seven – it was the first portrait that captured me without an interfering set of assumptions about how it should look. This photo represented me in a way that supported my identity at the time. Many more formal and perhaps more technically proficient pictures of me were influenced by photographic portrait practices such as a formal pose, a forced smile, appropriate dress, and so forth. Many people I have talked with about this share a similar experience.

Photography is a process of selection; "it appears that there is nothing more regulated and conventional than photographic practice and amateur photographs: in the occasions which give rise to photography, such as the objects, places and people photographed or the very composition of the pictures" (Bourdieu 1990: 7). The family photograph – an icon of living rooms and holiday greeting cards – is an important item in any discussion of photography as representational practice and ideology (Belk 1995; Berger 1972). Further, "advertising also relies heavily on images of the family, although rather than following domestic photography it holds out aspirations of how families *should* look, act, and consume" (Williamson 1986a: 125). Photographs help construct and constitute childhood memories. They reveal identity, not only to ourselves, families, and friends but also to the government in terms of identification cards, driver's licenses, and passports (Tagg 1989).

Early criticisms of photography as an art form described the new technique as one that directly reproduced reality (Clarke 1997; Goldberg 1996; Newhall 1982; Rosenblum 1994; Szarkowski 1989). However, the gap between the photographic record and perceptual experience reveals the artistic, political, and representational potential of photography – "it is just these differences that provide film with its artistic resources" (Arnheim 1957: 9). This is not to imply that photography cannot create realistic images, or that there is a real visual world out there that photography cannot capture. Rather, photography is both a critical part of the visual world and an important process of representing identity. Photography is a crucial important site in the crisis of representation. Several theorists suggest that photographs may be read like texts (e.g., Barrett 1990; Barthes 1981; Kozol 1994; Scholes 1989). This approach – one of many reflected in the growing academic interest in visual studies (Heller 1996) – is used below to draw links between identity narratives (life as text) and photographic narratives.

To interpret a photograph is to acknowledge its representational power both as artifact and as bearer of meaning. Many interpretative stances are possible, including psychoanalytic, semiotic, Marxist, feminist, and formalist (Barrett 1990). Barthes (1981) identified two signifying practices present in all photographs – denotation and connotation – that capture photography's appeal and representational power. Drawing upon semiotics, this system is "basic to any reading of the photographic image and underpin[s] its status as a text" (Clarke 1997: 222). Denotation, the literal meaning or significance of the image and its constituent elements, makes photography a complex medium of representation, for what the photograph shows or depicts has historically been considered a record of reality (Szarkowski 1989). However, a photograph's connotative meanings reflect broad societal, cultural, and ideological codes (see Mick and Politti 1989).

For example, in a recent *National Geographic* photograph by Jodi Cobb, two Tahitians carry French tourists from an outrigger canoe to the shore (see Plate 7.1). This photograph's meanings are overdetermined, in that decades of representational practice inform us how to read it. Furthermore, the identification of how one's photographs come to signify what they do is a path to self-understanding. Much like personal identity, photographs consist of surface and depth and can be appreciated only if one makes the effort to learn their life story.

Although interpretations of photographs are difficult to fit into a positivist, truth-seeking, research framework, the critic "cannot say just anything at all" (Barthes 1987: 81). Rather, good interpretations are resonant, interesting,

Plate 7.1 Tourists in Polynesia (Jodi Cobb 1997), courtesy *National Geographic* Image Collection

Plate 7.2 Brothers sailing, Michigan (c. 1950), collection of author

insightful, revealing, and ring true. Less successful ones are strained, off, unlikely, absurd, or a stretch (after Barrett 1990). Furthermore, personal significance and meaning often elude social confirmation – what a treasured photograph means to me may be personal, subjective, and idiosyncratic (cf. Richins 1994). Photographic collections and albums, posters, and popular culture photos in one's possession also reveal parts of the life story. We select particular photographs – to enlarge, to send as holiday greeting cards, to make into refrigerator magnets, to frame – to represent ourselves to others as well as to ourselves. For example, many of the photographic examples I chose to write about here are of water and boats, which represent an important and emotionally charged thematic line of my life story. My father and uncle are both deeply connected to boats – sailing, skiing, and fishing – and one of my favorite photographs is the two of them in a small sailing boat, taken about 1950 (see Plate 7.2). It frames two men who have been influential and contentious figures in my life story. I spent time growing up around boats and have lived near the coast for most of my adult life. For this consumer/interpreter/ researcher, these photographs of water and boats are compelling, interesting, and important as the ideological setting of my life story.

Visual consumer research

Like Belk (Chapter 11 in this book), I believe that a visual approach assumes an appreciation of photography and the visual arts from within an art-centered discourse. The use of photographs and photography in consumer research repre- sents a departure from traditional information-processing approaches in that it allows photographs to serve as stimuli or data for researchers. However, the complex nature of photography as a representational practice underscores the problems of relying on traditional methods in representing consumers. Techno- logical advances that enable photographs to be digitally manipulated are making more apparent the fact that photographs depend on context for meaning and do not necessarily create objective records of reality. I suggest that consumer researchers, rather than treating photographs and photography as vehicles to discover truth, instead turn to photography to complicate and disrupt ways of representing consumers. Part of this turn to photography ought to invoke the critical discourse of aesthetics and art history – the humanities disciplines that investigate art and its objects as cultural documents. Photographic practice is an essential component of the consumer's self-representation. Photographs represent an important path to understanding identity, one that is constructed by the assumptions and uses of photography that developed along with the medium. In this discourse, photographs can be considered objects that reflect and shape the culture that produces and preserves them, and critical attention can be focused on the social and cultural contexts in which artists have worked and the technical factors that affect artistic execution. Central issues to be addressed include evaluation, aesthetics, classification, identification, comparison, and monetary value. Like literary criticism, art criticism is characterized by a myriad of schools employing a variety of approaches to the subject, context, meaning, and production processes (Stern 1989). Photography and photographs are much more than secondary data – they are crucial issues in consumer identity construction. In the next sections, I move from issues of representing consumers to those of consuming representation.

The gaze

The *gaze* is one of the most influential concepts in the study of photography. Gaze has been written about from feminist, psychoanalytic, historical, and psychological perspectives (Adams 1996; Olin 1996). To gaze implies more than to look at – it signifies a psychological relationship of power, in which the gazer is superior to the object of the gaze. For example, film has been called an instrument of the male gaze, producing representations of women, the good life, and sexual fantasy from a male point of view (Mulvey 1989). Royalty gaze upon their subjects, viewed as property in the kingdom. Explorers gaze upon newly discovered land as colonial resources (Pratt 1992). Interpersonally, the gaze "corresponds to desire, the desire for self-completion through another" (Olin 1996: 215). Photographs represent the gaze through subject matter and its relationship to the viewer and photographer. John Urry extended the concept of gaze in his work on tourism – he calls attention to status differences by referring to the tourist gaze. The tourist gaze is not a static entity, for:

> . . . the gaze in any historical period is constructed in relationship to its opposite, to non-tourist forms of social experience and consciousness. What makes a particular tourist gaze depends upon what it is contrasted with; what the particular forms of non-tourist experience happen to be.
>
> (Urry 1990: 2)

In his study of Kenyan safari tourism, anthropologist Kenneth Little concludes that:

> the metaphor of the gaze generates the tourist perspective . . . mass tourism colonizes the imagination through the construction of the tourist perspective and the consequences of tourist colonialism are no less deep-seated or penetrating than the more familiar economic and political expression of colonialism.
>
> (Little 1991: 149–50)

Recent writers on the gaze urge us to turn the gaze upon ourselves, so that we see ourselves as we gaze, but warn that "to visualize looking is not as easy as it might appear. What might seem to be a purely visual theory, or a theory of pure vision, has become lost in the mysteries of human relationships" (Olin 1996: 218). Gaze, then, relates to the identity of the one who gazes and the object of the gaze. Let us gaze on this project.

Consumer research has turned its gaze to many exotic fields recently, visiting various humanities and social science fields as resources. Just as I am the tourist in representations of Hawaii, I also am a tourist in the field of art and photography. Although I am aware of the problems of the tourist gaze, I am not prepared to stay home for the rest of my days. I introduce this metaphor as a travel advisory for consumer researchers venturing into foreign fields. We often have differing (and perhaps conflicting) goals, methods, and theories from those of native researchers on home turf. Are your bags packed? For insights into representing consumers, let us look at two contemporary artists who represent identity in their work.

Artistic approaches to photographing identity

With the rise of photography departments in prominent museums, most notably the Museum of Modern Art in New York, photography has established itself as an art form. Artists, at first interested in photography as an aid to sketching and preparatory work, began to appropriate it as an expressive medium and invented many new forms, including the photo montage, the surrealist photo, the manipulated photo, and film (Stokstad 1995). Many contemporary photographers deal directly with consumer behavior in their work. Two, Barbara Kruger and Peter Menzel, seem especially relevant to issues of representing consumers. Whereas Kruger's work is viewed as fine art and comments on the use of propaganda (see Hupfer 1997), Menzel's work is seen as popular and straightforward. Nonetheless, each offers consumer researchers a wealth of material and a distinct vantage point from which to consider representational issues (Zaltman 1991).

Barbara Kruger

Buy me, I'll change your life.
(Barbara Kruger)

Perhaps best known for her photograph "I shop therefore I am," Barbara Kruger's photo montages combine text and found images to address a host of representational issues relevant to consumer culture, economic power, gender identity, and ethics. Formerly a picture editor for the Condé Nast publishing house, her work has appeared on billboards, book covers, shopping bags, and in museums worldwide. She is also a writer – her columns appear regularly in *Art Forum* and other outlets and have been collected in a book (Kruger 1994). Her message resonates with consumer researchers whose work reflects the notion that consumption is a critical component of identity. The work resembles an advertisement or a flyer for an event, but defies typical genres: "her wily manipulations elude aesthetic categorization: no formal criteria can explain them, just as they do not lodge easily within the established traditions of posters, art photography, and so on" (Linker, in Kruger 1990: 13). She focuses on the power of representation, for by means of "her arsenal of visual devices, Kruger proposes to intervene in stereotypical representations, disrupting their power, displacing their hold, and clearing a space for enlightened awareness" (Linker, in Kruger 1990: 12).

The linking of culture and consumption mimics marketing discourse by appropriating peppy slogans, juxtaposing image and text, and combining with persuasive consumption directives to provide a complex web of meaning and representation. Kruger's work subsumes publicity for its own purposes, "invoking the snares and innuendoes by which the viewer is beckoned and captivated" (Linker, in Kruger 1990: 75). She calls attention to the strategies of the marketplace, much as Andy Warhol marketed himself as a brand name (Schroeder 1997a). Yet unlike Warhol, she seems to maintain a critical stance toward commodification and consumer culture. However, the works of both are readily appropriated by the market (Schroeder 1992). Much of the irony of her "I shop therefore I am" was lost when the *New York Times Magazine* reprinted it to publicize its advertising possibilities. Still, Kruger's work remains optimistic in its power to reshape representation: "if sexual roles are constructed in representation, they can also be revised and restructured in discourse" (Linker, in Kruger 1990: 63). Kruger's work interrogates consumer culture by highlighting its role in representing identity. If consumers create themselves by shopping, what kinds of identities are available to them? Of course, "I shop therefore I am" appropriates Descartes famous maxim "I think therefore I am." For hundreds of years, philosophers have argued over the implications of that statement – perhaps Kruger's words will provide as much insight for consumer researchers.

Peter Menzel

Material World: A Global Family Portrait (Menzel 1994) was published in time for the holiday season in 1994. It is a book of photographs of "average" families in thirty countries around the world, showing their possessions, living quarters, and family members "to capture, through photos and statistics, both the common humanity of the peoples inhabiting our Earth and the great differences in material goods and circumstances that make rich and poor societies" (Kennedy 1994: 7). The book also presents information about each family's country that includes economic, health, and demographic statistics. In addition, a ranking of each country on various measures such as population density, infant mortality, and the level of affluence is provided. The book presents a detailed methodology section, articulating the way that each family was selected to represent "a cross-section of the world with special emphasis on fast-growing Pacific Rim economies, former enemies of the United States . . . " (Menzel 1994: 11). The book has been quite successful and has spawned a CD-ROM, a sequel entitled *Women in the Material*

World (D'Aluisio and Menzel 1996), a paperback edition, and a video series (see Belk, Chapter 11 in this book).

Material World is a provocative source of secondary data about consumer representation dealing with crosscultural issues, the relationship between economic conditions and materialism, and the way consumers from diverse cultures are represented in photography (see Belk, Chapter 11). Moreover, the book exemplifies photographers' representation of consumers and their possessions, previously elicited in similar projects by documentary photography researchers such as Lutz and Collins (1993), Rabinowitz (1994), Rosler (1989), and Tagg (1989), and useful for consumer researchers who probe into concerns of representation and identity. Readers of *Material World* consume representations of identity largely shaped by the photographer's gaze.

In Menzel's book, the main photo of each family shows the family outside its house, with all of their possessions piled around them as if in a massive yard sale. The cover of the book contrasts a U.S. family from Texas – posed outside a ranch house surrounded by photographs, furniture, appliances, pickup trucks, electronic goods, and the family dog – with a family from Bhutan, surrounded by goats, metal bowls, hand-held farming implements, and bright clothes. Each family photograph is indexed by the authors, and all possessions are listed (including some that are not shown in the photo), along with commentary by the photographer and members of the family. This enables the book to serve as an excellent data source that represents consumers as seen by a particular team of talented photographers.

However, straightforward content analysis limits our ability to engage in thick description (Geertz 1973). That is, a scooter in one country may be the main form of transportation for the entire family, whereas in another country it is merely a teenager's toy. An interpretive approach informed by photographic criticism offers consumer researchers a frame to describe, disrupt, and deconstruct a project such as *Material World*. Note that I consider *Material World* an excellent book and I believe that the author and photographers took care to present their subjects in a humane and fair manner. However, issues of representation offer insight into how people are represented (as consumers, as owners, as family members) by others within society (Rook 1991). Menzel and his team of photographers specifically set out to represent countries in the project. Therefore, the representativeness of these photos is a critical issue. Moreover, the choices made in selecting the individual families, photos, material goods, and the nuclear family unit are political and ethical choices. Whether these photographs create, confirm, or disrupt negative cultural stereotypes is a compelling issue.

Although these photographs differ from personal family photographs in terms of their purpose, their setting, and their technical perfection, "all the ideologies incorporated into domestic photography – democracy, choice, fun, leisure – are reproduced on a large scale in public photographs that, in modeling themselves on the family photograph's format, can more easily tap 'family values'" (Williamson 1986a: 125). The dominant representational theme in *Material World* is its emphasis on the family as the core organizing unit, for the family represents the natural form of social organization and the center of identity. Certainly the family is a critical influence in these matters. However, the family is normalized by privileging it over other identifiers in human life (social group, couple, individual, tribe). These representations have implications for researchers interested in family decision-making, social influence, and family values. Furthermore, the book provokes an implicit comparison of poorer countries to the US by means of selection of the cover photos, choice of photographers, and, more subtly, emphasis on mass-produced possessions in the photos and text. Much like *National Geographic*, the *Material World* project allows us to gaze at the "other" (Lalvani 1995; Torgovnick 1990; Urry 1990).

Consuming representations in the construction of identity

> If the photographer's attitude is open, frank and friendly, all barriers will come down and he will capture on film his impression of a person, a people, and a nation.
>
> (*Time-Life Guide to Travel Photography* 1972: 199)

> A photograph is an artifact that can be analyzed with some reference to – but not reducible to – its makers' institutional context, constraints, intentions, and unconscious motives on the one hand, or, on the other, its readers' constructions of meaning.
>
> (Lutz and Collins 1993: 88)

> What those of us who study visual representations need right now – if we are going to continue to produce new and unsettling questions rather than just tacitly reproduce canonized knowledge – is the disorderliness of spaces in conflict, the mayhem of the unknown, even if the resulting intellectual fracas sometimes feels like hell.
>
> (Holly 1996: 41)

When the photographer Garry Winogrand died in 1984, he left over 100,000 undeveloped photographs behind. A team of curators is slowly processing them – chemically, aesthetically, and psychologically – discovering that "Winogrand has given us a body of work that provides a new clue to what photography might become, a body of work that remains dense, troubling, unfinished, and profoundly challenging" (Szarkowski 1988: 41). In publishing some prints from this work, curator John Szarkowski states that any selection will not be representative of Winogrand's work: "we might say instead that these pictures were chosen because they are consonant with and yet different from his earlier work" (1988: 9). The question of how to represent someone through photography, through a research report, or through writing is a complex one, with implications beyond the scope of

212

this chapter. However, photography allows consumers to participate in the practice of representing identity. In the following sections, representation in photography will be discussed, with particular focus on identity.

Winogrand photographed everything he saw – he always carried a camera or two, loaded and ready to go. He wanted to make his photographs more interesting than whatever he photographed (Clarke 1997). Unlike many well-known photographers, he never knew what his photographs would be like: "he photographed in order to see what the things that interested him looked like as photographs" (Szarkowski 1988: 23). His photographs resemble snapshots – street scenes, parties, the zoo. A critical artistic difference between Winogrand's work and snapshots has been described this way: "the snapshooter thought he knew what the subject was in advance, and for Winogrand, photography was the process of discovering it" (Szarkowski 1988: 31). If we recall tourist photographic practice, the distinction becomes clear: tourists know beforehand what photographs of the Kodak Hula Show will look like. In contrast, Winogrand produced photographs of subjects that no one had thought of photographing. Often his subjects were unaware of his camera or indifferent to it. Winogrand was a major figure in post-war photography, yet his pictures often seem as if they are captured by chance. To him and other photographers in the 1950s, "the old pictures seemed planned, designed, conceived, understood in advance; they were little more than illustrations, in fact less, since they claimed to be something else – the exploration of real life" (Szarkowski 1988: 12). In this sense, the work of Garry Winogrand makes an interesting comparison to Ziller's research participants. Although Winogrand lived through photography, his work seems to depict everything but himself. His stated intention was not to document particular states or ideas, but to show what things looked like photographed. Winogrand's work remains central to his identity and now, of course, represents the photographer, for his photographs live on after his death.

Winogrand's use of photography was psychological, for he was a photographer "whose ambition was not to make good pictures, but through photography to know life" (Szarkowski 1988: 45). His teacher, Alexey Brodovitch, "fired his students with the idea that each of them was unique, and if they could describe their own perceptions their photographs would be good" (Szarkowski 1988: 12). Insistence that each person is unique counters the social science goals of classifying and categorizing, as well as mass-market segmentation practices. However, uniqueness is crucial in understanding the intersection of representation, identity, and photography, and the implications of stereotyped representations.

In Winogrand's "Circle Line Ferry, New York" (1971) (Plate 7.3), the two upper decks of a ferry are crowded with people straining to look at the sights and take in the summer scene: "like the photographer, everybody seems to be involved in the act of looking, so that we begin almost to see the world as a series of photographs" (Clarke 1997: 217). Two people seem isolated and more formally dressed and stiffly posed than the others – they are a couple, separated from the crowd, standing near the center of the boat, drinking from paper cups. They look as if

Plate 7.3 "Circle Line Ferry, New York" (Garry Winogrand 1971), courtesy Fraenkel Gallery, San Francisco, and the Estate of Garry Winogrand

they are attending a party, she carrying a white purse and sweater, he in a dark suit and tie. Amidst the crowd, they seem lost in thought, focused on themselves apart. The photo is balanced formally, for the couple are framed by the upper deck of the ferry and flank a supporting pole, which centers them in a classical manner. Winogrand shot straight at the crowd, focusing on the couple as the psychological and compositional center of the shot. They almost appear like rulers surrounded by their court attendants or the peasants under their care. We are left to wonder whether they are enjoying the ride and why they are not looking at the view. Are they tourists? Do they disdain the others, who appear to be of a lower class, and less aloof, more casually dressed than the couple? Even though the photo would make a nice souvenir of the journey, we realize that Winogrand did not take it for the couple, but for himself. Why was he interested in this scene? Perhaps the answer is because the scene says so much about Winogrand's own use of photography and the way he sees us seeing the world. In 1955 Winogrand made the first of many journeys across America: "there were pictures to be made out there" (Szarkowski 1988: 18). The photograph makes it seem as if he is not engaged in the ferry trip but, rather, is playing the role of the observer. The photograph also is interesting for consumer researchers, I think, in terms of recent calls for producing knowledge by turning to art (Belk 1998; Hupfer 1997; Schroeder 1997a).

Winogrand's picture happens to be a famous one – it is in the New York Museum of Modern Art's collection, is widely reproduced in textbooks on photography, and has been called "a definitive image of late twentieth-century life" (Clarke 1997: 217). What does this photo represent? More specifically, why did I choose to talk about this particular Winogrand photograph, one among hundreds of thousands of images? For I am consuming this representation through appropriation, discussion, and reproduction. How does this photo fit into my identity as a person and as a researcher? I must admit, when I began researching "Circle Line Ferry," I was surprised to discover it was so well known. Does this fame make this photograph more representative or less? For me, it was some confirmation of my eye or taste perhaps and meant I might need to do less to justify the discussion here. After all, it is an important image. As for its narrative meaning to me, it reminds me of a photograph of myself taken during an Istanbul marketing conference boating excursion on the Bosphorus. That photo captures important aspects of my identity as a traveler in an exotic land, a researcher presenting at an international conference, and a passenger on a boat. It represents an important ideological setting, a central theme, and an imagoe in my life story. Again, a family connection to boats is made in my choice of a representative photo – an academic who sails around the world presenting his research. Thus, this photograph and my choice of the Winogrand photograph represent my identity in complex ways – some pleasing, some troubling. I identify with the tourist and the tourist scenario: vacationing, being served, traveling to exotic lands. My identification is compelling but also unsettling. Who has constructed this image of tourism for me? What are its echoes in colonialist discourse and practice (Pratt 1992)? What are my objectives in assuming the tourist guise in travel and in research?

Often, when observing photographers on vacation, I notice a once-removed quality of their interactions. Each event is experienced as a photo opportunity, every new place a backdrop for a family picture. Postmodern theorists have also noted the spectacle of media-led society (Debord 1994). Since its invention, photography has been intimately connected with travel, and travel photographs have largely replaced travel logs as a method of remembering trips. Moreover, travel has become an excuse to take photographs: "we travel not just to be on the way, but to take pictures along the way" (Time-Life Editorial Staff 1972: 18). Photography provides direction and structure to travel. Consuming representation through showing, displaying, and discussing photographs of travel is important in establishing one's identity as a traveler, adventurer, sophisticate, or purist. Travel photographs, then, become chapter headings in the life story, helping to establish setting, character, and mood (McAdams 1985).

In the following sections, I review several research projects on representations of identity that integrate a social science perspective with photographic practice and criticism to enrich our understanding of critical issues in consumer representation.

Representing gender identity

> The rendition of structurally important social arrangements and ultimate beliefs which ceremony fleetingly provides the senses, still photography can further condense, omitting temporal sequence and everything else except static visual arrays. And what is caught is fixed into permanent accessibility, becoming something that can be attended anywhere, for any length of time, and at moments of one's own choosing.
>
> (Goffman 1976: 10)

In Bruce Weber's photograph "Bruce and Talisa on my Chris Craft, Bellport" (1982), a good looking couple sit perched on the rear deck of a small powerboat (see Plate 7.4). They are under way – the boat's wake trails off into a large, calm body of water. Deep in thought, the man sits in a pose reminiscent of Rodin's "The Thinker," his head resting gently on his hand, which is in turn propped on his thigh. The woman is in a position that Goffman describes as "licensed withdrawal." She is leaning into the man, her head is thrown back onto his shoulder, and her eyes are closed. They appear to be lovers enjoying a warm weather ride on the ocean. What strikes me about this pose is its irony: while appearing natural and realistic, it is actually quite ritualized. Weber, a well-known advertising photographer, is noted for his work for Calvin Klein. His work is characterized by its provocation, and he crosses the traditional boundary between commercial

Plate 7.4 "Bruce and Talisa on my Chris Craft, Bellport" (Bruce Weber 1982), courtesy of the artist and Robert Miller Gallery, New York

photography and art photography. I am drawn to this image for its sheer beauty as well as for its power to summon up my memories of Lake Michigan boat rides – memories that are well represented in photographs. I suppose that I identify with the male figure and all that he seems to enjoy, yet I also find the stereotypical pose problematic. For now, let it serve as an example of sociologist Erving Goffman's brilliant comments on representations of gender identity.

Goffman's study of gender advertisements in photographs grounds a technique for deftly combining nonverbal, symbolic, sociological, and biological analyses. His technique uses close observation of pervasive sex differences in advertising photographs in terms of posture, gesture, touching, and gaze. His central insight is that photographs serve as markers of identity by representing status and power. Advertising confirms social stereotypes about gender roles and the relations of power in depictions of body posture and stereotypical posing conventions. For example, women in ads are consistently posed in deferential positions, lying down or physically below men. Goffman focuses our attention on standard advertising poses that signal women's vulnerability to men, magnified by disparities between the physical power of the sexes. Thus, men are portrayed as larger, more powerful, and dominant, whereas women are represented as smaller, weaker, and submissive. A conventional posture for a woman is reclining: on a bed, a couch, the floor, or the ground. This is a tremendously vulnerable pose: "a recumbent position is one from which physical defense of oneself can least well be initiated . . ." (Goffman 1979: 41). The woman is exposed and defenseless, serving only to advertise the product's and her own availability. Moreover, her identity is obscured and trivialized.

Many advertisements show play or mock assaults – men are engaged in what appears to be playful aggression toward women, either carrying them, grabbing them, or covering their eyes from behind in the guise of play. These poses demonstrate the male's power and potential aggression (Goffman 1979), made less threatening because we know that they are "only playing" (the upbeat ad copy and the woman's smiles and apparent lack of fear). However, even though "mock assault" represents play at one level, at a deeper symbolic level it reinforces the relation between men and women. Goffman encourages us "to attend to how those who compose (and pose for) pictures can choreograph the materials available in social situations in order to achieve their end, namely, the presentation of a scene that is meaningful, whose meaning can be read at a flash" (Goffman 1979: 27). Representations of gender are a critical site in contesting and interrogating the issue of control over representation. Gender identity is a charged, important concept for consumer researchers interested in representation.

Representations of identity in National Geographic magazine

If you want to save something from exploitation, *don't photograph it.*
(John Szarkowski, in Goldberg 1997: B2)

Szarkowski's curious statement refers specifically to wilderness. Photographs of Western marvels such as the Old Faithful geyser and Yosemite were a powerful tool in the creation of the national park system (Newhall 1982). Szarkowski, an influential photography curator at the Museum of Modern Art in New York,

stands in contrast to the goals of social documentary photographers, early anthropologists, and the National Geographic Society, which in one way or another have
sought to preserve or change by calling attention to vanishing ways of life (Becker
1992; Guimond 1991; Rabinowitz 1994; Stange 1989). *National Geographic*, as an
icon of travel photography throughout the world, is an excellent vehicle for
investigating representations of identity in popular and widely circulated images.

An interesting and powerful analysis of the popular iconic magazine that is
cluttering up basements all over the world is presented in a book called *Reading
National Geographic*, coauthored by an anthropologist and a sociologist (Lutz and
Collins 1993). The researchers read the magazine and its production and consumption as a cultural text of difference, identity, representation, and domination.
They specifically focus on *National Geographic*'s famous and respected photographs.
Lutz and Collins attend to "the formal features of the shot such as composition
and point of view, but . . . interpret them in the historical and cultural context
that gives the photograph and its elements their meaning and significance" (Lutz
and Collins 1993: 5). They emphasize that:

> . . . ultimately, the evaluation should be based not on the intentions of
> the magazine's makers but on the consequences of its photographic
> rhetoric. In what ways do these photos change or reinforce ideas about
> others held by their readers? . . . how might these photos influence the
> practices of readers – as voters, neighbors to new immigrants, as white
> male coworkers with blacks and women, as consumers of products
> marketed as exotic?
>
> (Lutz and Collins 1993: 117)

Lutz and Collins conducted interviews with production staff, executives, photographers, and readers, and engaged in a critical analysis of the formal properties
of individual and collective photographs. Several themes emerged that resonated
with other descriptions of the representational processes of exoticism and primitivism (Borgerson and Schroeder 1997; Chow 1997; Lalvani 1995; Rushing 1992;
Torgovnick 1990; Urry 1990). In representing a world brightly different, "the
people of the third and fourth worlds are portrayed as *exotic*; they are *idealized*; they
are *naturalized* and taken out of all but a single historical narrative; and they are
sexualized" (Lutz and Collins 1993: 89). Dress, pose, gaze, and nudity are important photographic sites of difference in the photographs. For example, *National
Geographic* has a tradition of depicting naked women from so-called primitive
societies. Lutz and Collins point out that

> . . . none of the hundreds of women whose breasts were photographed
> were white-skinned . . . In this regard, then, their photographs play a
> central role in allowing the art of photography to exist silently beneath
> a scientific agenda and thereby increase readership and further legit-
> imate the *Geographic*'s project as one of both beauty and truth. All of this

elaborate structure of signification, however, is built on a foundation of racial and gender subordination: in this context, one must first be black and female to do this kind of symbolic labor.

(Lutz and Collins 1993: 115).

Reading National Geographic is as an exemplar of consumer research on photographic representations of identity. According to Lutz and Collins, *National Geographic* represents fine color photography itself and has served as an impetus in the marketing of photographic equipment and activities since its inception. At the same time, it reifies distinctions between the worlds of the West and the East, the primitive and the modern, the tourist and the native.

The June 1997 issue of *National Geographic's* cover story is "French Polynesia: Charting a New Course." The cover photo, the winner of a *National Geographic* web site contest, shows a woman in profile, wearing a garland of flowers on her head, a necklace of black pearls, softly backlit by the Polynesian sun. She is immediately recognizable as a representative of a type: an exotic native on a tropical island (Williamson 1986b). Inside the magazine, the story opens with a spectacular photograph (Plate 7.1) of a tourist scene captioned: "With strong arms and obliging souls, Tahitians usher ashore French vacationers after a lagoon cruise on an outrigger canoe" – an important clue to how this representation should be read (Benchley 1997). This image is a rich source for investigating the meanings conveyed by and about the post-colonial world. Its denotative meaning is clear: the tourists are visiting a beautiful tropical island and are being helped ashore, perhaps to prevent their clothes from getting wet even though the water is only ankle deep. Connotations of this photograph include issues of enjoyment, post-colonial economics, power and domination, inequity, consuming the exotic, and representations of the "other." For example, the photograph depicts a relationship between the French couple and the Tahitians marked by service, support, and subordination. The French couple represent the colonial history of France, the West, and whiteness. Furthermore, their corpulent state signifies abundance and gluttony. The Tahitians are represented as happy; their smiles signify pleasure in performing their role; and their authentic dress signifies the primitive. Moreover, by selecting this shot, the photographer and the editors portray tourists and natives interacting, a rare event, typified by the tourist gaze. The Tahitians play a role scripted by the economically important tourist industry and are portrayed in a stereotypical and clichéd manner that imparts representational power to the photograph. It is clear with whom the viewer is meant to identify (Lutz and Collins 1993).

This is not to suggest an essentialist view of identity representation, however, for it is difficult to disrupt this photograph's meaning without resorting to irony or parody, qualities largely absent in *National Geographic*. Aesthetically satisfying as this photo is, its connotative meanings bring up many disturbing issues of representation. The identities it contains look necessary, "as if the identity naturally befitted the people, rather than the people's being fitted to it through many social facts and practice, including representational ones" (Walker 1997: 303). To focus on one example, try to imagine the French and the Tahitians trading roles (Stern 1993). By considering the psychological, social, economic, and cultural relations between the two couples depicted in the photograph, we gain a greater appreciation and understanding of its hidden structure (Clarke 1997).

Influenced by the *National Geographic*'s marketing department and cognizant of its prestige in the world of media, Lutz and Collins under-emphasize the influence of advertising in the magazine's pages. The consumer world represented in the advertising photographs – automobiles, camera equipment, tourist destinations – assures the affluent Western viewers that the world welcomes them. The authors report that the marketing department would prefer more stories on cute animals and fewer about environmental destruction or political issues. Lutz and Collins's contribution lies in detailing the way that a seemingly banal popular magazine with beautiful pictures contributes to problematic representational practices that preserve the global status quo of the haves and the have-nots. *Reading National Geographic* is an exemplar of research that uncovers a complex web of meaning in photography as representation and representation through photographic practice. Conventions of photography – editorial selection, subject selection, pose – interact to produce stereotypical representations that influence our conceptions of the world.

Film

> Learning to read books – or pictures, or films – is not just a matter of acquiring information from texts, it is a matter of learning to read and write the texts of our lives.
>
> (Scholes 1989: 19)

Film is an important research technique for studying human behavior that represents by means of images, story, and sound. In this section, I focus on two studies of popular filmed representation, Holbrook and Grayson's analysis of the film *Out of Africa* and E. Ann Kaplan's analysis of Music Television (MTV). Kaplan's study brings out issues of representing identity by narrative analysis, and Holbrook and Grayson's article is open to reinterpretation in terms of issues of representation, gaze, and identity raised in this chapter. In writing about film, I am reminded of my first encounter with interpretive consumer research, one which became central to my identity.

My first attendance at a marketing conference was the American Marketing Association winter conference in 1988 in San Diego. A graduate student in social psychology at the time, I attended as a "tourist" at the invitation of Professor Franco Nicosia. One sight I particularly remember was Morris Holbrook's talk on semiotic research, in which he performed an analysis of the film *Gremlins* as an illustrative example. Holbrook (1988) found anti-consumption themes in the film and showed excerpts of the gremlins engaged in consumer mayhem as they terrorized the heroes. Although I realize now that the conference theme of "A Return to Broader Dimensions" was dominated by interpretive researchers, I was struck by the opportunities and threats inherent in Holbrook's approach (see Campbell 1996). Coming from an experimental background, I wondered about issues of validity, generalizability, and accuracy. I now find inspiration in Barthes' point that "criticism is not science. Science deals with meanings, criticism produces them" (1987: 79). Looking back, I realize that that conference is an important nuclear event in my life story. My interest in psychometric matters is still with me, but it was overwhelmed by questions of interpretation and representation raised that day.

Film remains an important yet understudied resource for consumer researchers. Holbrook and Grayson's (1986) analysis of *Out of Africa*, a film based on the Isak Dinesen novel, remains a key work in this area. Representations of Africa as an exotic, natural continent are reflected in Hillary Clinton's report in *Vogue* about her 1997 continental visit:

> . . . as a child, I imagined exploring the Blue Nile, Victoria Falls, the Serengeti, and other exotic places I discovered through books and movies . . . after I read Isak Dinesen, I longed to sleep in a tent where I could hear the lions roar at night.
>
> (Clinton 1997: 188)

Her representation of Africa exoticizes and obscures African identity by leaving out the people who live there and ignoring the political strife that has plagued Africa in the post-colonial period.

Holbrook and Grayson analyze *Out of Africa's* narrative elements of plot, character, setting, and themes to illustrate "the role that an in-depth analysis of symbolic consumption can play in clarifying the meanings conveyed by a work of art" (1986: 375). The goal of this project is to use consumer behavior to understand art. This is characteristic of the tourist gaze in that the goals of the tourist/researcher may be quite different from the artist/native. Consumption symbolism may clarify certain meanings relevant to Holbrook and Grayson's experience, but these meanings may not represent the work to interested others. Recognizing this concern, the researchers ask "which is more important, valuable, or otherwise central to consumer research: using artworks to understand consumption or using consumption to understand works of art?" (ibid.: 380). Holbrook and Grayson favor the latter, the pursuit of consumer research for its own sake. My position is that works of art help us understand how we live in a consumer society, how we construct our identities, and how we represent ourselves through consumption (Schroeder 1997b). In reviewing their *Out of Africa* analysis, I note that Holbrook and Grayson ignore issues of colonialism, oppression, and domination of Africa by Europeans, and fail to acknowledge the colonialist gaze (Pratt 1992). To be more inclusive and insightful, visual consumer research needs to incorporate an ethics of representation informed by social historical, art historical, and political factors. An example of this type of research is found in Kaplan's study of the Music Television channel (MTV).

In one of the first books to analyze MTV as an important popular culture form, Kaplan (1987) distinguishes five types of rock music videos – romantic, socially conscious, nihilist, classical, and postmodernist – to which most MTV videos can be linked. Representation of desire, class struggles, gender and sexuality, and identity centers Kaplan's analysis, which is informed by interdisciplinary postmodern thought. She looks at male and female performer videos and finds that "only those female representations considered to be the most marketable are frequently cycled . . . what is most marketable is obviously connected to dominant ideology . . . " (Kaplan 1987: 115).

Although MTV features stereotyped representations of gender identity, the medium is a forum for questioning, interrogating, and playing with gender roles. Kaplan cites Madonna's videos as an example of the male gaze turned back on men (Kaplan 1983; Traube 1992). She shows that

> . . . more than other programs, MTV positions the spectator in the mode of constantly hoping that the next ad-segment (of whatever kind) will satisfy the desire for plenitude: the channel keeps the spectator in the consuming mode more intensely because its items are all so short.
> (Kaplan 1987: 143)

She adds that insofar as "MTV constantly comments upon the self in relation to image (especially the TV image) . . . that may be seen as its main 'content'" (Kaplan 1987: 151).

Kaplan's study of MTV brings together many theoretical strands – film studies, feminist thought, literary studies, and marketing. She emphasizes MTV's institutional matrix, popular music's historical background, youth culture, and postmodern approaches to culture. Therefore, she is able to situate her analysis within the broader cultural context to draw out implications of representation. She also acknowledges the role of the viewer in creating story lines. Insofar as video is central to the lives of consumers, an understanding of photographic practice and the cultural forces that produce and consume images is critical for discussing issues of representation. Film produces life stories and cultural meaning – representations on film help shape broader cultural representations, which "figure in distorted interactions between people, patterned in ways that transcend individual whims, tastes, blind spots, or biases" (Walker 1997: 302). In her analysis of contemporary Chinese film, literary theorist Rey Chow sums up the relationships between film and representation this way:

> What needs to be theorized and articulated is the fact that more so than literature and art, film – even mainstream film – . . . contributes ever more urgently to the ongoing process of "writing culture" that have

become such a daily phenomenon in the *shared*, common visual spaces of our postcolonial, postmodern world.

(Chow 1997: 28)

Conclusion

> Across the social sciences and humanities [scholars are investigat-ing] the question of how people represent various kinds of human differences – racial/ethnic, gender, historical and class – to them-selves and each other. Most important is the fact that those under-standings or strategies for describing human differences have helped create and reproduce social hierarchies. At the least, those hierarchies have created small humiliations and rejections, and have lessened opportunities. At the worst, they have abetted wars of exterminations, lynchings, and rape. Representations may be deployed for or against such horrors or indifferently in relation to them, but they are never irrelevant, never unconnected to the world of actual social relations.
>
> (Lutz and Collins 1993: 3)

In her discussion of representational practices and moral recognition, the philosopher Margaret Urban Walker develops the concept of stereo-graphy to refer to the interrelationship of representation to ethical issues. Stereo-graphy refers to ways of representing groups of people in particular ways that "school us in perceiving certain patterns of human expression and comportment in particular ways or not at all" (Walker 1997: 313). Walker discusses Orientalist representa-tions (Said 1978 and 1993), pornography, and images of African famines as cogent examples of "practices of representing certain people in certain ways, where these ways are consistently different from the ways *other* people are represented" (Walker 1997: 309). She takes pains not to suggest that these representational practices "are the sole or even primary causes of moral mis-recognition or mis-treatments [and] might be symptomatic or expressive of prejudices propagated and sustained by other means" (ibid.: 313). Walker's theory is an important component of the ethics of representation that takes the signifying power of photographs seriously (Borgerson and Schroeder 1997). Certain groups are portrayed in stereo-graphed ways in cultural representations that undermine their identities and contribute to biased understandings about them. Consumer researchers are uniquely poised to address the contribution of consuming representation to these phenomena by bringing expertise in consumption processes to bear on a critical issue.

Those of us who represent others through our research need to question what it means to have that power. The gaze in its tourist and researcher guise is an important concept to address in consumer research, for it creates an awareness of the process of surveying, looking, and consuming the visual world (Hudson and Ozanne 1988). The metaphor is a useful reminder to consumer researchers on safari, out to collect useful trophies from other fields. The lesson is that we must avoid focusing on the details of our gaze, to the exclusion of the objects of the gaze, lest we undermine the gaze's moral intention and interpretive power (Chow 1997). A start might be to reconsider representing people solely as consumers, for our identities and life stories surely comprise more than consumption. Further, our focus on consuming representation underscores the political and ethical implications of this practice. Every representation of a woman, an African, or a consumer has the potential to construct the way society represents those categories, "and some of those representations can in fact do extraordinary powerful – or harmful – cultural and political work" (Bérubé 1997: B4). Representations are part of the lived experience; they construct reality. "Whose representation?" is a critical question framed by the use of photography in the dominant cultural discourse that consistently misrepresents as much as it represents (cf. Minh-Ha 1991; Rosler 1989; Goldberg 1996). Consumer research has come far in describing, predicting, and interpreting the ways that people consume and the influence of consumer culture worldwide. Representation remains a vital area for discussion, discourse, and disagreement.

Approaching visual representation within consumer research via semiotics offers researchers a grounded method that is able to account for political and ethical issues. As art historian Keith Moxey argues:

> . . . semiotics makes us aware that the cultural values with which we make sense of the world are a tissue of conventions that have been handed down from generation to generation by the members of the culture of which we are a part. It reminds us that there is nothing "natural" about our values; they are social constructs that not only vary enormously in the course of time but differ radically from culture to culture.
>
> (Moxley 1994: 61)

Representing consumers is always a political act. Consumer researchers ought to recognize this as part of the crisis of representation and work toward discussing ethical issues in representation as a key concern within the discipline.

Photography clearly highlights representation as a central issue in understanding consumers' lives, and underscores problems in the attempt to represent "reality." Photographs show many realities and help construct narratives of existence. In this chapter I have tried to blend personal and theoretical approaches to interpret photographs, describe identity construction, and discuss my own consumption of representation in order to sketch a theory of consuming representation. Moreover, I played the role of the tourist as I traveled to several areas far away from information-processing consumer research. By interrogating our own roles as consumers, tourists, and researchers, we start on the path of recognizing the power of representation – a key process of experiencing the world.

Consumers consume representations through watching, seeking, photographing, and remembering. Photography as a product, process, practice, and popular art form exists as a fundamental vehicle for constructing identity through the life story. As such, it serves as an important resource for consumer researchers beyond its usefulness as experimental data. The research reviewed here brims with relevance to the consumer research project and provides evidence of the possibilities of visually oriented consumer research. Although photography is not the objective technique for representing truth that was promised, it turns out to be much more than this ephemeral positivist phenomenon. Photography is a critical element in both forming and representing our individual and cultural identities.

Acknowledgments

Thanks to Barbara Stern and Russell Belk for support, encouragement, and suggestions on this chapter. Also, thanks to Judith Tolnick, Curator, University of Rhode Island Fine Arts Galleries for help with photo research. Preparation of this chapter was supported by the University of Rhode Island Center for the Humanities and the University of Rhode Island Alumni Association Faculty Fund.

References

Adams, L.S. (1996) *The Methodologies of Art*, New York: Harper Collins.

Arnheim, R. (1957) *Film as Art*, Berkeley: University of California Press.

Barrett, T. (1990) *Criticizing Photographs: An Introduction to Understanding Images*, Mountain View, CA: Mayfield Press.

Barthes, R. (1981) *Camera Lucida: Reflections on Photography*, trans. R. Howard, New York: Noonday.

—— (1987) *Criticism and Truth*, trans. K.P. Keuneman, Minneapolis: University of Minnesota Press.

Baxandall, M. (1987) *Patterns of Intention: On the Historical Explanation of Pictures*, New Haven, CT: Yale University Press.

Bearden, W.O., Netemeyer, R.G., and Teel, J.E. (1989) "Measurement of Consumer Susceptibility to Interpersonal Influence," *Journal of Consumer Research*, 15: 473–81.

Becker, K. (1992) "Picturing Our Past: An Archive Constructs a National Culture," *Journal of American Folklore*, 105, 415: 3–18.

Belk, R.W. (1986) "Art versus Science as Ways of Generating Knowledge about Materialism," in D. Brinberg and R.J. Lutz (eds) *Perspectives on Methodology in Consumer Research*, New York: Springer-Verlag, 3–36.

—— (1990) "The Role of Possessions in Constructing and Maintaining a Sense of the Past," in M.E. Goldberg, G. Gorn and R.W. Pollay (eds) *Advances in Consumer Research*, vol. 17, Provo, UT: Association for Consumer Research, 669–76.

—— (1995) *Collecting in a Consumer Society*, London: Routledge.

Benchley, P. (1997) "French Polynesia: Charting a New Course," *National Geographic*, 191 (June): 2–29.

Berger, J. (1972) *Ways of Seeing*, London: Penguin/BBC.

Bérubé, M. (1997) "The Cultural Representation of People with Disabilities Affects Us All," *Chronicle of Higher Education*, May 30, B4.

Borgerson, J.L. and Schroeder, J.E. (1997) "The Ethics of Representation – Packaging Paradise: Consuming the 50th State," *Colley Law Review*, 14 (3): 473–89.

Bourdieu, P. (1990) *Photography: A Middle-brow Art*, trans. S. Whiteside, Stanford, CA: Stanford University Press.

Campbell, C. (1996) "Romanticism, Consumption, and Introspection: Some Comments on Professor Holbrook's Paper," in R.W. Belk, N. Dholakia, and A. Venkatesh (eds) *Consumption & Marketing: Macro Dimensions*, Cincinnati, OH: South-Western, 96–103.

Chow, R. (1997) *Primitive Passions: Visuality, Sexuality, Ethnography, and Contemporary Chinese Cinema*, New York: Columbia University Press.

Clarke, G. (1997) *The Photograph*, Oxford: Oxford University Press.

Clinton, H.R. (1997) "African Odyssey," *Vogue* (June): 186–99, 280.

Collier, J. Jr. and Collier, M. (1986) *Visual Anthropology: Photography as a Research Method*, Albuquerque: University of New Mexico Press.

Coulter, R.H. and Zaltman, G. (1994) "Using the Zaltman Metaphor Elicitation Technique to Understand Brand Images," in C.T. Allen and D. Roedder John (eds) *Advances in Consumer Research*, vol. 21, Provo, UT: Association for Consumer Research, 501–7.

D'Aluisio, F. and Menzel, P. (1996) *Women in the Material World*, San Francisco: Sierra Club Books.

Debord, G. (1994) *The Society of the Spectacle*, trans. D. Nicholson-Smith, New York: Zone Books.

Durgee, J.F., Holbrook, M.B. and Sherry, J.F. (1991) "The Delivery and Consumption of Vacation Performances," in R.W. Belk (ed.) *Highways and Buyways: Naturalistic Research from the Consumer Behavior Odyssey*, Provo, UT: Association for Consumer Research, 131–40.

Edwards, E. (ed.) (1994) *Anthropology and Photography 1860–1920*, New Haven, CT: Yale University Press.

Frye, N. (1957) *Anatomy of Criticism: Four Essays*, Princeton, NJ: Princeton University Press.

Geertz, C. (1973) *The Interpretation of Cultures*, New York: Basic Books.

Goffman, E. (1979) *Gender Advertisements*, New York: Harper & Row.

Goldberg, V. (1996) "Photographs in History's Shifting Gaze," *New York Times*, section 2: 1, 16.

—— (1997) "A Photography Curator Narrows His Focus," *New York Times*, April 7: B1, B2.

Guimond, J. (1991) *American Photography and the American Dream*, Chapel Hill: University of North Carolina Press.

Havlena, W.J. and Holak, S.L. (1996) "Exploring Nostalgia Imagery through the Use of Consumer Collages," in K.P. Corfman and J.G. Lynch (eds) *Advances in Consumer Research*, vol. 23, Provo: UT: Association for Consumer Research, 35–42.

Heilemann, J. (1997) "Annals of Advertising: All Europeans are not Alike," *The New Yorker*, April 28/May 5: 174–81.

Heisley, D.A. and Levy, S.J. (1991) "Autodriving: A Photoelicitation Technique," *Journal of Consumer Research*, 18 (December): 257–73.

Heilsley, D.A. McGrath, M.A. and Sherry, J.F. (1991) " 'To Everything There is a Season:' A Photoessay of a Farmers' Market," in R.W. Belk (ed.) *Highways and Buyways: Naturalistic Research from the Consumer Behavior Odyssey*, Provo, UT: Association for Consumer Research, 141–66.

Heller, S. (1996) "Visual Images Replace Text as Focal Point for Many Scholars," *Chronicle of Higher Education*, July 19: A8–A9, A15.

Holbrook, M.B. (1988) "The Positivistic and Interpretive Sides of Semiotic Research on Artistic Consumption," paper presented at the American Marketing Association Winter Marketing Educators' Conference, San Diego, CA.

Holbrook, M. and Grayson, M.W. (1986) "The Semiology of Cinematic Consumption: Symbolic Consumer Behavior in Out of Africa," *Journal of Consumer Research*, 13 (December): 374–81.

Holly, M.A. (1996) "Saints and Sinners," *October*, 77 (Summer): 39–41.

Holt, D.B. (1995) "How Consumers Consume: A Taxonomy of Consumption Practices," *Journal of Consumer Research*, 22 (June): 1–16.

Hudson, L.A. and Ozanne, J.L. (1988) "Alternative Ways of Seeking Knowledge in Consumer Research," *Journal of Consumer Research*, 14 (March): 508–21.

Hupfer, M. (1997) "A Pluralistic Approach to Visual Communication: Reviewing Rhetoric and Representation in World War I Posters," in D. MacInnis and M. Brucks (eds) *Advances in Consumer Research*, vol. 24, Provo: Association for Consumer Research.

Kaplan, E.A. (1983) "Is the Gaze Male?" in A. Snitow, C. Stanell, and S. Thompson (eds) *Powers of Desire: The Politics of Sexuality*, New York: Monthly Review Press, 309–27.

—— (1987) *Rocking Around the Clock: Music Television, Postmodernism, & Consumer Culture*, New York: Routledge.

Kennedy, P. (1994) "Introduction," in Peter Menzel, *Material World: A Global Family Portrait*, San Francisco: Sierra Club Books.

Kozol, W. (1994) *Life's America: Family and Nation in Postwar Photojournalism*, Philadelphia: Temple University Press.

Kruger, B. (1990) *Love For Sale: The Words and Pictures of Barbara Kruger* [Text by Kate Linker], New York: Abrams.

—— (1994) *Remote Control: Power, Culture and the World of Appearances*, Cambridge: MIT.

Lalvani, S. (1995) "Consuming the Exotic Other," *Critical Studies in Mass Communication*, 12, 3: 263–75.

Little, K. (1991) "On Safari: The Visual Politics of a Tourist Representation," in D. Howes (ed.) *The Varieties of Sensory Experience: A Sourcebook in the Anthropology of the Senses*, Toronto: University of Toronto Press.

Lutz, C.A. and Collins, J.L. (1993) *Reading National Geographic*, Chicago: University of Chicago Press.

McAdams, D.P. (1985) *Power, Intimacy, and the Life Story*, Homewood, IL: Dorsey Press.

MacCannell, D. (1976) *The Tourist: A New Theory of the Leisure Class*, New York: Schocken.

McCracken, G. (1988) *Culture and Consumption: New Approaches to the Symbolic Character of Consumer Goods and Activities*, Bloomington: Indiana University Press.

Menzel, P. (1994) *Material World: A Global Family Portrait*, San Francisco: Sierra Club Books.

Mick, D.G. and Politti, L.G. (1989) "Consumers' Interpretations of Advertising Imagery: A Visit to the Hell of Connotation," in E.C. Hirschman (ed.) *Interpretive Consumer Research*, Provo, UT: Association for Consumer Research, 85–96.

Minh-Ha, T.T. (1991) *When the Moon Waxes Red: Representation, Gender, and Cultural Politics*, New York: Routledge.

Moxey, K. (1994) *The Practice of Theory: Poststructuralism, Cultural Politics, and Art History*, Ithaca, NY: Cornell University Press.

Mulvey, L. (1989) *Visual and Other Pleasures: Theories of Representation and Difference*, Bloomington: Indiana University Press.

Nash, D. (1996) *Anthropology of Tourism*, New York: Pergamon.

Newhall, B. (1982) *The History of Photography*, 5th edn, New York: Museum of Modern Art.

O' Guinn, T.C. and Shrum, L.J. (1997) "The Role of Television in the Construction of Consumer Reality," *Journal of Consumer Research*, 23 (March): 278–94.

Olin, M. (1996) "Gaze," in R.S. Nelson and R. Schiff (eds) *Critical Terms for Art History*, Chicago: University of Chicago Press, 208–19.

Pratt, M.L. (1992) *Imperial Eyes: Travel Writing and Transculturation*, New York: Routledge.

Rabinowitz, P. (1994) *They Must be Represented: The Politics of Documentary Photography*, London: Verso.

Richins, M.L. (1994) "Special Possessions and the Expression of Material Values," *Journal of Consumer Research*, 21 (December): 522–33.

Rook, D. (1991) "I Was Observed (In Absentia) and Autodriven by the Consumer Behavior Odyssey," in R.W. Belk (ed.) *Highways and Buyways: Naturalistic Research from the Consumer Behavior Odyssey*, Provo, UT: Association for Consumer Research, 48–58.

Rosenblum, N. (1994) *A History of Women Photographers*, New York: Abbeville Press.

Rosler, M. (1989) "In, Around, and Afterthoughts (On Documentary Photography)," in R. Bolton (ed.) *The Contest of Meaning: Critical Histories of Photography*, Cambridge: MIT Press, 303–42.

Rubenstein, H.R. (1982) "Collecting for Tomorrow: Sweden's Contemporary Documentation Program," *Museum News*, 63 (August): 55–60.

Rushing, W.J. (1992) "Marketing the Affinity of the Primitive and the Modern: René d'Harnoncourt and 'Indian Art of the United States'," in J. Berlo (ed.) *The Early Years of Native American History*, Seattle: University of Washington Press, 191–236.

Said, E. (1978) *Orientalism*, New York: Vintage.

—— (1993) *Culture and Imperialism*, New York: Vintage.

Scholes, R. (1989) *Protocols of Reading*, New Haven, CT: Yale University Press.

Schroeder, J.E. (1992) "Materialism and Modern Art," in F. Rudmin and M. Richins (eds) *Meaning, Measure, and Morality of Materialism*, Provo, UT: Association for Consumer Research, 10–14.

—— (1997a) "Andy Warhol: Consumer Researcher," in D. MacInnis and M. Brucks (eds) *Advances in Consumer Research*, vol. 24, Provo: Association for Consumer Research, 476–82.

—— (1997b) "Roots of Modern Marketing in Italian Renaissance Art," in A. Falkenberg (ed.) *Proceedings of the Macromarketing Seminar*, Bergen, Norway: Norwegian School of Economics and Business Administration.

Scott, L.A. (1994) "Images of Advertising; The Need for a Theory of Visual Rhetoric," *Journal of Consumer Research*, 21 (September): 252–73.

Sontag, S. (1977) *On Photography*, New York: Noonday.

Stange, M. (1989) *Symbols of Ideal Life: Documentary Photography in America 1890–1950*, Cambridge: Cambridge University Press.

Stokstad, M. (1995) *Art History*, New York: Abrams.

Stern, B.B. (1989) "Literary Criticism and Consumer Research: Overview and Illustrative Analysis," *Journal of Consumer Research*, 16 (December): 322–34.

—— (1993) "Feminist Literary Criticism and the Deconstruction of Ads: A Postmodern View of Advertising and Consumer Research," *Journal of Consumer Research*, 19 (March): 556–66.

—— (1995) "Consumer Myths: Frye's Taxonomy and the Structural Analysis of Consumption Text," *Journal of Consumer Research*, 22 (September): 165–85.

Stern, B.B. and Schroeder, J.E. (1994) "Interpretive Methodology from Art and Literary Criticism: A Humanistic Approach to Advertising Imagery," *European Journal of Marketing*, 28 (September): 114–32.

Summers, D. (1996) "Representation," in R.S. Nelson and R. Schiff (eds) *Critical Terms for Art History*, Chicago: University of Chicago, 3–16.

Szarkowski, J. (1988) *Winogrand: Figments from the Real World*, New York: Museum of Modern Art.

—— (1989) *Photography Until Now*, New York: Museum of Modern Art.

Tagg, J. (1989) *The Burden of Representation: Essays on Photographies and Histories*, Minneapolis: University of Minnesota.

Taylor, L. (ed.) (1994) *Visualizing Theory: Essays from Visual Anthropology Review, 1990–1994*, New York: Routledge.

Time-life Editorial Staff (1972) *Travel Photography*, New York: Time-Life.

Torgovnick, M. (1990) *Gone Primitive*, Chicago: University of Chicago Press.

—— (1997) *Primitive Passions: Men, Women, and the Quest for Ecstasy*, New York: Knopf.

Traube, E. (1992) *Dreaming Identities: Class, Gender, and Generation in 1980s Hollywood Movies*, Boulder, CO: Westview.

Urry, J. (1990) *The Tourist Gaze: Leisure and Travel in Contemporary Societies*, London: Sage.

Walker, M.U. (1997) *Moral Understandings: Feminist Studies in Ethics*, New York: Routledge.

Williamson, J. (1986a) *Consuming Passions: The Dynamics of Popular Culture*, London: Marion Boyers.

—— (1986b) "Women is an Island: Femininity and Colonization" in T. Modleski (ed.) *Studies in Entertainment: Critical Approaches to Mass Culture*, Bloomington: Indiana University Press, 99–118.

Zaltman, G. (1991) "Fellows Award Speech: One Mega and Seven Basic Principles of Consumer Research," in R.H. Holman and M.R. Solomon (eds) *Advances in Consumer Research*, vol. 18, Provo, UT: Association for Consumer Research, 8–10.

Zaltman, G. and Coulter, R.A. (1995) "Seeing the Voice of the Customer: Metaphor-Based Advertising Research," *Journal of Advertising Research*, 35 (July/August): 35–51.

Ziller, R.C. (1990) *Photographing the Self*, Newbury Park, CA: Sage.

8

JOURNEY TO KROYWEN

An ethnoscopic auto-auto-auto-driven stereographic photo essay

Morris B. Holbrook

The magical beliefs and practices of the Nacirema present such unusual aspects that it seems desirable to describe them as an example of the extremes to which human behavior can go.

(Miner 1956: 503).

Preview

Pursuing the tradition established by Samuel Butler's study of *Erewhon* ([1872] 1970), this chapter presents the author's subjective, personal, introspective insights concerning the transitional market economy found in the developing consumer culture of Kroywen – a Nacireman society that has been little studied and remains poorly understood, in part because of the harsh and even danger-ous conditions that exist therein. To overcome these barriers to investigation, the author reflects his long-term, immersive participant observation in the Kroywe-nese culture in the form of a *photo essay* (i.e., a photographically documented, self-reflective account) that uses *stereography* (i.e., three-dimensional images) for purposes of *auto-auto-auto-driving* or *auto^3-driving* (i.e., a self-expression of his own reactions to stereo pairs taken by himself) in order to construct a coherent *ethnoscopy* (i.e., a pictorial record of the relevant consumer culture). Hence, the example of Kroywen serves both to introduce and to illustrate an approach by means of the ethnoscopic auto^3-driven stereographic photo essay that may be of use in a wide variety of anthropological or sociological applications to marketing and consumer research.

Introduction

Perhaps because of its comparatively small size (a population of roughly nine million), its location in a remote region on the eastern border of Nacirema (Gatewood 1996; Miner 1956), its virtual inaccessibility to surface vehicles (with an average traffic speed of less than five miles per hour over rough and congested terrain), and its problematic access by plane (via the most dangerous of the world's airports), the society of Kroywen has typically received less attention from cultural anthropologists, ethnographers, sociologists, and marketing or consumer research-ers than it might deserve, although it is potentially appropriate as an illustration of many extreme cultural and market-oriented phenomena associated with the struggling emergence of a developing economy. Specifically, though under-developed or backward in many respects – its crumbling infrastructure of pothole-filled roadways and vehicle-crammed access routes; its conspicuous popu-lation of destitute derelicts and homeless beggars; its visible evidence of social malaise or ennui; its proliferation of garbage, inundation by pollution, and pervasiveness of decay in its private buildings and public structures; its slow efforts to rebuild amidst rampant inefficiency – Kroywen affords many neglected oppor-tunities to study the visible traces of a society in transition. To bridge this gap in our understanding of Kroywen, its evolving market structure, and its awakening culture of consumption, this chapter presents an *ethnoscopic auto-auto-auto-driven stereographic photo essay* on the nature and scope of consumer behavior and market-ing institutions in this little-studied society.

Ethnoscopy

As used here, the term *ethnoscopy* refers to an approach borrowed from cultural anthropology (Ball and Smith 1992; Bateson and Mead 1942; Collier 1967; Collier and Collier 1986) and visual sociology (Becker 1986, 1995; Chaplin 1994; Wagner 1979) that makes use of photographs or other pictorial records as a means of collecting data, eliciting responses from informants, documenting research results, or expressing the researcher's introspective insights (Harper 1988). "Ethno" refers to the intended focus on a society's *culture*. "Scopy" refers to the researcher's ability to *see* or to *visualize* the key phenomena of interest in pictorial form. Such ethnoscopic methods have gained increased usage by those studying consumer behavior and other aspects of a society's consumption system (Belk 1991; Belk *et al.* 1988; Heisley *et al.* 1991; Wallendorf and Belk 1987).

Auto-auto-auto-driving or auto[3]-driving

Via a process sometimes called *auto-driving* (Heisley and Levy 1991), visual anthro-pologists and sociologists have used photographs to elicit responses from infor-mants who have been asked to comment on the meanings found in pictorial representations of their own environments or behaviors (Collier and Collier 1986; Harper 1987, 1989). Further, in what we might refer to as *auto-auto-driving*, researchers have sometimes asked their informants to take the appropriate photos themselves (Ziller 1990), to instruct the researchers on how best to capture the relevant phenomena on film (van der Does *et al.* 1992), or to combine such photographic images into self-revelatory collages (Zaltman and Higie 1993). In this study, the researcher himself introspects on the significance of his own impressions prompted by photographs taken by himself – hence, the term *auto-auto-auto-driving* or $auto^3$*-driving.*

Stereography

The techniques of *stereography* permit the researcher to transcend the traditional two-dimensionally flat surface of the printed page or computer screen to achieve a three-dimensional view of the relevant visual materials. Numerous commentators agree that 3-D stereography greatly enhances the vividness, clarity, realism, and depth of visual representations (Holbrook 1996, 1997b). Though stereo 3-D images appear in a wide variety of formats – for example, computer-generated diagrams, random dot stereograms, View-Master slide reels, red-and-green-or-blue anaglyphs, single-image stereograms, lenticular prints, holograms, computer graphics, or virtual reality (Holbrook 1997b) – this chapter focuses on the format most appropriate to the print media in which most ethnographic research currently appears: namely, *photographic prints* that lend themselves to reproduction in the pages of journals or books (Holbrook 1996). In this connection, the author takes *stereo pairs* to be the most accessible and useful format for displaying 3-D stereographic pictorial representations of ethnoscopic material.

Photo essay

The *photo essay* is a mode of self-expressive presentation that lends itself to conveying insights gained via ethnoscopic auto-auto-auto-driven stereography. In this case, the approach parallels that sometimes referred to as Subjective Personal Introspection or SPI (Holbrook 1995). Here – following such examples as those provided by Holbrook (1987, 1997a), Mead (1994), Peñaloza (1994), and Rook (1991) – the photo essay makes use of pictorial images to document the visual evidence for those aspects of objective reality that have shaped the author's subjective impressions (Bachand 1988; Heisley *et al.* 1991; Stern 1994). Hence, though the style of writing is personal in tone, the pictures provide corroboration of the bases for the relevant introspections (Bertrand 1988; Holbrook 1988; Joy and Venkatesh 1994; Kaushik and Sen 1990). This approach thereby overcomes some of the objections sometimes raised against SPI as a potential source of knowledge by critics who are wedded to the older more quasi-positivistic approaches to the social sciences in general (Calder and Tybout 1987) or to ethnography in particular (Wallendorf and Brucks 1993).

Method

Stereo pairs

Stereo pairs are taken by two camera lenses separated by a suitable distance – for example, the distance between the human eyes or about two and a half inches. These lenses may be mounted on one camera (e.g., the popular Stereo Realist or Kodak versions); may belong to two cameras arrayed side-by-side and fired simultaneously (either by hand or by some appropriate synchronizing device); or may consist of one camera lens shifted from left to right (over an interval of time during which nothing in the picture moves). Whichever method is employed, the result is two images that capture the binocular disparity or parallax shift typical of the two eyes in ordinary stereoscopic vision. When mounted side-by-side and viewed in a way that fuses them back into one stereoptical view, these two images permit the recreation of a true 3-D experience. Good discussions on the art of photographing, cropping, and mounting stereo pairs appear in a wide variety of sources (Burder and Whitehouse 1992; Ferwerda 1990; Waack 1987; White 1996).

Viewing

Viewing of the sort of stereo pair just described may occur without the help of any mechanical assistance (*free-viewing*) or with the aid of some optical device (*aided viewing*).

Free-viewing

To free-view a stereo pair, place the page close to your face and look straight ahead, with each eye aimed at its appropriate image. Probably the picture will be out of focus and everything will look blurred. Then relax the eyes and continue to look straight ahead while slowing pulling the page away from your face. As the distance between the page and your eyes increases, the two pictures should become clearer and should seem to float together, ultimately fusing into a true 3-D image. Learning to free-view stereo pairs in this manner requires a certain amount of practice and patience. The reason for this is that one must learn to overcome the natural and habitual tendency of the eyes to converge (i.e., to toe inwards) and to accommodate (i.e., to focus) at the same time. Normally, when seeing something close to the face, we tend to look cross-eyed (convergence) while trying to bring it into focus (accommodation). However, in free-viewing a stereo pair, we must learn to *decouple* these two responses – that is, to focus *without* converging. Some viewers acquire this skill quite rapidly and easily; for others, it takes hours, days, or even weeks of practice to achieve stereopsis in this manner. The fact that most people *can* attain success in this endeavor is attested to by the worldwide popularity of the *Magic Eye* and other "stereogram" books (Grossman and Cooper 1995). Meanwhile, for those willing to invest the needed time and effort, excellent tutorials on free-viewing are available from a number of helpful sources (Alderson 1988; Best 1979; Brown [1903]1994; Ferwerda 1990; Girling 1990; Grossman and Cooper 1995; Johnstone 1995; Norton 1994; Richardson 1994; Waack 1987; Waldsmith 1991). Internet-connected readers might also wish to consult the material found at http://www.columbia.edu/~mbh3 and http://takeo.kulab.sfc.keio.ac.jp/~morris.

Aided viewing

Those not willing or able to invest the time and effort required to master the art of free-viewing as just described may wish to rely on some form of optical assistance in achieving successful stereopsis. Toward this end, the most effective viewing aid that the author has found is the prismatic lorgnette consisting of a hand-held pair of magnifying prisms that enlarge the two pictures slightly while causing them to fuse. Such a "prism-lens" viewer is available for under five dollars (including postage) from the original manufacturer (The Added Dimension, P.O. Box 15325, Clearwater, FL 34629, 813–446–9106); from Cygnus Graphic (P.O. Box 32461, Phoenix, AZ 85064, 602–277–9253); from Reel 3-D Enterprises (P.O. Box 2368, Culver City, CA 90231, 310–837–2368); or, in the United Kingdom, from the Stereoscopic Society (c/o Eric Silk, 221 Arbury Road, Cambridge, CB4 2JJ, UK). Further details appear at the Web sites specified in the last paragraph.

Fieldwork

Fieldwork underlying the present ethnoscopic auto-auto-auto-driven stereographic photo essay has entailed a deeply immersive period of participant observation over the past thirty years. During this extended time frame, the author has lived and worked among the Kroywenese, always maintaining a sort of fascinated detachment or studied distance even while sharing in their local rituals and customs. Some of his preliminary conclusions were reported in a subjective, personal, introspective essay on this theme (Holbrook 1994). More recently, however, he has worked toward reflecting his impressions of this unique culture by taking numerous field tours of the local terrain while carrying a pair of disposable cameras taped together for purposes of stereo photography. Thus, he has eschewed his conventional stereographic gear – the twin 35 mm single-lens reflex cameras, the dual shutter release, the bracket mounted on a tripod – in favor of a more portable and flexible photographic method that permits him to maneuver freely through the difficult and dangerous terrain of Kroywen. Carrying more cumbersome equipment would have rendered him defenseless and vulnerable to attack by some vicious animal or angry native. Hence, he has opted for portability at the expense of the greatest possible resolution or optimal exposure settings in capturing his stereographic images. Fortunately, good 3-D effects rely on maximum depth of field (consistency of focus from the foreground to the background) via minimum apertures (lens openings) (Burder and White-house 1992; Ferwerda 1990; Waack 1987). Hence, the tendency of disposable cameras to employ small lenses requiring bright light fits well with the ethnoscopic auto^3-driven stereographic agenda pursued here.

Ethnoscopic auto^3-driven stereographic photo essay

For purposes of expressive documentation via the present ethnoscopic auto^3-driven stereographic photo essay, we may divide our experience of the Kroy-wenese culture into a number of salient categories that appear to reflect the transi-tional nature of this society, captured at the moment of its evolving transformation from a relatively primitive to a more modern market economy. Indeed, every-where we look in Kroywen, we find symptoms of the old customs and norms juxtaposed against the more recently emerging values and technologies. Thus, old habits of farming struggle to survive amidst the pavement of city streets. Modern equipment races to overcome the accelerated crumbling of an outmoded infra-structure. Primitive means of communication strive to make sense of the surround-ing chaos. Destitute vendors sell their shabby wares by the sides of congested avenues. Waste products pile up faster than sanitation teams can remove them.

Specifically, a careful examination of the visual record suggests that these phenomena may be captured under the headings of the following seven categories:

1   *Commerce.*
2   *Communication.*
3   *Transportation.*
4   *Flora – forestation and agriculture.*
5   *Fauna – pets and wildlife.*
6   *Waste – refuse, garbage, trash, and litter.*
7   *Miscellaneous institutions – education, sanitation, law enforcement, and housing.*

In considering the visual evidence that bears on these seven themes, we shall examine seven photographic montages (Plates 8.1–8.7), each of which presents four stereo pairs intended to illustrate the relevant category. In each montage, these stereo pairs will be referred to as UL, LL, UR, and LR to designate the upper left, lower left, upper right, and lower right corners, respectively. For example, "UR3" indicates the stereo pair in the upper right-hand corner of the third montage. Readers who wish to view the stereo pairs in color or to see them as red-and-blue 3-D anaglyphs should pursue the appropriate links provided by the author's Web site (http: //www.columbia.edu/~mbh3) or should access these links directly:

• http://www.geocities.com/MadisonAvenue/2506 for the color stereo pairs;
• http://takeo.kulab.sfc.keio.ac.jp/~morris/kroywen/kroywen.htm   for   the   red-blue 3-D anaglyphs.

Montage 1: Commerce

UL1

Only a small proportion of the Kroywenese population is literate enough to require the widespread availability of books. Hence, when a new bookstore moves into any given area, the ones already there tend immediately to fail commercially. For this reason, most of the society's needs for real literature are met by various itinerant street vendors who dig discarded volumes out of trash or garbage receptacles and recycle them for use at a small fee by those who have not yet read them. As shown in UL1, such a recycling project requires no more than a small card table or stand set up by the side of the road. The stereographic view clearly captures the plastic containers – originally intended to hold milk cartons – stashed under the card tables and used to store the books at night or when it rains.

LL1

Meanwhile, most Kroywenese confine their reading primarily to pamphlets or magazines that contain large numbers of pictures of such things as sports heroes, movie stars, naked women, and disgraced members of the Royal Family. As shown in LL2, these – along with daily newspapers that also contain many photographs – can be bought from kiosks scattered throughout the city. Such vendors also supply other essential products like cigarettes, chewing gum, or candy (main staples in the Kroywenese diet). Notice here how the stereo effect makes it possible to examine individual magazine covers, to recognize particular newspapers, or to identify individual brands of candy bars in what would otherwise seem like a hopeless jumble of pictorial clutter.

UR1

Ordinary household goods such as toothpaste, scouring powder, or checkered shirts may be purchased from Kroywenese street merchants who spread out their wares on the sidewalk to attract passers by. In UR1 the 3-D experience calls attention to signs that say "Special 99" located in both the foreground and the background of the stereo picture. In Kroywenese, the word "special" serves as a commonly understood warning that a quoted price (in this case, 99 cents in Kroywen's currency) is considerably higher than what the object in question is actually worth. For example, when dining at a restaurant in Kroywen, one must listen patiently while the waiter or waitress rattles off a long list of "specials" that the chef has prepared for that particular occasion. These are invariably cooked in bulk, are soggy from having sat on the back burner for hours, are totally lacking in character or flavor, and are exorbitantly priced at a considerable premium over what one would expect to pay for comparable items listed on the everyday menu. (In another context, a Kroywenese celebrity named Churchlady – who used to

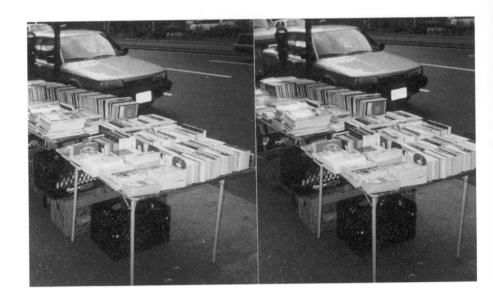

Plate 8.1 Montage 1: Commerce

Plate 8.2 Montage 2: Communication

Plate 8.3 Montage 3: Transportation

Plate 8.4 Montage 4: Flora – forestation and agriculture

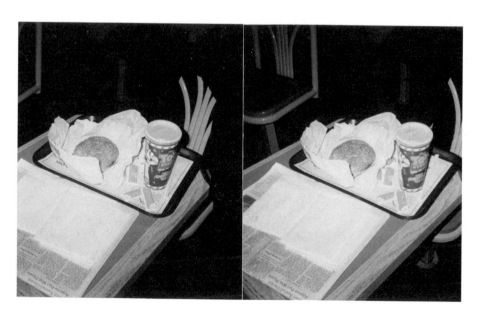

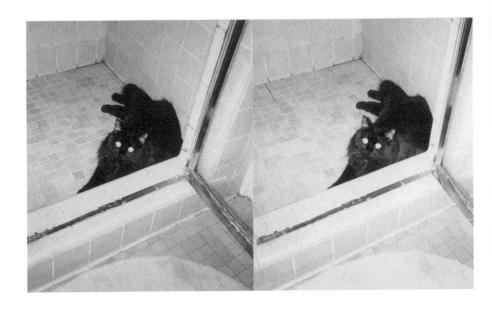

Plate 8.5 Montage 5: Fauna – pets and wildlife

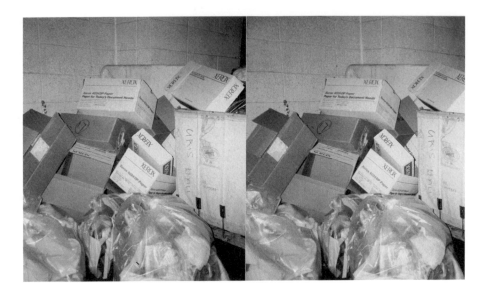

Plate 8.6 Montage 6: Waste – refuse, garbage, trash, and litter

Plate 8.7 Montage 7: Miscellaneous institutions – education, sanitation, law enforcement and housing

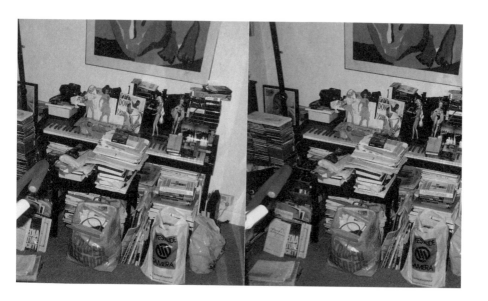

appear on a weekly television broadcast called *Saturday Night Live* – has further deconstructed the word "special" by applying that term to anything she can think of that is truly awful; hence, in Kroywenese, "special" has also come to mean "inane," "stupid," or "absurd.")

LR1

Kroywenese grocers sell fruits, vegetables, and flowers from stands built out onto the sidewalk, often so far that they virtually choke off pedestrian traffic and thereby help to ensure a "captive audience" of potential customers. LR1 shows the intrusive effect of such a massive array. Notice how the in-depth 3-D experience calls attention to the hanging roll of plastic bags in the foreground as well as the assortment of flowers that in only two dimensions seem to hide in the background.

Montage 2: Communication

UL2

To a tourist, the most visually impressive system of communication in Kroywen consists of pictorial messages composed in the native iconography and inscribed on the walls of buildings or in other public places. Indeed, one sometimes gets the impression that the Kroywenese mind abhors a blank space and contrives to fill any available flat surface with a visibly manifested outpouring of creative effort. Such markings serve to document interpretations of local history, to reinforce territorial boundaries, or to support other native customs. Thus, as shown in UL2, the closed doors to a public building afford a mural-sized space onto which to inscribe a collection of important totemic emblems such as the Lion King, the Frog Prince, and the Space Ship. In the latter connection, legend has it that in prehistoric times Kroywen was visited by aliens from outer space who mingled with the people and thereby fostered some of the distinctive appearances and behavior patterns that remain to this day.

LL2

Kroywenese citizens also engage in various rituals of self-inscription. In LL2 we observe a native woman who descends into a "subway" (translated later under "UR3") and who wears a complex Kroywenese insignia on her back. Such markings on one's personal attire help to guard against loss or theft. Sometimes they convey important messages about the owner's self-image. Equally often, however, they merely announce the name of the designer who produced the clothing in question. Apparently, many Kroywenese do not realize or care that by wearing apparel publicly identified by its brand name, they are in effect serving without pay as human billboards to provide free advertising for the manufacturer.

UR2

During the formative years of its history over the last four centuries, Kroywen has been settled by immigrants from a number of disparate cultures – Naeporue, Nacirfa, Naisa, Onital – each of which now claims certain territorial rights that often remain hotly contested and constitute the object of ceaseless tribal skirmishes or even large-scale internecine warfare. Visible signs of this multi-cultural strife appear ubiquitously in public places. Thus, in a complex system of writing that makes use of the unique Kroywenese alphabet, members of warring factions stake claims of local dominion or inscribe warnings to competing tribes on virtually any flat surface that becomes available for this purpose. For example, those who erect large monuments or other edifices at great communal expense (the Statue of Ytrebil, the Tomb of Tnarg, the Garden of Nosidam, the Theater of Ynos) are often amazed by how promptly their facades become covered with these Kroywenese inscriptions. On a reduced scale, UR2 shows how the same principle applies to smaller windows of opportunity such as the electric utility box pictured here. Sometimes called a *graffito* (singular) or *graffiti* (plural), such signage expresses the writer's view of the local social conditions and is generally displayed in close proximity to the work of other contributing social commentators. In this illustration, though this particular Kroywenese dialect defies easy translation into English, the message posted here might be read: "My name is HKeor7; I own this street corner; go away or I will kill you." Obviously, such a warning signals danger for the unwary pedestrians approaching from the distance, as clearly seen in the depth perspective emphasized by the stereoscopic view.

LR2

For those who speak the relevant dialects and can therefore understand such messages, even more frightening warnings appear – larger than life – on the walls of unguarded buildings. For example, in LR2 someone who identifies himself only as "Sef" has posted the hostile words "Mene Fu Aton Cend" or, in English, "I'm a meanie who says "F*** Y**" to anyone who wants to see this end of town." Notice here how stereopsis helps us to read the otherwise obscured, and inherently untranslatable, but nonetheless terrifying postscript: "Navev."

Montage 3: Transportation

UL3

Earlier we noted the difficulty of reaching Kroywen by land or air. Not surprisingly, similar impediments to transportation appear inside Kroywen itself. As depicted in UL3, travel in Kroywen by means of its city streets or roads is all but impossible due to the poor condition and ill-repair in which these thorough-fares are kept, especially when combined with the excessive number of motor vehicles and self-propelled modes of transportation that crowd and clog the main routes. This stereo pair shows the equipment needed to resurface some of the "potholes" (Kroywenese for "craters in the pavement") that bring traffic to a virtual standstill on one major artery that runs from north to south. Of course, while the repairs proceed (often for several weeks or even months at a time), the equipment itself forestalls any possibility of traffic moving through the affected area. The typical Kroywenese response to such circumstances is to honk one's horn, thereby creating a noise-pollution problem that is as insufferable for local residents as it is difficult to capture on film.

LL3

Construction work on the crumbling infrastructure also chokes pedestrian traffic to a crawl throughout Kroywen. For example, LL3 shows one of the countless tunnel-shaped scaffolds that snake through the city. Though these structures do have the advantage of protecting those on foot from the debilitating effects of Kroywen's notoriously inclement weather, they force such pedestrians to proceed single-file, often at a snail's pace behind one little old lady who has ill-advisedly set forth to buy some milk for her cat. Notice here how the 3-D depth effect emphasizes the interminable length of this particular tunnel, with barely a glimmer of light at its other end.

UR3

Due to the severe problems with pedestrian and automotive traffic just described, many Kroywenese rely on a complex subterranean system of tunnels that permit them to reach most destinations in the city by train without the need to travel above ground – with the advantage of further avoiding some of the more extreme discomforts of the notoriously grim Kroywenese climate (oppressive heat and tropical storms in the summer, bitter cold and waist-high blizzards in the winter). UR3 shows an entrance to this underground tunnel system, which is found at the bottom of a stairway that leads through a hole in the sidewalk. The local term for such an access route is "subway" (see also LL2). Ordinary English lacks a true synonym for this expression. However, roughly translated, it connotes the "sub"-standard conditions experienced in this mode of travel and conveys that such a means of transportation is "way" below par. As one might expect when descending stairs that plunge into underground caverns, the subways are inhabited by rats, defiled by human waste, and polluted by other ubiquitous forms of filth. For this reason, many Kroywenese prefer to transport themselves by means of bicycles.

LR3

A pair of such bicycles appears in LR3. The 3-D view clarifies how they are chained securely to a tree to avoid theft and calls attention to the thick treads on their bulging tires. The latter are needed to negotiate the rough terrain of the "pothole"-filled Kroywenese streets. A further boon to bicycle travel is that people riding on these self-propelled vehicles feel completely at liberty to ignore all traffic regulations such as stop signs, cross walks, or the directions of one-way streets. Such flouting of conventions makes walking by foot a very dangerous mode of travel for those few pedestrians brave enough to venture forth into Kroywen's downtown areas.

Montage 4: Flora – forestation and agriculture

UL4

Heavily wooded in many places, Kroywen offers its citizens numerous sylvan scenes in which to walk or sit while admiring the beauties of nature. For the convenience of such naturalists, as shown in UL4, Kroywenese woodsmen have cleared paths through the forest and have installed comfortable benches illuminated by overhead lamps. At night these benches are covered with the bodies of homeless people who find that they provide a convenient place to sleep. In viewing this stereo pair, notice how the trees along the path – which look like an undifferentiated clump of tangled branches when seen in just two dimensions – clearly stand apart as isolated units when seen three-dimensionally.

LL4

The Kroywenese farm in LL4 occupies a small plot of land nestled between the wall of a building and the adjacent sidewalk. In a culture famous for its so-called "vest-pocket" parks, such a modest-sized farm emphasizes the need to make maximum use of every potential site for agriculture. This particular farmer raises flowers of the type sold by a neighboring street vendor (shown in UR4). Elsewhere in the city, however, comparable agricultural operations specialize in growing tomatoes, turnips, pumpkins, cabbages, carrots, marijuana, and other edible or smokable fruits or vegetables (see also the fresh produce stand in LR1). In stereo, the depth in LL4 clearly indicates the spatial relationship between the long but narrow farm and the bordering footpath for passing pedestrians.

UR4

As just mentioned, flowers like those grown on farms such as that shown in LL4 are brought to market by the street vendor whose offerings appear in UR4. It seems remarkable that this impressive variety of floral species can be made available in such a cramped and crowded milieu. But, by virtue of having learned to live in crowded places, the Kroywenese are masters at the organization and utilization of small spaces. Notice here how the 3-D effect lets each flower emerge with its own individual identity.

LR4

Despite their access to plentiful fruits, vegetables, and other agricultural products – as shown in LR1, LL4, and UR4–most Kroywenese prefer a diet based on "hot dogs" and "hamburgers" of the type featured in LR4. Paradoxically, a "hot *dog*" is made not from dog but rather from pig, whereas a "*ham*burger" is made not from pig but from cow, horse, or worms. (Alternate versions are also available in forms made from turkey, veal, fish, beans, or other vegetables – including something called "tempeh" that consists of soybeans fermented with a rhizopus and that is imported from the neighboring community of Notpmah Tsae.) As indicated with special vividness in three dimensions by the stereograph in LR4, the Kroywenese hamburger consists mostly of paper packaging and a thick bun, encouraging local diners to cover its paltry contents with massive amounts of mustard or ketchup and to inquire plaintively, "Where's the beef?" As also indicated, the milkshake container features a picture of Toy Story – a masterwork by the guru Yensid Tlaw, who is as renowned in Kroywen as he is in other parts of Nacirema, Naeporue, and Naisa.

Montage 5: Fauna – pets and wildlife

UL5

The most popular pet in Kroywen – whether because of this animal's intelligence and tolerant disposition toward humans, its talent for taking care of itself and living in cramped quarters, or its ability to help control the pest population – is the house cat. The feline shown in UL5 lives primarily in a shower stall and spends most of his time hunting for cockroaches that crawl up through the drain pipe. Because he is black, many Kroywenese – strongly superstitious people who associate black cats with witchcraft – will have little to do with him. However, his owners value him highly for his help with the roach-control problem.

LL5

Second in degree of popularity, though not nearly as smart or discriminating as cats, dogs provide good protection from burglars or muggers. The only disadvantage is that they must be walked several times a day – or, as shown in LL5, tied to a convenient post at a bus stop where they can pathetically beg for food from passing strangers. Notice in LL5 how stereography clarifies the spatial relationship between the post, the dog, the leash, and the photographer. The depth effect indicates that the dog has moved as far toward the camera as its leash will permit. It is wise to maintain such a safe distance when photographing animals on the streets of Kroywen.

UR5

In Kroywen, the pigeon is often viewed as the unofficial State Bird. In UR5, a flock of these creatures forages for food on the outskirts of the forest shown in UL4. The in-depth 3-D view calls attention to the park benches in the distance where, on sufficiently warm and sunny days, many elderly Kroywenese citizens like to sit and feed legions of pigeons such as these. Because the ubiquitous pigeons live among filth and garbage, many Kroywenese find this practice disgusting; but others – perhaps because they are lonely – gladly seek the companionship of these feathered friends.

LR5

Another species of Kroywenese wildlife is the oft-maligned squirrel. Some regard squirrels as little better than rats with bushy tails. But given half a chance, as shown in LR5, such creatures will sit charmingly on a bench in the forest and beg ingratiatingly for scraps of food, especially nuts. The stereo effect in LR5 conveys the in-your-face charm of the squirrel in the foreground, while also alerting us to its companion located on the left in the background of the picture. Thus, as elsewhere, the 3-D view deepens our ability to perceive important details in the relevant scene.

Montage 6: Waste – refuse, garbage, trash, and litter

The waste products generated by Kroywenese consumers occupy a hierarchy of cultural worth ranging from high to low in stature. Specifically, on a continuum of prestige: refuse > garbage > trash > litter. We shall review each in turn.

UL6

Refuse consists of waste produced as a by-product of respectable activities such as the operations that occur in an office building. In UL6 we find a mountain of refuse generated by one of the paper-intensive service industries. Here, the 3-D view allows us to look into each plastic bag in depth and to peer deeply into each empty cardboard box.

LL6

Meanwhile, waste from ordinary household consumption accumulates on the sidewalks of Kroywen in huge piles of black plastic bags filled with *garbage*. In LL6, the 3-D effect clearly reveals the contours of each garbage bag. Though the black color obscures the contents within, the distinctive shapes permit us to speculate on the nature of the discarded material inside these "baggies." For example, the bulging bag in the immediate foreground appears likely to contain a dead body.

UR6

When they are not too busy with other distractions, the Kroywenese sometimes deposit their portable *trash* – such as cigarette, chewing-gum, or candy wrappers – in large receptacles located for this purpose on nearly every corner. Stereography reveals that the trash can shown in UR6 contains empty plastic bags, food packages, tin cans, and something that looks ominously white and fluffy – as if a baby in its swaddling clothes might have been casually tossed into this trash container. Distressing as it may seem to members of some other cultures, many young Kroywenese parents dispose of unwanted infants in this manner – often because excessive procreation imposes severe demands on the economic resources of their families or because they are too embarrassed to tell their mothers and fathers that they have conceived a child out of "wedlock".

LR6

When waste fails to wind up in the refuse pile, the garbage bag, or the trash receptacle, it becomes *litter* – perhaps the most common form of "disposal" found in Kroywen. Generally speaking, when a Kroywenese citizen finishes using some product, he or she just drops whatever remains after consumption right down onto the sidewalk or into the nearest gutter. As a result, almost every available nook and cranny of Kroywen is filled to overflowing with litter. For example, the stereo effect in LR6 helps us peer down into the crevice between the "oice" box on the left and the lamppost on the right, where we find two empty beer bottles in brown paper bags. In Kroywenese, "oice" means "recycling bin." Those who have failed to cultivate the appropriate distance and detachment born of a thoroughgoing cultural relativism might be tempted to wonder how much harder it would have been for those anonymous and long-departed beer drinkers to place their litter into the oice box where it would have been elevated to the status of trash.

Montage 7: Miscellaneous institutions – education, sanitation, law enforcement, and housing

UL7

Given the severely limited resources with which it has to work, education in Kroywen remains quite undeveloped and improves at only the most painfully slow pace. Thus, UL7 shows the dismal conditions that prevail in the author's dimly lit classroom. An overhead projector in the center of the picture fails to function (as usual), while the instructor's lecture notes must be propped up on a makeshift podium made from a cardboard box retrieved from the refuse heap shown in UL6. Moreover, the 3-D effect helps us to observe that, on the left and right as well as farther back in the picture, several people have brought bottles of water to class. This underscores the impotability of the local drinking water, which contains dangerous impurities and biological waste products. The huge rivers that border the outskirts of Kroywen are so polluted by health hazards as to make drinking from them unthinkable. Swimming in them would also produce devastating ill effects. Indeed, the water cannot even be used safely for purposes of doing one's laundry – a circumstance that forces many citizens to send their dirty clothing to predaceously expensive Kroywenese dry cleaners who use harsh chemicals to remove the ingrained dirt picked up from all corners of the filthy environment.

LL7

Sanitation practices in Kroywen also suffer by comparison with more developed societies. For example, as shown in LL7, many Kroywenese toilets function improperly, if at all, and require frequent replacement. This particular pile of discarded "potties," revealed in vivid detail by the 3-D stereographic view, was removed from service because flushing them wasted too much of the admittedly problematic Kroywenese water – which, paradoxically, is in scarce supply even though it is not fit for human consumption in the first place.

UR7

Not surprisingly, given the primitive status of such public services as education and sanitation, the Kroywenese system of law enforcement also falls far behind more civilized standards. Indeed, crime is rampant throughout Kroywen; and – thanks to a bizarre system of jurisprudence in which innocent citizens collectively spend more time on jury duty than do criminals behind bars – such transgressions go largely unpunished. For example, even though Kroywenese streets are too crowded to permit navigation by automobiles, many young Kroywenese enjoy stealing cars just for the fun of it. As shown in UR7, most Kroywenese guard against auto theft by attaching a device to their steering wheels called a "club." In the three-dimensional view, stereography permits us to examine the interior of this particular car in a way that is not possible in just two dimensions. In particular, the 3-D effect enables us to peer inside and to see why the club makes it difficult to turn the steering wheel, thereby discouraging all but the most ambitious criminals from taking this vehicle.

LR7

Finally – if the streets of Kroywen are unsafe, unclean, and overpopulated by uneducated thieves – nothing much more flattering can be said about the interior of the typical Kroywenese dwelling. As an example, consider the cluttered interior space shown in LR7, which depicts a corner of the author's own cramped living quarters. Here, stuffed into a pitiably tiny chamber – one that must serve simultaneously as a study, a music room, a home gym, and a storage closet – we find books and periodicals stacked in haphazard piles, an inaccessible piano buried under a mountain of disorganized stuff, the handlebars of a stationary exercise bike, and a collection of Barbie dolls, not to mention a huge heap of compact discs, scattered video tapes, packages of half-eaten candy, and some camera equipment of use in projects such as the one presently under consideration. In LR7 observe how the 3-D experience helps one to make sense of all this clutter and to visit the scene by moving visually through the space in an inquisitive fashion while simultaneously thanking one's lucky stars for the blessing that one does not have to live and work amidst such a depressing array of debris.

Discussion

As the potentially perplexed reader has doubtless noticed by now, this chapter conforms to the ethos of postmodernism by simultaneously pursuing at least two somewhat contradictory though not altogether incompatible purposes. First, on the serious side, the author has attempted to demonstrate convincingly how stereography tends to enhance the vividness, clarity, realism, and depth in the visual representations that anthropologists, sociologists, and marketing or consumer researchers use to discover, to document, and to present ethnographic findings. But second, on a lighter note, the author has satirized what he takes to be the undercivilized aspects of living conditions in at least one modern metropolis. If the power of the 3-D experience has helped to convince the reader that life in Kroywen is scarcely more advanced than what one might reasonably expect to find in the developing economy and transitional culture of some destitute but emerging consumer society, then the author has accomplished both of his otherwise competing objectives. Thus, through the eyes of this ethnoscopic auto-auto-auto-driven stereographic photo essay, the author hopes to have shown that Kroywen is an interesting place to visit and a visually striking place to photograph, but at best a rather problematic place in which to live.

Acknowledgments

The author thanks Stephen Brown and Barbara Stern for their helpful comments on a draft of this chapter. He also gratefully acknowledges the support of the Columbia Business School's Faculty Research Fund.

References

Alderson, T. (1988) "Everyone's Guide to Freevision," *Stereo World*, 15, 4: 12–17.
Bachand, D. (1988) "The Marketing of Ideas: Advertising and Road Safety," *International Journal of Research in Marketing*, 4, 4: 291–309.

Ball, M.S. and Smith, G.W.H. (1992) *Analyzing Visual Data*, Newbury Park, CA: Sage Publications.

Bateson, G. and Mead, M. (1942) *Balinese Character: A Photographic Analysis*, New York, NY: New York Academy of Sciences.

Becker, H.S. (1986) "Photography and Sociology," in H.S. Becker (ed.) *Doing Things Together: Selected Papers*, Evanston, IL: Northwestern University Press, 221–72.

—— (1995) "Visual Sociology, Documentary Photography, and Photojournalism: It's (Almost) All a Matter of Context," *Visual Sociology*, 10, 1–2: 5–14.

Belk, R.W. (ed.) (1991) *Highways and Buyways: Naturalistic Research from the Consumer Behavior Odyssey*, Provo, UT: Association for Consumer Research.

Belk, R.W., Sherry, J.F., Jr., and Wallendorf, M. (1988) "A Naturalistic Inquiry into Buyer and Seller Behavior at a Swap Meet," *Journal of Consumer Research*, 14, 4: 449–70.

Bertrand, D. (1988) "The Creation of Complicity: A Semiotic Analysis of an Advertising Campaign for *Black & White* Whiskey," *International Journal of Research in Marketing*, 4, 4: 273–89.

Best, S.R. (1979) "Free Vision," *Stereo World*, 6, 4: 8–10.

Brown, T. ([1903] 1994) *Stereoscopic Phenomena of Light & Sight*, Culver City, CA: Reel 3-D Enterprises, Inc.

Burder, D. and Whitehouse, P. (1992) *Photographing in 3-D*, 3rd edn, Surrey, UK: The Stereoscopic Society.

Butler, S. ([1872] 1970) *Erewhon*, Harmondsworth: Viking Penguin.

Calder, B.J. and Tybout, A.M. (1987) "What Consumer Research Is," *Journal of Consumer Research*, 14, 1: 136–40.

Chaplin, E. (1994) *Sociology and Visual Representation*, London: Routledge.

Collier, J., Jr. (1967) *Visual Anthropology: Photography as a Research Method*, New York, NY: Holt, Rinehart and Winston.

Collier, J., Jr. and Collier, M. (1986) *Visual Anthropology: Photography as a Research Method*, revised and expanded edition, Albuquerque, NM: University of New Mexico Press.

Ferwerda, J.G. (1990) *The World of 3-D: A Practical Guide to Stereo Photography*, 2nd edn, Borger, The Netherlands: 3-D Book Productions.

Gatewood, J.B. (1996) "Ignorance, Knowledge, and Dummy Categories: Social and Cognitive Aspects of Expertise," paper presented at the 95th Annual Meeting, American Anthropological Association, San Francisco, CA, November 19–23 (http://www.lehigh.edu/~jbg1/liquors.htm).

Girling, A.N. (1990) *Stereoscopic Drawing: A Theory of 3-D Vision and Its Application to Stereoscopic Drawing*, London: Arthur N. Girling.

Grossman, M. and Cooper, R. (1995) *Magic Eye: How to See 3D – The 3D Guide, A Training Manual by N. E. Thing Enterprises*, Kansas City, MO: Andrews and McMeel.

Harper, D. (1987) *Working Knowledge: Skill and Community in a Small Shop*, Chicago, IL: University of Chicago Press.

—— (1988) "Visual Sociology: Expanding Sociological Vision," *The American Sociologist*, 19, 1: 54–70.

—— (1989) "Interpretive Ethnography: From 'Authentic Voice' to 'Interpretive Eye,'" in R.B. Flaes (ed.) *Eyes Across the Water: The Amsterdam Conference on Visual Anthropology and Sociology*, Amsterdam: Het Spinhuis, 33–42.

Heisley, D.D. and Levy, S.J. (1991) "Autodriving: A Photoelicitation Technique," *Journal of Consumer Research*, 18, 3: 257–72.

Heisley, D.D., McGrath, M.A., and Sherry, J.F., Jr. (1991) "'To Everything There Is a

Season:' A Photoessay of a Farmer's Market," in R.W. Belk (ed.) *Highways and Buyways*, Provo, UT: Association for Consumer Research, 141–66.

Holbrook, M.B. (1987) "An Audiovisual Inventory of Some Fanatic Consumer Behavior: The 25–Cent Tour of a Jazz Collector's Home," in M.R. Wallendorf and P.F. Anderson (eds) *Advances in Consumer Research*, vol. 14, Provo, Utah: Association for Consumer Research, 144–49.

—— (1988) "Steps Toward a Psychoanalytic Interpretation of Consumption: A Meta-Meta-Meta-Analysis of Some Issues Raised by the Consumer Behavior Odyssey," in M.J. Houston (ed.) *Advances in Consumer Research*, vol. 15, Provo, Utah: Association for Consumer Research, 537–42.

—— (1994) "Loving and Hating New York: Some Reflections on the Big Apple," *International Journal of Research in Marketing*, 11, 4: 381–85.

—— (1995) *Consumer Research: Introspective Essays on the Study of Consumption*, Thousand Oaks, CA: Sage Publications.

—— (1996) "Breaking Camouflage: The Role For Stereography in Consumer Research," working paper, Graduate School of Business, Columbia University, New York.

—— (1997a) "Feline Consumption: Ethography, Felologies, and Unobtrusive Participation in the Life of a Cat," *European Journal of Marketing*, 31, 3/4: 214–33.

—— (1997b) "Stereographic Visual Displays and the Three-Dimensional Communication of Findings in Marketing Research," *Journal of Marketing Research*, 34 (November): 526–36.

Johnstone, T. (1995) *Magic 3D: Discover the Revolutionary World of Photographic Free-Viewing*, London: Stanley Paul.

Joy, A. and Venkatesh, A. (1994) "Postmodernism, Feminism, and the Body: The Visible and the Invisible in Consumer Research," *International Journal of Research in Marketing*, 11, 4: 333–57.

Kaushik, M. and Sen, A. (1990) "Semiotics and Qualitative Research," *Journal of the Market Research Society*, 32, 2: 227–42.

Kinsman, A. (1992) *Random Dot Stereograms*, Rochester, NY: Kinsman Physics.

Mead, R. (1994) "Where Is the Culture of Thailand?" *International Journal of Research in Marketing*, 11, 4: 401–4.

Miner, H. (1956) "Body Ritual Among the Nacirema," *The American Anthropologist*, 58: 503–7 (http://www.musespace.com/musings/articles/nacirema.html).

Norton, R. (1994) *Stereoviews Illustrated – Volume I: Fifty Early American*, New Haven, CT: Stereoviews Illustrated Press.

Peñaloza, L. (1994) "Crossing Boundaries/Drawing Lines: A Look at the Nature of Gender Boundaries and Their Impact on Marketing Research," *International Journal of Research in Marketing*, 11, 4: 359–79.

Richardson, D. (1994) *Create Stereograms on Your PC: Discover the World of 3D Illusion*, Corte Madera, CA: Waite Group Press.

Rook, D.W. (1991) "I Was Observed (*In Absentia*) and Autodriven by the Consumer Behavior Odyssey," in R.W. Belk (ed.) *Highways and Buyways*, Provo, UT: Association for Consumer Research, 48–58.

Stern, B. (1994) "Authenticity and the Textual Persona: Postmodern Paradoxes in Advertising Narrative," *International Journal of Research in Marketing*, 11, 4: 387–400.

van der Does, P., Edelaar, S., Gooskens, I., Liefting, M., and van Mierlo, M. (1992) "Reading Images: A Study of a Dutch Neighborhood," *Visual Sociology*, 7, 1: 4–67.

Waack, F.G. (1987) *Stereo Photography: An Introduction to Stereo Photo Technology and Practical Suggestions for Stereo Photography*, trans. L. Huelsbergen, Berlin, Germany: F.G. Waack.

Wagner, J. (ed.) (1979) *Images of Information: Still Photography in the Social Sciences*, Beverly Hills, CA: Sage Publications.

Waldsmith, J.S. (1991) *Stereo Views: An Illustrated History and Price Guide*, Radnor, PA: Wallace-Homestead Book Company.

Wallendorf, M. and Belk, R.W. (1987) "Deep Meaning in Possessions," videotape, Cambridge, MA: Marketing Science Institute.

Wallendorf, M. and Brucks, M. (1993) "Introspection in Consumer Research: Implementation and Implications," *Journal of Consumer Research*, 20, 3: 339–59.

White, S. (1996) "The Medium of Stereo Cards," *PSA Journal*, 62, 3: 26–9.

Zaltman, G. and Higie, R.A. (1993) "Seeing the Voice of the Customer: The Zaltman Metaphor Elicitation Technique," report no. 93–114, Cambridge, MA: Marketing Science Institute.

Ziller, R.C. (1990) *Photographing THE SELF: Methods for Observing Personal Orientations*, Newbury Park, CA: Sage Publications.

Part 4

PRAGMATICS, INNOVATION AND CRITICAL ISSUES

9

ADVERTISING NARRATIVES

What are they and how do they work?

Jennifer Edson Escalas

Introduction

Much of advertising tells stories. Ads show homemakers solving household problems with powerful cleaning products, families reunited through telephone calls, and even ongoing epics where the brand of coffee somehow becomes a critical prop in the storyline or looking at the back of a card becomes the basis of a relationship. Consumer research has studied story-based advertising from a variety of perspectives. Advertising narratives have been examined under the rubric of drama (Stern 1994; Deighton *et al.* 1989), transformation (Puto and Wells 1984), and story grammars (Mick 1987). A content analysis conducted for this chapter shows that nearly a quarter of current television ads are in the form of narratives (see p. 275). Why do so many ads tell stories? I argue that ads tell stories because stories are able to involve, captivate, and entertain consumers. More importantly, stories are able to communicate, persuade, demonstrate, and model the products that should be used and the way to use them.

In this chapter I extend the stream of research that contends that the form of advertising matters as much as its content (see McQuarrie and Mick 1996). In this case the form being examined is narrative structure. I begin with a discussion of narratives in general, focusing on the specific aspects of stories that make them useful to advertisers. Next, I explore the role of narratives in advertising and conduct a content analysis of recent television ads, examining the degree to which the ads tell a story. I propose that marketers can use narrative advertising to elicit narrative thought, generate emotion, create brand meaning, and model usage experiences. Finally, I identify directions for future research.

Narratives

Although a great deal of research in cognitive psychology has examined how people process information, form mental categories, encode and retrieve information, and so forth, there has only recently been an interest in narrative thought.

Scholars use the analogy of science and literature to propose two different modes of thought: the rigorous world of logical deduction, labeled paradigmatic thought, and the imprecise world of aesthetic intentions, labeled narrative thought (Bruner 1986). Narrative thought creates stories that are coherent accounts of particular experiences, temporally structured, and context sensitive (Baumeister and Newman 1994). The narrative mode of thought does not necessitate that individuals form elaborate, complex novels in their minds. Rather, under conditions of narrative processing, people think about incoming information as if they were trying to create a story. In day-to-day living, individuals continuously attempt to impose narrative structure on occurrences in order to understand them.

The structure of narratives

What makes a story a story? An important aspect of narrative thought is its structure. This structure consists of two important elements: chronology and causality.

First, narrative thought organizes events in terms of a temporal dimension; things occur over time. Time is configured in narratives as episodes, whereas time in reality is an undifferentiated, continuous flow. The human perception of events with a beginning, middle, and end, known as experienced time, is structured time. Polkinghorne (1991) theorizes that temporality is the primary dimension of human existence. Kerby (1991) asserts that the general objective of narrative to achieve closure (by framing the story with a beginning, middle, and end) is a fundamental way in which human events are understood.

Second, narrative thought structures elements into an organized framework that establishes relationships between the story's elements and allows for causal inferencing. Narrative story organization incorporates general knowledge about human goal-oriented action sequences; events are organized according to the causal and intentional relations among them. Episode schemas are one way to characterize narrative structure (Pennington and Hastie 1986 and 1992). Figure 9.1 illustrates an abstract episode schema, which represents a standard sequence of events in both the real world and in stories. To interpret the figure, an event, or series of events, initiates a psychological reaction and activates goals in a main character. The goals may be formulated in response to the initial event, or may be pre-existing goals that are activated by the initial event. The protagonist's psychological state and goals provide reasons for his or her subsequent actions. These actions lead to an outcome or result. Accompanying physical states may be the main character's state at the time of the initiating events or the result of the initiating events. The physical states may also contribute to the activation of mental states or goals. The direct links shown between elements in the episode schema may or may not all be utilized in any given interpretation or retelling of an action sequence. Because these narrative elements are organized through time, causal inferences can be made. What happens in time one (for example, the protagonist feels jealous) causes what happens in time two (he kills his rival).

268

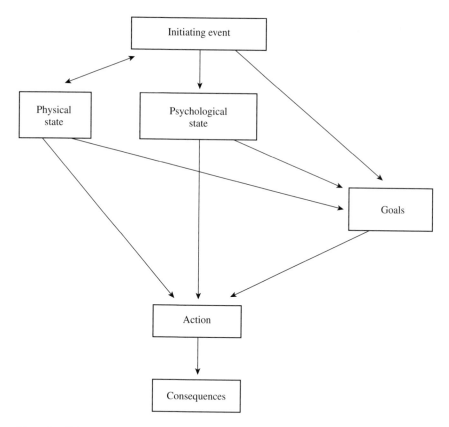

Figure 9.1 Episode schema

Source: N. Pennington and R. Hastie (1986) "Evidence evaluation in complex decision making," *Journal of Personality and Social Psychology*, 51, 2: 242–58. Copyright © 1986 by the American Psychological Association. Reprinted with permission.

While I have proposed some generalities, there is no universal agreement on narrative structure, particularly across differing academic fields. In psychology, Bruner (1990) contends that there are four necessary elements of narrative structure. First, narratives must contain agents engaged in actions undertaken to achieve goals. Second, sequential order must be established and maintained. Events and states are linearized in a standard way; there is a causal sequence of events. These first two elements correspond to the chronology and causality components described above. Bruner's third and fourth elements deal less with narrative structure and more with the focus of narrative. In his third required element, Bruner contends that narratives must be canonical; they must conform to general rules. Narratives often pay attention to unusual events, with the goal of explaining such events in a way that conforms to accepted standards. Finally, narrative is never voiceless; it always comes from a narrator's perspective.

Alternatively, in the field of rhetoric, Burke (1969) defines a "pentad" of five essential elements of narrative. He asserts that any complete statement about motives will answer the following five questions, which correspond to his five elements of narrative. First, what was done? (The action.) Second, when or where was it done? (The scene.) Next, who did it? (The actor.) Fourth, how did the actor do it? (The instrument or agency.) And finally, why? (The purpose or intention.) Except for the scene, these elements correspond to the components of the episode schema developed by Pennington and Hastie (1986). Furthermore, the "when" aspect of Burke's scene can be thought of as contributing to the chronology of narrative.

Story grammarians such as Mandler (1984) assert that stories have an underlying structure that remains relatively invariant in spite of differences in content from story to story. Stories consist of a setting and a series of episodes with a final ending event. These episodes are further decomposed into smaller and smaller units. An episode consists of a beginning, development, and ending. The development, in turn, consists of reactions and goals. Essentially, story grammars postulate a set of categories that must be included in a story and provide rules that specify the relations between categories (Brewer and Lichtenstein 1981). While these theories about the necessary elements of narrative structure vary as to the fine points of what constitutes a narrative, they consistently agree on the necessity of a temporal dimension (chronology) and defined relationships between story elements (causality).

Story quality

Beyond the basic structure of narrative, other theories have identified story characteristics that contribute to a narrative's quality. These characteristics answer the question, "What makes a *good* story?" In one such theory, Bruner (1986) proposes two dimensions to narrative: the landscape of action and the landscape of consciousness. The former is the causal sequence of events while the latter is the degree to which the viewer is made aware of the protagonist's psychological state. The landscape of action consists of events that are visible to the casual observer: the initiating event, resulting action(s), and outcome(s). The landscape of consciousness allows the reader/viewer to "get inside the head" of the story's character(s). The audience learns what the character is thinking and feeling. There is an emphasis on attitudes, motivations, goals, and personal development. Whereas a landscape of action is necessary for any narrative, a landscape of consciousness has been shown to make a narrative more compelling. Readers make more inferences and exert a greater effort to construct an interpretation when a story has a well-developed landscape of consciousness (Feldman *et al.* 1990). Thus a story with both a landscape of action and consciousness is a better story than one that contains only a landscape of action.

In addition to Bruner's landscape of consciousness, other aspects of narrative have been identified as contributors to a story's quality. Gergen and Gergen (1988) theorize that the dramatic engagement of a narrative depends on the evaluative slope of the story. The events in a story are evaluated over time (as it occurs in the narrative) for the degree to which they improve or worsen the state of the protagonist. Stories that have a steep incline or decline in evaluative slope, and those that alternate in sign (e.g., rising, falling, then rising again), evoke the most emotion. The classical tragedy, *Oedipus Rex*, is an example of a narrative with rapidly deteriorating events, from the perspective of the protagonist. Gergen and Gergen would contend that this steep, downward, evaluative slope creates drama and generates emotion.

Finally, a narrative imbalance has also been shown to improve a story's quality (Lucariello 1990; Feldman *et al.* 1990). This imbalance can take the form of a breach in canonical expectations about how people should behave or how stories should unfold (e.g., throwing water on birthday cake candles breaches one's cultural expectations about birthday party behavior). A narrative imbalance can also be tension between story elements, such as actions that fail to achieve goals (e.g., the love of Romeo and Juliet fails to bring them and their feuding families together). These narrative imbalances lead to increased elaboration by readers as they attempt to explain the imbalance (Lucariello 1990; Feldman *et al.* 1990).

The function of narratives

In order to make sense of what goes on in the world, people naturally think about things, people, and events in the form of narratives. By constructing stories, individuals organize their experiences, create order, explain unusual events, and gain perspective and make evaluations (Bruner 1990). Narratives place events into framing contexts so that the parts can be understood in relation to the whole. Thus, for example, the meaning of an event is the result of its being a part of a plot (Polkinghorne 1991). As a result of this emplotment, people can make meaningful evaluations (Pennington and Hastie 1992), form judgments (Gergen and Gergen 1988), and inform action (Olson 1990). This format for experienced events also makes them memorable and sharable (Olson 1990).

Narrative thought also informs emotional experiences. First, narratives play a role in emotion appraisal (Shweder 1994). Since narrative thought provides an interpretive scheme to organize the world and one's relationship to it, they help determine the self-relevancy of events, which is a necessary precursor to emotion (Lazarus 1991). Some scholars assert that emotions have different "plots" that are matched to current situations, leading to different emotional responses (Shweder 1994). Second, stories help people understand, evaluate, and cope with emotions once they have been aroused. Narratives make emotions meaningful by placing them in the context of an individual's personal history and goals (Averill 1994). Others assert that to be intelligible, emotion must be a constituent of a recogniz-able narrative (Gergen and Gergen 1988). Finally, people may even have a narrative understanding of what is the best way to cope with or respond to emotion (Clore 1994).

Given this narrative understanding of the world, it is not surprising to learn that people also think of themselves in terms of self-stories. When asked "Who are you?", people give a narrative account of the past. The self is given content through narrative constructions (Kerby 1991). Different aspects of the self are illustrated with different stories about the past. Moments in time are not unrelated; rather there exist goal-directed, coherent sequences linking one's past, present, and future into a present identity. Thus, who one is is embedded in an ongoing, narrative history (Kerby 1991).

Narratives as a constructive organizing process

Narratives are similar to the general concepts of schemas or scripts in that they are organizing mental structures or frameworks. Whereas narratives serve as a cognitive organizing process (Polkinghorne 1991), schema are defined as the general knowledge a person possesses about a particular domain (Alba and Hasher 1983). A story schema is the knowledge about the structure of stories that underlies an individual's intuitions about what a story is (Brewer and Lichtenstein 1981; Mandler 1984). A story schema consists of a set of expectations about the way in which stories proceed, reflecting regularities from past encounters (Mandler 1984). It may contain information that differentiates a comedy from a tragedy, for example.

Narratives are distinct from schemas in that narratives have a more narrowly defined form and function. Narratives are also different from scripts, a category which may be considered a subset of schemas. Scripts represent commonly experienced events as an abstraction (Abelson 1981). Narratives, however, often vary significantly from scripts, with specific details and unusual events. In fact, stories conforming strictly to scripts have been given low story-ratings by subjects (Brewer and Lichtenstein 1981). Therefore, narratives are a unique concept, used by individuals to make meaning of the world at an intermediate level of abstraction. (See Table 9.1 for a summary of narrative terms.)

In this chapter I focus on the narrative mode of thought as a process, not a mental representation. Narratives are constructive. The typical story consists of interrelated episodes describing human action sequences; people are willing to make inferences and even delete (or forget) information in order to make their stories coherent and complete (Baumeister and Newman 1994). Narrative thinking does not lead people to ignore contradictions, but it provides a way for the inevitable inconsistencies that people observe in human behavior to be interpreted and remembered more easily (Baumeister and Newman 1994). In the narrative mode of thought, meaning is fluid and contextual (Reissman 1993). The human mind is a creative model-builder. Building stories is an ongoing process; people fit characters and episodes together in a narrative form to render the world and their lives meaningful.

Many scholars now assert that people naturally tend to think about and interpret the world around them through narrative thought (Bruner 1986 and 1990;

Table 9.1 Narrative definitions

Narrative	One or more episodes consisting of actors engaged in actions to achieve goals. Sequence initiated by some event and actions result in outcome(s). Linear chronology. Causality implicit or inferred. Often focus on particular and unusual events.
Story	Synonymous with narrative.
Story grammar	Grammatical rules that specify canonical story components and their order.
Story Schema	Abstract knowledge about the structure of stories.
Script	Abstract representation of commonly experienced events.
Schema	Abstract general knowledge about a particular domain
Plot	Synonymous with narrative (Elsewhere, emphasis on causality (Stern 1994).)
Drama	Narrative in a visual or spoken medium (e.g., stage, cinema, television, radio). (Elsewhere, classical drama consists of beginning, rising action, turning point, falling action, and resolution (Stern 1994).)
Narrative processing	The mode of thought where individuals process incoming information as if they were trying to create a story. The imposition of narrative structure on occurrences, the creation of stories.
Narrative thought	Synonymous with narrative processing.

Kerby 1991). Narrative is the mode of thought that best captures the experiential aspect of human intention, action, and consequences; it involves reasons and goals (Reissman 1993). The narrative process is so pervasive that people spontaneously create stories to explain the random movement of colored rectangles, attributing causality to the movement (Michotte 1963 in Hermans 1996). Bruner (1986) suggests a genetic proclivity for narrative. He proposes that the reason people have no early infancy memories is that they are unable to organize events in narrative form at that stage of development.

As story builders, people do not record the world but rather create it, mixing in cultural and individual expectations, and combining sensory input and schematic knowledge (Chafe 1990). Narratives are a construction; they require creativity (Olson 1990). Stories are also greatly influenced by the social setting in which a person exists (Kerby 1991). The stories that people tell one another and themselves are determined in part both by shared language and the genre of storytelling inherited from traditions.

Summary

Overall, narrative structure helps people organize and understand events, situations, and others, as well as their emotional responses to them. Individuals think in terms of stories, linking what occurs in their lives in a goal-oriented fashion that provides meaning and purpose. Narratives provide the temporal and relational structure and context necessary for people to make sense of who they are, what they feel, what they own and use, and what their place in the world is.

Advertising narratives

Many advertisements tell stories. Most often, an ad is a self-contained narrative. For example, a recent ad for Pizza Hut has all the narrative elements described above. The initiating event is the commencement of a Little League baseball game. The main character, a young red-headed boy, is sent out to play right field (physical state). The boy looks a little confused and does not appear to be paying attention to the game (psychological state). The action begins when a ball is hit in the boy's direction. He raises his glove and miraculously catches the ball (accomplishing his goal). His face first registers shock, then joy. The cheering team runs out to celebrate this game-winning catch (the outcome). These consequences continue at Pizza Hut, where the team is shown celebrating its victory, with the rightfielder at the center of attention.

In addition to ads that are complete stories in and of themselves, ad campaigns can have varying degrees of storytelling. For example, some ad campaigns tell the same basic story over and over again with different characters and in different settings. In ads for the pain killer Aleve, for example, the protagonist is a hard-working individual who suffers from arthritis. He or she used to need many doses of other pain-relief medicine to make it through the day, but with Aleve he or she is able to take just two pills in the morning and work pain free for the entire day. The characters may be cowboy hat manufacturers, electricians, or seamstresses, but the narrator is always a caring loved-one.

Other ad campaigns tell ongoing stories in serial form. These are the melo-dramas of advertising. Again, there are varying degrees of this structure. The Sprint "Dime Zone" campaign is loosely tied together from one ad to the next. These ads tell a series of independent stories about the way that different characters' lives are changed for the better when they discover the Sprint dime-a-minute rate. The stories are connected when the dime is passed on to another lucky customer, who becomes the protagonist in the next Sprint ad. The quintessential continuing story campaign is that of Taster's Choice. These ads are nearly soap operas, with each successive ad building on the story-line presented in the last ad (or episode). The ads all end on a suspenseful note: for example, what will happen to the couple who fell in love over Taster's Choice coffee when the woman's ex-husband appears on the scene? The success of the Taster's Choice campaign has led to other continuing story campaigns, including Hallmark cards (a young woman tries to teach her boyfriend the importance of looking at the back of cards) and Miracle Whip (a detective has an unsteady relationship with a woman who makes him sandwiches with Miracle Whip).

While these examples of storied advertisements show some variety, they all contain the basic narrative elements of chronology and causality. The definition of a narrative ad is simply an ad that tells a story. The extent to which an ad tells a story, however, is a matter of degree (Mick 1987). Some ads may not have all the elements required to be a story. Others may focus on what happens but not why. Others may not allow viewers into the hearts and minds of the characters. Thus, the narrative structure of advertising runs along a continuum, with completely non-narrative ads on one end, and well-developed, complete, and moving stories on the other end. Furthermore, non-narrative ads take many forms. The proto-typical non-narrative ad can be categorized as lecture (Deighton *et al.* 1989; Wells 1988), informational (Puto and Wells 1984), or rational/cognitive advertisements (Aaker and Norris 1982).

Based on Laskey *et al.*'s (1989) typology of main message strategies, narrative ads can be found in all four classes of transformational ads. Narrative ads are often used to associate the experience of using a brand with psychological char-acteristics (Puto and Wells 1984). Stories in ads focus on the user (character), brand image, usage occasion, and product class (Laskey *et al.* 1989). However, not all transformational ads tell stories. Vignettes, which show a series of scenes or actions (see discussion below), are an example of transformational advertisements that typically do not tell a story. Celebrity endorsements may also be transforma-tional, but are not typically narratives (Qualls and Puto 1998). Another example of a non-narrative, transformational ad is the Coca-Cola campaign that shows a red button with lively music lyrics against colorful, ever-changing backgrounds. This ad may be well liked, it may evoke emotion and set a mood, it may even enhance Coke's brand image, but it doesn't tell a story. (Table 9.2 highlights some advertising definitions.)

The pervasiveness of advertising narratives

In order to make assertions about the importance of advertising narratives, I conducted a content analysis of 323 television advertisements that aired in Tuc-son, Arizona, during the three week period: 6.22.97, 6.29.97, 7.6.97. Ten hours of television programming was taped, covering: a broad range of prime time, day time, and late evening hours; the five major networks (ABC, CBS, NBC, FOX, and UPN), cable networks (TBS, A&E), and local affiliates; sports, situation comedy, drama, talk show, and news formats; and white and African American target audiences (see Table 9.3 for a description of the shows taped). The commercials advertised major corporations and local businesses, as well as pro-moting public service issues. The ads promoted many product classes: other television shows (50 ads, 17.8 percent of the total); automobiles (33, 11.7 percent); beverages (25, 8.9 percent); food products (22, 7.8 percent); medicine/first aid products (19, 6.8 percent); personal hygiene products (14, 5.0 percent); movies (12, 4.3 percent); and restaurants (10, 3.6 percent). The fifty ads promoting other television shows and forty-two repeat ads were eliminated from the analysis, leaving a set of 231 advertisements.

All ads were coded by the author for the degree to which the ad contained the

Table 9.2 Advertising definitions

Narrative ad	An ad containing a narrative (typically one episode, although may be more).
Drama ad	Synonymous with narrative ad. (Elsewhere, emphasis on show v. tell (Wells 1988)), absence of narration (Deighton *et al.* 1989), inclusion of classical drama elements (see Table 9.1) (Stern 1994).
Story ad	Synonymous with narrative ad. (Elsewhere, emphasis on character, plot, and narration (Deighton *et al.* 1989)).
Vignette ad	A series of scenes and people, edited together in rapid succession, no chronology, no causality (Stern 1994).
Transformational ad	An ad that causes the experience with the product/brand to be different than the same experience would be without the ad (Puto and Wells 1984).
Slice of life ad	An ad with story-like scenarios (Mick 1987).
Informational ad	An ad that provides consumers with factual, relevant brand data in a logical manner (Puto and Wells 1984).
Lecture ad	An ad that tells the consumer about the product/brand (as opposed to showing) (Wells 1988).
Argument ad	A narrated ad with no characters and no plot (Deighton *et al.* 1989).
Rational/Cognitive ad	Synonymous with informational ads (Aaker and Norris 1982).

narrative elements discussed above and the degree to which the ad unfolded over time on two separate five-point scales. The scales are as follows:

- Is this a well-developed story in terms of its elements (scene, actor, purpose/ intention/goal, action, response, outcome)?
- Does this ad have a temporal dimension (beginning, middle, end, occurs over time)?

The scores on these two scales were averaged to form one narrative structure score. When analyzing the ads, the scales were applied conservatively. In order to achieve a five on temporality, an ad had to show a distinct beginning, middle, and end and a progression through time, such as a child growing up. To receive a five on structural elements, the ad had to show actors engaged in actions to achieve goals. This scale item also required a distinct initiating event and outcome. I found that many ads neither begin at the beginning of a story nor provide a well-defined conclusion. Based on this conservative approach, ads were considered to be well-developed narratives if they scored four or more on the combined five-point narrative structure scale. By that criterion, 21.6 percent (55) of the ads reviewed contained well-developed stories. Additionally, 40.3 percent (93) of the ads were equal to or above the midpoint ($\geq$ 3) in terms of narrative structure.

An ANOVA model was run to test whether the shows in which the ads were

Table 9.3 Programming taped for content analysis

Program	Network	Show type	Time/date	Length taped
WNBA	NBC	Sports/weekend	1.30 p.m. 6.22.97	1 hour
60 Minutes	CBS	News/primetime	6.00 p.m. 6.22.97	1 hour
Caroline in the City	NBC	Situation comedy/primetime	8.00 p.m. 6.23.97	$^1/_2$ hour
Suddenly Susan	NBC	Situation comedy/primetime	8.30 p.m. 6.23.97	$^1/_2$ hour
Voyager	UPN	Sci-fi, drama/syndicated	8.00 p.m. 6.25.97	1 hour
Seinfeld	NBC	Situation comedy/primetime	8.00 p.m. 6.26.97	$^1/_2$ hour
Rosie O'Donnell	NBC	Talk show/daytime	3.00 p.m. 6.30.97	1 hour
Home Improvement	ABC	Situation comedy/primetime	8.00 p.m. 7.1.97	$^1/_2$ hour
Spin City	ABC	Situation comedy/primetime	8.30 p.m. 7.1.97	$^1/_2$ hour
Biography	A&E	Documentary, drama/cable	9.00 p.m. 7.1.97	1 hour
Wimbledon	NBC	Sports/weekend	9.30 a. m. 7.5.97	$^1/_2$ hour
The Beverly Hillbillies	TBS	Situation comedy/cable	1.00 p.m. 7.6.97	$^1/_2$ hour
Living Single	FOX	Situation comedy/primetime	7.30 p.m. 7.10.97	$^1/_2$ hour
Local News	NBC	News/local affiliate	6.00 p.m. 7.11.97	$^1/_2$ hour
Late Night (Letterman)	NBC	Talk show/late night	10.35 p.m. 7.11.97	$^1/_2$ hour

embedded, or the product categories being advertised, were significantly related to the degree to which the ads had a narrative structure (8 categories × 15 shows). Only product category had a significant effect on narrative structure (F[7,210]=3.62, p < 0.001). This result appears to be driven by the high narrative structure of ads for beverages – alcoholic and non-alcoholic – (μ=3.24), and the low score for commercials advertising movies (μ=1.58). In fact, if ads for movies are deleted from the set (it can be argued that ads for movies are creatively constrained by the fact that they must condense a two-hour narrative into a thirty-second advertisement), the percentage of commercials that tell a story (narrative score ≥ 4.0) increases to 22.8 percent.

Although the shows in which the ads were embedded did not have a significant relationship to narrative structure, the ads shown during the *Seinfeld* episode had the highest average narrative score (μ=3.0). Others (Deighton *et al.* 1989) have argued that television commercials can be considered to be good ads because firms are willing to invest in them. By that criterion, the ads on *Seinfeld* should be especially good, as *Seinfeld* is the highest rated show in America (and therefore the most expensive to air advertisements). Furthermore, the lowest average narrative structure score corresponded to ads aired during an afternoon rerun of *The Beverly*

Hillbillies on TBS (μ=1.79), in all likelihood the least expensive air time. This implies that narrative advertisements are considered by advertisers to be good ads – that is, ads that provide the company benefits that exceed the high cost of running them. Overall, based on the findings of the content analysis of television ads, it can be argued that narrative advertising plays a substantial role in current advertising campaigns. Therefore, it is of both practical and theoretical interest to understand the effects of this structural form.

Related advertising research

Narrative ads have been studied by some consumer researchers looking at drama in advertising (Stern 1994, Deighton *et al.* 1989), and by others who applied story grammar analysis to advertising (Mick 1987). In drama advertising research, however, the definitions of drama are not completely synonymous with the necessary elements of a story, as outlined above. Deighton *et al.* (1989) define drama ads as unnarrated ads, with characters and a plot. They contrast drama ads with story ads (narrated, character, plot), demonstration ads (narrated, no character, plot), and argument ads (narrated, no character, no plot). Narrative theory argues, however, that all stories have a narrator presence, or at least a perspectival stance (Bruner 1990). In a film or play, the audience may feel that they are "directly witnessing" the action, in which case the narrator may be substituted by a point of view (Chapman 1978). In non-narrated story ads, people view the action through a character's perspective which replaces, in some sense, an overt narrator (see also Stern 1994). Thus, Deighton *et al.*'s distinction between drama ads and story ads is not entirely clear. Both forms can be considered to be narrative ads.

Although Deighton *et al.* develop a four-level ad structure taxonomy, their empirical work contrasts only drama and argument ads. The authors find that drama advertising affects persuasion by evoking feelings and by verisimilitude, which they operationalize as drawing the viewer into the ad and the ad being perceived with authenticity. Argument ads, on the other hand, affect persuasion by presenting convincing arguments that do not evoke a great deal of counter-arguing. Thus, drama ads, which I would argue are synonymous with the definition of narrative ads presented in this chapter, work by generating affect, personally involving the viewer in the ad, and appearing to be realistic or believable stories.

In terms of Stern's research on drama advertising, narrative ads are, in essence, classical dramas (Stern 1994). Stern refers to Freytag's pyramid (in Sternberg 1978) to define the elements of classical drama. A classical drama consists of a beginning, rising action, turning point, falling action, and resolution. This is entirely consistent with the way stories have been defined by narrative research. Stern distinguishes classical drama ads from vignettes, which she defines as a series of "stories." I would assert that these are not stories by the criteria set up here, for they have no beginning, middle, and end. Vignettes are better referred to as a sequence of scenes or actions. Vignettes are also distinguished from classical drama by the way that they occur in time. Classical dramas, as narratives, have a linear chronology, whereas vignettes are discrete, unconnected pieces of time – further evidence that vignette ads are not narrative ads. However, some vignette ads may be organized around a story-like theme, making the relationship between vignettes and narratives a matter of degree.

Stern (1994) theorizes that classical dramas, which are essentially narratives, are persuasive because they provide consumers with a coherent cause–effect progression. In response, consumers are able to make causal attributions about the product/person/situation interaction. Additionally, she claims that classical dramas work through empathy. Consumers are actively drawn into classical dramas and therefore experience affective reactions. This is consistent with Deighton *et al.*'s (1989) empirical findings that drama persuades through emotional responses.

Mick (1987) applied the formal structural analysis of story grammars to advertising, despite the fact that story grammars have primarily been used to study folktales and tend to have limited applicability (Mandler 1984). Mick found that the grammaticality of story ads was a matter of degree. In this type of analysis, ads are broken down into their "base structure," which consists of the grammatical story components, primarily a series of episodes (further deconstructed, see above). He asserts that by analyzing story ads via the story grammar approach, advertisers can identify whether ads are story-like or not, as well as determine the influence of story ad structure on cognitive ad responses such as recall.

In his story grammar article, Mick points out three interesting differences between traditional stories (found in books and movies, for example) and televised advertising narratives. First, consumers have preconceived ideas about the persuasive intent of the advertiser (see also Friestad and Wright 1994). Viewers approach advertising with more skepticism than they do a book or movie. Second, advertising narratives are pictorial. Therefore, they are more like movies than books. Finally, stories in ads are compressed to just 30 to 60 seconds. They typically can consist of one or two episodes at most.

In conducting the content analysis for this chapter, I found that many ads do not begin with an initial event, but instead tend to "throw you into the action," allowing the viewer to pick up the story-line quickly via inferencing. Because narrative processing occurs naturally and requires little effort, consumers are able to understand fairly complex stories rapidly. This makes advertising narratives appealing for two reasons. First, they are able to overcome the time constraint of advertising; second, they can be understood in a low involvement setting.

Story quality in advertisements

Although all advertising narratives tell stories, some ads tell "better" stories than others. The Pizza Hut ad described above (p. 274) is likely be judged as a better story than many story ads that demonstrate simple product usage scenarios. (Three independent coders gave the Pizza Hut ad a score of five on the two five-point scale items used in the content analysis, compared to lower narrative scores for a variety of product usage scenario ads – Escalas 1996). For example, a typical pain relief product ad shows a character in pain (the initial event, or the result of some other initial event). To solve this problem, the character uses the pain relief product (goal and action). The outcome is a happy, pain-free protagonist. Even though this ad is in the form of a story (it would have received a narrative score between a three and a four in the content analysis), it is not very compelling.

Why is one advertising narrative better than another? The answer is: for the same reason that one story is more compelling than another. Providing the consumer with a landscape of consciousness is one way that an advertising narrative can be more interesting and entertaining. When people are able to relate to a character's thoughts and feelings and observe personal development, they are more likely to be drawn into the ad story. Furthermore, ads that evoke emotion can move or touch consumers in a personal way. Gergen and Gergen's (1988) research on dramatic engagement suggests that an advertising narrative in which the protagonist's situation rapidly improves or worsens, or alternates between the two, should be especially good at generating feelings responses in consumers.

Another aspect of ad story quality is the extent to which the ad is novel. Story ads with a narrative imbalance should be more interesting and provocative than those that conform too rigidly to expectations. Additionally, ads that follow repetitive story-lines may become abstractions to consumers. Rather than focusing on the particular events, the story may be perceived as mechanistic. Narrative research has shown that scripts score low on measures of story quality (Brewer and Lichtenstein 1981). Therefore, overdependence on the use of story "formulas" may eliminate the benefits of advertising narratives. However, if a story ad is too novel, or if it departs from expectations too much, then the advertiser may sacrifice ease of understanding (Mandler 1984). People have expectations about how stories will unfold, and too large a breach in those expectations can lead to incomprehensibility, particularly in a 30 to 60 second ad.

In addition to the quality of the story in the ad, marketers are interested in the types of responses that advertising narratives evoke from consumers. Literary analysts have long assumed that an audience's response to a presentation is shaped by its form (see Deighton et al. 1989). How does the narrative form of ads affect consumers' responses? I propose that narratively structured advertisements lead to narrative thought processes. Narrative processing, in turn, results in a variety of affective, cognitive, and behavioral responses to the ad and the product/brand.

Priming narrative thought using advertising

There are a variety of methods by which an ad can invoke narrative thought. Ads may be presented to consumers in the form of a story, which is likely to prime narrative processing of the ad. For example, a recent Visa Gold Card ad tells the story of a young woman who took a dream vacation alone to Venice because her American boyfriend refused to leave work to join her. Once there, she fell in love with an Italian man. The fact that the ad is in the form of a story may prime the ad viewer to think in narrative form, processing the ad's events in keeping with the episode schema presented above, by piecing the elements together over time and focusing on causality. Alternatively, the individual may be drawn into the story, imagining himself or herself in Venice as the woman or the Italian man, or perhaps even the forgotten boyfriend, and experiencing the story events. Or the consumer may relate the externally presented story to a personal story and begin to think in a self-generated, narrative way about the last romantic vacation he or she took. In the first case, the ad is processed narratively, but the story is external to the ad viewer. The interaction is quite distant. In the second case, the viewer is drawn into the story, becoming personally caught up in the events. Self-referencing occurs as the viewer imagines himself or herself to be one of the characters. In this third case, the external narrative provides what can be considered a narrative shell or script; it provides an initial narrative direction or starting point for self-generated thought.

Another way in which advertising can elicit narrative thought is by directly encouraging self-generated narratives, for example stimulating autobiographical memories or mental simulation of product use. Both autobiographical memories and mental simulations are usually in the form of stories (Polkinghorne 1991; Fiske 1993). Here, rather than presenting a complete story, the ad may present songs or images designed to evoke memories of the past (Sujan *et al.* 1993), or the ad may be filmed from the first person perspective, encouraging imaginings about the future (Meyers-Levy and Peracchio 1996). Ads also present direct exhortations to think about the past (e.g., "Remember the times of your life," for Kodak film) or to imagine the future (e.g., "Imagine yourself in a Mercury"). Thus, ads may prime mental simulation and autobiographical memory retrieval indirectly with images, music, and so forth, or directly with specific instructions or cues for the consumer to follow.

What advertising narratives can do for ad responses

Based on the assertion that advertising narratives prime narrative thought, there are a variety of ways in which ads that tell stories can affect consumers. First, narrative advertisements can influence viewers' cognitive responses. They may be able to capture a viewer's attention and draw him or her into an ad. This personal involvement (or "hook") can be the result of an interesting and relevant plot, a familiar setting, or characters with whom the viewer can relate (Escalas *et al.* 1997). Similarly, advertising narratives can enhance character identification. Research has shown that the quality of a story in general leads to increased elaboration by the readers or listeners (Feldman *et al.* 1990). Ad viewers will engage in the cognitive activities necessary to comprehend the story, such as establishing relationships among the narrative elements, fitting the story to their story schemas, and developing causal inferences. This increased elaboration is likely to result in better recall about the ad and the brand.

Narrative thought also plays a role in creating, interpreting and understanding emotions. In advertising research, four types of feelings have been identified as capturing the majority of affective responses to ads: upbeat feelings, warm feelings, uneasy feelings, and disinterested feelings (Goodstein *et al.* 1990). Upbeat feelings, warm feelings, and uneasy feelings are likely to be positively related to narrative structure. However, narrative thought may be negatively related to disinterested feelings. As narrative structure improves, story quality improves, and hence subjects may be more interested in the ad, rather than distancing themselves and becoming skeptical.

It has been argued that emotions such as warm feelings arise in reaction to people or situations (Aaker *et al.* 1986; Escalas *et al.* 1997). These feelings may develop in response to stories. Narratives provide the characters and situations necessary to create an interpersonal or situational interaction. These "interpersonal" feelings can be contrasted with emotions that are more stimulus-driven such as upbeat feelings (see Zajonc 1980). Although story ads may evoke stimulus-driven feelings, other types of advertising (such as vignettes) may do so equally well. Overall, better stories in ads are likely to evoke more emotion, particularly "interpersonal feelings," than less well-developed narratives.

Since people naturally create meaning in the world based on stories, it is logical to assume that advertising narratives will help to create brand meaning for consumers. Narrative research has shown that people are very good at establishing the relationship between story elements and extrapolating meaning (Carr; 1986, Polkinghorne 1991). Thus, a story ad that provides a brand with a series of linkages to certain types of characters, settings, and usage scenarios creates meaning for that brand. If one of the connections built through the advertising narrative is to the consumer him/herself, then the brand's meaning may be especially compelling.

Finally, advertising narratives and narrative responses in consumers should have an impact on attitudes towards the ad and brand. Story ads are often judged to be good ads (with correspondingly high attitudes towards the ad (A_{ad})) because stories are an interesting and entertaining form of communication. Furthermore, narrative thought may provide a more enjoyable form of processing. These factors may favorably influence consumers' assessments of story ads. Favorable attitudes towards an ad have been shown to influence attitudes towards the advertised brand (A_B) positively (see Brown and Stayman 1992). There are also other mechanisms through which advertising narratives may favorably affect A_B. First, the positive emotions generated during narrative thought may be transferred to the brand. Second, narrative processing may evoke less criticism of the ad and brand than analytical thought. Third, consumers may understand and appreciate the way that the brand is to be used based on an advertising narrative. Lastly, because people often think of themselves in the form of narratives, narrative thought may create a link between the brand and the self, which contributes to a brand's meaning and value.

What advertising narratives can do for product experiences

The stories provided in narrative ads may do more than influence ad viewers' cognitive, affective, and attitudinal responses. The content of a narrative ad may set up a narrative shell or script that the viewer can use in subsequent purchase situations. One AT&T ad stars a businessman who is traveling alone, apparently homesick for his family. The ad shows the man feeling better after he calls his wife from the plane. The next time the consumer is on a plane feeling lonely, his or her narrative thoughts may be guided by the AT&T episode, particularly the positive outcome, and the consumer may be more favorably disposed to using the "air-fone." AT&T ad campaigns may have, over time, increased the primary demand for telephones in general as consumers have seen story after story highlighting the positive results of communicating by phone. When these consumers think about making phone calls, their own narrative enactment may be favorably inclined. Thus an ad can influence viewers' construction of narratives in the future. This ability to affect consumer narratives may allow marketers to make their brands more meaningful and valuable.

Narrative ads can also serve as "generic plots" that actually frame or influence subsequent consumption experiences with the brand. The externally provided narratives serve as a template enabling consumers to evaluate and make sense of their later experiences with the brand. If a consumer sees a story in which a worker thwarts her overbearing boss's criticism by using Federal Express, the consumer may feel more secure the next time he or she sends a package via Fed Ex (e.g., Deighton 1984). This is more than mere recall of an advertising narrative in a purchase setting; what I propose here is an effect on actual usage evaluations. A generic plot may affect the way that consumers cognitively inter-pret their experiences. For example, the woman in the Fed Ex ad may earn a promotion. This is not interpreted as a random event if the story in the ad indicates that the promotion was caused by her adept use of Fed Ex. But more than that, the next time consumers ship packages from work, they may actually believe that they are is doing a better job because they used Federal Express. Thus, consumers may come to construct their personal consumption experiences using the generic plots presented in narrative ads.

Many consumer behavior researchers have alluded to the power of stories in guiding and constructing subsequent consumption experiences. For example, Puto and Wells (1984) assert that transformational ads can "transform" product usage experiences, and Deighton (1984) argues that advertising suggests a hypothesis for consumers regarding what their consumption experiences will be like. When consumers later encounter ambiguous evidence (the consumption experience), confirmatory biases (Slovic et al. 1977) may lead them to evaluate those experi-ences in keeping with the hypotheses created in the advertising. Since many consumption experiences are subjective and ambiguous, consumers may construct stories to interpret such experiences using narratives suggested in advertising.

I do not mean to imply that only narrative ads are able to transform or guide consumption experiences. Other advertising structures may accomplish the same thing via different processes. However, story ads may be particularly well suited for "teaching" consumers what they should expect to experience (which then becomes what they actually perceive they experience though narrative interpretation). Scott (1994) asserts that narratives are more palatable than exhortation for changing beliefs. Narratives provide parables or exemplary stories that embody cultural expectations and values. Thus, advertising narratives can show consumers how to use the brand, how they will feel when they use the brand, and how they should evaluate their brand experience.

Summary

Advertising narratives allow marketers to achieve a variety of goals. Narrative advertising can prime narrative processing, generate feelings, increase involvement in and elaboration about the ad, create brand meaning, and improve ad and brand attitudes. Advertising narratives may also be more effective than non-narrative ads in affecting purchase decisions and transforming consumption experiences by providing a narrative shell or generic plot that guides future narrative processing.

Conclusion

In general, narrative structure helps individuals organize and understand situations, others, and themselves. People think in terms of stories, imposing a temporal and relational structure on events. This chapter extends narrative research to the realm of advertising. Many ads tell stories. Nearly a quarter of the ads reviewed in the content analysis of current television ads had a high level of narrative structure. I propose that advertising narratives evoke narrative processing in consumers which positively affects their cognitive, affective, attitudinal, and behavioral responses to the ad and the brand/product.

Theoretical contributions

The narrative processes discussed throughout this chapter provide new insights into the way that consumers actually think about and understand advertising. First, the distinction between narrative and paradigmatic thought, although relatively new to consumer research, is very important. People are not objective fact finders; rather, they are story builders. They understand the world around them by relating events temporally and building narrative relationships to attribute causality. There may be some cases where consumers research a problem, gather information, and integrate that information somewhat scientifically but, on a day-to-day basis, I claim that most of what consumers feel, think, and do is based on the stories they hear and create.

More specifically, narratives are able to create meaning via their structure. The relational structure and temporal dimension of stories are the enabling factors of meaning creation. Other consumer research involving narrative notions (e.g., Thompson *et al.* 1990; Kleine *et al.* 1995) has theorized that consumers use narratives to understand their consumption experiences and to create their self-identities. This chapter extends their research by elucidating precisely how narratives are able to do this.

Additionally, I have extended narrative research to the realm of advertising. The narrative framework allows consumer researchers to understand many different types of advertising that have been studied by others, such as drama ads, transformational ads, slice of life ads, ads that evoke autobiographical memory, ads that induce mental simulation, and so forth, from a single perspective. All of these ad types elicit narrative thought. While there may be subtle differences in the degree to which narrative thought is evoked, and its subsequent effects, an overall framework based on the way that narrative processing works, and its general effects, contributes to our understanding of these ad types.

Directions for future research

In closing, I suggest four potential avenues for future research into this important topic.

In this chapter I have made a variety of claims about the effects of advertising narratives on consumers. Future research examining the relationship between narrative advertisements and viewers' affective, attitudinal, and cognitive responses (including narrative processing) is necessary to provide empirical support for these assertions.

A particularly interesting prediction made in this chapter regards the power of stories in ads to guide and transform subsequent consumption experiences, building on the research of Puto and Wells (1984) and Deighton (1984). Do narrative ads "transform" subsequent consumption experiences better than ads that are not narratives? Are these later interactions with products influenced in manners consistent with the stories shown in narrative advertising? Do consumers use stories to interpret their experiences with brands? Are these stories affected by the stories told in ads? Future research can examine the way that narrative ads that serve as generic plots influence subsequent brand experiences.

Another interesting avenue for future research involves vignette advertising. Of the ads that scored low on narrative structure in the content analysis, not all were traditional lecture or argument ads. Many were vignette ads, with a rapid succession of scenes, perhaps with music tying the images together. In some ways, vignettes are like stories, but in other ways they are not. For example, vignettes have scenes and characters, but they typically have neither a temporal dimension nor causal relationships between elements. Stern (1994) asserts that this type of ad persuades through exposure to multiple observations. Based on these multiple observations, consumers make causal attributions about the product/person/situation interaction. Remember that with narrative ads, one instance is enough to allow for causal inferencing due to the temporal and relational structure of stories. In terms of emotional reactions, Stern argues that vignettes engender sympathy, with viewers more detached and in control of their emotions. Sympathy can be considered a less "interpersonal" emotion than empathy, which is evoked by classical drama ads (i.e., narrative ads).

The temporal dimension of narratives is a critical distinction between story ads and vignettes. Stories unfold over time, but vignettes are often temporally disjointed. However, this categorization is not completely dichotomous. It is possible to imagine ads that present a story in the form of vignettes by showing either the same characters in different settings or different characters in similar plots. A recent McDonald's ad told approximately three stories in one vignette ad. The ad quickly circulated through three different stories, each with a beginning, middle, and end and three sets of characters engaged in actions to achieve goals. The ad thus told three stories simultaneously. Future research can empirically examine the mechanisms by which narrative and vignette advertising persuade consumers, including the role of the types of attributions made and emotions generated as mediating factors. Experimental research provides the opportunity to examine the effect of structural narrative elements such as temporal unfolding and goal-oriented action sequences.

Finally, one of the compelling rationales for studying the role of narratives in advertising is the fact that narrative thought is natural and pervasive in human thought. As a communication device, narratives require little involvement and processing effort, making them especially well suited for advertising. However, a great deal of advertising research is based on the notion that by increasing the degree of consumer elaboration, advertisers can positively influence recall and brand attitudes (e.g., Greenwald and Leavitt 1984; Kardes 1988). Future research can examine what this implies for advertising narratives. Are stories in ads less effective because they require lower levels of elaboration for comprehension? Or are they a more effective way to achieve the same level of recall? Prior research has been inconclusive (Escalas 1996). I hypothesize that stories in ads reduce the elaboration and involvement threshold necessary to achieve a positive effect on recall and attitudes. However, the central role of the brand in the story may prove to be a key moderator of this effect.

In this chapter I hope I have demonstrated that the narrative approach to advertising has important implications for the study of consumer behavior by conceptualizing what advertising narratives are, providing a theoretical framework for how they work, and putting forward ideas for future research.

Acknowledgments

I would like to thank Jim Bettman, Barbara Stern, and George Zinkhan for their thoughtful comments and suggestions.

References

Aaker, D., and Norris, D. (1982) "Characteristics of TV Commercials Perceived as Informative," *Journal of Advertising Research*, 22, 2: 22–34.

Aaker, D., Stayman, D.M., and Hagerty, M. R. (1986), "Warmth in Advertising: Measurement, Impact, and Sequence Effects," *Journal of Consumer Research*, 12, 4: 365–81.

Abelson, R.P. (1981) "The Psychological Status of the Script Concept," *American Psychologist*, 36, 7: 715–29.

Alba, J.W. and Hasher, L. (1983) "Is Memory Schematic?" *Psychological Bulletin*, 93, 2: 203–31.

Averill, J.R. (1994) "I Feel, Therefore I Am – I Think," in P. Ekman and R. J. Davidson (eds) *The Nature of Emotion: Fundamental Questions*, New York, NY: Oxford University Press, 379–85.

Baumeister, R.F. and Newman, L.S. (1994) "How Stories Make Sense of Personal Experiences: Motives that Shape Autobiographical Narratives," *Personality and Social Psychology Bulletin*, 20, 6: 676–90.

Brewer, W.F. and Lichtenstein, E.H. (1981) "Event Schemas, Story Schemas, and Story Grammars," in J. Long and A. Baddeley (eds) *Attention and Performance IX*, Hillsdale, NJ: Lawrence Erlbaum Associates, 363–79.

Brown, S.P. and Stayman, D.M. (1992) "Antecedents and Consequences of Attitude Toward the Ad: A Meta-analysis," *Journal of Consumer Research*, 19, 1: 34–51.

Bruner, J. (1986) *Actual Minds, Possible Worlds*, Cambridge, MA: Harvard University Press.

—— (1990) *Acts of Meaning*, Cambridge, MA: Harvard University Press.

Burke, K. (1969) *A Grammar of Motives*, Berkeley, CA: University of California Press.

Carr, D. (1986) *Time, Narrative, and History*, Bloomington, IN: Indiana University Press.

Chafe, W. (1990) "Some Things that Narratives Tell Us About the Mind," in B.K. Britton and A.D Pelligrini (eds) *Narrative Thought and Narrative Language*, Hillsdale, NJ: Lawrence Erlbaum Associates, 79–98.

Chapman, S. (1978) *Story and Discourse: Narrative Structure in Fiction and Film*, Ithaca, NY: Cornell University Press.

Clore, G.L. (1994) "Why Emotions are Felt," in P. Ekman and R.J. Davidson (eds) *The Nature of Emotion: Fundamental Questions*, New York, NY: Oxford University Press, 103–11.

Deighton, J. (1984) "The Interaction of Advertising and Evidence," *Journal of Consumer Research*, 11, 3: 763–70.

Deighton, J., Romer D., and McQueen, J. (1989) "Using Drama to Persuade," *Journal of Consumer Research*, 16, 3: 335–43.

Escalas, J.E. (1996) "Narrative Processing: Building Connections between Brands and the Self," unpublished dissertation, Duke University, Durham, North Carolina.

Escalas, J.E., Moore, M.C., and Edell, J.A. (1997) "Fishing for Feelings: Having a Hook Helps!" working paper, Duke University, Durham, North Carolina.

Feldman, C.F., Bruner, J., Renderer, B., and Spitzer S. (1990) "Narrative Comprehension," in B.K. Britton and A.D. Pelligrini (eds) *Narrative Thought and Narrative Language*, Hillsdale, NJ: Lawrence Erlbaum Associates, 1–78.

Fiske, S.T. (1993) "Social Cognition and Social Perception," *Annual Review of Psychology* 44: 155–94.

Friestad, M. and Wright, P. (1994) "The Persuasion Knowledge Model: How People Cope with Persuasion Attempts," *Journal of Consumer Research*, 21, 1: 1–31.

Gergen, K.J. and Gergen, M.M. (1988) "Narrative and the Self as Relationship," *Advances in Experimental Social Psychology* 21, 1: 17–56.

Goodstein, R.C., Edell, J.A., and Moore, M.C. (1990) "When are Feelings Generated? Assessing the Presence and Reliability of Feelings Based on Storyboards and Animatics," in S.J. Agres, J.A. Edell, and T.J. Dubitsky (eds) *Emotion in Advertising: Theoretical and Practical Explorations*, Westport, CT: Quorum Books, 175–93.

Greenwald, A.G., and Leavitt, C. (1984) "Audience Involvement in Advertising: Four Levels," *Journal of Consumer Research*, 11, 1: 581–92.

Hermans, H.M. (1996) "Voicing the Self: From Information Processing to Dialogical Interchange," *Journal of Personality and Social Psychology*, 119, 1: 31–50.

Kardes, F.R. (1988) "Spontaneous Inference Processes in Advertising: The Effects of Conclusion Omission and Involvement on Persuasion," *Journal of Consumer Research*, 15, 2: 225–33.

Kerby, A.P. (1991) *Narrative and the Self*, Bloomington, IN: Indiana University Press.

Kleine, S.S., Kleine, R.E., III, and Allen, C.T. (1995) "How is a Possession 'Me' or 'Not Me'? Characterizing Types and the Antecedents of Material Possession Attachment," *Journal of Consumer Research*, 22, 3: 327–43.

Laskey, H.A., Day, E., and Crask, M.R. (1989) "Typology of Main Message Strategies for Television Commercials," *Journal of Advertising*, 18, 1: 36–41.

Lazarus, R.S. (1991) "Progress on a Cognitive-Motivational-Relational Theory of Emotion," *American Psychologist*, 46, 8: 819–34.

Lucariello, J. (1990) "Canonicality and Consciousness in Child Narrative," in B.K. Britton and A.D. Pelligrini (eds.) *Narrative Thought and Narrative Language*, Hillsdale, NJ: Lawrence Erlbaum Associates, 131–50.

McQuarrie, E.F., and Mick, D.G. (1996) "Figures of Rhetoric in Advertising Language," *Journal of Consumer Research*, 22, 4: 424–38.

Mandler, J.M. (1984) *Stories, Scripts, and Scenes: Aspects of Schema Theory*, Hillsdale, NJ: Lawrence Erlbaum Associates.

Meyers-Levy, J., and Peracchio, L. (1996) "Moderators of the Impact of Self-Reference on Persuasion," *Journal of Consumer Research*, 22, 4: 408–23.

Mick, D.G. (1987) "Toward a Semiotic of Advertising Story Grammars," in J. Umiker-Sebeok (ed.) *Marketing and Semiotics: New Directions in the Study of Signs for Sale*, Berlin, Germany: Walter de Gruyter & Co., 249–78.

Olson, D.R. (1990) "Thinking About Narrative," in B.K. Britton and A.D. Pelligrini (eds) *Narrative Thought and Narrative Language*, Hillsdale, NJ: Lawrence Erlbaum Associates, 99–112.

Pennington, N. and Hastie, R. (1986) "Evidence Evaluation in Complex Decision Making," *Journal of Personality and Social Psychology*, 51, 2: 242–58.

—— (1992) "Explaining the Evidence: Tests of the Story Model for Juror Decision Making," *Journal of Personality and Social Psychology*, 62, 2: 189–206.

Polkinghorne, D.E. (1991) "Narrative and Self-Concept," *Journal of Narrative and Life History*, 1 (2 and 3): 135–53.

Puto, C.P. and Wells, W.D. (1984) "Informational and Transformational Advertising: The Differential Effects of Time," in T.C. Kinnear (ed.) *Advances in Consumer Research*, 11, Proto, UT: Association for Consumer Research, 572–6.

Qualls, W.J., and Puto, C. P. (1998) "Celebrities and Transformation: Using Cultural Icons to Create Brand Perceptions," paper presented at a special session on "Popular Culture and Marketing Effects: An Examination of Processes Influencing Consumers'

Brand Perceptions" at the American Marketing Association Winter Educators' Conference, Austin, TX, 20 February.

Reissman, C.K. (1993) *Narrative Analysis* (Qualitative Research Methods, 30), Newbury Park, CA: Sage Publications.

Scott, L.M. (1994) "The Bridge from Text to Mind: Adapting Reader-Response Theory to Consumer Research," *Journal of Consumer Research*, 21, 3: 461–80.

Shweder, R.A. (1994) "You're Not Sick: You're Just in Love," in P. Ekman and R.J. Davidson (eds.) *The Nature of Emotion: Fundamental Questions*, New York, NY: Oxford University Press, 32–44.

Slovic, P., Fischoff, B. and Lichtenstein, S. (1977) "Behavioral Decision Theory," *Annual Review of Psychology*, 28: 1–39.

Stern, B.B. (1994) "Classical and Vignette Television Advertising Dramas: Structural Models, Formal Analysis, and Consumer Effects," *Journal of Consumer Research*, 20, 4: 601–15.

Sternberg, M. (1978) *Expositional Modes and Temporal Ordering in Fiction*, Baltimore, MD: Johns Hopkins University Press.

Sujan, M., Bettman, J.R., and Baumgartner, H. (1993) "Influencing Judgments Using Autobiographical Memories: A Self-Referencing Perspective," *Journal of Marketing Research*, 30, 4: 422–36.

Thompson, C.J., Locander, W.B., and Pollio, H.R. (1990) "The Lived Meaning of Free Choice: An Existential–Phenomenological Description of Everyday Consumer Experiences of Contemporary Married Women," *Journal of Consumer Research*, 17, 2: 346–61.

Wells, W. D. (1988) "Lectures and Dramas," in P. Cafferata and A. Tybout (eds) *Cognitive and Affective Responces to Advertising*, Lexington, MA: Lexington Books, 13–20.

Zajonc, R.B. (1980) "Feeling and Thinking: Preferences Need No Inferences," *American Psychologist*, 35, 2: 151–75.

10

POETRY AND REPRESENTATION IN CONSUMER RESEARCH

The art of science

Barbara B. Stern

with poems by George M. Zinkhan and John F. Sherry, Jr.

> Poets, by creating new ways of feeling and perceiving, help to create the new ways of thinking that bring us to terms with a changing world . . . It is one thing to describe these new develop-ment in the language of science, but how are we to take these new and urgent realities into our hearts as well as our minds, unless poets give us new images with which to experience them?
>
> (Hayakawa 1964: 270–1)

History of poetry in consumer research

This will be brief. Ten years after Belk argued for poetry's "contribution to knowledge" about consumer behavior (1986: 19), one poem has been published in the journal of record – the *Journal of Consumer Research*. The poem is Sydney Levy's "Awash in Ideas," included in his article, "Stalking the Amphisbaena" (1996: 173). In 1993–4, the *International Journal of Research in Marketing* published four poems, and in 1997 *Consumption, Markets, and Culture* will publish three poems. The count is more robust in the *Journal of Advertising*, where nine poems have been published since September 1992. In view of the paucity of items published, submitting this chapter to a scholarly journal would probably invite negative evaluations of the "length to contribution" ratio and the "contribution to disciplinary knowledge" criterion. In addition, the intrusion of poetry in a scientific journal might offend as many readers as the intrusion of a scientific study in a literary publication. As Northrop Frye comments, in one of his rare uncharitable pronouncements, "I understand that there is a Ph.D. thesis somewhere which displays a list of Hardy's novels on the order of the percentages of gloom they contain, but one does not feel that that sort of procedure should be encouraged" (1973: 19).

Indeed, Frye continues, "there is nothing to be gained by confusing the standards of the two subjects" (1973: 19). According to the standards of social science, poetry does not measure anything, represents but one person's voice, and cannot be evaluated in terms of reliability and validity. Its nearest analog is introspective research, which also generates knowledge about universal habits of human thinking and feeling by closely examining individual experiences. Although introspection has made some inroads into consumer behavior research (Holbrook 1995; Gould 1991), it is currently stalled, perhaps because it has been the object of vigorous criticism (Wallendorf and Brucks 1993). The criticisms apply to poetry as well, which falls equally short as a social science research tool by fusing the roles of researcher and introspector, by relying exclusively on the insights of a single individual, and by conveying ambiguous meaning. Poetry has barely entered the consumer behavior literature in journals that, in a word, "speak" to the entire field.

Undaunted by the scarcity of exemplars, I nonetheless propose a reconsideration of poetry as a representational mode that can enrich understanding of consumers. This chapter's "defense of poesy" borrows freely from literary criticism, a rich source of information about the nature of specialized poetic language, its difference from scientific statements (Brooks and Warren 1960), and its capacity to convey a texture of experience exceeded only by the reality of the experience itself. It is based on the close association between poetry and advertising and its historical legitimacy as a respectable way of knowing (Belk 1986). Following the defense, there is a selection of poems written by George Zinkhan and John F. Sherry, Jr.

"The poet makes silk dresses out of worms" (Wallace Stevens)

Poetry occupies a special place as a contributor to knowledge about consumption because of its kinship with advertising. Burnett's definition of advertising creativity – "the art of establishing new and meaningful relationships" (Blasko and Mokwa 1986: 48) – merely restates Stevens's line. The creative talent of copywriters resembles that of poets (Zinkhan 1993), as Orwell points out in *Keep the Aspidistra Flying* (1936). The character Gordon Comstock, a former poet, translates his talents into copywriting as a result of an agency personnel shift. When Mr Erskine finds himself in charge of the New Albion advertising agency and discovers that Gordon Comstock has published some verses in a magazine, he decides that Comstock would make a suitable copywriter trainee:

> Wrote poetry, did he? Oh yes? Hm. And had it printed in the papers? Hm, hm. Suppose they paid you for that kind of thing? Not much, eh? No, suppose not. Hm, hm. Poetry? Hm. A bit difficult that must be. Getting the lines the same length, and all that. Hm, hm. Write anything else? Stories, and so forth? Hm. Oh yes? Very interesting. Hm!
>
> (Orwell 1936: 66–7)

In creative endeavors (Pandya 1994), poetry and advertising are allied arts. As early as 1923, the Russian poet Mayakovsky pointed out that "great ad lines were poems" (Harnett 1988: 7). Closer to our day, Hayakawa (1964) called advertising *"the poeticizing of consumer goods."* He pointed out that advertising can be considered "sponsored poetry," in contrast to poetry neither produced on demand nor paid for by advertisers – the "unsponsored" poetry that is little read nowadays. It is advertising that allows Americans to "have more access to poetry (or perhaps we should say that poetry has more access to us) than at any other time in history" (ibid.: 262). Access is no longer peculiarly American, for as Sherry and Camargo pointed out, most of the labels in their study of Japanese advertising "exhibit a poetic structure . . . most often that of the prose poem, with cadence, imagery, and figurative language contributing to an overall effect" (1987: 180).

In much of the world, advertising has displaced unsponsored poetry as the prime vehicle for expressing a culture's ideals and sentiments. It is the poetry of relevance for ordinary people, increasingly disinterested in any other kind of poetic expression. Hayakawa does not castigate advertising as a cultural excrescence, but instead compares it to the work of a poet laureate in those nations that still have one. Looked at this way, commercial institutions hire copywriters to express a product's spiritual essence just as political institutions hire poet laureates to express a country's soul.

However, copywriters are far more influential. Advertising is the prime "symbol-manipulating occupation" of our era, responsible for creating new ways of thinking and feeling that facilitate adjustment to change. Indeed, Hayakawa views advertising as "a tremendous creator and devourer of symbols" (1964: 267), the engine of symbol production and consumption that dominates postmodern life (Firat and Venkatesh 1995; Holbrook and Hirschman 1982). In particular, advertising provides a conduit to the consumer, serving as "a kind of dictionary constantly keeping us apprised of new consumer signifieds and signifiers" (McCracken 1987: 122). Commercial symbols (Leiss *et al.* 1986) endow daily life – "the data of everyday experience" (Hayakawa 1964: 260) – with significance by investing products with rich meaning beyond themselves. Poetry provides more than raw data, for it sums up to a thick description of distilled experience. Its prevalence enables advertising communication to serve as a "reflection of dominant cultural values and a shaper of cultural values" (Belk 1986: 8).

The reflection/shaping process is influenced by what we call "poet-researchers" (although "researcher-poets" would do as well) – consumer behavior researchers who write and publish poetry. Among these are Morris Holbrook, John Sherry, John Schouten, and George Zinkhan. Holbrook advocates the use of representational forms borrowed from the humanities, urges researchers to remain open to aesthetic perspectives (1987), and writes poetry himself (1995). Yet even though the past decade has witnessed borrowings of analytical modes from literature and the pictorial arts (Scott 1994; Stern 1988, 1989), there has been little in the way of representation with experimentation. The acceptance of poetry as a legitimate research form lags behind the acceptance of poetics as a source of research analysis. Thus, the poet's way of knowing is still considered "other" compared to the researcher's way. To bolster the argument for reconnecting poetry and research, let us now turn to historical precedent.

Poetry and ordinary life

The coopting of poetry by advertising has crystallized its role in daily life. Nonetheless, however important sponsored poetry may have become, unsponsored poetry has been shunted aside by the modern predilection for science. The twentieth century inherited the dualism of poetry versus science, with science acquiring the sacredness that formerly was attached to poetic language. To Matthew Arnold, in the mid-nineteenth century, poetry was expected to "assume something of the character of religion, as did the poetry of the ancients . . . .of religion as an agency which binds life into a whole" to combat disunity, the "great problem of modern life" (Trilling 1963: 32). Arnold foresaw a grand future for poetry as a "criticism of life" – "the highest expression of the imaginative reason" (Trilling 1963: 178). About a century later, I.A. Richards announced the "more representative modern view . . . that the future of poetry is *nil*" ([1926] 1970: 20). The contemporary view of poetry as peripheral to society's main concerns stems from the tension between art and science dating to the classical era (Belk 1986).

Classical values

Although Plato denounced the truth value of poetry, Aristotle considered it the prime source of knowledge about human life. He praises the representational power of poetry ("imitation"), claiming that "the reason why men enjoy seeing a likeness is that in contemplating it they find themselves learning or inferring, and saying perhaps, 'Ah, that is he'" (Fergusson 1961: 55–6). By the end of the Roman era, Aristotle's view prevailed, summed up in Horace's maxim: the mission of poetry is to "instruct with delight." Up until the end of the eighteenth century, this mission was accepted, and poetry and prose were used as vehicles of critical commentary about all things in life. If anything, poetry was the more respected locus of "man's most exalted thoughts" (Ciardi and Williams 1975: 14) – the kind of writing best suited to express serious ideas. However, because the poet's reach for divine language often exceeded his (rarely her) grasp, poetry also became the medium of satire, devastating in the hands of skilled social satirists.

Alexander Pope was the last and greatest commentator whose poetry critiqued everyday affairs ("The Dunciad") and philosophical matters ("Essay on Man," "Essay on Criticism"). His poems eschewed neoclassical rules of decorum in poetic diction (elevated usage derived from earlier poets, deemed superior to ordinary conversation) in favor of "language really spoken by urbane and cultivated people of the time" (Abrams 1993: 163). The language was suited to the subject and genre, for "The Dunciad" was written "as an attack . . . on the abuses against knowledge" in Pope's time (Wimsatt 1951: 48). Published in 1742, the fourth and

293

last book is a critique of the major social institutions of Pope's day – language, politics, schools and universities, the aristocracy, the Church, and the arts and sciences.

Despite the constraints of the heroic couplet – rhymed iambic lines – Pope used poetry to comment not only on society but also on science. His work praises science as a corrective to the goddess who rules the "Kingdom of the Dull" and seeks "to destroy Order and Science and to substitute the Kingdom of the Dull on earth." She effects her goal when she "leads captive the Sciences, and silenceth the Muses," instead encouraging the prattling of her children: "Half-wits, tasteless Admirers, vain Pretenders, the Flatterers of Dunces, or the Patrons of them." She is assisted by the "Geniuses of the Schools," who advance the cause of stupidity by ensuring that the doors of learning are never allowed "to stand too wide" (Wimsatt 1951: 431). By the end of the eighteenth century, poetry was no longer a vehicle for serious criticism. The two-culture binary that pits "the sciences" against "the poetries" (Richards [1926] 1970) was dominant, and poetry was relegated to its own restricted domain.

New criticism

In the succeeding two centuries, modernist thinking codified the antipathy between the scientific perspective (rational, positivist) and the poetic one (emotional, experiential). Language expressed the separation, with scientific writing grounded in the concept of fixed meaning waiting to be comprehended correctly. By the twentieth century, science was viewed as the repository of truth and the acknowledged forum for generating and testing knowledge. Poetry was out of favor as a form capable of conveying the kind of meaning that I.A. Richards ([1926] 1970) calls "sense" – the communication of thoughts (as distinct from that of "feeling," p. 175). Most of the New Critics accepted Richards's pronouncement – "the language of poetry is not the language of science" (ibid.: 33).

Nonetheless, poetry had a more elevated place as the "guardian of the suprascientific myths" (Richards [1926] 1970: 78) – "the highest form of language . . . the unique, linguistic instrument by which our minds have ordered their thoughts, emotions, desires" (Richards 1929: 301). Although the New Critics evaluated their critical methods as scientific (in the empirical Aristotelian tradition), they kept veering toward poetry as a superior way of representing truth. As Richards points out, "poetical descriptions often seem so much more accurate than prose descriptions. Language logically and scientifically used cannot describe a landscape or a face" ([1926] 1970: 33). New Critical ambivalence is a consequence of tension between the insistence on scientific methods of analysis (a reaction against the symbol-hunting idiosyncratic critics of the inter-war period) and the deep conviction that poetry was the most exalted mode of writing.

Deconstruction

> ... literary writing is best understood not as a diacritical or
> disengaged activity but instead as one of the many forms of cul-
> tural production by which men and women have made their
> world. Far from being divorced from the world, literary produc-
> tion is itself a form of social practice: texts do not merely reflect
> social reality but create it.
>
> (Patterson 1990: 260)

The modernist tension based on a schism between literary and non-literary writing has been challenged in the past generation by the postmodernists (Keller 1995). They do not accept clear boundaries between art and science, instead viewing all writing as "literary" (Stern 1993, 1996). Language is construed as a cultural production that creates reality and that requires interpretation, not as an opaque medium for universal truth. Looked at this way, the nature, function, and value of poetry in research is not necessarily antithetical to prose, but merely another way of representing knowledge.

Hillis Miller (1976: 335–8), a leading "Yale School" critic, sums up the older critical dichotomy as scientific versus deconstructive, calling the former "canny" and the latter "uncanny." The canny critics – scientific, modern, and theoretical – take as their province "the human sciences," placing faith in rationality, cognition, and logic, "with agreed-upon rules of procedure, given facts, and measurable results." Miller terms their methods and results "a happy positivism."

The uncanny critics – deconstructive, postmodern, and symbolic – find that logic ultimately fails. At "the moment when logic fails in their work . . . the moment of their deepest penetration into the actual nature of language" occurs (Miller 1976: 338). The mystery of an uncanny moment is "the manifestation of a hidden order" (Culler 1982: 24), revealing laws deeper than those of logic. The postmodern bias is toward the uncanny, for those "who have no faith in logic, are rewarded with deep penetration into the nature of language" (ibid.: 24).

Consumer research

In consumer research, the canny critics were dominant until the 1980s. None-theless, the discipline is so new that it cannot help but being influenced by the self-reflexive "science studies" of the last three decades as well as the precepts of universalist science (Keller 1995). At first, in the 1960s, the discipline borrowed traditional social science methods (surveys, experiments) and quantitative tools. More recently, innovative methods (participant observation, in-depth interviews, content analysis) and qualitative tools have become legitimized. Nonetheless, despite a waning of adherence to positivism and its mathematical underpinnings, the disciplinary community is still governed by the modernist assumption that prose is the only correct form for representing scientific reality.

Interestingly, this same community makes use of poetic language – notably metaphors – to express itself. One of the great strengths of poetry is metaphor-creation. As Zaltman and Coulter (1994) point out, metaphors are key windows for viewing consumer thought and feelings and for understanding behavior. The essence of a metaphor (Lakoff and Johnson 1980) is the transformation of experience from one domain to another that sparks insight into the first in terms of the second. Psychologists currently view metaphors as the foundation of learning – essential units of thought and communication (Ortony 1993).

One striking example in our own field is the approach to consumer behavior known as "information processing," a metaphor based on a comparison of humans to machines:

humans:intellectual operations:computers:data processing

The metaphoric transfer applies the mechanical processes of computing to human thought. Metaphoric creativity is a distinctively human activity, for no matter how competently computers perform cognitive operations, they have no imagination. Ironically, only a human being is capable of inventing the figurative language that expresses his or her machine-like nature.

The use of metaphors in scientific writing lends credence to the postmodern view of all writing as literary and open to interpretation, rather than the division of writing into that which is literal and truthful (science) versus that which is figurative and ambiguous (art). Looked at this way, one need not construe scientific and humanistic inquiry as mutually exclusive (Hirschman 1986) routes to meaning. If meaning is seen as an evolutionary process rather than as a finite product, poetry is at least as well suited as prose to convey flux, ambiguity, and connotation.

Art has the potential to generate knowledge about consumer behavior (Belk 1986) as a source and validation of hypotheses, a compendium of data, and a more gestalt picture. In addition, poetry can serve as a form for critical commentary. The rationale is that poetry (indeed, all verbal art) has narrative capability for "telling" (Wells 1989) as well as for "showing" – that is, for representing data (description) and comment on data (interpretation). This dimension of poetry is implicit in an all-embracing definition of text proposed by Hirschman and Holbrook – "a mental schema, often shared by a group of researchers, used to represent material phenomena" (1992: 56). These schemas are presumed to shape the research process, determining not simply the content of the written outcome but also the form. If we define a research work as *an object that has been generated, analyzed, edited, and recorded to inform the audience about an aspect of consumption,* poetry is as viable a vehicle for communicating information as is prose.

One example is Holbrook's "On Reading Wallendorf and Brucks" (1995: 250–4), which he terms a "gentle and friendly" reply to authors whom he feels have "inexplicably slighted" his work (p. 251). The poem expresses his "essentially romantic orientation" in using subjective personal introspection "to explore the experiential aspects of consumption" (p. 250). He defends his view of the "Human Condition" by reversing Descartes' comment on reality: "I am; therefore, I feel" (p. 254). The subject of the long poem (twenty-two stanzas) is Holbrook's counter-argument against Wallendorf and Brucks's "six big claims," presented in quatrains with an "abab" rhyme scheme in ballad measure rather than heroic couplet. The meter replicates Holbrook's intent, for although ballad rhythm has many uses, it is associated with "light" verse rather than the poetry of high seriousness. In this way, the poem critiques scholarly prose – the venue of high seriousness – by satirizing both its content and its form. The poem challenges research assumptions not only by what it says but also by how it says it, spoofing the empowered prose form in a burlesque that treats serious issues lightly.

The poetic performance

Although Holbrook's theme is serious, the poetic performance is playful, engaging readers in wordplay, the special property of poetic language. Its power to perform or dramatize experience, to evoke reader identification with other lives, and to defamiliarize the mundane rests on attributes such as rhythm, rhyme, imagery, tone, diction, and economy of expression. The tendency of poetic language to involve readers makes it especially complex "text" (Stern 1996), a postmodern construct broad enough to include products (Derrida [1967] 1976), consumers (Holbrook and Hirschman 1993), and all of consumption itself (Hirschman and Holbrook 1992). Poetic text can represent data (Belk 1986) from any consumption-related domain – tangible entities (products, humans, objects in nature) as well as intangible ones (institutions, electronic impulses, exchange processes), and current as well as historical phenomena. Let us turn to some of the poems published between 1992–6 to describe two ways that poetry as an art form comments on advertising and consumption.

Brand names

The first and most explicit delineation of the poet-researcher's turf is the image domain of brand names. Clusters of names serve as images that convey "sensory suggestion . . . by the device called the catalogue, which consists simply of a list of names of things . . . that tends to become a mixture of both names and metaphors" (Ciardi and Williams 1975: 244). The source of imagery reveals the area of experience most central to a poet's observations. For example, Dana Lascu's "Of Cigarettes" (1992: 56) describes advertising for cigarettes in newly capitalist Romania (brands such as Kent, Camel, Marlboro, Gitanes, Gauloises, and Carpati), where home decor consists of "empty cartons . . . framed as art" as replacements for portraits of Lenin and Communist slogans.

John Schouten's "Recommended Daily Allowance" (1993: 24) points out that "These are the days of boxed wine and branded roses." The poem lists brand names such as Ford, Chevrolet, Infiniti, Hostess, and Michelob as examples of advertising's "crumpled words," and Schouten asks, "Who makes the promises we live by?" Brand lists reference the transformation of brands from product identifiers to recognizable cultural symbols, already found in novels (Friedman 1985), films, and video games (Pope 1994). Slogans also enter poetic imagery in Schouten's poem, for the line "the night belongs to Michelob" raises the question: "Who bought it back from the stars and the wind?" Insofar as the principle of image selection reflects the poet's attitudes to subject and audience (authorial "tone"), unsponsored poetry by researchers serves as Dorian Gray's mirror to sponsored poetry, reflecting the dark side of symbol manipulation to connote the good life.

Sin products

Poetry has long expressed the dark side of human behavior, in consequence of its capacity to evoke strong emotional responses. In consumption poetry, Rick Pollay's "The Cowboy and Genital Joe" (1994: xii) uses limerick rhythm to describe the Marlboro Man and Joe Camel, product spokescharacters rendered as heroes "to those partly grown." The characters are symbols aimed at "touching the dreams of the young" insofar as their suggestiveness and ambiguity stimulate envy on the part of vulnerable audiences. Joe Camel performs the sponsor's message by posing in scenes that elicit teen envy, ostensibly on account of his odd nose – the face of "Genital Joe." The poem reinforces the symbolism of sin by representing culturally resonant product personifications in a rhythmic pattern associated with ribald "light" verse.

Poet-researchers: George Zinkhan and John F. Sherry, Jr.

Let us turn to Zinkhan's and Sherry's poems to see the representational mode in action. Zinkhan's cycle of poems captures aspects of consumer behavior centered on themes of materialism, situational effects of consumption (the home, the city), the meaning of possessions, consumer behavior at the extreme (skydiving, mountain climbing), remembered consumption, and the impact of social effects and family dynamics on consumer behavior. Sherry's poems deal with darker themes, using a variety of verse forms to represent anger, poverty, and world-weariness.

Time and timelessness through consumption:
a reflection on the social meaning of things

George M. Zinkhan

My Grandmother's Clocks

The grandfather clock at my grandmother's house strikes eight times
    when it is only four o'clock
    in the afternoon.

The kitchen clock is sixteen minutes fast
    at least and grandma's
    bedroom clock has no discernible pattern.

It may show two
    (in the morning!?)
    when I think that it is seven (at night).

On other clocks
    the hands don't visibly turn
    at all.

At the age of 81
    my grandmother seems not to notice
    this confusing contradiction of clocks.

She is quite advanced
    in her approach
    to the years.

Cockeysville, MD
August 1993

Sonnenchein Dragon: Visiting at the Chicago Art Institute

Undulating outline of Chinese dragon
    forming a crescent-shape with his nose
    and horn and lower jaw

Enduring image of the dynamic,
    creative force of nature:
    the supernatural

Energetic thought cast from jade
    in the third century
    before Christ

Startling fresh visitors
    with his energy and timelessness:
    green hero of the Sonnenchein collection

Surprising especially this middle-aged dragon son
    visiting from the distant south
    standing agape for hours

Understanding for the first time
    his clawed dragonhood
    and jade exterior . . .

Chicago, IL
August 1992

City Climbing: Scenes from a Chicago Health Club

> At the health club . . . (at high noon)
>   suited men from Amoco Tower
>   come to climb the indoor wall
>   slanted here and there
>   and stretching up: six stories tall.
>
> Formal skins are shed, spidermen emerging
>   with long ropes and webs
>   suspended from distant ceilings.
>
> The determined creatures climb high,
>   pausing at odd angles
>   with open mouths.
>
> After climbing
>   there are showers and soap
>   and powder and hair spray
>   to reassemble the corporate veneer
>   lost (temporarily) in the curious ascension.
>
> When the lunch hour ends
>   suited men from Amoco Tower
>   (newly coifed) run for elevators
>   rising toward their work desks
>   fifty-one stories above the asphalt.

Chicago, IL
August 1992

Mountain Climbing: Walking on the Edge

> Come,
>   let us walk . . . slowly
>   to the edge
>   of the precipice.
>
> See,
>   it is not so frightening
>   now
>   that we are near.
>
> Feel
>   the wind on your face
>   and in your hair
>   flowing wildly.
>
> Imagine
>   what
>   it would be like falling
>   drifting
>   in that realm
>   of amber reminiscence.

Long's Peak, Colorado
Summer 1992

The Old Man and His Garage

"You might as well get some kerosene
   and put that whole garage

To the torch," the old man told his
   daughter over breakfast.

Later that afternoon the old man
   looked out his bathroom window

To see sixty-five years of accumulated
   papers and memories

Blowing here and there across the yard
   and out into the street.

"What the hell do you think you're
   doing?"

Shouted the old man to his daughter,
   cleaning out the garage.

Detroit, Michigan
April 1988

Dead Rat Tomorrow

"Son, get the shovel.
   There's a dead rat stinking in the backyard."

"Why do we have to now, Dad?
   It was out there yesterday.
   It'll be there tomorrow."

"Let's go now.
   Turn off the TV."

"It's raining, Dad
   And the rat is shrinking.
   It used to be more of a rat."

"More of a rat?"

"Tomorrow, Dad."

"Tomorrow?"

Houston, TX
October 1989

Tape Talk

My sister, Allison, talks and talks too much
 all of the time about what I don't know.
Mommie says that she's going to get some tape
 and seal her mouth shut.
Or, I wish that Mommie would say that
 before Allison gives me a headache again
And I have to swallow two more chunks
 of that bitter Bayer Aspirin.

Houston, TX
March 1991

. . . who were boys

Three brothers who were boys together
 wrestling on the lawn with balls
 trying to forget that they are forty and beyond

 huffing and puffing
  erupting into an ice cream fight
 with chocolate and vanilla mixed
  melting on their balding heads and
 rolling down their graying beards

The young children of three brothers . . . who were boys together
 stare and wonder:
 "What's got into them?"

Sparks, MD
July 1991

Three poems

John F. Sherry, Jr.

One Tuna Caught this Day in Diamant

"Pas des yeux!"
The withered scold
In arid voice as parched
As her wise skin
Cuts through chorales of frugal wives,
Strains to conduct
In cadence kinder to her purse,
(Mindful of unhaggled mangoes,
Okra, cane)
The dull cleaver,
Thumbs already on the scales,
To slow the beats per measure
Slapped down on her cleft fish,
Rapped smart as dominoes
On a weathered barrelhead.
Quivered gill slits seal in the sun.
Unwanted eyes cloud quickly
To their stock fate.
The bargaining beguine resumes
At the next beached boat.
His tuna parsed
Among the most insistent,
The fisher turns to
Mending nets.

market music

i've felt mick
　shill for sympathy
　　before first light
　　　in oude markt
　　　　in louvain
　　　　　at decibels that make
　　　　　　a belgian endive
　　　　　　　vendor wilt
　　　　　　　a ululating elvis
　　　　　　　mourn blue christmas
　　　　　in chatuchak
　　　　in hot bangkok october
　　　threatening to distract
　　the earnest dance step
　of a thai boy sweating
to an asian ice ice baby
in a neighboring
　stall
　　the technopulse of
　　akihabara
　　　that goads the shinjunrui
　　　　to retroritual
　　　　　in harajuku
　　　　　　before their outraged
　　　　　　elders
　　　　　　and hammer pound the zapotecs
　　　　　in a oaxacan zocalo
　　　　where girls too young
　　　and tired to dance
　　hawk chiclets
　with their marble
rabbits
each market
　has a music
　　beyond the gold coast
　　　on the miracle mile
　　　　the grounded lyric
　　　　　rhythm tone and beat
　　　　　　of petty produce
　　　　　　　penny capital
　　　　　　　locked in a jewel box
　　　　　　saved in shrinkwrapped skin
　　　　　mark time until
　　　　the sale

hump flute

if i see kokopelli dance
    through one more fucking coffee shop
in one more midwest campus town
    across a fissured plaster wall
bereft of choreography
    beyond a miles davis tape
autoreversed eternally
    i might have to foreswear caffeine
and seek serenity somewhere
    less aromatic and intense

References

Abrams, M.H. (1993) *A Glossary of Literary Terms*, 6th edn., New York: Holt, Rinehart and Winston.

Belk, R.W. (1986) "Art Versus Science as Ways of Generating Knowledge About Materialism," in D. Brinberg and R.J. Lutz (eds) *Perspectives on Methodology in Consumer Research*, New York: Springer-Verlag, 3–36.

Blasko, V.J. and Mokwa, M.P. (1986) "Creativity in Advertising: A Janusian Perspective," *Journal of Advertising*, 15,4: 48–51.

Brooks, C. and Warren, R.P. (1960) *Understanding Poetry*, New York: Holt, Rinehart and Winston.

Ciardi, J. and Williams, M. (1975) *How Does a Poem Mean?* 2nd edn, Boston: Houghton Mifflin.

Culler, J. (1982) *On Deconstruction: Theory and Criticism After Structuralism*, Ithaca: Cornell University Press.

Derrida, J. ([1967] 1976) *Of Grammatology*, trans. G. Chakravorty Spivak, Baltimore: Johns Hopkins University Press.

Fergusson, F. (1961) *Aristotle's Poetics*, trans. S.H. Butcher, New York: Hill and Wang.

Firat, A.F. and Venkatesh, A. (1995) "Liberatory Postmodernism and the Reenchantment of Consumption," *Journal of Consumer Research*, 22,3: 239–67.

Friedman, M. (1985) "The Changing Language of a Consumer Society: Brand Name of Usage in Popular American Novels in the Postwar Era," *Journal of Consumer Research*, 2,1: 927–37.

Frye, N. (1973) *Anatomy of Criticism: Four Essays*, Princeton: Princeton University Press.

Gould, S.J. (1991) "The Self-Manipulation of My Pervasive, Perceived Vital Energy through Product Use: An Introspective-Praxis Perspective," *Journal of Consumer Research*, 18,2: 194–207.

Harnett, J.W. (1988) "A Dawning Market? Russia's Roots in Advertising," *Marketing Communications*, 13,4: 7.

Hayakawa, S.I. (1964) *Language in Thought and Action*, 2nd edn, New York: Harcourt, Brace & World.

Hirschman, E.C. (1986) "Humanistic Inquiry in Marketing Research: Philosophy, Method, and Criteria," *Journal of Marketing Research*, 23,3: 237–49.

Hirschman, E.C. and Holbrook, M.B. (1992) *Postmodern Consumer Research: The Study of Consumption as Text*, Newbury Park, CA: Sage.

Holbrook, M.B. (1987) "What Is Consumer Research?" *Journal of Consumer Research*, 14,1: 128–32.

—— (1995) *Consumer Research: Introspective Essays on the Study of Consumption*, Thousand Oaks, CA: Sage.

Holbrook, M.B. and Hirschman, E.C. (1982) "The Experiential Aspects of Consumption: Consumer Fantasies, Feelings, and Fun," *Journal of Consumer Research*, 9,2: 132–40.

—— (1993) *The Semiotics of Consumption: Interpreting Symbolic Consumer Behavior in Popular Culture and Works of Art*, Berlin: Mouton de Gruyter.

Keller, E.F. (1995) "Science and Its Critics," *Academe*, 81,5: 10–15.

Lakoff, G. and Johnson, M. (1980) *Metaphors We Live By*, Chicago: The University of Chicago Press.

Lascu, D. (1992) "Of Cigarettes . . .," *Journal of Advertising*, 21,3: 56.

Leiss, W., Kline, S., and Jhally, S. (1986) *Social Communication in Advertising: Persons, Products, & Images of Well-Being*, Toronto: Methuen.

Levy, S.J. (1996) "Stalking the Amphisbaena," *Journal of Consumer Research*, 23,3: 163–76.

McCracken, G. (1987) "Advertising: Meaning or Information," in M. Wallendorf and P. Anderson (eds) *Advances in Consumer Research*, vol. 14, Provo, UT: Association for Consumer Research: 121–24.

Miller, J.H. (1976) "Steven's Rock and Criticism as Cure," *Georgia Review* (30): 330–48.

Ortony, A. (1993) *Metaphor and Thought*, 2nd edn, New York: Cambridge University Press.

Orwell, G. (1936) *Keep The Aspidistra Flying*, London: Secker & Warburg.

Pandya, M. (1994) "They're in a Position to Mix Metaphors With Business," *The New York Times*, 27 November, 3–9.

Patterson, L. (1990) "Literary History," in F. Lentricchia and T. McLaughlin (eds) *Critical Terms for Literary Study*, Chicago: The University of Chicago Press: 250–62.

Pollay, R. (1994) "The Cowboy and Genital Joe," *Journal of Advertising*, 23,3: xii.

Pope, K. (1994) "Product Placements Creep into Video Games," *The Wall Street Journal*, 224, 5 December: B5.

Richards, I.A. (1929) *Practical Criticism: A Study of Literary Judgment*, New York: Harcourt Brace.

—— ([1926]1970) *Poetries and Sciences*, New York: W.W. Norton.

Schouten, J.W. (1993) "Recommended Daily Allowance," *Journal of Advertising*, 22,1: 24.

Scott, L. (1994) "Images in Advertising: The Need for a Theory of Visual Rhetoric," *Journal of Consumer Research*, 21,3: 252–73.

Sherry, J.F., Jr. and Camargo, E.G. (1987) "'May Your Life Be Marvellous': English Language Labeling and the Semiotics of Japanese Promotion," *Journal of Consumer Research*, 14,3: 174–88.

Stern, B.B. (1988) "How Does an Ad Mean? Language in Services Advertising," *Journal of Advertising*, 17,2: 3–14.

—— (1989) "Literary Criticism and Consumer Research: Overview and Illustrative Analysis," *Journal of Consumer Research*, 16,3: 322–34.

—— (1993) "Feminist Literary Criticism and the Deconstruction of Advertisements: A Postmodern view of Advertising and Consumer Responses," *Journal of Consumer Research*, 18,4: 556–66.

—— (1996) "Deconstructive Strategy and Consumer Research: Concepts and Illustrative Exemplar," *Journal of Consumer Research*, 23,3: 136–47.

Stevens, W. (1973) "Selections from *Adagia*," in G. Geddes (ed.) *Twentieth Century Poetry*, 2nd edn, Toronto: Oxford University Press, 581–7.

Trilling, L. (1963) *Matthew Arnold*, Cleveland: Meridian Books.

Wallendorf, M. and Brucks, M. (1993) "Introspection in Consumer Research: Implementation and Implications," *Journal of Consumer Research*, 20,3: 339–59.

Wells, W.D. (1989) "Lectures and Dramas," in P. Cafferata and A.M. Tybout (eds) *Cognitive and Affective Responses to Advertising*, Lexington, MA: Lexington Books, 13–20.

Wimsatt, W.K., Jr. (ed.) (1951) *Alexander Pope: Selected Poetry and Prose*, New Haven: Yale University Press, 361–449.

Zaltman, G. and Coulter, R.H. (1994) "Seeing the Voice of the Customer: Metaphor-Based Advertising Research," working paper, Harvard Business School, Harvard University.

Zinkhan, G.M. (1993) "Creativity in Advertising," *Journal of Advertising*, 22,2: 1–4.

—— (1994) "Poetry in Advertising," *Journal of Advertising*, 23,4: iii – vii.

11

MULTIMEDIA APPROACHES TO QUALITATIVE DATA AND REPRESENTATIONS

Russell W. Belk

It has become the task of . . . social scientists to acquire an intimate knowledge, not only of the subject matter they hope to illuminate, but of the media through which they intend to represent it, for more than ever, the visual media is not just a tool for the study of culture but an integral part of the culture we study.

(Griffin 1993: 21)

This preoccupation with the medium – Alfie Gell's "enchantment of technology" – has led to the major use of ethnographic film being in classroom teaching, not in research. From all the current signs it seems that IMM [Interactive Multimedia] – like ethnographic film – will find its major use in undergraduate teaching rather than professional research . . . Abandoning linearity signals a return to Radcliffe-Brownian butterfly collecting: the arbitrary and decontextualized pursuit of comparison and connection for its own sake, or worse, the sheer observation of data for little more than immediate entertainment.

(Banks 1994)

[in answer to Banks] Audiovisuals are important epistemologically because they open the empirical problematics of fieldwork to unprecedented scholarly inspection; second, they make a significant contribution . . . by providing unique opportunities in textual and audiovisual research; third, they play a crucial ethical role [through establishing intimacy with subjects] in . . . struggles against racism.

(Biella 1994)

The Little Prince

Human behavior is inherently multimodal and human experience is inherently multisensory. Driving a car is not a purely tactile experience, eating a meal involves more than tasting flavors, and having a conversation is not simply about listening. Through the process of synesthesia we are sometimes able to more or less successfully perceive an experience in one sensory mode via another sensory mode. For example, when we hear the phrase "red rose," we may be able to visualize and perhaps even imagine the feel and smell of the flower this phrase denotes. Even in this case, however, we lose something in the decontextualized verbal description. We must fall back on the generic assumption that a rose is a rose. This assumption is challenged in Antoine de Saint Exupéry's (1943) enduring story *The Little Prince*. Having lovingly cared for the single rose on his asteroid, the Little Prince is devastated when he visits another asteroid and finds a garden filled with five thousand roses. His rose suddenly seems quite ordinary and common. But he is befriended by a fox who helps him realize that his rose is unique in all the world. It is unique because of the Little Prince's loyalty to it and because of the time and effort he has devoted to caring for it. Our informants and research sites in qualitative research are similarly unique, and part of what we ideally seek to preserve and convey about them is their uniqueness. This is a key difference from quantitative research which presents only faceless and placeless numbers.

Saint Exupéry is also instructive about this difference in the humanism of alternative research epistemologies if we read his "grown-ups" as quantitative researchers in the following passage:

> Grown-ups love figures. When you tell them that you have made a new friend, they never ask you any questions about essential matters. They never say to you, "What does his voice sound like? What games does he love best? Does he collect butterflies?" Instead, they demand: "How old is he? How many brothers has he? How much does he weigh? How much money does his father make"? Only from these figures do they think they have learned anything about him.
>
> (Saint Exupéry 1943: 16–17)

Instead of relying on numbers, Saint Exupéry's narrator fills his charming and insightful fable with drawings. These drawings are of the Little Prince, the sheep he desires to have, and the people and sights he encounters in visiting seven other asteroids. On the sixth of these asteroids he finds that the sole resident is a geographer who may be seen to provide another portrayal of the quantitative researcher. The Little Prince compliments the man on the beauty of his planet and asks if it has any oceans. The geographer tells him he has no idea. Nor, in response to the Little Prince's questions, does he know if it has mountains, towns, rivers, or deserts. For, as the geographer explains, it is the job of the *explorer* to go out and find things; the geographer is much too important to ever leave his desk. As qualitative researchers we are the explorers who leave our desks and go out and observe and talk to consumers in their natural environments. And it is up to us to preserve and present some of the richness and humanity of the consumers we encounter and their worlds, despite the grown-ups and geographers who would reduce this complexity to numbers.

If a quantitative researcher were to write up experimental results in a paper that included a photograph of one of the research subjects, or write up regression results from a survey in a paper that included a sketch of a particular respondent's living room, these papers would no doubt be criticized and rejected for including irrelevant personal information; data that do not belong in a scientific report. But in qualitative research we use a personal (rather than impersonal) approach to data collection and our research reports strive to be experiential, intimate, and evocative. We try, with varying degrees of success, to present a rich, full, thick description of the people, places, and events we study. Multisensory information can potentially help us to achieve these ends better by helping us convey what informants and sites look like and sound like, what aromas smell like, how foods taste, how objects feel, and what ambience characterizes an event.

One of the tools that may be especially helpful in pursuing these goals is the increasing array of multimedia techniques at our disposal for preserving and presenting more of the fullness of people, places, and consumption events. We are no longer limited to the paper and pencil drawings of the narrator of *The Little Prince*. However, rather than feel compelled to use these dazzling new technologies, we should keep in mind that the purpose of multimedia data collection and presentation is to enhance our ability to preserve and convey the essential humanity of those whom we study. Since the majority of the multimedia techniques available or becoming available emphasize the visual, it is also well to remember that there are four or five other sensory modes (depending on whether we recognize the sixth sense of intuition). Furthermore, it is important to keep in mind that we may ultimately be most interested in things that, like the Little Prince's sheep, are not visible at all. Finally, it is necessary to recognize that visual information also has a positivist legacy. Since imaginary constructs, like imaginary sheep, do not fare well within positivism, it is useful to begin to consider multimedia possibilities by examining how visual data have been construed by positivist science. Then we may better understand how such data might instead be used to present richer, more unique, and more human views of consumers.

Positivist versus non-positivist uses of the visual

As the last sentence's reference to "views of consumers" suggests, our language is steeped in visual metaphors which suggest that "seeing is believing" (Dundes 1972). Not just in English, but in other languages as well, expressions like these are common:

- See for yourself.
- It all depends on how you look at it.
- Great leaders have great vision.
- I see what you mean.

- Do you have any insights?
- The doctor will see you now.

In each of these cases we are using seeing as a metaphor for investigating, interpreting, or understanding. This common equation of knowing with seeing derives from various versions of positivism that emerged from the empiricism of the Enlightenment. As Slater explains, in this view:

> We can only know what we see. Ideas – theories, concepts, general-izations, and so on – either can or must arise only from perceptual experiences of the materiality of the world. Scientific methods of obser-vation, experimentation, evidence and verification/falsification all oper-ationalize the primary notion that ideas (subjectivity) must be anchored in materiality . . . Most crucially, the criterion of visibility places mean-ings and values on the side of subjectivity: unlike such things as color, weight and mass, the meaning of an object is not an observable property and therefore not a proper object of positivist thought.
>
> (Slater 1995: 220–1)

Slater goes on to note that reducing the knowable to discrete measurable facts is a key part of the disenchantment of the world and drains the world of much of its interest and meanings. The key question in knowledge seeking is thereby changed from: "What is the essence or meaning of the world?" to "What exists in the world and how does it behave?" This orientation also leads to experimentation in order to control events. And such instrumental rationalism also seeks to evacuate values from the scientific quest for knowledge. Thus, early uses of the visual in positivist research pursued a "trivial realism" that attempts to reduce the world to visable facts (Slater 1995), just as the grown-ups in *The Little Prince* wish to reduce the world to numbers. For example, the pursuit of trivial realism and facts led behavioralism to focus on the observable stimulus and response, and to leave the unobservable processes of behavior as a black box. More recently cognitive psychology has focused on observable behavioral, verbal, and written responses to represent what supposedly goes on in the mind, while ignoring the feelings of the body (Berman 1989; Romanyshyn 1989; Turner 1984).

Although this is a somewhat overstated view of science which in reality often hypocritically sacrifices trivial visual realism in order to aestheticize its own mean-ings and romanticize its own values (Lynch and Edgerton 1988; Schaffer 1993; Slater 1995), it is a good starting point for considering how visual images might instead be used in non-positivist consumer research. Whereas science disavows an interest in symbolic meanings and embraces a supposedly value-free neutrality, non-positivist research seeks to discover symbolic meanings and admits the impos-sibility of value-free inquiry. As I have stressed, non-positivist research attempts to remain in touch with the uniqueness and humanity of our informants and thereby to preserve at least some of the richness and complexity of their lives. One key way in which visual images can aid in this objective is by giving a face to our informants and sites. While verbal images can also humanize subjects, words do not allow the direct and immediate identification and empathy that is possible with visual images. Such is the power of the visual image. Freedberg cites as evidences of this power:

> People are sexually aroused by pictures and sculptures; they break pictures and sculptures; they mutilate them, kiss them, cry before them, and go on journeys to them; they are calmed by them, stirred by them, and incited to revolt. They give thanks by means of them, expect to be elevated by them, are moved to the highest levels of empathy and fear.
>
> (Freedberg 1989: 1)

This was especially true in the middle ages of Europe when all but the most élite were illiterate and cathedral stained glass windows, morality plays, and the friezes of public architecture not only told stories but evoked powerful emotions. Today the power of the visual image remains especially strong, but for another reason. The visual retains its power because, while largely literate, the world's population has succumbed to photos, videos, television, and films. These are easier and more engrossing sources of stimulation than books, journals, magazines, newspapers, and the other forms of the printed word. This is true of the personal computer as well. It has quickly evolved from verbal commands and source codes to graphical user interfaces, sound, music, clip art, digital photographs, animation, and movies. The overlap and synthesis of television, telephone, computer, camera, cinema, Internet, fax, and related technologies promise even more visual and multimedia dominance in the future. Not only has the visual become the key contemporary mode of mass media representation and consumption, it is also the key mode of personal representation within the family where the photo album is our chief biographic and autobiographic form (see Chalfen 1987; Hirsch 1981; King 1984; Musello 1979; Spence and Holland 1991; Walker and Moulton 1989).

But there is nothing new about visual images. They predate known written languages by tens of thousands of years. It is now estimated that some of the surviving rock art in Australia may be 100,000 years old. There is something compelling about visual images in helping us reflect on things, people, events, and their interrelations. The visual, whether petroglyphs or family videos and photo albums, helps us remember and reconstruct the past. And the visual may help us achieve a different type of knowledge especially conducive to the goal of non-positivist research to capture the unique human texture of our informants, phenomena, and sites. This is the type of knowledge that Langer (1963) called *knowledge of* (versus *knowledge about*) an experience. Denzin (1989) termed it *emotional understanding* (versus *cognitive understanding*). And I (Belk 1989) prefer to think of it as *experiential knowledge* (versus *propositional knowledge*). The concepts are similar in each case. *Propositional, cognitive, knowledge about* a person, place, or phenomenon helps convey declarative statements of fact – e.g. "This is X;" "This is how X happened." But *experiential, emotional, knowledge of* something prompts us to consider and perhaps vicariously feel a part of a particular person, situation, or event – e.g. "What was it like to experience X?", "What is it like to be X?". The maxim that a picture is worth a thousand words rings true because of the non-verbal (and perhaps non-verbalizable) but significant details that visual images can convey. They help provide a context for understanding. We see what people are like, their regard toward one another, and the emotions they convey through their facial expressions, gestures, and postures. We can look at historical images as well and reflect on what it might have been like to be there. While words can also shape vicarious experiences and cause us to imagine what something unseen is like, such words require more work and more trust on the part of the audience. Visual material has an immediacy that lends itself to greater and easier accessibility, and an apparent veracity that can help to erase doubts and uncertainties. "Seeing is believing" is a saying in which we place considerable faith. It is possible to deceive with visual images, but it is also possible to capture and more effectively sustain attention and to convey essential features of human existence through visual representations.

Roland Barthes (1984) suggests that good photographs induce us to think. While photographs from our personal past may transport us back in a Proustian sense to the people, places, and events they represent ("I recognize, with my whole body" writes Barthes 1984: 45), even photographs of distant and unseen landscapes can engage us experientially:

> For me, photographs of landscape (urban or country) must be *habitable*, not visitable. The longing to inhabit, if I observe it clearly in myself, is neither oneiric (I do not dream of some extravagant site) nor empirical (I do not intend to buy a house according to the views of a real-estate agency); it is fantasmatic, deriving from a kind of second sight which seems to bear me forward to a utopian time, or to carry me back to somewhere in myself . . . it is as if *I were certain* of having been there or of going there.
>
> (Barthes 1984: 39–40)

As with Proust, it is not just the visual that can prompt such feelings, but tastes, smells, sounds, and tactile sensations as well (e.g., see Cohen 1988). Clearly more than just thinking, in the cognitive sense of dispassionate meaning-making, is involved here. We empathize and feel what such a place is like. Good photographs spur us to imagine ourselves there and to reflect on what we might feel in such circumstances. As Susan Sontag recalls:

> One's first encounter with the photographic inventory of ultimate horror is a kind of revelation: a negative epiphany. For me, it was

photographs of Bergen-Belsen and Dachau which I came across by chance in a bookstore in Santa Monica in July 1945. Nothing I have seen – in photographs or in real life – ever cut me as sharply, deeply, instantaneously. Indeed, it seems plausible to me to divide my life into two parts, before I saw those photographs (I was 12) and after, though it was several years before I understood fully what they were about.

(Sontag 1977: 19–20)

Even with the immediacy of these photographs' emotional impact, it took the youthful Sontag time in order to understand fully their meaning. At the very least, information about the context of the photos is needed. When we make the photograph we are at least partly aware of this context. But when someone else has made the photograph we need some contextualization.

When we remember our own past with the aid of photographs, and certainly when we attempt to experience vicariously other people, places, and times, it is not simply positivist facts that we call up. Wright Morris observes:

When we say "How well I remember!" invariably we remember poorly. It is the emotion that is strong, not the details. The elusive details are incidental, since the emotion is what matters. In this deficiency of memory do we have the origins of the imagination . . . Artifacts mystically quickened with sentiment await their reappearance in the imagination, a reenactment and a confirmation. Each time these tokens are handled they give off sparks.

(Morris 1989: 75–7)

Visual and other sensory stimuli can also "give off sparks" when they come from someone else's life rather than our own (see Belk 1991b). Perhaps this is why museums (and now virtual museums) continue to fascinate us.

Thus, while photographs may in some ways act like memory in preserving traces of events, they fall short of memory in other respects, as Berger explains:

Unlike memory, photographs do not in themselves preserve meaning. They offer appearances – with all the credibility and gravity we normally lend to appearances – prised away from their meaning . . . Photographs in themselves do not narrate.

(Berger 1980: 51)

For this reason, even with ethnographic arguments for empowering informants by helping them to represent themselves, often through photos or video (e.g., Clifford and Marcus 1986; Clifford 1988; Ruby 1995), we would not normally expect a consumer ethnography to be composed solely of unnarrated uncaptioned photos, film, sound recordings, or video. Captions help orient the viewer and in so-doing help the polysemic photograph (Ball and Smith 1992) convey *particular* meanings (Signorelli 1987). They also help to contextualize the image. Bourdieu argues:

> Refusing the meaningless (*insignificant*) picture (in the twofold sense of being devoid of meaning and devoid of interest) or the picture which is ambiguous and anonymous, actually means refusing photography as an endless finality. The value of a photograph is measured above all by the clarity and the interest of the information that it is capable of communicating as a symbol, or preferably, as an allegory . . . The *legibility* of the picture itself . . . includes the expectation of the title or the caption which states the signifying intention and allows one to judge whether the realization is in accord with the explicit ambition.
>
> (Bourdieu 1990: 92)

The argument I wish to make is for using multimedia methods as an expansion of written textual data collection and representation. For representation we should most often expect to use some form of written, spoken, or visual narration attempting to guide the audience to particular (though possibly multiple) interpretations of meanings. With interactive multimedia presentations the audience is given greater, though not total, latitude to construct its own meanings.

I have sought above to distinguish positivist and non-positivist uses of the visual. Whereas positivism seeks to use the visual as facts to convey propositional knowledge, non-positivist uses of the visual seek to convey experiential knowledge – to use the power and immediacy of the visual in order to spur the audience to feel, think, and reflect on the persons, places, and things that are the focus of research attention. Visuals in non-positivist research are not intended as mere illustrations ("This is X"). Rather, non-positivist use of visuals should prompt us or "prick us" (Barthes's (1984) *punctum* rather than *studium*) to feel, think, imagine, and empathize. It is significant that we are at the apparent dawn of a digital multimedia age. Even though there is a qualitative interpretive turn underway in consumer research, marketing, management, communications research, and related fields, this is no guarantee that new multimedia possibilities will be strictly allied with non-positivist research. Robbins presents an alternative scenario:

> Positivism may be seen as a preliminary attempt to rationalize the image (though now we will say that it lacked the means, and that its ideas of cognitive truth were simplistic). The "digital revolution" (with its new means and new approach to cognition) takes the Cartesian project in image culture to a "higher stage."
>
> (Robbins 1995: 38)

Whatever the accuracy of this forecast for positivist uses on new multimedia technologies, there is a great opportunity to use multimedia possibilities in order to pursue more successfully the non-positivist goal of preserving and presenting the essential uniqueness and humanity of the consumers we study. The remainder of this chapter explores these possibilities and some of their implications for our research.

Multimedia data and representation

In contrast to verbal printed text, multimedia might mean several things in today's technological environment and are likely to mean more things in the future. While they are not exhaustive, Tables 11.1 and 11.2 show the major current alternatives for collecting and presenting qualitative consumer research data, along with major advantages and disadvantages of each (see also Farnell and Huntley (1995) for another assessment of many of these media). As the epigraphs at the start of this chapter suggest, there is debate as to whether the enhanced multimedia presentation possibilities of local and distributed access digital presentations evaluated at the bottom of Table 11.2 represent a research breakthrough as much as a pedagogical advance. It is my position that these enhanced multimedia possibilities can be both if they are used effectively. But they will not

Table 11.1 Comparison of data collection media

Medium	Advantages	Disadvantages
Fieldnotes/ transcriptions (in computer format)	Immediate record of multiple sensory impressions Researcher as instrument benefits from skills, judgment Nonlinearly searchable Can preserve narratives and processes	Privileges verbal over non-verbal Slippage, errors, forgetting Researcher as instrument may disempower informants Transcription is tedious
Audiotape	Accurately records what was said and how it was said Easy and inexpensive	Privileges aural Linearly searchable (but slow, even in digital format)
Artifacts	May preserve detail of what was consumed Can inspect carefully	Privileges visual/tangible May decay (e.g., foods) Costly, storage problems
Photographs, slides	Preserves detail of what, who, and perhaps how May preserve humanity of informants Can be made by informants Can be used in presentation and reports	Privileges visual Slow searches or searches limited to indexing May decay (albeit slowly) unless in digital format Intrusive and threatens informant anonymity
Film, videotape	Same as photographs and audiotape Most engaging	Same as photographs and audiotape, but more costly Most intrusive

316

Table 11.2 Comparison of data presentation media

Medium	Advantages	Disadvantages
Printed Text	Can describe multiple sensory impressions Can present abstract constructs and narratives Accepted and inexpensive Can incorporate photos	Not user searchable unless part of a full text database Ability to humanize informants requires skill and audience involvement Non-interactive
Live lecturer	Highly interactive Can incorporate all other presentation media Can be spontaneous and vary content and sequence according to audience	Expensive to reproduce and transport May decay with time Idiosyncratic variability over presenters and occasions
Audiotape	Same as in audiotape data collection (Table 11.1) Can incorporate sound and musical effects May be audio broadcast	Same as in audiotape data collection (Table 11.1) Generally boring Seldom used by itself or with photographic slides
Photographs, slides	Same as in photographic data collection (Table 11.1) Engaging immediacy Potential random access by user	Same as in photographic data collection (Table 11.1) No easy stand-alone access Access fixed, except when combined with digital (below)
Film, videotape	Same as in video data collection (Table 11.1) May be video broadcast if of high enough quality Stand-alone user can rewind, fast forward Strong emotional potential	Same as in video data collection (Table 11.1) Film is difficult to access; video formats differ internationally and evolve More expensive for single user access Expensive to produce
Local access digital (e.g., CD-ROM)	Can incorporate other media, except live lecturer, and their benefits Nonlinear access may allow active audience participating in analysis and interpretation Individual or group access	Requires computer with multimedia drive Group presentation requires projection device Nonlinear access partly depends on maker-created electronic hyperlinks
Distributed access digital (e.g., Internet, World Wide Web)	Same as local access digital Potentially limitless access to related material No storage medium cost unless material is downloaded Can be continuously updated No cost to equipped user	Requires web access Nonlinear access partly depends on maker-created electronic hotlinks Currently slower than local access digital Potential for getting lost in electronic links

soon, if ever, replace lecturers, video, and printed texts (with or without photographic material). Since these lecturers, videos, and printed sources can each potentially incorporate other media as well, and since any multimedia presentation requires multimedia data collection, the following discussion will attempt to show how we might broaden our media literacy as consumer researchers through various of these multimedia formats. Because there are still limited multimedia examples to draw upon in consumer research, some applications will be cited from other social sciences and humanities as well. Following a discussion of each medium below, I conclude by briefly addressing questions of how we move from multimedia data collection to multimedia presentation, and how the process of analyzing and interpreting multimedia data differs from analyzing and interpreting printed text.

Photographic examples

The simplest and most common type of multimedia presentation in consumer research is the photo-aided journal article, book, or book chapter. Examples of ethnographic consumer studies employing photographs include: Belk *et al.*'s (1988) study of a swap meet (see Plate 11.1); Hirschman's (1988) study of WASPs; Heisley *et al.*'s (1991) study of a farmer's market; Costa and Belk's (1990) study of *nouveaux riches*; Hill's (1991) and Hill and Stamey's (1990) studies of the homeless; O'Guinn's (1991) study of Barry Manilow fans; Peñaloza's (1994) study of Mexican immigrants to the U.S.; and Schouten and McAlexander's (1995) study of Harley-Davidson bikers. While the Heisley *et al.* (1991) study may be seen to humanize the informants for readers and to explore the intimacy of the photographer–informant relationship via these photos, for the most part such photo-aided consumer studies have been focused as much on propositional knowledge ("This is X") as on experiential knowledge ("This is what it is like to be X").

Better examples of experiential studies of consumption can be found farther afield, such as the book *Rich and Poor* by the then art student Jim Goldberg (1985) and by former suburban newspaper photographer Bill Owens (1973) in his book *Suburbia*. Jim Goldberg preceded Heisley and Levy (1991), and Dennis Rook (1991 – interviewed by John Sherry) in using visual elicitation methods. He first photographed the (poor) residents of a transient hotel, and later the (rich) trustees of the art school he attended. In each case he brought the photos back to those portrayed and asked them to write a caption for the photo as if it were the final memorial of their lives. The results are evocative both emotionally and comparatively, as Plates 11.2 and 11.3 suggest. Bill Owens employed a different tactic in using his access as a suburban newspaper photo-journalist to capture telling scenes of consumption by the residents of a new suburb in California. These scenes are of Tupperware parties, Christmas decor, and garages overflowing with possessions. As with Jim Goldberg's work, the role of possessions in portraying identity, lifestyle, and sense of worth is often quite striking.

Several other photographic studies of consumption deserving note (all published in book format) include: Aaland (1981); D'Aluisio and Menzel (1996); Evans (1990);

Hansen and Blüher (1993); Levinson (1983); Menzel (1994a); Pratt (1994); Putnam and Newton (1990); Rand and Bird (1984); Reddy (1993); Riis (1971); Rousseau (1981); Rutkovsky (1992); Salinger (1995); and Tuchman (1994). The Aaland (1981) and Pratt (1994) studies of county fairs offer a nice contrast to each other in terms of social class and regional differences. Other examples are cited in Belk (1986).

Archives of historical photographs also offer potential treasure troves for consumer research, including the Farm Security Administration photos (housed in the Library of Congress) directed by Roy Stryker and continued under funding from Standard Oil of New Jersey (housed in the Ekstrom Library of the University of Louisville) – e.g. Agee and Evans (1941); Hagen (1985); Keller (1985); Lange (1987); Stange 1989; commercial photographers' plates (e.g. Lesy 1973); and historical society records (e.g., Belk 1992, see Plate 11.4). The SAMDOK program in Sweden (centered in the Nordiska Museet in Stockholm) is an on-going ethnographic photo archive with much to offer consumer researchers.

A particularly clever use of historical visual evidence is Morris *et al.*'s (1979) study of the origin of southern Italian gestures using both contemporary photo portraits in southern Italy and Greece, and ancient Greek literary descriptions. They found that while the verbal language of Greek sailors visiting this region of Italy had totally disappeared, the nonverbal language of gestures persists in the similarity of current Greek and southern Italian gestures (but not further north where Greek influence did not intrude), and in references to a head-tossing ("no") gesture called *ananeuo'ing* in Homer's *Iliad*. Collett (1984) cites a similar study by Di Jorio in 1832 that related the contemporary gestures of Neapolitans in Italy to those depicted in ancient Greek pottery. It appears that unlike verbal language and certain consumption patterns, nonverbal communications are much slower to change with globalization and culture contact (Archer 1997).

Giving the camera to informants is another technique that has begun to enter consumer research, for instance in work underway by Kelly Tepper (see also Becker 1981; Ziller 1990). An interesting use of a natural consumer-generated archive – the family photo album – is Chalfen's (1988) study of Japanese American family acculturation through such photos. Scrapbooks form a related visual resource (e.g., Katriel and Farrell 1991). There has also been some similar work on tourist photographs (e.g., Albers and James 1988; Bensen and Silberman 1987; Little 1991).

In evaluating and interpreting photos like these it is important to consider the photographer's and researcher's intent and the resulting genre of representation (see Becker 1995). As Bourdieu notes of French photographs:

> The effort of recognition is accomplished by classification within a genre or – which amounts to the same thing – the attribution of social use, as the different genres are defined primarily with reference to their use and their users: "It's a publicity photo", "It's a pure document", "It's a laboratory photo", "It's a competition photo', "It's a professional photo", "It's an educational photo", etc.
>
> (Bourdieu 1990: 89)

Plate 11.1 The sacred and profane: seller at a swap meet (Belk *et al.* 1988)

Thus, we might well wish to contextualize our interpretations of a photo with the knowledge or assumption of its purpose: to document, to remember, to critique, to create art, to sell, and so forth. Classifying photographs as art versus records (Schwartz 1989) is both too simple and too mutually exclusive. Harper's (1988) classification of visual images as "scientific," "narrative," "reflexive," or "phenomenological" is more satisfactory and corresponds to types of text-based ethnography. These genre categorizations not only specify an intent, but also an audience.

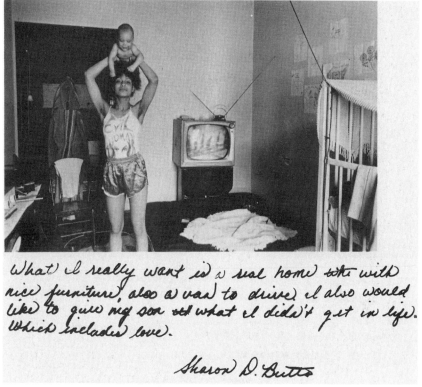

What I really want is a real home with with nice furniture, also a van to drive I also would like to give my son what I didn't get in life. Which includes love.

Sharon D. Butts

Plate 11.2 Transient hotel resident (Goldberg 1985)

Thus, it is useful to recognize that Jim Goldberg's photos are not simply aimed at artistic representation of his subjects, but also at critical commentary on what it means to be rich and poor in American society. He succeeds, in my judgment, in showing the comparable levels of materialism, desperation, and unhappiness among both the rich and poor, but this is presumably informed by an intent to challenge the stereotypes that poverty brings misery and wealth brings happiness. (See Schroeder's Chapter 7 in this book for further examples of the uses and analysis of photographs in consumer research.)

Videographic examples

Film and videotape are media that have thus far seen limited use in ethnographic consumer research, at least in comparison to the extensive use of these media by anthropologists (see Heider and Hermer 1995). There are several examples nevertheless. Wallendorf and Belk (1987) produced *Deep Meaning in Possessions*, which serves both as an early explication of qualitative methods in consumer research and a report of the Consumer Behavior Odyssey – a multimedia research project that traveled from coast to coast in the U.S. during 1986 (see Belk 1991a).

321

I am trapped – in this very consuming game where I can't have anything that is average.

I have to have a super car, a super wife, a super house.

I have at the bottom of everything a lack of self-confidence.

I am afraid of being a loser.

RON

Plate 11.3 Surburban resident (Goldberg 1985)

A summary of the video can be found in Wallendorf *et al.* (1988). The Marketing Science Institute not only distributes the video, but also houses an archive of photos and computerized fieldnotes from the project. A subsequent project, the Odyssey Downunder, in Aboriginal communities of Australia led to a fourteen-part video series on qualitative consumer research methods narrated by Robert Armstrong, Russell Belk, Ronald Groves, Ronald Hill, Geoffrey Keil, and Melanie Wallendorf. The final two-part video entitled *From Dreamtime to Screentime: The Impact of Consumer Culture on Australian Aborigines*, constitutes an analytical report of project results (Groves and Belk 1994). A summary of this video can be found in Groves and Belk (1995). There are other relevant videos on advertising, Indian

Plate 11.4 Mormon pioneer families, American Fork Canyon – courtesy Utah State
Historical Society (Belk 1992)

weavers, Australian Aboriginal art, and other topics involving marketing, but they
are either not ethnographic or do not focus on consumers primarily. There is a
video underway by Thomas O'Guinn on fans of popular musicians and musical
groups that involves ethnographic consumer research. There are, as well, consumer-related ethnographic videos from other disciplines such as Michael Lucas's
Welcome Home (1985) on satellite television viewing and his *No Illusions* (1986) on
deer hunting. Having coproduced *Deep Meaning in Possessions*, it is easy to see one
reason that there have not been more consumer video ethnographies made. It is a
time-consuming and potentially expensive process. With digital video equipment

323

becoming easier to use and less expensive to acquire, these barriers may well be declining. Nevertheless, it is a joy to have a professional crew to handle video, sound, direction, and post-production, as was the case in the Odyssey Downunder.

Even more limited use has been made thus far of film and video documents produced by consumers. Perhaps the only consumer research project to do so is Dennis Rook's (1985) study of consumer Christmas celebrations recorded on 8 mm film and video. Another consumer home video and film archive has been assembled by anthropologist Rick Prelinger (see local access digital section below). Given the prevalence, price decline, and quality improvements in home-use camcorders, there are untapped opportunities to analyze such already available data, as well as to obtain consumer-produced video documents focusing on activities specified by the researcher. While not prepared by consumers, television programs offer another video archive that has begun to be analyzed by consumer researchers (e.g., Wells and Gale 1995; Wells and Anderson 1996).

Subjectively, virtually all of the several video applications noted here are successful in creating audience empathy with the humanity of the research informants and their situations, thereby creating experiential as well as propositional knowledge. This is apparently true of Wallendorf and Belk (1987) for example, where several scenes such as those involving an old man with three garages full of possessions occasionally bring student audiences to tears, while others like a bird owner's dialogue about breeding his pet bird bring laughter, but not at this informant's expense. Such audience emotions also arise in films like those of Lucas (1985, 1986) that take a more critical view of the consumer activities investigated: satellite television viewing and deer hunting. While it would certainly be possible to create less sympathetic renderings of informants, and it is as important to note the genre of films and videos as it is with photographs, the more three-dimensional portrayal of informants moving, speaking, and engaging in various activities is necessarily engaging. Although selective filming, framing, and editing leave ample room for producer creativity and points of view, the videos that let subjects speak for themselves with a minimum of voice-over (e.g., Groves and Belk 1994; Lucas 1985, 1985) seem to be most effective in allowing the audience to form its own impressions and conclusions. The researcher's decisions that continue to subtly, or not so subtly, mold these reactions are beyond the scope of this chapter (see Collier 1986; Dowrick 1991; Dowrick and Biggs 1983; Heider 1976; Rabinger 1987; Rollwagen 1993; Worth 1981).

Local access digital examples

If there are few consumer ethnographic research examples of videography, there are almost no current examples of CD-ROM or other local access digital media. A singular example is Peter Menzel's (1994b) interactive version of his (1994a) book. Because it offers an example of what is possible in this medium, as well as a comparison to the book version of the same material, the CD-ROM program is worth a bit of description. In an opening narrative about the project, narrated by

Charles Kuralt and featuring photographs and video from families around the world, we learn that Menzel and other photographers visited one family in each of thirty countries and interviewed family members about their lives and favorite possessions. As a part of the project, family possessions were taken outside and photographed with the family. Each family member's daily life is profiled on the CD-ROM, along with statistics such as income, distance to work or school, ages, work hours, and other descriptors. The user (IBM Windows or Macintosh) can subsequently bypass this introduction, or choose to go through it, before reaching the opening menu of options. At any point the user can return to prior screens, print a screen, or quit the program. There is no search procedure, but the opening menu allows the user to complete a questionnaire about his or her own material lifestyle (paralleling those informants completed), select a country, or go to comparative photos and statistics on the thirty countries (e.g., photo comparisons of bathrooms, kitchens, and transportation; statistics or graphs on birth rates, nutrition, and leisure activities). If an individual country is chosen, the user can hear and see photo and video clips on the country and on the family chosen within it, both also narrated by Kuralt with culturally appropriate introductory music.

The family is presented in the context of a "family album," the opening page of which contains the portrait of the family and its possessions (see Plate 11.5). At this point portions of the photo can be magnified and a list of the family's possessions can be displayed. Favorite possessions of various family members are highlighted in the possession list and by "clicking" on them the possessions are also highlighted in the photograph and a brief explanation of their meanings appears on the screen. The interactive user can also choose to examine the family's questionnaire responses, to see an encyclopedic narrative on the country, or to examine the photographer's journal concerning the family. On opening the "album" the user sees captioned photos of each family member in several scenes from daily life. It is also possible to click on a number of these photos in order to see further photos or videos of the family members. In the video clips there is background noise and conversation, but no on-camera dialogues, monologues, or voice-overs. By choosing various options the user can move from country to country or examine a given country and family in some depth. Country comparisons can be made via the summary statistics (available as numbers or bar charts) and photos in the categories of vital statistics, food, shelter, livelihood, and leisure – generally with two statistics and two photo possibilities in each category.

Comparing Menzel's book and CD-ROM (both cost about $35) shows that basically the same information is contained in each, except that the questionnaire data, country descriptions, and photographer's journal are more complete in the CD-ROM, and the narration, music, and videos are obviously missing in the print version. In a sense, a book also allows random access, since the reader can page through in any sequence, use the index or the table of contents, and "quit" the book whenever desired. But besides the additional media included in the CD-ROM, the presentation seems to be more engaging. It is quite possible that a user might pick up the book and look at a single country or a single set of photo comparisons (e.g., music-making around the world). But it seems far less likely that the CD-ROM user would do so without also examining something else a mouse click or two away. These links are clearly intertextual in a multimedia sense of the term. It is also possible to flip through the book more quickly than is the case with the CD-ROM. Farnell and Huntley describe some of the implications of this medium for researchers and users:

> If the results of scholarly production can be almost as multi-media as cultural events themselves, then conducting fieldwork with a CD ROM in mind means collecting data in as many forms as possible – video, sound tape, photographs, pictures, maps, drawings, songs, interviews – and imagining creative ways to re-present them, bearing in mind that the ethnography so produced will be structured somewhat differently each time, depending upon the inquisitive choice of the user. I find that exciting!
>
> (Farnell and Huntley 1995: 10)

In opposition to Banks (1994) – see epigraphs on p. 308 – Biella (1994) emphasizes that the user of such interactive media is freed from notions of linearity, at least to a degree. However, both Banks (1994) and Biella (1994) agree that simple programmed learning approaches to such presentations do not take full advantage of these media. And without boolean logic random search capabilities, the linkages that are possible are only those the author has built in. Thus CD-ROM is not an automatic improvement over single medium approaches; and the garbage-in-garbage-out adage applies as much here as it does anywhere (both in terms of the ethnographic data and the sophistication of the CD-ROM programming). But local access digital media clearly offer a more complete portrait of informants and sites, and a potentially quite engaging multimedia presentation. For further discussion of these points, see Biella (1995) and Danet (1997).

Historical material CD-ROMs with relevance to consumer behavior are illustrated by Rick Prelinger who uses advertising, educational films, and industrial films of the twentieth century to demonstrate the development of consumer culture in the U.S., as well as other cultural phenomena. Probably the most relevant for consumer research are volumes one (*The Rainbow is Yours*) and two (*Capitalist Realism*) of his twelve-CD series "Our Secret Century" (Prelinger 1996a, 1996b), although his earlier *Ephemeral Films* CD is also relevant (see http://www.voyagerco.com). Prelinger calls himself a media archaeologist and has assembled an archive of over 33,000 films on which these narrated and text-linked CD-ROMs are based. A CD-ROM demonstrating another potential of the medium is Dan Wardlow's (1998) *Principles of Marketing: An Interactive Approach*. This is clearly an instructional CD intended to supplement or replace introductory marketing texts. It incorporates films, animation, charts, text, and programmed learning, and allows the student to proceed through material in whatever order desired. This early entrant into CD-ROM-based instructional material also brings

Plate 11.5 Possessions of a Thai family, screen from *Material World* (Menzel 1994b)

us back to the Banks (1994) and Biella (1994) debate on whether interactive media are promising only for educational purposes or for research purposes as well.

Coffey and Atkinson (1996) offer a promising view of the use of interactive media for research, but also suggest that both researchers and their audiences must view the research and representation process differently in order to achieve this potential:

> We would not have separate phases of data storage, retrieval, analysis, and writing up. Instead, we would prepare the data sets of interviews, documents, and other representations together with our sociological commentary in such a way as to allow the reader to navigate her or his unique pathways through them all. The reader (working at a multi-media workstation rather than a book or journal) therefore would not be constrained to inspect only those extracts from the data that we had chosen for illustrative purposes. By activating links across all the data files (created by us or by the reader, or by both), readers become analysts in their own right. Furthermore, the full possibilities of hypertext and hypermedia mean that it is not too fanciful to think in the near future of hypertext-based ethnographies in which the reader can activate sound and visual playbacks, so that original documents can be inspected in the context of ethnographic analysis.
>
> (Coffey and Atkinson 1996: 183)

Indeed, some available CDs already allow these options. Whether or not they become more widely produced and consumed in the future in consumer research will depend on the field's willingness to make the required changes in order to create and meaningfully use such interactive media, academia's willingness to credit appropriately such work for promotion and tenure decisions, and researchers' abilities to overcome challenges to informant anonymity. For further discussion of these issues, see Lister (1995).

If we expand our conceptualization of what we mean by local access digital, we might also include other research and representation alternatives such as Zaltman's computerized ZMET collage technique for exploring consumer metaphors (Zaltman 1995; Zaltman and Coulter 1995; Zaltman and Higie 1993; Zaltman and Schuck 1995; Zaltman et al. 1995), as well as the use of computer-based presentation programs such as PowerPoint. With a computer and projection device, multimedia research and teaching presentations are possible that incorporate words, graphics, music, voices, animation, video, and photographs. Janeen Costa and I have been using such methods in qualitative marketing research classes we have taught over the past two years and we have also made these presentations available to students on a list server. This has allowed us to present these materials simultaneously to others in the U.S. and abroad whom we invite to subscribe to the list server. With the addition of a list server, we are beginning to shade into the last category of multimedia that I discuss in the following section.

Distributed access digital examples

The other common digital medium is the Internet. Although list servers and individual e-mail are capable of handling photos, graphics, sounds, artwork, and videos in appropriate formats, word-based text is currently most common in this medium as well. With the Web-based *Journal of Consumer and Market Research* having begun, there is one emerging forum already other than constructing your own home page or searching for others'. The intent is to submit, review, and publish research papers electronically, with the possible inclusion of raw ethnographic data as well as articles. In part, this has led Larsen and Wright (1996) to propose the establishment of a canonical body of qualitative consumer data in order to provoke multiple analyses and interpretations in the pursuit of ultimate consensual validation of this work. As an experimental demonstration of such methods, they have acquired an interview with an African-American university dean, "Ella," which they (Larsen and Wright 1998), Craig Thompson (1998), and I (Belk 1998) have all interpreted. The others' interpretations were independent, while mine was made in light of their interpretations and is oppositional in attempting to offer a conflicting interpretation. I also argue in my paper (the term may be becoming obsolete) that seeking a consensually validated canonical interpretation is undesirable, that multiple interpretations are ideal, and that analyzing secondhand data is clearly inferior to analyzing firsthand (personally collected) data. The last conclusion is based on the firsthand researcher's inevitable tacit knowledge of the informant and the ability to clarify, probe, and try alternative data collection methods. All of these opportunities are lacking with secondhand data. Nevertheless, the exercise with "Ella" is a useful one, and the interview text is, at this writing, available on the Web site http://cob.jmu.edu/wrightnd/canoncan/htm.

Another Web-based multimedia presentation in progress is the "Revealing Things" project by Judith Gradwohl of the Smithsonian Institution. The project is intended to "transcend traditional exhibitions in both content and design," according to the proposal. It will represent eleven American homes and possessions, with other homes from other countries and other historical periods also being included. Stories will be presented as first-person narratives and the Web site will allow users to examine ten different themes including important possessions, food, clothing, recreation and leisure, festival days and holidays, space use, family technology and resource use. There will be stories about single objects and their histories, who used them, and what it would be like to live in Kansas or in India. It is a central theme of the project that "Our possessions reflect our heritage, our personalities, our aspirations, ourselves." For example, blue jeans will be able to be examined as an historical object, a fashion statement, and (in Eastern bloc countries) a forbidden good. The designers also intend to monitor the Web site continually, and to incorporate material contributed by users as well as modify the presentation based on user suggestions. A variety of special programs and activities will also be a part of the changing Web site. Judith Gradwohl can be contacted at jag@ic.si.edu.

As Table 11.2 suggests, one of the advantages of distributed Web access versus local CD-ROM access to research material is the nearly limitless possibilities of linking to related material. At the same time, this lack of finite structure presents the possibility of getting lost in hyperspace. Unlike CD-ROM, where the only links possible are those the authors have specified, once a particular Web site is left (via an electronic link, addressing another site, backtracking, or through searches), the possibilities are virtually endless. While individualistic Western societies enshrine individual choice as being virtuous, and while exploring hyperspace can be stimulating to a greater degree than with local access digital media, the Web surfer will probably not know what lies ahead. In addition to current time delays during such exploration, there is also the question of when the exploration should be concluded. Unlike reading a book, there is no fixed ending. But like much qualitative interpretation, the explorer is likely to reach a point of saturation (or exhaustion) where nothing new is being learned. Apart from marking various Web locations in order to return to them in the future, material from the Web (text, photos, video, sounds) can be downloaded and stored for future access. Perhaps the largest limitation of the Web, when not used in conjunction with a known source like the *Journal of Consumer and Market Research*, is the uncertain quality of the material that may be encountered. The researcher putting data up on a Web site also must anticipate a variety of possible users and uses to which these data might be put. No doubt both changing technology and ethical and legal arguments about intellectual property will continue to shape these considerations in the future.

Discussion and conclusions

This has necessarily been a short overview of the multimedia forms currently available to consumer researchers. I have presented or discussed some of the few current examples of consumer research projects using such media. Interested readers are encouraged to explore both the existing material and multimedia possibilities in their own research. As suggested at the beginning of this chapter, the existence of multimedia research tools does not mean that they must or should be used. The medium or media should match the goals of the project and what is feasible for a particular researcher. There is clearly more work involved in creating a good multimedia presentation than there is in preparing a paper or book containing only written text.

That said, these are exciting times in terms of the possibilities we now have available for gathering and representing consumer research in multiple sensory modalities. As with all innovations, the innovators must lead before others can follow. Journals, promotion and tenure committees, and professional associations are among the important gatekeepers that will also affect the rate and degree of adoption of multimedia technologies by consumer researchers. Given the curious nexus of multimedia vehicles within the territory between art and science, it may also be the case that either positivist or non-positivist consumer researchers will be the first to dominate CD-ROM and Web vehicles. At this point, however, it seems most likely and most suitable that qualitative consumer researchers will seize the opportunity to expand the modalities of our data collection and representation media. Those of us doing qualitative research have a great opportunity for making our research more interesting, open, humanizing, and compelling by using more of the array of multimedia tools.

Producing interesting theoretical perspectives is, I think, a matter of rejecting the premises of science and embracing those of art (see Belk 1986 and Brown 1998). That is, in our data collection and representation we should eschew the cold precision and hollow mechanical language of science in order to become both literary and visual artists in crafting compelling documents for today's visual world. Consumer desire depends on the visual both for stimulation and, as with the Little Prince's sheep, for visualization (e.g., see Buck-Morss 1989; Friedberg 1993; Tester 1994). Thus, if it is consumer desire that we ultimately seek to understand, we too must turn our attention more to the visual, to multiple sensory modalities, and to multimedia methods of capturing and portraying truths about consumption.

In suggesting that we become better artists in gathering and preparing multi-media representations of consumers, I am not suggesting that we abandon our attempt to study naturally occurring behaviors. We might imagine a continuum with positivist laboratory research at one end and art for art's sake at the other end. Traditional non-positivist ethnography might be thought to occupy the midpoint of this continuum. While there is a potential role for multimedia at each point along the way, I am arguing for an ideal somewhere between traditional ethnography and art for art's sake. In the case of photography, for instance, this means that rather than think of photos as data for later analysis and trying to sample representatively the people, time, and space under study, we would instead think of photos as ideally capturing the essence of the behavior we seek to portray. We should make visual images with this in mind and look for the most effective image rather than the most typical one. We should learn how to make good photos in both a technical and artistic sense. The camera and photographer are not neutral tools recording what they see, but creative tools potentially able to convey essential truths about the behaviors of interest. There are other roles for photography in consumer research, but to use it and other non-textual media in non-creative ways is to assure that these media will play only a trivial role in the future of consumer research.

There is a parallel between the uses I am advocating for non-textual multi-media and the uses Wolcott (1994) discusses for text-based data and representa-tions. He suggests that data are never presented in purely raw form, but that the researcher always "cooks" the data in some way. The simplest way of cooking the data and the one most used by novice researchers, is to analyze it descriptively, in the sense of data-constrained and supposedly objective and confirmable accounts.

But whereas analysis *transforms* data, interpretation *transcends* data with more speculative, data-distant, abstract, and intuitive researcher insights. It is this interpretive mode that Wolcott (1994) sees as more characteristic of seasoned and mature researchers. Similarly, in the case of multimedia representations of consumer behavior, an interpretive account involves the more artistic creative use of the tools that I am calling for. It seeks to transcend propositional knowledge and mere description in favor of the effective presentation that provides experiential knowledge and essential truths about the phenomenon under study. To do this it is not enough to simply randomly record sights and sounds. This might suffice for description, but it is unlikely (except by chance) to lead to good interpretation and artistically effective representation. Rather, these images must be captured either thoughtfully or intuitively with an interpretive stance or position already framing them. In this sense the distinction between data and representation collapses. The cooking takes place, in part, as the images are gathered. These images will be further refined in preparing them for presentation, but the interpretative and creative process has begun in the field.

And what of the audience for multimedia consumption representations? Do such representations offer a more closed text than the printed word? That is, are they less open to further audience interpretation? The answer depends on the representation. The heavy authorial voice of a video using a voice-over soundtrack to tell the audience what everything depicted is, and what it means, is indeed a closed text. But the video that lets the voice of the informants speak for itself is far more open. Non-linear interactive digital media can provide extremely open texts to their audiences. Thus there is a range of possibilities depending on the medium and how it is used by the researcher. There is also a partial interaction between the openness of the multimedia text and the aims of the researcher. Purely descriptive data representations provide a very open text that requires much active sense-making by the audience. Purely interpretive representations leave little room for audience interpretations beyond accepting or rejecting the interpretation offered. Of the various ways of handling this dilemma, perhaps the polyvocal perspective of presenting multiple points of view and multiple possible interpretations offers the most satisfactory resolution. This is also consistent with the view that there exist multiple truths rather than a singular truth. And it allows the representation of conflicting perspectives of different informants, groups, and researchers. Nevertheless, as a creative pursuit, different researchers will need to find their own ways of dealing with presenting open versus closed multimedia texts.

I hope that the few examples and discussion presented here encourage more multimedia ideas and a broadened palette of research and representational techniques. I hope that the challenge to preserve the uniqueness of our informants and research sites is one that resonates with other researchers. And I hope that the call to avoid striving for better science in favor of striving for better art is found to be creatively liberating. For like our research subjects and the Little Prince's rose, we are each unique and have distinctive points of view that should be evident in our research.

Acknowledgments

I am grateful to Susan Spiggle for her helpful comments on a draft of this chapter. I am also grateful to the *Journal of Consumer Research* for permission to reproduce Figures 11.1 and 11.4, Jim Goldberg for permission to reproduce Figures 11.2 and 11.3, and *Material World* for permission to reproduce Figure 11.5. Further multimedia examples can be found on my home page: http://www.business.utah.edn/~mktrwb/.

References

Aaland, M. (1981) *County Fair: Portraits*, Santa Barbara, CA: Capra.

Agee, J. and Evans, W. (1941) *Let Us Now Praise Famous Men*, Cambridge, MA: Riverside Press.

Albers, P. and James, W.R. (1988) "Travel Photography: A Methodological Approach," *Annals of Tourism Research*, 15: 134–58.

Archer, D. (1997) "Unspoken Diversity: Cultural Differences in Gestures," *Qualitative Sociology*, 20,1: 79–105.

Ball, M.S. and Smith, G.W.H. (1992) *Analyzing Visual Data*, Newbury Park, CA: Sage.

Banks, M. (1994) "Interactive Multimedia and Anthropology – A Skeptical View," http://www.rsl.ox.ac.uk/isac/marcus.banks.01.html, June, University of Oxford.

Barthes, R. (1984) *Camera Lucida: Reflections on Photography*, trans. R. Howard, London: Fontana (original *La Chambre Claire*, Paris: Editions du Seuil, 1980).

Becker, H. S. (ed.) (1981) *Exploring Society Photographically*, Chicago: University of Chicago Press.

—— (1995) "Visual Sociology, Documentary Photography, and Photojournalism: It's (Almost) All a Matter of Context," *Visual Sociology*, 10,1–2: 5–14.

Belk, R.W. (1986) "Art Versus Science as Ways of Generating Knowledge About Materialism," in D. Brinberg and R.J. Lutz (eds) *Perspectives on Methodology in Consumer Research*, New York: Springer-Verlag, 3–36.

—— (1989) "Visual Images of Consumption: What You See and What you Get," in T. Childers *et al.* (eds) *1989 AMA Winter Educators' Conference: Marketing Theory and Practice*, Chicago: American Marketing Association, 122.

—— (1991a) "The History and Development of the Consumer Behavior Odyssey," in R.W. Belk (ed.) *Highways and Buyways: Naturalistic Research from the Consumer Behavior Odyssey*, Provo, UT: Association for Consumer Research, 1–12.

—— (1991b) "Possessions and the Sense of Past," in R.W. Belk (ed.) *Highways and Buyways: Naturalistic Research from the Consumer Behavior Odyssey*, Provo, UT: Association for Consumer Research, 114–30.

—— (1992) "Moving Possessions: An Analysis Based on Personal Documents from the 1847–1869 Mormon Migration," *Journal of Consumer Research*, 19,3: 339–61.

—— (1998) "Ella's Elephants and the Three Blind White Guys," in W. Hutchinson and J. Alba (eds) *Advances in Consumer Research*, vol. 25, Provo, UT: Association for Consumer Research.

Belk, R.W., Sherry, J.F., Jr., and Wallendorf, M. (1988) "A Naturalistic Inquiry into Buyer and Seller Behavior at a Swap Meet," *Journal of Consumer Research*, 14,4: 449–70.

Bensen, J. and Silberman, R. (1987) "Tourist Photographs as Souvenirs," in J. Salzman (ed.) *Prospects: An Annual of American Cultural Studies*, vol. 11, New York: Cambridge University Press, 261–71.

Berger, J. (1980) *About Looking*, New York: Pantheon.

Berman, M. (1989) *Coming to Our Senses: Body and Spirit in the Hidden History of the West*, New York: Simon and Schuster.

Biella, P. (1994) "Codifications of Ethnography: Linear and Nonlinear," http://www.usc.edu/dept/elab/welcome/codifications.html, November, University of Southern California.

—— (1995) "Interactive Media and the Visual-Digital Horizon," *Anthropology Newsletter*, December: 32–3.

Bourdieu, P. (1990) *Photography: A Middle-brow Art*, trans. S. Whiteside, Stanford CA: Stanford University Press.

Brown, S. (1998) *Post Modern Marketing II: Telling Tales*, London: Routledge.

Buck-Morss, S. (1989) *The Dialectics of Seeing: Walter Benjamin and the Arcades Project*, Cambridge, MA: MIT Press.

Chalfen, R. (1987) *Snapshot Versions of Life*, Bowling Green, OH: Bowling Green State University Popular Press.

—— (1988) "Japanese American Family Photography: A Brief Report on Home Visual Mode Communication in Cross-Cultural Contexts," *Visual Sociology Review*, 3, Fall: 12–16.

Clifford, J. (1988) *The Predicament of Culture: Twentieth-Century Ethnography, Literature, and Art*, Cambridge, MA: Harvard University Press.

Clifford, J. and Marcus, G.E. (eds) (1986) *Writing Culture: The Poetics and Politics of Ethnography*, Berkeley: University of California Press.

Coffey, A. and Atkinson, P. (1996) *Making Sense of Qualitative Data: Complementary Research Strategies*, Thousand Oaks, CA: Sage.

Cohen, E. (1988) "The Broken Cycle: Smell in a Bangkok Soi (Lane)," *Ethnos*: 52, 37–49.

Collett, P. (1984) "History and the Study of Expressive Action," in K.J. Gergen and M.M. Gergen (eds) *Historical Social Psychology*, Hillsdale, NJ: Lawrence Erlbaum, 371–96.

Collier, J., Jr. (1986) *Visual Anthropology: Photography as a Research Method*, 2nd edn, Albuquerque: University of New Mexico Press.

Costa, J.A. and Belk, R.W. (1990) "Nouveaux Riches as Quintessential Americans: Case Studies of Consumption in an Extended Family," in R.W. Belk (ed.) *Advances in NonProfit Marketing*, vol. 3, Greenwich, CT: JAI Press, 83–140.

D'Aluisio, F. and Menzel, P. (1996) *Women in the Material World*, San Francisco: Sierra Club Books.

Danet, B. (1997) "Books, Letters, Documents: The Changing Aesthetics of Texts in Late Print Culture," *Journal of Material Culture*, 2, March: 5–38.

de Saint Exupéry, A. (1943 [1971]) *The Little Prince*, trans. K. Woods, San Diego: Harcourt Brace Jovanovich.

Denzin, N.K. (1989) *Interpretive Interactionism*, Newbury Park, CA: Sage.

Dowrick, P.W. (1991) *Practical Guide to Using Video in the Behavioral Sciences*, New York: Wiley.

Dowrick, P.W. and Biggs, S.J. (eds.) (1983) *Using Video: Psychological and Sociological Applications*, New York: Wiley.

Dundes, A. (1972) "Seeing is Believing," *Natural History*, 81, May: 8+.

Evans, C. (1990) *In The Money*, London: Blue Window Books.

Farnell, B. and Huntley, J. (1995) "Ethnography Goes Interactive," *Anthropology Today*, 11, October: 7–14.

Freedberg, D. (1989) *The Power of Images: Studies in the History and Theory of Response*, Chicago: University of Chicago Press.

Friedberg, A. (1993) *Window Shopping: Cinema and the Postmodern*, Berkeley, CA: University of California Press.

Goldberg, J. (1985) *Rich and Poor*, New York: Random House.

Griffin, M. (1993) "The Millstone of Popular Culture: Competing with the Commercial Mass Production of Cultural Imagery," *Visual Sociology*, 8,2: 32–7.

Groves, R. and Belk, R.W. (1994) *From Dreamtime to Screentime: Consumer Culture and Australian Aborigines*, (two-part video), Perth, Western Australia: Edith Cowan University.

—— (1995) "The Odyssey Downunder: A Qualitative Study of Aboriginal Consumers," in F.R. Kardes and M. Sujan (eds) *Advances in Consumer Research*, vol. 22, Provo, UT: Association for Consumer Research, 303–5.

Hagen, C. (1985) *American Photographers of the Depression: Farm Security Administration Photographs, 1935–1942*, New York: Pantheon.

Hansen, U. and Blüher, K. (1993) *Handel Und Konsumkultur*, Hannover: Fackelträger.

Harper, D. (1988) "Visual Sociology: Expanding Sociological Vision," *American Sociologist*, 19: 54–70.

Heider, K.G. (1976) *Ethnographic Film*, Austin: University of Texas Press.

Heider, K.G. and Hermer, C. (1995), *Films for Anthropological Teaching*, 8th edn, Arlington, VA: American Anthropological Association, Special Publication 29.

Heisley, D.D. and Levy, S.J. (1991) "Autodriving: A Photoelicitation Technique," *Journal of Consumer Research*, 18,3: 257–72.

Heisley, D.D., McGrath, M.A. and Sherry, J.F., Jr. (1991) "'To Everything There Is a Season;' A Photoessay of a Farmer's Market," in R.W. Belk (ed.) *Highways and Buyways: Naturalistic Research from the Consumer Behavior Odyssey*, Provo, UT: Association for Consumer Research, 141–66.

Hill, R.P. (1991) "Homeless Women, Special Possessions, and the Meaning of 'Home': An Ethnographic Case Study," *Journal of Consumer Research*, 18,3: 298–310.

Hill, R.P. and Stamey, M. (1990) "The Homeless in America: An Examination of Possessions and Consumer Behaviors," *Journal of Consumer Research*, 17,3: 303–21.

Hirsch, J. (1981) *Family Photographs: Content, Meaning, and Effect*, New York: Oxford University Press.

Hirschman, E.C. (1988) "Upper Class WASPs as Consumers: A Humanistic Inquiry," in E.C. Hirschman and J.N. Sheth (eds) *Research in Consumer Behavior*, vol. 3, Greenwich, CT: JAI Press, 115–47.

Katriel, T. and Farrell, T. (1991) "Scrapbooks as Cultural Texts: An American Art of Memory," Text and Performance Quarterly, 11, January: 1–17.

Keller, U. (1985) *The Highway as Habitat: A Roy Stryker Documentation, 1943–1955*, Santa Barbara, CA: University Art Museum.

King, G. (1984) *"Say Cheese"! Looking at Snapshops in a New Way*, New York: Dodd, Mead, & Company.

Lange, D. (1987) *Dorothea Lange: Aperture Masters of Photography, Number Five*, New York: Aperture.

Langer, S.K. (1963) *Philosophy in a New Key: A Study of the Symbolism of Reason, Rite, and Art*, 3rd edn, Cambridge, MA: Harvard University Press.

Larsen, V. and Wright, N. (1996) "Community and Canon: A Foundation for Mature Interpretive Research," in M. Brucks and D.J. MacInnis (eds) *Advances in Consumer Research*, vol. 24, Provo, UT: Association for Consumer Research, 310–14.

—— (1998) "The Mirror and the Lamp, the Mask and the Elephant: A Close Reading of 'Ella'," in W. Hutchinson and J. Alba (eds) *Advances in Consumer Research*, vol. 25, Provo, UT: Association for Consumer Research.

Lesy, M. (1973) *Wisconsin Death Trip*, New York: Pantheon.

Levinson, J.D. (1983) *Fleamarkets*, Berlin: Braus.

Lister, M. (ed.) (1995) *The Photographic Image in Digital Culture*, London: Routledge.

Little, K. (1991) "On Safari: The Visual Politics of a Tourist Representation," in D. Howes (ed.) *The Varieties of Sensory Experience: A Sourcebook in the Anthropology of the Senses*, Toronto: University of Toronto Press, 148–63.

Lucas, M.A. (1985) *Welcome Home: A Satellite Dish Survey of South East Ohio* (video), Columbus, OH: M.A. Lucas.

—— (1986) *No Illusions: A Deer Hunting Experience* (video), Columbus, OH: Ohio Arts Council.

Lynch, M. and Edgerton, S.Y., Jr. (1988) "Aesthetics and Digital Image Processing: Representational Craft in Contemporary Astronomy," in G. Fyfe and J. Law (eds) *Picturing Power: Visual Depiction and Social Relations*, London: Routledge, 184–220.

Menzel, P. (1994a) *Material World: A Global Family Portrait*, San Francisco: Sierra Club Books.

—— (1994b) *Material World: A Global Family Portrait*, (CD-ROM), San Francisco: StarPress Multimedia.

Morris, D., Collett, P., Marsh, P., and O'Shaughnessy, M. (1979) *Gestures: Their Origins and Distribution*, London: Jonathan Cape.

Morris, W. (1989) "On Memory, Emotion, and Imagination," and "Origins," in W. Morris (ed.) *Time Pieces: Photographs, Writing, and Memory*, New York: Aperture Foundation, 33–6, 75–82.

Musello, C. (1979) "Family Photography," in J. Wagner (ed.) *Images of Information: Still Photography in the Social Sciences*, Beverly Hills, CA: Sage, 101–18.

O'Guinn, T.C. (1991) "Touching Greatness: The Central Midwest Barry Manilow Fan Club," in R.W. Belk (ed.) *Highways and Buyways: Naturalistic Research from the Consumer Behavior Odyssey*, Provo, UT: Association for Consumer Research, 102–11.

Owens, B. (1973) *Suburbia*, San Francisco: Straight Arrow Books.

Peñaloza, L. (1994) "Atravesando Fronteros/Border Crossings: A Critical Ethnographic Exploration of the Consumer Acculturation of Mexican Immigrants," *Journal of Consumer Research*, 21,1: 32–54.

Pratt, G. (1994) *In Search of the Corn Queen*, Washington, D.C.: National Museum of American Art.

Prelinger, R. (1996a) *Capitalist Realism* (CD-ROM), Irvington, NY: Voyager.

—— (1996b) *The Rainbow is Yours* (CD-ROM), Irvington, NY: Voyager.

Putnam, T. and Newton, C. (eds) (1990) *Household Choices*, London: Futures Publications.

Rabinger, M. (1987) *Directing the Documentary*, Boston: Focal Press.

Rand, P. and Bird, E. (1984) *The Private Rich: A Family Album*, New York: Crown.

Reddy, G.P. (1993) *Danes are Like That! Perspectives of an Indian Anthropologist on the Danish Society*, Mørke, Denmark: Grevas Forlag.

Riis, J.A. (1971) *How the Other Half Lives*, New York: Dover (original 1901).

Robbins, K. (1995) "Will the Image Move us Still?," in M. Lister (ed.) *The Photographic Image in Digital Culture*, London: Routledge, 29–50.

Rollwagen, J. (ed.) (1993) *Anthropological Filmmaking: Anthropological Perspectives on the Production of Film and Video for General Audiences*, 2nd edn, New York: Harwood.

Romanyshyn, R.D. (1989) *Technology as Symptom and Dream*, London: Routledge.

Rook, D. (1985) "Consumers' Video Archives and Household Rituals," presented at Conference of the Association for Consumer Research, Las Vegas, NV, 19 October.

—— (1991) "I Was Observed (*In Absentia*) and Autodriven by the Consumer Behavior Odyssey," in R.W. Belk (ed.) *Highways and Buyways: Naturalistic Research from the Consumer Behavior Odyssey*, Provo, UT: Association for Consumer Research, 48–58.

Rousseau, A.M. (1981) *Shopping Bag Ladies*, New York: Pilgrim.

Ruby, J. (1995) "The Moral Burden of Authorship in Ethnographic Film," *Visual Anthropology Review*, 11, Fall: 77–82.

Rutkovsky, P. (1982) *Commodity Character*, Rochester, NY: Visual Studies Workshop Press.

Salinger, A. (1995) *In My Room: Teenagers in Their Bedrooms*, San Francisco: Chronicle Books.

Schaffer, S. (1993) "The Consuming Flame: Electrical Showmen and Tory Mystics in the World of Goods," in J. Brewer and R. Porter (eds) *Consumption and the World of Goods*, London: Routledge, 489–526.

Schouten, J.W. and McAlexander J.H., (1995) Subcultures of Consumption: An Ethnography of the New Bikers," *Journal of Consumer Research*, 22,1: 43–61.

Schwartz, D. (1989) "Visual Ethnography: Using Photography in Qualitative Research," *Qualitative Sociology*, 12, Summer: 119–53.

Signorelli, V. (1987) "Capitulating to Captions: The Verbal Transformation of Visual Images," *Human Studies*, 10: 281–310.

Slater, D. (1995) "Photography and Modern Vision: The Spectacle of 'Natural Magic'," in C. Jenks (ed.) *Visual Culture*, London: Routledge, 218–37.

Sontag, S. (1977) *On Photography*, New York: Delta.

Spence, J. and Holland, P. (eds) (1991) *Family Snaps: The Meaning of Domestic Photography*, London: Virago.

Stange, M. (1989) *Symbols of Ideal Life: Social Documentary Photography in America, 1890–1950*, Cambridge: Cambridge University Press.

Tester, K. (ed.) (1994) *The Flâneur*, London: Routledge.

Thompson, C. (1998) "A Hermeneutic Interpretation of an Interview with Ella," in W. Hutchinson and J. Alba (eds) *Advances in Consumer Research*, vol. 25, Provo, UT: Association for Consumer Research.

Tuchman, M. (1994) *Magnificent Obsessions: Twenty Remarkable Collectors in Pursuit of Their Dreams*, San Francisco: Chronicle Books.

Turner, B.S. (1984) *The Body and Society: Explorations in Social Theory*, Oxford: Basil Blackwell.

Walker, A.L. and Moulton, C. (1989) "Photo Albums: Images of Time and Reflections of Self," *Qualitative Sociology*, 12, Summer: 155–82.

Wallendorf, M. and Belk, R.W. (1987) *Deep Meaning in Possessions: Qualitative Research from the Consumer Behavior Odyssey* (video), Cambridge, MA: Marketing Science Institute.

Wallendorf, M. and Belk, R.W. and Heisley, D. (1988) "Deep Meaning in Possessions: The Paper," in M. Houston (ed.) *Advances in Consumer Research*, vol. 15, Provo, UT: Association for Consumer Research, 528–30.

Wardlow, D.L. (1998) *Principles of Marketing: An Interactive Approach*, (CD-ROM), Cincinnati, OH: South Western.

Wells, W.D., Anderson, C.L. and Gale, K.L. (1995) "Fictional Subjects in Consumer Research," in F. R. Kardes and M. Sujan (eds) *Advances in Consumer Research*, vol. 22, Provo, UT: Association for Consumer Research, 306–10.

Wells, W.D. and Anderson, C.L. (1996) "Fictional Materialism," K.P. Corfman and J.G. Lynch, Jr. (eds) *Advances in Consumer Research*, vol. 23, Provo, UT: Association for Consumer Research, 130–46.

Wolcott, H.F. (1994) *Transforming Qualitative Data: Description, Analysis, and Interpretation*, Thousand Oaks, CA: Sage.

Worth, S. (1981) *Studying Visual Communication*, L. Gross (ed.), Philadelphia: University of Pennsylvania Press.

Zaltman, G. (1995), "Amidword: Anthropology, Metaphors, and Cognitive Peripheral Vision," in J.F. Sherry, Jr. (ed.) *Contemporary Marketing and Consumer Behavior: An Anthropological Sourcebook*, Thousand Oaks, CA: Sage, 282–304.

Zaltman, G. and Coulter, R.A. (1995) "Seeing the Voice of the Customer: Metaphor-Based Advertising Research," *Journal of Advertising Research*, 35, July–August: 35–51.

Zaltman, G. and Higie, R.A. (1993) "Seeing the Voice of the Customer: The Zaltman Metaphor Elicitation Technique," Marketing Science Institute Report Number 93–114, September.

Zaltman, G. and Schuck, L.J. (1995) "Sensing the Voice of the Customer," paper presented at the Harvard Business School Colloquium, "Multimedia and the Boundaryless World," 16–17 November.

Zaltman, G., Zaltman, A., Crameri, N., Finkle, M., and Randel K. (1995) "The Dimension of Brand Equity for Nestle Crunch Bar," report for QUEST and Associates, Cambridge, MA.

Ziller, R.Z. (1990) *Photographing the Self: Methods for Observing Personal Orientations*, Newbury Park, CA: Sage.

12

CONDUCTING THE CHOIR

Representing multimethod consumer research

Linda L. Price and Eric J. Arnould

The power of group song lies largely in the chorus, even though the role of the individual solo is a pivotal one, showing that the significance of the individual is not overshadowed by this group demonstration. The fact that there are points in dancing when every individual chants his one *mioc* [individual praises, or "he does his thing"] shows the significance of songs and dances to the ego of each person.

(Anthropologist Francis Deng, recalling the Yoruba "Dance of the Tortoise," in Lienhardt 1985: 145)

We must think like musicians.
(Edgar Morin, 1996, Philosopher of Complexity)

Overture

The use of multiple methods associated with disparate epistemological paradigms is still rare in consumer research. To realize the potential of multimethod research, we draw on examples that show the theoretical and practical importance of employing different assumptions about doing multimethod science. To convey these assumptions and their consequences, *we use the metaphor of representing research as conducting a choir.* Lakoff and Johnson summarize the value of a good metaphor:

There is a similarity induced by the metaphor that goes beyond the mere similarities between the two ranges of experience. The additional similarity is a structural similarity. It involves the way we understand how the individual highlighted experiences fit together in a coherent way . . . The metaphor, by virtue of giving coherent structure to a range of our experiences, creates similarities of a new kind.

(Lakoff and Johnson 1980: 150–1).

Thus, we use musical metaphors as a way of giving a different kind of coherence to the research experience and of representing different, hopefully enlightening, patterns of similarity and difference in research phenomena.

Many other researchers have explored various issues associated with the notorious crisis of representation in the social sciences. For example, some explore the issues of reflexivity raised by the encounter between alternative scientific paradigms (Ashmore 1989; Bleier 1986; Clough 1992; Woolgar 1988), and others examine the possibilities of more fully representing the complexity of social practices through alternative textual forms (Calas and Smircich 1991; Gubrium and Holstein 1997; Richardson 1994; Van Maanen 1988) and through performance (Finley and Knowles 1995; Paget 1995). Our References section also lists accounts of some more technical workbench issues involved in multi-person, multimethod research (Creswell 1994; Jick 1979; Mason 1994; Miles and Huberman 1994; Olesen *et al.* 1994; Nau 1996; Sells *et al.* 1995). In this chapter our concerns are pragmatic but not narrowly technical. Our choir metaphor is an answer to the question: "How shall we think about linking and representing data rooted in different paradigmatic premises?"

Announcing a theme

> Perhaps one of the reasons for this lack of accumulation in marketing thought is due to the nature of the paradigm in use. We have assumed that our inability to develop a body of coherent theory is due to the incorrect usage of . . . methods. However, the problem may be less in the method and more in the paradigm.
>
> (Rohit Deshpande 1983: 106)

In the spirit of Deshpande's (1983) critique, we offer an alternative for conducting and representing multimethod research that is based on our research practice rather than on normative prescriptions. We think the metaphor of conducting a choir provides a useful alternative "paradigm" to Shelby Hunt's (1991) revised convergence model. His model seems to be based more on fears of nihilistic relativism than on an examination of what embracing multimethod research relativistically might accomplish (Thompson *et al.* 1997). Through the choir metaphor we hope to embrace the mystery and paradox that surround music. As Levi-Strauss writes, "Since music is the only language with the contradictory attributes of being at once intelligible and untranslatable, the musical creator is a being comparable to the gods, and music itself the supreme mystery of the science of man" (1969: 18). Our metaphor is also an alternative to the late Paul Anderson's critical relativism (1986) in that we see no necessity why, once the paradigmatic assumptions guiding different research practices are bracketed, the findings also should be compartmentalized. Ours differs from Hudson and Ozanne's (1988) dialectical metaphor because we see no need to insist on the modernist criteria of "progress" as a driving force in moving from one way of doing research to another.

Music is not superseded, nor are views about its meaning and significance. Modern choral masterpieces enlarge our sensibilities; but they do not surpass or replace those masterpieces which have preceded them (Storr 1992).

Our choir metaphor also differs from the puzzle metaphor that is sometimes used to describe multimethod research (Morgan 1980; Mick et al. 1996). A puzzle is no more and no less than the sum of its parts. It implies that the pieces always connect and do not overlap; it allows neither for pieces that do not connect, nor those that may be connected or overlap in different, equally interesting ways. The voices of a choir create forms that are greater than the sum of their parts and make for themselves experiences of empathy that would be unlikely to occur in ordinary social intercourse (Blacking 1987: 26). Moreover, by contrast with a puzzle, choral patterns exist in time and require duration for development and completion. As such they more aptly represent behavioral processes which appear to be in constant motion (Storr 1992). We think that multimethod research, like the voices in a choir, can yield something more than the sum of its disparate parts, does allow for multiple scientifically compelling ways of ordering, and permits us to practice and represent discovery-oriented research.

Finally, our choir metaphor differs from the jazz metaphor sometimes used to describe research (Oldfather and West 1994; Holbrook 1984). As studies of jazz performances make clear, jazz is a form designed to facilitate improvisational solos; it privileges individual voices (Bastien and Hostager 1988). Our metaphor for representing multimethod research is about finding ways to blend voices (paradigmatic ones, as well as those of individual researchers) into a complex whole that does not necessarily privilege the solo voice. Choral singing aims to create a harmony of gesture and expression (Levi-Strauss 1969: 29). While our choir metaphor differs from the jazz metaphor, both share a musical frame, and in our discussion of multimethod research the more general metaphor of music also figures prominently.

Elaborating a theme: the choir

Consider then a choir, simply defined as a company of singers, especially in a church. A choir is made up of multiple voices. Singing differs from spoken language in demanding the participation of the whole body, but according to the strict rules of a particular vocal style (Levi-Strauss 1969: 28). Singers in a choir read and interpret musical scores according to the skills and view of the singers and the conductor. Rather than being redundant, the voices may sing in harmony, may sing partially overlapping melodic lines, may sing in different octaves, and may carry entirely different themes. It makes no sense to speak of one part being better or worse than another. Themes may be announced, disappear, recur, and be reworked. Different voices play different roles. The bass parts are always the ground. Soprano voices usually bear the melody. Alto and tenor voices are like the mortar between bricks. Some well-rounded individual voices mix especially well with other voices. Voices lean on one another to achieve resonant effects. Interplay between voices constitutes a whole that is greater than the sum of the parts

341

and cannot be constituted by separate parts in isolation. Partial parts may seem incongruous without the addition of other parts, although consistent articulation or coloration among voices is often important in achieving a harmonious sound. And there is no competition between voices, always a blending of them. Hence, simultaneity in performance of the parts is crucial to achieve desired musical effects. Last but not least, an audience listens to the choir. Experience and interpretation of the music is ultimately a collaboration among the composer, players, conductor, and audience (Levi-Strauss 1969). Choral works are inescapably dependent on performance. An unfamiliar performance of a familiar work may throw new light on it and open or alter one's perception of it, and a particular concert may provoke many varied reactions. In fact, an individual may find that the same choral work arouses different emotions on different occasions. Appreciation of both form and emotional significance enters into the experience of a choral work and cannot be separated (Storr 1992).

Elaborating a theme: composition

A choral metaphor can influence the design of a research presentation by broadening our understanding of the role of theory in composing multimethod research presentations. First, an analogy with musical theory invites a researcher to include maximal consideration of related theory, just as developing and performing choral music includes consideration of, and choice between, a range of structural types such as motets, chorales, and oratorio, and styles within each of them. These structures provide a framework for composition that reduces uncertainty for composer, performers, and audience. But notice that even when we think about musical composition at the most basic level, choice of key, for example, really provides us only with a minimal exclusionary principle. Choice of a key tells us what will be excluded rather than included. As Hans Keller (1970) notes, the form or background of the composition is shared by many pieces and elucidates the cultural expectations of the listener, whereas the foreground is the individual structure which happens instead of the form and serves to heighten expectation and postpone resolution in unexpected ways. A compelling score "can seem to its audience full of indefinably familiar things – and at the same time invested with godlike power of 'understanding' that is far indeed from the daily round" (Moore 1984: vii). Great composers arouse our emotions because they are experts in heightening expectation and postponing resolution (Meyer 1956).

A musical metaphor suggests then that planning a study only identifies the rules for generating generic types of representation or choral combination that one wishes to explore. Thus Palestrina (Renaissance), Bach (baroque), Mozart (classical), Brahms (romantic), and Britten (twentieth century) all wrote choral masses. However, they differ dramatically (Brahms and Britten added secular content) while responding to the structure of the Catholic Mass. Similarly, if we conduct a statistical research study we know we will make statements about means, tendencies, and frequencies in a population, but this merely opens up a vast range of expression. Similarly a literary critical analysis will be concerned with narratives and their basic building blocks (Stern 1989), but the range of narrative forms is vast. In short, in music as in research, although we must play by certain rules, these rules mostly reduce uncertainty without constraining compositional creativity. Further, writing or playing one kind of music does not preclude writing or playing another kind. Winton Marsalis composes and plays both jazz and classical trumpet, for example.

A second level of structure is provided by the idea of choral composition. In addition to forms, choral music includes songs, or *lieder*, in the German tradition. Again, choice of song reduces uncertainty for composer, performer and audience. But one cannot imagine exhausting the possibilities of a choral song; multiple performances of *lieder* are common. Even a simple song, like one based on a twelve-bar blues progression, offers multiple interpretive possibilities. If one listens to a master, like saxophonist Charlie Parker (Holbrook 1984), one realizes the enormous possible variations in which even a single song may be played by a single performer. Consider then the interpretive possibilities that manifest from multiple voices and parts as in a choral composition. Thus, why not consider the genre of research reports that represent consumer behavior as a songlike form with equivalent performative potential?

Finally, composition also includes consideration of the social norms that structure music and performances. Although music is sometimes referred to as a universal language, this is an entirely misleading description (Storr 1992: 50; Pole 1924). It is extremely difficult to appreciate music from different periods of history or from different cultures (Ellis 1885). Which sounds are consonant (hence need no resolution) are determined at a given historical moment by the prevailing musical style, and vary radically according to the musical system developed in each culture (Rosen 1975). Performance too is culturally and stylistically informed. For example, due to differences in social norms, American choral performances tend to emphasize blended, yet distinct individual voices, while Danish choral performances emphasize group voices – voices leaning against one another to make a unified, well-rounded sound. The use of vibrato in choral performances also differs both by culture and by style, or era of choral music. Similarly, in multimethod research presentations we might write to emphasize phenomenological results in one case, cultural results in another, and causal relationships in a third, while still incorporating results stemming from each method.

Composing and performing a score allow for trial and error and make room for discovery. To achieve a well-rounded composition or performance sometimes requires the composer or conductor to identify and fill in gaps with a human or musical voice. By altering the combinations of instruments and voices, composers enhance, modify and suppress the overtones that are produced and change the sound (Storr 1992). Composers use repetition, elaboration of pattern, contrapuntal techniques and symmetry as defining structure, often in order to relate human stories (Rowell 1984; Storr 1992) Well-rounded research does something similar when multiple experiments enrich the melodic line, or multiple examples of a phenomena provide coloration, or multiple data sets provide resonance. For example, in our multi-year research on white water river rafting, both immersion in our data (a kind of practicing), and chance and deliberate encounters with other scholars' theoretical and empirical work led us to additional compositional possibilities. Combining new data with old, we elaborated new themes including play (Arnould and Price 1994), the social construction of nature (Arnould, Price and Tierney 1997), and consumer magic (Arnould, Price and Tierney 1995). Why not grant researchers the freedom to compose different kinds of studies, and think of consumer research and its representation as an array of compositional and performative possibilities?

An experimental sketch

To sketch out some of our ideas about the value of the choral music metaphor for representing consumer research, we draw on examples from a number of our research projects. We would like readers to think of this as a musical experiment. Here the appropriate analogy is to think of data as sounds represented in notes, chords, and choral voices as the raw materials from which multimethod representations of consumption phenomena are composed. The rules of composition are like musical theoretical structures (choral forms, chord progressions, melody, harmony, dissonance, etc. – see Glossary on page 359). We organize this sketch around three themes (although many others are possible):

1   adding parts, echoes, and multiplication of meanings;
2   developing cross rhythms and embracing polyphony;
3   counterpoint and dissonance.

Adding parts, echoes, developing cross rhythms, embracing polyphony

Just for the sake of our thought experiment, let us suspend the pervasive visual metaphor of demarcation in social science (Stoller 1989), the linear correspondence model of reality (Ashmore 1989; Woolgar 1988), and the assumption of a unitary reality. This sounds challenging, but in fact people do this whenever they listen to music. First we rely on our hearing rather than our vision to define reality. And choral music may address compelling issues and emotions, but it hardly does so in a linear way. And, as emphasized earlier, different listeners often experience different realities when they listen to a piece of music. Yet, human attitudes and ways of thinking are shaped by dance and song and we can be fairly confident that listeners to great music which is familiar to them share a high degree of consensus. In fact, Marcel Proust (1981) argued that music may provide a unique means of communication between souls. So think of a multimethod research presentation as if it were choral music, with the potential to be both profoundly meaningful while still diverse, artificial and even capricious in form and style (Levi-Strauss 1969; Pears 1987). Multimethod research, like choral music, adds parts, incorporates echoes, and conveys multiple meanings, without requiring correspondence to another order of reality. Choral music defies the dichotomy between the thing which is known and the knower, and moves beyond the Cartesian division of physical and mental and transcends human categories of space, time and causality (Peat 1987; Schopenhauer 1966).

Adding parts: melody and harmony

Different data sets, as well as different kinds of data, can provide melody and harmony in a research presentation. In music, melody is defined as the rational progression of single tones and harmony is defined as the rational combination of several tones (Baker 1895; Cooper 1971). (In both cases, "rationality" refers to the delimited constructed rationality particular to a musical form or genre, not to a presumably universal epistemological order.) Melody and harmony are indifferent to key, and the same notes may make up either a melodic or harmonic progression depending upon the overall compositional structure.

For an example of what adding parts means in representing research data, we consider our multi-year study of commercial white water river rafting. Some additions were planned and others unplanned. We began by studying the inter-action between professional river guides and their commercial clients with the aim of understanding the satisfaction process. A river outfitter originally presented the satisfaction process to us as an outcome of functional benefits: safety, boat hand-ling, and camping skills. We can think of this as a melodic line, one consistent with early survey research on services. Through participant observation, we learned that satisfaction was primarily affected not by functional service provision, but by the guides' emotion work (Arnould and Price 1993; Tierney, et al. 1994). So we added the theme of emotion work to the orchestration of our study. We found that this harmonic addition provided a richer understanding of both satisfaction in particular and the consumption of river rafting in general (Price, et al. 1995). Also, in research on white water river rafting we tested a structural model of the relationship between guide performance, affect and satisfaction. At odds with product-based studies, we did not find a relationship between guide performance and negative affect. Participant observation reveals that customers generally believe guides have control over factors that influence positive affect, but do not believe they control factors that produce negative affect. Together, structural model and participant observation facilitate a more harmonic whole.

Music often proceeds by the introduction of musical themes that recur in the composition. The use of certain instruments to represent specific characters in the musical play *Peter and the Wolf* is a familiar example. Virgil Thompson's musical invention to introduce children to the orchestra and how different musical voices contribute to the orchestral sound – *Tubby the Tuba* – is another example. Our research is similar to a chorus in that we add a voice, or a harmony, a chord, an instrument, or double an instrument in both planned and opportunistic ways. Data sometimes functioned for us as melody. Two pieces of data, collected at different points in time, repeated the same melodic line although with different coloring or timbre. The first verbatim evokes the idea of *communitas* that so often emerges between customers and guides during a river trip:

> And at the top of this hike there was a beautiful fresh spring waterfall. And it was fabulous. And it felt so good for everybody because everybody's been in dirty water since yesterday when we embarked on this trip . . . one of the college girls organized a group shot . . . And in that group shot there was a clear intermingling of groups that included hugging and having arms around people who I think under other conditions would be considered strangers . . . And we were all huddling in there and at the same time sharing space with each other so that no one was hogging the water.
> (Price, participant observation notes, June 1992, cited in Arnould and Price 1993: 34).

The second, collected four years later from a different trip with different guides and participants restates the same theme:

> We then made our way over to Bum Dam Falls . . . a little waterfall . . . and people dam it up with their butts, and stop up the water, build up the water pressure, and create a big wall of water to pour over those below. It's a lot of fun, really a lot of *fun*. So, everybody took turns stripping down to the bathing suits, trunks, skivvies, or what have you, and getting wet. It was real *fun* because there was a big push to get [a female guide] to strip down to her suit and [a male guide] to jump in, so all the guides . . . got in the stream too. It was pretty cool, for the fans, there was a lot of *cheering, clapping, hugging* in the falls, and sputtering, *laughing and running*. So, it was kind of a *play* in nature phenomena going on . . . made up *with people*, of people, and it was certainly in nature.
> (Arnould, participant observation notes, June 1996)

Notice in the first verbatim the researcher writes as an embodied participant; in the second as a more distant observer. This exemplifies the characteristic coloration of our two styles of representing data.

Data can also function as melody and harmony. For example, interviews with river guides told a story that captured a consistent melodic structure in multi-day white water river trips. In the following verbatim, one guide evoked the melodic figure that recurs on the third day of a multi-day trip:

> Another thing about Day 3 is that, Day 1 everyone walks way upstream, or walks way downstream to pee, by Day 3, people are

just peeing right there. Sorta, that's what I think, when I think of Day 3, people have just sorta *given up* anything that happened on Day 1.

(River guide, mwm30s, June 1996, interviewer Price)

In participant observation field notes collected at the same time in a different place by a different researcher, an example of this sort of development is recorded in the following verbatim. It provides both melodic restatement and harmonic counterpoint:

When I went down to the river bank just a few minutes ago, I said, "Hey, is this a public bath house? Can anyone come?" And, Sinead said, "Oh, you're very welcome." . . . So, I noticed there is this kind of *emotional opening up* that goes on. [But] not everyone participates . . . But, I think some have hung back from doing things, some have also hung back emotionally – it's interesting.

(Arnould participant observation notes, June 1996).

Melodic lines that make a whole

Sometimes music requires that multiple melodic lines be joined to comprise a whole. We found an example of this in our research on satisfaction, for fulfilling white water river rafting customers' pre-trip expectations does not predict post-trip satisfaction. Pre-trip, people express concerns about safety and the functional competence of the boatman. But post-trip measures diverge from these pre-trip criteria. One might conclude that the results of the two survey measures are incommensurate or unstable. But by adding participant observation data, one gets inside the black box of the "treatment" to identify emergent, emotional changes that provide an explanation linking the two results (Arnould and Price 1993). Thus, the two melodic lines of survey and participant observation data add up to a harmonic whole.

Echoes

Musical voices can call to one another across a composition, amplifying and doubling one another. As in advertising, by combining words and pictures the resonant effect is more than mere repetition (McQuarrie 1989). For example, in the context of a study of ordinary service encounters, we presented a conventional three-way table of complicated relationships between service provider performance dimensions and customers' positive affective responses by service encounter type (Price, *et al.* 1995) (see Table 12.1). For service encounters marked by positive affective customer responses, the table shows some relationships between service encounter types shown as columns, and service provider performance dimensions shown as rows. We employ boxes to highlight significant relationships.

Notice that when we present the data as in Table 12.1 readers can easily lose

Table 12.1 Service encounters marked by positive affective customer responses

Service performance dimensions	Service encounter types			
	Brief impersonal	Brief personal	Extended impersonal	Extended personal
Mutual understanding				
Beta	0.10	0.22	0.07	0.08
T value	1.5	3.4[1]	0.48	0.83
Caring about the customer				
Beta	0.28	0.22	0.05	0.49
T value	3.7[1]	3.1[2]	0.34	3.6[1]
Authenticity				
Beta	0.13	0.09	0.09	0.00
T value	1.9	1.5	0.48	0.02
Competence				
Beta	0.07	0.11	0.28	0.17
T value	1.0	1.6	1.9	1.0
Failing to meet minimum standards				
Beta	−0.28	−0.21	−0.22	0.00
T value	−3.5[1]	−3.4[1]	−1.5	0.04
Adjusted R^2	0.33	0.38	0.26	0.40
F value	27.82[1]	30.20[1]	6.05[1]	11.11[1]

Source: Author's survey data

Notes 1 $p < 0.001$; 2 $p < 0.005$

sight of the fact that we are dealing with *variables*, since the numbers seem to proclaim an authoritative kind of identity. The single figures, like a chord, do not represent variation very well. But when we add verbatim comments from open-ended probes (shown in Table 12.2) to the representation of the relationships, the meaning of the figures echo through the verbatim quotes and the meaning of the verbatim quotes is echoed back in the statistical results. In a figurative sense, the verbatim quotes act like a series of solo parts, the statistics like a chord or even a melodic line.

In Table 12.2 the evident particularity of the verbatim comments doubles without duplicating the numbers. And, of course, the textual examples in each category could be multiplied. We get more than the sum of the parts when we present two resonant, echoing portions of data together.

Table 12.2 Informant comments related to service performance dimensions

Service provider dimension	Verbatim
Caring about the customer	My brother and his family and my family all went out for a big family breakfast. I had some coupons which we used. Laura (waitress) was very busy and yet patient, understanding, and very nice and relaxed. She gave us a bonus by applying one coupon to all of the kids (5x) meals. So we got all five kids' meals free + one adult meal free.
Mutual understanding	I've known Kelly for four years now. She sat down at our table and told a joke. It was more like we were at her house and not at a pub/restaurant. She was very spontaneous because the conversation was casual and light, we were kidding all the time. Me and my friends were very rowdy at times, and she actually would get rowdy with us. Throughout the encounter she would get very close to all of us.
Authenticity	Provider was incredibly excited and happy – very bubbly – tossing info at me right and left. Very observant, very knowledgeable and personable – seemed to very much enjoy his position, or at least dealing with people. Made sure I was comfortable, both while waiting and with his diagnostic of my car – joked and basically very friendly.
Competence	After the CC sneak run, I was starved so a friend and I went to a small cafe for brunch . . . Our waitress was a young girl who had at least ten other tables. She came bouncing up to us relaxed and smiling asked if we were ready. We said we would be in one minute and she was back sixty seconds later. I ordered the omelet which came in minutes. It was wonderful. This put me in a great mood. Looking back I realized we had a wonderful conversation between the two of us and great service. She saw that we were happy and relaxed so she was put at ease.

Source: Author's fieldnotes

Multiplications of meanings between theoretical schemas

Playing a musical score in a variety of ways (*legato, obligato, a tempo*) encourages different interpretations, and many musical compositions are available in multiple interpretations. For example, Charlie Parker's *Now's the Time* has been reorchestrated and re-recorded by many jazz artists over a forty-year period (Holbrook 1984). Even pop tunes such as those of the Beatles can be orchestrated to create a kind of classical sound, or a classical melody can be adapted to make a pop anthem. The 1940s pop song *I'm Always Chasing Rainbows* is from a theme by

Chopin. And Procul Harem based the 1960s hit *A Whiter Shade of Pale* on a theme by Bach. Analogously, there is no defensible ontological principle to uphold the belief that data support a unitary interpretation. As the late Paul Anderson argued nearly ten years ago (1989), the history of scientific controversies shows precisely the reverse. The meaning of data, like the meaning of music, is filtered through the interpreter and the compositional (theoretical) framing adopted.

A few examples will illustrate this. We began a paper based on our white water river rafting data as follows:

> Three main organizing themes associated with satisfying raft trips emerged early in our research . . . communion with nature, communitas . . . and extension and renewal of self.
>
> (Arnould and Price 1993: 31)

Several years later we began a manuscript on consumer magic based on additional data collected in the same context as follows:

> Packaged river magic like all magic depends for its effects on: The *condition of the performer*: e.g., readiness to experience transcendent powers; a *rite*: for example, the river becomes a mediator between the visible and invisible; a *formula*: e.g., symbolic means of inducing cooperation with forces that respond only to symbols.
>
> (Arnould *et al.* 1995)

These two introductions indicate the compositional score or theoretical structure through which the data will be organized. Now consider two verbatim quotes from the river rafting data. The first comes from an interview with a river guide:

> I think, river magic . . . I see it all the time . . . I saw it when I guided. Just the spell that the river environment can cast on people, and just bring them – pulling away from that urban 9 to 5 lifestyle that most people live – and, you know, just bring them back to the basics . . . The moon rise, listening to the water, sitting on a sandy beach and a warm breeze blowing through the cottonwoods, seeing wildlife. That, to me, is river magic.
>
> (Interview, river guide, swm40s, June 1996)

The second is an excerpt from fieldnotes tape-recorded in the moment of experience and later transcribed for analysis:

> It was really nice hiking up the trail, all the different rocks tumbled down, the gnarled, ancient junipers and stumps of old dead junipers gnarled into the rocks. I have to admit that I began to have kind of a flow feeling . . . a kind of little endorphin flowing kind of experience at

this point. It seemed like others did too, the others were too. It certainly seemed like Sinead [a rafting customer] and [a female guide] were.

(Arnould participant observation fieldnotes, June 1996).

Like these fieldnotes, taken out of context, a B flat is just a musical note. Depending upon how the notes or the data are combined into a structure, however, we either get a concerto for violin in B flat, or a Dixie Land band jazz rave-up by Sidney Bechet. We would neither mistake one for the other; nor could we simply put a passage from one into the other. Analogously like musical notes or phrases, we can use these two fieldnotes to develop different meanings in the data, by organizing them in terms of different compositional (theoretical) schemas: communion with nature, an interpretation we offered in one article (Arnould and Price 1993), or mediation between visible and invisible worlds that we offer in a second paper (Arnould and Price 1994). The two interpretations stem from different theoretical structures or scores that provide both of these isolated "notes" with meaning. One structure concerns the social construction of nature; the other, consumer magic. Notice, however, that these fieldnotes, just like a solitary B flat, are not amenable to every compositional purpose. We think that both representations of the market offering and its consumption are credible and informative. Is one rendering of the market offering correct, and the other not? The idea seems absurd, just as it would seem absurd, to argue for a definitive B flat blues or performance of Chopin's C flat *étude*.

Developing cross-rhythms and embracing polyphony

Now let us suspend the conventional expectation that multiple methods render only redundant meanings either via refinement and replication in the experimental tradition, or triangulation in the ethnographic tradition (Thompson *et al.* 1997). Instead, let multimethod research develop cross-rhythms and embrace polyphony as in choral work.

Developing cross-rhythms: men and women

Data from several studies indicate that a full choral story requires accepting cross-rhythmic elements. In music, rhythm refers to the measured movement of similar tone-groups, defined as the effect produced by the systematic grouping of tones with reference to regularity both in their accentuation and in their succession as equal or unequal in time value. Therefore, a rhythm is a tone-group serving as a pattern for succeeding groups identical with it as regards the accentuation and duration of tones. The rhythm is thus a thing apart from tonal melody or harmony (Baker 1895; Cooper 1971). An example from multimethod research is data that, indicate that, across generations, North American women consistently experience U.S. Thanksgiving Day as a consumption event that they make and do, whereas men experience it as something that happens (Wallendorf and Arnould 1991).

Both rhythm lines are part of the song, irreducibly completing and complementing one another.

Similarly, in white water rafting data, we discovered that men's and women's experiences express complementary rhythms. For example, when men are told to urinate in the white water river, this is a minor reinforcer of men's sense of liminality, of being part of a ritual community; for women, it raises existential issues about the boundaries of the self (Arnould and Price 1994). The same experience is linked to two different themes (liminality and selfhood) that both genders experience in river rafting but in different circumstances. The rhythms of their experience are complementary. In both cases, we would lose richness if we tried to reduce men's and women's experiences to a unique measure of central tendency.

Developing cross-rhythms: experts and novices

The experiences of expert and novice consumers may also tell differently patterned but complementary stories. For example, in our rafting data, river guides seem to revel in all kinds of weather. Our guides interpret violent weather as evidence of nature's majesty, a common musical theme (Haydn's *Creation*, Stravinsky's *Rite of Spring*).

> S (a river guide) went out [in the freezing downpour] to check the tent. Had her rain gear handy, she was prepared. Came back and [I] asked how it was and she talked about oh, it's so beautiful up the canyon. The rain was coming down. But, uh, it was coming down in big sheets, it looked so beautiful. S is always like right on the surface with those kind of [very genuine] comments.
>
> (Arnould participant observation notes, June 1996)

In an interview, a river guide also expressed the North American view of nature as character-building (Arnould, *et al.* 1997):

> the last day of our last trip, . . . we stopped to go look at these wonderful petroglyphs. And we had to walk through knee high grass . . . It was very wet, it had been raining for days. And, it started raining pretty hard when we started to go on the walk . . . And they [the customers] were just like . . . and they went through the mud and moaned and complained about it. But I think that, too will add to their experience.
>
> (River guide, swf30s, September 1996)

However, novice rafters experience things differently for they hum a different tune. Evidence of two such counter-rhythms is found in participant observation notes recorded on the bad weather trip. In one case, a theme of marital conflict is used to interpret the bad weather experience:

> So, there's like an undercurrent of, you know, "it's a fine mess *you've* gotten us into" (from the husband to the wife) . . . he said, hey, this is not so bad. Could be colder. And Gary piped in with yeah, and you've got company.
>
> (Arnould participant observation notes, June 1996)

In the other fieldnote excerpt, another theme comes through:

> Taken from my theory that this [rainy] trip had become a story about "making it through," I heard Shelly (the wife) refer to it today, as well, a night *we* can "celebrate making it through the week." Although everyone seemed to be cheered up by the sunshine.
>
> (Arnould participant observation notes, June 1996)

These contrasting rhythms conjoin to present a more complete choral portrait of the experience of bad weather on a river trip, just as the various instruments in the orchestra allow Stravinsky to represent both violence and peace, struggle and tranquillity.

Embracing polyphony

In musical composition, polyphony refers to the combination in harmonious progression of two or more independent parts (Baker 1895; Cooper 1971). Thus, unlike cross-rhythms that combine, here independent stories coexist. For example, depth interviews conducted with Hausa women handicraft potters in the Niger Republic reveal their insistence that potting activities diminish during the farming season. They say that during the rainy season (June to August) the quarry floods, it is too humid to dry the pots during this period, and besides farming is more important. In contrast, ten months of observation of the rhythm of the actual firings of pots in which counts were made of the vessels fired, revealed no diminution of pottery production during the rainy, farming season. Additional participant observation data provided knowledge about gender norms, gender conflicts, ritualized proscriptions on quarrying clay, and myths about household agricultural self-sufficiency that decode the apparent discrepancy between the interview and observational data (Arnould 1989). Participant observation data do not resolve an apparent conflict between the researcher's data and the informants' representation of their practice, but instead provide a framework that supports the polyphony.

Another example comes from research on Thanksgiving Day in the US. In depth interviews, informants often say that Thanksgiving always brings the whole family together. The following verbatim is typical:

INTERVIEWER: I just wanted to ask you a few questions about Thanksgiving. Who you spend your holiday with, where, and what you usually eat?

RESPONDENT: We *always* had Thanksgiving at our house. *All* the kids would come and bring their husbands and children. Sometimes we would have up to 24 people over for dinner. The kids would usually sit in the foyer for dinner because the floor was marble and they could spill and nobody would care. You could mop the floor with a special chemical that they recommended. The parents would sometimes sit on the stairs that overlooked the foyer and watch their children eat. My husband was *always* the initiator in family gatherings. They called him "leader", he *always* made sure *everyone* came home for Thanksgiving. It was a lot of work, sometimes it took over two days to do the preparations for the dinner. My daughters would bring salads usually. I *always* cooked the turkey. The turkey was the center of attention. *Always* the main focus of the meal.

(Depth interview, November 1988, emphasis added)

Sadness is expressed when the ideal of togetherness is not realized, especially when it becomes impossible because of death, divorce, or migration. Survey data reinforce the impression that family togetherness is a universal Thanksgiving ideal, and travel industry data show that the Thanksgiving Day weekend is the busiest U.S. travel period. Nonetheless other data, casual visits to inexpensive cafeteria-style restaurants, indicate that not everyone is "always" together on Thanksgiving Day. These restaurants are almost exclusively filled with senior citizens. Participant observation provides an additional "voice," providing data about middle-class U.S. household form, function, and mythos that demystifies contradictory, polyphonous themes without reducing them to a singular melodic line (Wallendorf and Arnould 1991).

Counterpoint and dissonance

Finally, let us suspend the convention of conducting scientific studies by conducting and presenting results sequentially. Building a corpus of data sets, and independent interpretations that are then presented together, can produce a kind of counterpoint. In music, the term "counter" is used in a variety of contexts. Generally it refers to any vocal part that contrasts with the principal part or melody. More specifically, it refers to counter-exposition, the re-entrance of the subject or subjects of a fugue, either directly following the exposition or after the first episodes. The term "counterpoint" is more specific still, meaning note against note. In the restricted sense, counterpoint refers to the art of adding one or more melodies to a given melody *according to certain rules*. In a wider sense, counterpoint refers to the genre of polyphonic composition of which the canon and the fugue are the most highly developed contrapuntal forms. These counterpoints may appear to be dissonant, which refers to a combination of two or more tones requiring resolution (Baker 1895; Cooper 1971).

All these musical terms evoke the ideas of simultaneous contrast, opposition, and resolution in accordance with certain rules. Consideration of counterpoint has certain virtues in both music and the representation of multimethod consumer research. Just as it would be absurd for the members of a chorus to sing their (counter-)parts individually or sequentially, so there is something to be gained from simultaneous presentation of research results. A multimethod research presentation can highlight first one data set, then another contrasting one, and finally allow a melodic ensemble to reassert itself.

At a more complex compositional level, research may be conducted or analyses composed on the basis of multiple, paradigmatic assumptions that do not necessarily converge (dissonance). It becomes a matter of combining them according to certain rules or "bridging epistemologies" (Grimes and Rood 1995). Sometimes a third term or third data set provides the resolution, just as dissonant notes or phrases can be resolved by a third note or phrase. Unlike music, the rules of counterpoint still must be worked out in multimethod research (Thompson, *et al.* 1998). Multimethod research on preference formation and commercial friendships illustrates the way that a simultaneous interplay of individual voices creates theoretically interesting dissonance and counterpoint.

Consider two paired texts presented in Table 12.3. The pair presented on the left are excerpts from extensive ethnographic fieldnotes on preference formation collected in 1986 in the Niger Republic (Arnould 1989). The pair presented on the right come from a feminist literary critical reinterpretation that illustrates, among other things, that the fieldnotes are already a descriptive representation of a consumption phenomena (Thompson, *et al.* 1998).

The dissonant extended feminist critique on the right departs from and exposes the structure of patriarchal conventions guiding the ethnographic narrative and defining its voice of scientific objectivity. Rather than assuming that scientific texts stand outside the operation of narrative power, the dissonant feminist reading examines the latent structure of binary oppositions that enable masculine cultural styles to dominate feminine ones. By exposing the tensions between the dominant/suppressed voices, the feminist critique provides insights into the way that scientific narratives "write" social reality in terms that privilege some interests and social positions while simultaneously obscuring others.

The dissonant critique sets up a narrative tension that can be resolved in the same sense as a musical resolution that throws unexpected nuances in other parts of the data into greater clarity (Holbrook 1984). In this case, the critique sensitizes the ethnographic analyst to the significance of puberty in Hausa women's lifecycle. For example, during puberty Hausa women gain a unique but temporary social license that helps to account for the rapid spread of foreign novelties and the agency of innovation. The premarital period is the only time when Hausa girls are freed somewhat from strict gender role conventions in this patriarchal society and are encouraged to be outgoing, spontaneous, and even aggressive. At this time Hausa women have a rare social space in which to pursue their desires and to

Table 12.3 Dissonant representations of Nigerien women's consumption behavior

Fieldnote excerpts	*Feminist deconstruction*
I asked Magaji's wife, Mariama, which of the enameled basins in her collection . . . she preferred . . . the last ones because they were so . . . "white" . . . I asked why women made such great collections . . . She replied simply . . . decoration . . . Magaji threw in his two cents. He says it's a bourgeois conceit . . . all women want to spend their money on now is enameled bowls, hangings, and beds.	"Notice that Mariama is quoted directly only twice . . . the absence of directly quoted informant speech reveals high authorial control . . . notice that there are two male authority figures conversing with a married woman in order to collect information . . . available only in the oral "gossip" system of women-to-women talk. We cannot assume the "knowers" are privy to the voices of the "known" . . . Magaji's interpolation illustrates the risks that women take in making personal revelations in male-female conversation . . . "
One older female informant, Nana Zobe, explained that the explosion of marriage goods can be explained by the desire to reinforce marriages in order to demonstrate a family's strength or prestige (*karfi*). Married women continue to acquire, collect, and decorate their homes with brilliant enamel ware and tapestries, to compete for prestige (*k'amiya*) with other women. Thus, in a society with few outlets for feminine expression, novel consumer goods fuel a Veblenesque competitive display for status.	To a Hausa wife, [enamel] bowls stacked on a table at the rear of a two-room adobe house represent the universe over which she has control. Women enjoined from leaving the family compound without permission live in narrow confines, and home decoration is central. When a woman moves up in class, she is more likely to be secluded and, hence, more likely to spend most of her time within the home. I suggest that the desire to acquire decorative objects expresses a need to make the tightly constrained space of seclusion more appealing. From the woman's perspective, control over home decoration signals an improved lifestyle, one that is easier and more luxurious."

exert a fleeting form of cultural capital over purchase decisions related to their marriage trousseaus.

The critical counterpoint between voices provides insights into why married women acquire novel enamel ware, decorate their homes with it, and use it to compete for prestige (*k'amiya*). They do so in part to claim a domestic space and assert a domestic aesthetic, and in part to signal the status of the households to which they belong. In turn, these signals can attract young girls to older women as their unpaid helpers in expectation of aid from their older sponsors as they reach marriage age. Hence, a conspicuous display that creates marital discord simultaneously creates and reinforces women's social networks. Together, competition and cooperation reinforce women's support networks and their maintenance of a distinctly feminine domestic space (Thompson, *et al.* 1998).

Another example of counterpoint and dissonance comes from a research project on commercial friendships. When we asked a sample of hairstylists if they develop friendships with customers, many said that they do. When we asked a sample of customers if they develop friendships with hairstylists, many also said that they do. A survey approach enables us to characterize these friendships in terms of a common measure insofar as both describe their relationships in accordance with cultural ideals about what friendship means. In other words, consistent with the representation of the stylists' shop in popular culture (films like *Hairspray* or *Steel Magnolias*), we are likely to conclude that commercial friendships sometimes develop between hairstylists and their clients. However, depth interviews show that in practice the term is used loosely and differently by stylists and customers. Moreover, particular stylists and customers often disagree about both the terms and degree of commercial friendship between them. One thinks that they are "best" friends, whereas the other denies that they are friends at all. One asserts they might exchange gifts or see each other socially, but the other doubts the likelihood of this happening. The voices in the choir seem dissonant. Depth interviews add a voice that permits an explanation of the complex interplay between cultural ideals and the lived experience of commercial friendships by revealing different schemas and rules for commercial friendships between hair stylists and their customers (Price, *et al.* 1996).

Finale

Our choir metaphor builds on previous explorations of musical metaphors in social science (Bastien and Hostager 1988; Eisenberg 1990; Holbrook 1984; Oldfather and West 1994). It is useful in thinking about the practice and representation of research, both of which are similar to composing and performing a chorale. While we try to obey the rules and conventions particular to certain paradigmatic forms, we also want to venture past the conventional bounds of the tunes we perform and experiment with alternate performances. We recognize that we like several kinds of choral music and many very different compositional styles. There is no point in trying to put them in some order of "greatness" or to establish an order of preference. They fall into separate categories according to the nature of the information they convey (Levi-Strauss 1969: 29). The choir metaphor is a comfortable one for us and others, although it may induce some discomfort as well. Common to both choral and multimethod research works is the blending of apparent oppositions, freedom and structure, mind and senses, knower and known, expectations and unborn fulfillments.

> The trick is to be able to feel the music. This ability comes through both understanding the deep structures of music and giving oneself the freedom to let go and apply those deep structures in new situations.
> (Oldfather and West 1994: 23)

We invite other researchers to play. Researchers can contribute to a choral performance in many ways. Researchers may act as composers to combine data into a synthesis of unified voices translating the realm of behavior into the realm of musical experience. We might also think about multiple researchers working together as members of a choir. Researchers may participate in a project as "musicians" adding collaborative voices. By working together, researcher voices may complement one another as harmony complements melody. Multiple researchers may also add different rhythms, harmonies, and melodies to a research composition and, like singers of different vocal range in a choir, can also extend the range of a research ensemble. The challenge here is assembling a choir of performers from an academic community noted for preferring to play solo. In addition, researchers might also rethink replication as performances or variations on a pre-existing theme. Thus, Stern (1994) reanalyzes some Thanksgiving Day stories from Wallendorf and Arnould (1991), adding her own concepts and choral voice. Finally, researchers may also work like sound engineers, recording and mixing the voices of other participants (informants or subjects) for presentation to an audience.

Concluding notes on the performance

The fundamental problem the choir metaphor addresses is the need to elaborate a way of thinking about and doing complex research involving ultimately indeterminate social systems and using data derived from presumably incommensurate paradigms. Reductionist methodological strategies that privilege some level of reality as ontologically superior – for example, sophisticated computational systems themselves quite immaterial and certainly not "empirical" – do not appeal to us. Nor do exclusionary models of research that assert their unique epistemological privilege and thereby fail to come to terms with the socially constructed, contingent nature of scientific representation (Ashmore 1989; Best and Kellner 1991: 256 ff.; Clifford and Marcus 1986; Foucault 1972; Woolgar 1988). Unlike the choir model that embraces contingency and complexity, scientific reductionism or exclusivism do not do justice to the nature of the complex problems in consumer research that interest us. Our choir metaphor is a response to the call for analytic approaches in consumer research that highlight the nuanced differences in consumption emergent under postmodern cultural conditions (Holt 1997).

The musical metaphor can help consumer behavior scholars accept that there are no ultimate formulas for human relations as the community of theoretical physicists does for the physical universe. As in music, atomic structure and biology, reducing social phenomena like consumption to *less* than complex systems (even at their elemental levels), is as much a distortion as reducing great choral works to their melodies.

Embracing the kind of orchestral complexity we advocate does not mean trading in order for disorder, logical certainty for logical uncertainty, Cartesian rationality for unreason, coherent discourse for Babel. A choral performance is both carefully structured and untranslatable. It is complex and able to embrace polyphony, dissonance, counterpoint, and other phenomena without for all that becoming chaotic. Of course in music, as in science, it need not be the mathematical dimension of a research presentation that compels and instructs. Further, many roles and combinations of roles are available in both music and science (Bastien and Hostager 1988; Traub 1996).

We recognize that composing, conducting, and performing multimethod research is not easy. Effective multimethod research, like choral masterpieces, forges a synthesis of competing desires and disparate elements into a unified and unique whole, evoking profound and exalted ideas and emotions. The researcher and composer are both well-drilled artisans who develop expertise in melding multiple elements into a meaningful whole. Moreover, like a choral masterpiece, the effect of multimethod research is inescapably dependent on performance. A particular interpretation depends on voices, instruments, conductor, audience and composer. Its style is culturally and historically informed. Like music, the best of multimethod research enhances and coordinates group feelings, recovers personal feelings, and informs and structures day-to-day actions. Like choral masterpieces, the best of multimethod research is likely to be routinely altered through varied performances and complemented by the addition of works with alternative styles, but it need not be supplanted or dismissed.

Ultimately this chapter is motivated by the fact that we think that we operate within a paradigm of science, but it is not one of those proposed by most contributors to the debate on method and theory development in consumer behavior. In contrast to the descriptive and prescriptive philosophy of science models put forth by thoughtful scholars, we compare our research process to making music (or at least trying). Even if scientific paradigms successively exhaust one another, music nonetheless appears to be an inexhaustible medium of expression, even in its simpler forms. Perhaps our metaphor can serve as a guide for new modes of representing multimethod consumer research.

To conclude, this chapter aims at making a contribution to using multiple kinds of data sources in consumer research. Our new point of departure for multimethod research captures our own research aspirations. But more importantly, as so many students of creativity propose (Holbrook 1984), we have tried to have fun, to improvise, to play with some ideas, and to endeavor to make them sing and dance.

Glossary of musical terms

Choir   (1) A company of singers, especially in a church (2) A choral society.

Color   (1) Timbre (tone-color). (2) The characteristic rhythms, harmonies, and melodies of a composition.

Counter   Any vocal part set to contrast with the principle part or melody; specifically *counter-exposition*, re-entrance of the subject or subjects of a fugue, either directly following the exposition, or after the first episodes.

Counterpoint   i.e. note against note. (1) In a wider sense the art of polyphonic composition . . . The canon and the fugue are the most highly developed contrapuntal forms. (2) In a more restricted sense, the art of adding one or more melodies to a given melody (*cantus firmus*) according to certain rules; hence, one of, or all, the parts so added. (3) The Theory of Counterpoint generally recognizes five species: (i) Note against note, whole notes in the counterpoint against whole notes in the *c.f.*; (ii) 2 against 1, half-notes in the counterpoint against whole notes in the *c.f.*; (iii) 4 against 1, quarter notes in the counterpoint against whole notes in the *c.f.*; (iv) with syncopation, syncopated half-notes in counterpoint against whole notes in the *c.f.*; (v) *florid, figuate*, or *figured*, the counterpoint written in irregular rhythms.

Dissonance   (1) In theory, the simultaneous sounding of tones so remotely related that their combination produces beats. (2) In practice, a combination of two or more tones requiring resolution. The dissonant intervals are the seconds and their inversion, the sevenths, also all diminished and augmented intervals.

Harmony   The rational combination of several tones.

Melody   The rational progression of single tones.

Polyphony   In musical composition, the combination in harmonious progression of two or more independent parts (as opp. to *Homophony*).

Rhythm   The measured movement of similar tone-groups, i.e. the effect produced by the systematic grouping of tones with reference to regularity both in their accentuation and in their succession as equal or unequal in time value. *A* Rhythm is, therefore, a tone-group serving as a pattern for succeeding groups identical with it as regards the accentuation and duration of the tones. The rhythm, being thus a thing apart from tonal melody or harmony, is reducible to a formula of notes without pitch, merely representing an orderly series of pulsations. Of the three basic constituents of music – rhythm, melody, and harmony – rhythm is the most instinctive, and essential to the existence of the other two.

(All definitions drawn from Baker 1895 and Cooper 1971)

Acknowledgments

Thanks to Kent Grayson and Ken Friedman for helpful comments on this chapter. Thanks also to Hanne Barlach and Lars Thoger Christensen, Odense University, for insight into the dynamics of choirs, and to Professors Hilton Jones and James Lewis, University of South Florida, for expert advice in the history of music.

References

Anderson, P.F. (1986) "On Method in Consumer Research," *Journal of Consumer Research* 13, 2: 155–73.

—— (1989) "On Relativism and Interpretivism – with a Prolegomena on the 'Why'

Question," in E.C. Hirschman (ed.) *Interpretive Consumer Research*, Provo, UT: Association for Consumer Research.

Arnould, E.J. (1989) "Toward a Broadened Theory of Preference Formation and the Diffusion of Innovations: Cases from Zinder Province, Niger Republic," *Journal of Consumer Research* 16, 2: 239–67.

Arnould, E.J. and Price, L.L. (1993) "'River Magic': Hedonic Consumption and the Extended Service Encounter," *Journal of Consumer Research* 20, 1: 24–45.

—— (1994) "Whitewater Framed by Canyon Walls: Playing Games in Nature," presented in the special topics session "Framing Consumption as Play," Annual Meetings of the Association for Consumer Research, Boston, MA, 20–23 October.

Arnould, E.J., Price, L.L., and Tierney, P. (1995) "Natural Magic: Packaging the Transformative Power of Nature," Annual Meetings of the Association for Consumer Research, Minneapolis, MN, 19–22 October.

—— (1998) "The Wilderness Servicescape," in J.F. Sherry, Jr. (ed.) *Encountering Servicescapes: Built Environment and Lived Experience in Contemporary Marketplaces*, Lincolnwood, IL: NTC Publications.

Arnould, E.J. and Wallendorf, M. (1994) "Market-Oriented Ethnography: Interpretation Building and Marketing Strategy Formulation," *Journal of Marketing Research* 31, 4: 484–504.

Ashmore, M. (1989) *The Reflexive Thesis*, Chicago: University of Chicago Press.

Baker, T. (1895) *Dictionary of Musical Terms*, New York: G. Shirmer.

Barry, D. (1996) "Artful Inquiry: A Symbolic Constructivist Approach to Social Science Inquiry," *Qualitative Inquiry* 2, 4: 411–38.

Bastien, D.T. and Hostager, T.J (1988) "Jazz as a Process of Organizational Innovation," *Communication Research* 15, 5: 582–602.

Best, S. and Kellner, D. (1991) *Postmodern Theory*, New York: Guilford Press.

Blacking, J. (1987) *A Commonsense View of All Music*, Cambridge: Cambridge University Press.

Bleier, R. (ed.) (1986) *Feminist Approaches to Science*, Oxford: Pergamon Books.

Calas, M. and Smircich, L. (1991) "Voicing Seduction to Silence Leadership," *Organization Studies* 12, 4: 567–602.

Clifford, J. and Marcus, G.E. (eds) (1986) *Writing Culture*, Berkeley, CA: University of California Press.

Clough, P.T. (1992) *The Ends of Ethnography: From Realism to Social Criticism*, Thousand Oaks, CA: Sage Publications.

Cooper, M. (ed.) (1971) *The Concise Encyclopedia of Music and Musicians*, London: Hutchinson.

Creswell, J.W. (1994) *Research Design: Qualitative and Quantitative Approaches*, Thousand Oaks, CA: Sage Publications.

Cvitanovic, P. (1996) personal communications, and "Complexity in Physics," remarks presented at "The Challenge of Complexity," a seminar in honor of Edgar Morin, Odense University, Odense, Denmark, 25 September.

Deshpande, R. (1983) "'Paradigms Lost': On Theory and Method in Research in Marketing," *Journal of Marketing* 47, 4: 101–10.

Eisenberg, E.M. (1990) "Jamming: Transcendence Through Organizing," *Communication Research* 17, 2: 139–64.

Ellis, A.J. (1885), "On the Musical Scales of Various Nations," *Journal of the Society of Arts* 33: 485–527.

Finley, S. and Knowles, J.G. (1995) "Researchers as Artist/Artist as Researcher," *Qualitative Inquiry* 1, 1: 110–42.

Fontana, A. (1994) "Ethnographic Trends in the Postmodern Era," in D.R. Dickens and A. Fontana (eds) *Postmodernism and Social Inquiry*, New York: Guilford Press.

Foucault, M. (1972) *The Archaeology of Knowledge*, New York: Pantheon Books.

Glaser, B.G. and Strauss, A.L. (1967) *The Discovery of Grounded Theory*, Chicago: Aldine.

Grimes, A.J. and Rood, D.L. (1995) "Beyond Objectivism and Relativism: Descriptive Epistemologies," in W. Natter, T.R. Schatzki, and J.P. Jones (eds) *Objectivity and Its Other*, New York: Guilford Press.

Gubrium, J.F. and Holstein, J.A. (1997) *The New Language of Qualitative Method*, Oxford: Oxford University Press.

Heidegger, M. (1977) *Poetry, Language, Thought* trans. A. Hofstadter, New York: Harper & Row.

Holbrook, M. (1984) "Theory Development is a Jazz Solo: Bird Lives," in P. F. Anderson and M.J. Ryan, (eds) *Proceedings 1984 AMA Winter Educator's Conference: Scientific Method in Marketing*, Chicago, IL: American Marketing Association.

Holt, D.B. (1997) "Poststructural Lifestyle Analysis: Conceptualizing the Social Patterning of Consumer in Postmodernity," *Journal of Consumer Research* 23, 4: 326–50.

Hudson, L. and Ozanne, J.L. (1988) "Alternative Ways of Seeking Knowledge in Consumer Research," *Journal of Consumer Research* 14, 4: 508–21.

Hunt, S.D (1991) "Positivism and Paradigm Dominance in Consumer Research: Toward Critical Pluralism and Rapprochement," *Journal of Consumer Research* 18, 1: 32–44.

Jick, T.D. (1979) "Mixing Qualitative and Quantitative Methods: Triangulation in Action," *Administrative Science Quarterly* 24: 602–11.

Keller, H. (1970) "Towards a Theory of Music," *Listener* June 11: 796.

Lakoff, G. and Johnson, M. (1980) *Metaphors We Live By*, Chicago: University of Chicago Press.

Levi-Strauss, C. (1969) *The Raw and the Cooked*, New York: Harper and Row.

Lienhardt, G. (1985) "Self: Public, Private. Some African Representations," in M. Carrithers, S. Collins and S. Lukes (eds) *The Category of the Person*, Cambridge: Cambridge University Press.

Lincoln, Y.S. (1995) "Emerging Criteria for Quality in Qualitative and Interpretive Research," *Qualitative Inquiry* 1, 3: 275–89.

Mason, J. (1994) "Linking Qualitative and Quantitative Data Analysis," in A. Bryman and R.G. Burgess (eds), *Analyzing Qualitative Data*, New York: Routledge.

McQuarrie, E.F. (1989) "Advertising Resonance: A Semiological Perspective," in E.C. Hirschman (ed.) *Interpretive Consumer Research*, Provo, UT: Association for Consumer Research.

Meyer, L.B. (1956) *Emotion and Meaning in Music*, Chicago: University of Chicago Press.

Mick, D.G., Fournier, S., and McQuarrie, E.F. (1996) "Truths, Half-Truths, and Opinions on Combining Qualitative and Quantitative Methodologies," special session presentation at the 26th Annual Association of Consumer Research Conference, Tucson, AZ, 10–13 October.

Miles, M.B. and Huberman, M.A. (1994) *Qualitative Data Analysis: An Expanded Sourcebook*, 2nd edn, Thousand Oaks, CA: Sage Publications.

Moore, J.N. (1984) *Edward Elgar: A Creative Life*, Oxford: Oxford University Press.

Morgan, G. (1980) "Paradigms, Metaphors, and Puzzle Solving in Organization Theory," *Administrative Science Quarterly* 25, 4: 605–22.

Natter, W., Schatzki, T.R. and Jones, J.P. III (eds) (1995) *Objectivity and Its Other*, New York: Guilford Press.

Nau, D.S. (1996) "Mixing Methodologies: Can Bimodal Research be a Viable Post-Positivist Tool?," (http://www.nova.edu/sss/QR/QR2-3/nau.html).

Oldfather, P. and West, J. (1994) "Qualitative Research as Jazz," *Educational Researcher* November, 22–6.

Olesen, V., Droes, N. Hatton, D. Chico, N. and Schatzman, L. (1994) "Analyzing Together: Recollections of a Team Approach," in A. Bryman and R.G. Burgess (eds) *Analyzing Qualitative Data*, New York: Routledge.

Paget, M.E. (1995) "Performing the Text," in J. Van Maanen (ed.) *Representation in Ethnography*, Thousand Oaks, CA Sage Publications.

Pears, D. (1987) *The False Prison*, vol. 1, Oxford: Clarendon Press.

Peat, D.F. (1987) *Synchronicity: The Bridge Between Matter and Mind*, New York: Bantam Books.

Pole, W. (1924) *The Philosophy of Music*, London: Kegan Paul Trench, Trubner.

Price, L.L., Arnould, E.J. and Hausman, A. (1996), "Commercial Friendships: Service Provider-Client Relationships Dynamics," paper presented at the Fifth Annual Conference "Frontiers in Services," Nashville, TN, 3–5 October.

Price, L.L., Arnould, E.J., and Deibler, S. (1995) "Consumers' Emotional Responses to Service Encounters: The Influence of the Service Provider", *International Journal of Service Industry Management*, 6, 3: 34–63.

Price, L.L., Arnould, E.J., and Tierney, P. (1995) "Going to Extremes: Managing Service Encounters and Assessing Provider Performance," *Journal of Marketing* 59, 2: 83–97.

Proust, M. (1981) *The Remembrance of Things Past, Vol. III, The Captive*, trans. C.K.S. Moncrieff, T. Kilmartin and A. Mayor, London: Chatto & Windus.

Richardson, L. (1994) "Writing as a Method of Inquiry," in N.K. Denzin and Y.S. Lincoln (eds) *Handbook of Qualitative Research*, Thousand Oaks, CA: Sage Publications.

Rosen, C. (1975) *Arnold Schoenberg*, New York: Viking Press.

Rowell, L. (1984) *Thinking About Music*, Amherst, MA: University of Massachusetts Press.

Sanjek, R. (1990) "On Ethnographic Validity," in R. Sanjek (ed.) *Fieldnotes: The Makings of Anthropology*, Ithaca: Cornell University Press.

Schopenhauer, A. (1966) *The World as Will and Representation*, trans. E.F.J. Payne, New York: Dover.

Sells, S.P., Smith, T.E. and Sprenkle, D.H. (1995) "Integrating Qualitative and Quantitative Research Methods: A Research Model," *Family Process* 34, 2: 199–218.

Smith, R.J. (1990) "Hearing Voices, Joining the Chorus: Appropriating Someone Else's Fieldnotes," in R. Sanjek (ed.) *Fieldnotes: The Makings of Anthropology*, Ithaca: Cornell University Press.

Stern, B.B. (1989) "Literary Criticism and Consumer Research: Overview and Illustrative Analysis," *Journal of Consumer Research* 16, 3: 322–34.

Stern, B.B. (1994) "Consumer Myths: Frye's Taxonomy and the Structural Analysis of Consumption Text," *Journal of Consumer Research* 22, 2: 165–85.

Stoller, P. (1989) *The Taste of Ethnographic Things*, Philadelphia: University of Pennsylvania Press.

Storr, A. (1992), *Music and the Mind*, New York: Ballantine Books.

Thomson, C.T. Arnould, E.J. and Stern, B.B. (1997) "Exploring the *Différance*. A Postmodern Approach to Paradigmatic Pluralism in Consumer Research," in S. Brown and D. Turley (eds) *Consumer Research: Postcards from the Edge*, London: Routledge.

Thompson, C.T., Stern, B.B. and Arnould, E.J. (1998), "Writing the Differences: Postmodern Pluralism, Retextualization, and the Construction of Reflexive Ethnographic Narratives in Consumer Research," *Culture, Markets and Consumption* 3 (1, June).

Tierney, P., Price, L.L., and Arnould, E.J. (1994) "Analysis of Expectations and Factors that Influence Satisfaction on Ecotourism Trips," paper presented at the Fifth International Symposium on Society and Resource Management.

Traub, J. (1996) "Passing the Baton: What C.E.O.s Could Learn from the Orpheus Chamber Orchestra," *The New Yorker* 26 August and 2 September: 100–5.

Van Maanen, J. (1988) *Tales of the Field: On Ethnographic Writing*, Chicago: University of Chicago Press.

Wallendorf, M. and Arnould, E.J. (1991) "'We Gather Together': The Consumption Rituals of Thanksgiving Day," *Journal of Consumer Research* 18, 1: 13–31.

Woolgar, S. (ed.) (1988) *Knowledge and Reflexivity: New Frontiers in the Sociology of Knowledge*, London: Sage.

13

UNLUCKY FOR SOME

Slacker scholarship and the well-wrought turn

Stephen Brown

Pre-text

Before we get down to business, let me ask you a simple question: what is the single most important publication in the history of marketing and consumer research? No, not your favorite; no, not the most influential; no, not the most cited or anthologized. And, no, not one of your own! (How dare you? Have you no shame? What on earth is the academy coming to?) I mean the most important, the most meaningful, the one that set tongues wagging, the one that calls down the years, the one that resonated at the time of publication and still resonates today, the one that registered 8.9 on the academic Richter scale and succeeded in decisively shifting the tectonic plates of the discipline.

Faced with this admittedly impossible choice, I suppose many people might be inclined to opt for the fairly obvious contenders – *Market Behavior and Executive Action,* "Marketing myopia," "Broadening the concept of marketing," "Marketing as exchange," "The nature and scope of marketing," "The sacred and profane in consumer behavior" and (how could I forget?) "Trinitarianism, the eternal evangel and the three eras schema." What do you mean, you've never heard of "Trinitarianism, the eternal evangel and the three eras schema"? It's a modern classic, I'll have you know. It has taken the academy by storm. It has repositioned the very parameters of post-war marketing scholarship. Yes, ok, it's one of my own (Brown 1996). Look, I make the rules around here and, if I want to bend them a bit, that's my prerogative. Don't mess with me, bro'.

Other people, by contrast, are liable to take this hypothetical interrogative opportunity to display their boundless erudition and learning. Denied the chance to nominate one of their own breakthrough papers, they'll either completely redefine the discipline's domain by, say, claiming *das Kapital, The Interpretation of Dreams* or *The System of Objects* as marketing publications *manqué,* or they'll anoint the most obscure contribution possible by portraying it as an undiscovered gem, a paper before its time, an enormously important yet inexcusably overlooked classic. You know the kind of thing I mean: Lazarsfeld's long-lost lucubrations on licking

Viennese lollipops (in the original German), Cova's incomprehensible cogitations on the postmodern condition (in the original French) or, indeed, Brown's apoplectic apocalyptism about trinitarianism, the eternal evangel and the three eras schema (in the original gobbledegook).

Anyway, to get back to what I was saying: what do you consider to be the most important publication in the field of marketing and consumer research? The answer – and I don't want to hear any insubordination from the ranks (stand up straight, Thompson; get a bloody hair cut, Belk; hit the deck, Holbrook, and give me fifty; you eyeballin' me, Arnould?) – is very simple, not to say blindingly obvious. It is, of course, *The Hidden Persuaders* by the late, great Vance Packard (1957).

Right, now just calm down for a second and let me try to explain. Yes, I know only too well that Packard's venomous tract comprised, and still comprises, by far the most devastating attack on marketing and its scholarly succubae. Yes, I appreciate that Packard's polemic is anathema to anyone who harbors a soft spot, however vestigial, for the marketing system and its associated intellectual apparatus (I suspect many business school academics fall into this category). Yes, I am the first to admit that Packard's absurd fantasies about brainwashed consumers have launched a thousand pointless dissertations on the auto-suggestive power of subliminal advertising (the less said about the implementation of ludicrous legislative controls, the better). And, yes, I realize that he is our field's favorite hate figure and hate figures are vitally necessary for our own sense of scholarly solidarity. If Packard didn't exist, we'd have to, well, you know . . .

Be that as it may, by intimating – from the top of the bestsellers list, remember – that marketers possessed some kind of magical power over, and hence had the ability to control, the unpredictable behaviors of consumers, Packard succeeded in selling (no, make that marketing) marketing to generations of managers and would-be managers, not to mention innumerable naive academics. You know the type: hey guys, the science/general theory/all-singing-all-dancing model of marketing is almost within our grasp – provided, of course, we try hard enough, crunch ever larger data sets through ever-faster computers, and at all times refuse to attend to the siren voices of postmodern marketing malcontents, degenerates, vulgarians, deviants, reprobates, delinquents, sodomites . . .

Packard's critique, in short, was the best advertisement that marketing ever had or is ever likely to have. Albeit totally erroneous, his rant did more for marketing than any number of heartfelt panegyrics to the importance of a marketing orientation ("Marketing myopia"), any number of ersatz assertions about its ineffable, all-encompassing applicability ("Marketing is everything"), any number of tub-thumping, look-ma-no-polysyllables textbooks on marketing "principles" (do I really need to name names?), or any number of obscure, arcane, abstruse cryptograms claiming to have transcended the quotidian concerns of practicing managers and transported the discipline to its rightful place in the ivy-clad ivory tower (who said "Trinitarianism, the eternal evangel and the three eras schema"?).

What, you don't agree with my assessment of Packard's place in the marketing anti-pantheon? You think I, how can I put this?, *mis*-represent him? You reckon I belittle our community of scholars? You don't like the irresponsible way I'm shaping up to write about these weighty, learned matters? So much the better! If everyone really hates this chapter – safely tucked away toward the back of the book, please note – maybe I'll be one day elevated to Packard's dizzy depths. I quite fancy the hate-figure function, just so long as you don't say anything nasty about me.

Cri-sis de coeur

Hold on a minute Stephen, I hear you say, what has all this self-indulgence got to do with the much-vaunted "crisis of representation" that, as the very existence of this book bears eloquent witness, is afflicting the social sciences in general and consumer research in particular? Well, a very great deal is the straightforward answer, though I bet you never thought you'd get one of those from me. But before I elaborate – and since representation is the focus of every other contribution to this path-breaking publication, this august anthology, this scholarly selection, this magnificent manual, this cerebral compendium, this encyclopedia of excellence, this . . . has my chapter been accepted yet, Babs? – let me just back up a little and expatiate for a moment on the concept of "crisis."

Now, I know some of the more cynical among you probably suspect a cunning postmodern plan is in the process of being hatched ("that son-of-a-bitch Brown is going to keep deferring the start of this chapter until he runs out of space or the editor intervenes"); I know my heinous record of serial textual harassment counts against me; and I know people are saying that I'm the kinda guy who's liable to leave readers lucklessly floundering in an intertextual intellectual limbo. So be it. See if I care. Nevertheless, I *do* think it is necessary to unpack the concept of "crisis" before we decide whether we're in the throes of one or not. (Don't you just love the word "unpack"? It's so postmodern, it's so preposterous, it's so ubiquitous, it's so unnecessary. It's the Volkswagen, the Visa, the Vosene of late-twentieth century verbiage.)

Appealing though "unpack" is to lovers of language, and aspirant pseudo-intellectuals such as myself, few would deny that "crisis'" is the *primus inter pares* of the postmodern lexicon – the Versace, the Valentino, the Louis Vuitton, if you will. It is, after all, an incredibly compelling, arresting, shock-jock word. It carries connotations of crying for help, purgatory, agonistics and all-purpose lachrymosity. It's second sibilant syllable is redolent of vampires, Vincent Price and mustachioed villains of Victorian melodrama. It literally screams at us from the panic-stricken page. It ought to be printed in scarlet, or allowed to flash on and off like a literary lighthouse, the pulsar of prose, a textual patrolcar in hot pursuit. Crisis, in effect, is the intellectual equivalent of Pavlov's bell. On hearing it, scholars slaver uncontrollably, cognizant of the self-aggrandizing opportunities sure to arise from a serious disciplinary schism.

Okay, I exaggerate a tad, but surely you won't deny that "crisis" is a resonant word, one which suggests that something important, something revolutionary, something terrible is happening or about to happen. Indeed, according to my well-thumbed, dog-eared, coffee-stained, broken-spined *Webster's Universal Collegiate Dictionary* – oh, all right, I bought it yesterday; give me a break, will you? – a crisis is variously: "a turning point for better or for worse"; "a condition of instability that leads to a decisive change"; "a personal tragedy or emotional upheaval"; "the point in a disease where a decisive change occurs"; and "the point in a play when antagonistic elements confront each other." I am reliably informed, what is more, that the word derives from the Greek verb *krinein*, to "decide," and the associated noun, *krisis*, meaning "judgment" (Ayto 1990). Intriguingly, the word "critic" is attached to the same root, as are "certain," "crime," "decree," "discern," "discrete," "discriminate," "excrement," "riddle," "secret," and "secretary." Now, that's what I call a meaningful etymological miscellany (but, then, I am a pretentious so-and-so).

What I'm trying to say, I suppose, is that the C-word pertains to a particular, an identifiable, a decisive point in time. Yet, it is more than a decade now since Marcus and Fischer (1986) announced their so-called "crisis of representation" and in that time the phrase has been uncritically parroted by almost every social science worth its salt (e.g. Brown 1995; Denzin 1995; Dickens and Fontana 1994). While allowances must be made for a certain time-lag in the intellectual diffusion process, the sad fact of the matter is that this ostensible crisis seems to be taking an awfully long time to come to a head, let alone resolve itself. If, of course, we are in an ongoing and – oxymoron alert! – *permanent* state of crisis, then we can only conclude that the concept of "crisis" is itself in crisis, though we must acknowledge the possibility that the crisis in crisis may also be crisis prone and, hence, the crisis in crisis in crisis is crisis-stricken and . . . is that an infinite regress in your pocket-edition or are you just pleased to "C" me?

Crisis de jour

Hmmm, let me try to come at this one from a different angle. Scrub the previous section. Block and delete, fellow cyberscribes. Once more from (over) the top. Accepting for a moment that the notion of "crisis" may be utterly devalued through over-use – and, personally, I'm much more worried by the prospect of uninterrupted academic stability than another round of weeping, wailing and dental delinquency – the possibility nonetheless remains that there is something unique about the, er, *événements* that we are experiencing or, rather, that everyone tells us we are experiencing. Regrettably, this contention does not withstand close scrutiny. The history of our discipline (assuming marketing and consumer research to be one and the same) contains any number of "crises" and homologous euphemisms – "ruptures," "breaks," "transitions," "shifts," "endings" and, Heaven help us, "*événements.*"

Thirty-five years ago, for example, Bartels (1962) was discussing the then crisis in marketing. Twenty-five years or so ago, Fisk (1971) and Bell and Emory (1971) were also crying crisis. Fifteen-odd years ago, Bennett and Cooper (1981) contributed their apocalyptic two-pennyworth. Ten years back, Belk (1987) was saying something similar. And, as you are well aware, the past five years have been all-but awash with crises de jour (Brady and Davis 1993; Brown 1995a; McDonald 1994). It sometimes seems that, like the buses of legend, you don't need to worry about missing one crisis, because another will be along in a minute.

Faced with the facts of marketing history, albeit the facts of history are constructions in themselves (LaCapra 1985; White 1973), it is tempting to respond with the claim that our crisis is so much worse than the ones that have gone before. We're in the grip of a *real* crisis this time, not one of your micro-crises, mini-crises, meso-crises, proto-crises, para-crises, pseudo-crises, crypto-crises, counterfeit-crises, call-that-a-crisis? crises, I've-had-worse-hangovers crises, pull-yourself-together-there's-nothing-wrong-with-you crises that marketing thinkers thought, or thought they thought, they were having in the past.

You don't need me to tell you, however, that this contention is complete nonsense. Granted, it is comforting, in a perverse sort of way, to think that *our* crisis, our macro-crisis, our mega-crisis, our meta-crisis, our super-crisis, our hyper-crisis is somehow deeper or more profound than its predecessors, since this implies that superior cerebral skills – fortunately possessed by ourselves – are necessary to overcome it. Nevertheless, the absurd claim that that "my intellectual crisis is worse than your intellectual crisis" is nothing less than unspeakably narcissistic at best and mind-bogglingly bombastic at worst, possibly both. Or, if you prefer suitably camouflaged academese, we could term it negative ontological one-upmanship (one-downpersonship, perhaps?). It is, to be brutally frank, an inverted instantiation of the modern, Western, today somewhat tarnished, progressivist worldview. It states, in effect, that we are better because we are worse.

Perhaps I'm being a little too hard on the crisis mongers of marketing. God only knows, I've mongered crises with the best of them and, as the bargain hunters among you may be pleased to hear, I think I've still got one or two in left in stock (special price, today only, everything must go, all major credit cards accepted, "nice to look at, lovely to hold, but if it gets broken, consider it sold"). Indeed, one only has to glance across the extant intellectual landscape – anthropology, history, sociology, geography, politics, philosophy, economics, cultural studies, etc. etc. etc. – to see that we are in the middle of a veritable crisis-fest, a conceptual close-out of massive proportions, the mother of all scholarly yard sales. True, some might consider it curious that we all seem to be experiencing crises at the same time but, for every one of those, several others are likely to point to the *fin de siècle* effect, that almost palpable sense of despondency, lassitude, stasis and, above all, *failure* that characterizes the dog days of the present century (see Brown 1995b).

As Kermode (1967; 1995) rightly notes, however, such pervasive pensive sentiments can strike at any time or place – and they do. The Western tradition is literally littered with intimations of intellectual mortality (yes, I know). Every generation, so it seems, lives in times of turbulence, of transgression, of turpitude, of transformation, of crisis. Whether it be the Baudrillards, Jamesons and Blooms of the 1990s, the Foucaults, Bells and Grahams of the 1960s, the Eliots, Pounds and Spenglers of the 1930s, or the Nordaus, Huysmans and Marmallés of the previous *fin de siècle*, it is clear that creative writers and thinkers in the Western tradition are preoccupied with, not to say addicted to, the concept of crisis. Isn't it remarkable, Kermode (1995: 261) wryly concludes, that crises, ends, transitions and the like seem to occur "at the very moment when Foucault, or whoever, happened to be around to witness and explain it."

For Kermode, in fact, this seemingly insatiable desire for crises, breaks, ruptures and endings is a fundamental correlate of the human condition. Human beings require consonance, they need things to make sense and are predisposed to impose structure on the existential flux and fragmentation of our daily lives. The idea that we live within a sequence of events between which there is no pattern, relation, progression or mutuality, is simply unthinkable. Hence, human-kind is inclined to impose beginnings, middles, ends and all manner of "breaks" upon time. Just as our individual lives have a clearly discernible plot structure, so too "we project our existential anxieties onto history" (Campion 1994: 346), "we hunger for ends and for crises" (Kermode 1967: 55), we can't avoid "a certain metaphysical valorization of human existence" (Eliade 1989: vii).

Crisis de trop(e)

Whoa, this is heavy stuff. From inconsequential academic anxieties to the End of the World. From alternative writing strategies to a projection of the baby-boom's collective mid-life crisis. From reverse gear to runaway truck. In less than three pages! Talk about exaggeration. Talk about extrapolation. Talk about excessive. Talk about, where on earth do we go from here?

Okay, let me just back up a little from the edge of the abyss. (Is that Philip Kotler I see down there? Surely not. Must be a trick of the light.) Yeah, yeah, I know, if I keep on backing up like this, I'm going to crash into the previous chapter, cause a ruckus and create all sorts of literary congestion. Keep your distance, Belk, you road hog! Yo, Hirschman, get a move on. It's people like you that cause RTAs (Representations Textual Accidents). Am I gonna have to call a cop from Routledge?

Right, let's try it again and remember to put on your seatbelt this time. Take it from me, there are some bad-ass auto-drivers in this part of the academy, though it's the eighteen wheelers of scholarship – the self-styled auto-auto-auto-drivers – that you really have to be wary of. Engine on, engage drive, check mirror, release brake . . . remove parking ticket, curse and swear, practice obscene gesture . . . right-hand side of the manuscript!!! Jeez, that was a close shave.

If we accept that the concept of crisis is abrogated through overuse, whilst acknowledging that it has always been prone to Peter and the Wolf-type propen-sities, then hackneyed or not, debased or not, negated or not, the notion of crisis must perform some useful purpose or fulfill a need. Far from being the unsettling, disruptive and nugatory occurence that it is traditionally taken to be, there may well be a positive side to crisis. Or, to put it another way, perhaps these unsettling, disruptive and nugatory occurences *are* the positive side to crisis. Just as Packard's critique of the marketing system. . . .

Hold on a minute, I hear you say, this chapter has just gone well and truly off the rails. Surely we reversed away from Packard a couple of sections ago and we have been reversing ever since. How can we possibly have got to Packard when we've been going backwards all this time? What's more, the business about there being a positive side to crisis. Surely, one of our earlier definitions of 'crisis' emphasized the possibility of a positive or negative outcome. 'A turning point for better or worse', wasn't that it?

Look you, I don't like being interrupted when I'm driving, especially on a highway strewn with Freudian potholes and metaphysical road works. But in order to avoid any more disruption, please note that: (a) we've done a complete circuit of the text and are now backing into VP from the front – there he is in the rear-view mirror; (b) my point is not that a crisis may have a positive or negative *outcome* but that the crisis *itself* may somehow prove advantageous; and (c) your off-the-rails allusion is completely inappropriate. Don't mix metaphors with me, sister. (By the way, what is it with railroads and marketers? From Ted Levitt to Dominque Bouchet – the Casey Jones of the marketing academy – it's railroads, railroads, railroads. The iron horse trope has been flogged to death, folks. Make way for the open road, I say. Wind in your hair, flies in your teeth, carbon monoxide in your lungs. (I love the smell of exhaust fumes in the morning.)

Time out for a second. Hey, I'm not such a bad guy. I have a sensitive side too, you know. I appreciate that you have a bit of a hang-up about Vance the Man. I mean, for more than a generation he has been the Antichrist of marketing and consumer research and I know it's not easy for you to come to terms with the fact that he's been our savior all along. Hell, I was as surprised as you are when the Vancian vision, the Packard prophesy, manifested itself to me. True, it wasn't a numinous light, speaking in tongues, Eureka-type experience, but it was a revelation, albeit a subliminal revelation, all the same. So, take it from me cybros and sisters, you've gotta accept the fact that we can't keep deferring the Packard issue. Out of the goodness of my heart I'm prepared to back off just a little while longer. But this is the very last time, *comprende*? What's more, there's a price to pay for prevarication, because I'm gonna have to fill this yawning textual gap by getting downright mean and nasty.

Just as Kermode (1967) suggests that the insatiable human desire for crises and ruptures has been with us since the very dawn of civilization, so too Lifton (1985) contends that it comprises nothing less than a primordial thanatic impulse, a universal urge towards the void. There is, let's be honest, a kind of orgiastic excitement associated with crying crisis, with the unleashing of wild forces, with the thought of total destruction. After all, it is only by letting slip the dogs of war, by destroying everything, by deliberately pressing the auto-destruct button, that we come to know what it really feels like to be alive. It is, as Ronell (1994) observes, part of a human, all-too-human desire for deep pain.

Crisis, in other words, implies conflict. The term carries connotations of schism, rupture, division, disruption, disputation, discontinuity, disaffection, defeat, death. It is, as noted earlier, a condition of instability, a personal tragedy, an emotional upheaval, the point in a play where antagonistic elements confront one another. But – and this is a very big but – it is important to appreciate that conflict is not necessarily a bad thing, at least not in intellectual life.

Friedrich Nietzsche, for instance, famously avers that "he who has to be a creator always has to destroy" (1961) and "if a temple is to be erected, *a temple must be destroyed*: that is the law" (1956). For Nietzsche, in fact, conflict, animosity and the naked exercise of will-to-power is the very hallmark of modern civilization. It is what has enabled us higher men – sorry, but Freddy mad dog Nietzsche wasn't exactly pro-feminist – to rise above the herd (Nehamas 1985). Likewise, our leading, living literary critic, Harold Bloom (1973), posits that thinkers generally and poets in particular are involved in a quasi-Oedipal, life or death struggle with their prodigious predecessors – Milton begat Blake, Blake begat Shelley, Shelley begat Yeats, etc. – and it is only by successfully overcoming (or, strictly speaking, sidestepping) the titanic forerunner that a distinctive poetic voice can begin to emerge. As one of Bloom's literary biographers makes clear, his life-long project of antithetical criticism comprises nothing less than a "poetics of conflict" (Allen 1994).

In a similar vein, Deleuze and Guattari (1988) employ the metaphor of the barbarian invasion – what they term "nomadology" – to describe developments in latter-day academic discourse. Distinguishing between "state thought," which is rigorous, disciplined, objective and continually monitored by the apparatus of power, and "nomadic thought," which is fluid, flexible, disconcerting (to the establishment) and invariably espoused by "outsiders," Deleuze and Guattari draw upon the time-worn dialectic of barbarian hordes versus civilized society to suggest that, contra the myth of primitivism, nomadic bands are remarkably innovative in many respects (warfare, science, technology, social arrangements). They represent a vital Dionysian spur to the uncivilized advance of "civilization."

Nomadic thought, then, is an attempted experiment in creativity and becoming; it is anti-traditional and non-conforming; it is opposed to stultifying orthodoxy; it involves breaking with convention; it seeks emancipation from totalizing or accepted modes of discourse; it revels in the proliferation of radically different perspectives and philosophies; it postulates a return to pre-cognitive forms of understanding (desire, intuition, spirituality, flow); it stresses the need to challenge disciplinary limits, canonical restrictions, extant ideologies and hegemonic critical practices. And, that's just for starters!

Crisis de ville

Sorry, folks, got a bit carried away there. Exceeding the intellectual speed limit. You know how easy it is when the road is clear, the top is down, the music's on and you're driving a conceptual Cadillac. What's that? Damn! Must have gone through a right-brain radar trap back there. Academic cop car's sitting on our tail. Oh shit, looks as though they're state tropers. Yes, *tropers*. Maybe they're from the marketing patrol, or possibly consumer research division – it's so hard to tell them apart. Whatever, most of those guys are dyed-in-the-wool positivists. Washed in the blood empiricists, or their necks are, at least. Boy, we *are* in trouble. Pull over slowly, I'll do the talking. Yes, officer, I know it's illegal to reverse down an interstate at seventy miles per hour, but we were being chased by a crazy guy in a Packard. Yes, officer, I appreciate that it's against the law to carry an automatic intellectual weapon in this state. But, hey, the Kalishinkov of continental philosophy is just a toy, a replica, a simulacrum made out of postmodern plastic, believe me. Let me try to put it to you in marketing terms.

You know and I know that just about everyone in marketing and consumer research pontificates about peace, love and understanding (e.g. Hirschman and Holbrook 1992; Hunt 1991; Sherry 1991); about how it is necessary to set our differences aside, to recognize that there are many different forms of knowledge, to learn to compromise and give a little for the greater good of the discipline, especially when there are so many idolaters and apostates out there who have yet to be converted to the marketing cause. After the desperate, distracting and ultimately debilitating paradigm wars of the 1980s, we sorely need a period of peace and quiet, of epistemological stability, of *pax intellectualis*, and, if we manage to maintain a methodological truce for a while, very real theoretical and practical rewards will undoubtedly come our way. With our radical new tools, techniques and conceptualizations (LISREL, relationship marketing, comprehensive consumer databases and all the rest), the breakthrough that we have patiently waited for will finally transpire. The bright uplands of marketing understanding are beckoning, glimmering on the horizon, almost visible to the naked eye. Provided, of course, we all stick together and nobody rocks the boat.

Are these aging hippies for real – *man*? Say what you like, but as far as I am concerned, the paradigmatic battles of the 1980s were our discipline's finest hour. Prior to Anderson's (1983; 1986; 1989) seminal contention that what counts as knowledge is *relative* to different times, contexts and research communities, the academic standards of marketing and consumer research – the all-round caliber of theoretical contributions – were somewhat wanting, to put it politely (have you read "The nature and scope of marketing" lately?; perused "Broadening the concept of marketing" possibly?; tell me, was Aspinwall (1958) on hallucinogenics when he wrote "The characteristics of goods" or does it just seem that way?).

More importantly perhaps, it was Hunt's (1984; 1989; 1990) ferocious rejoinders, his admittedly fatuous reds-under-the-bed assertion that *relativism* would lead inexorably to nihilism, irrationalism, incoherence, irrelevance, transgression, fornication, self-abuse, blindness, brain-disease and – *gasp* – the abandonment of extant academic standards, that placed Anderson on his not inconsiderable mettle and attracted the attention of interested onlookers. After all, there's nothing like a cerebral boxing match among the heavyweights of the discipline to draw a gawping crowd, particularly when the pugilists attempt to retain a degree of academic decorum ("I welcome the comments by" and what have you) whilst desperately slugging it out. True, the altercation got a little bit cab-ballistic at times – I'm still not quite sure if we finally sorted out the issues of "reification" and "incommensurability" – but the very fact that the leading lights of the field felt it necessary to cross swords in this manner ensured that everyone else was required to reflect on their own philosophical position or, to be more precise, to reflect on the fact that what they do without reflection, what they do day-and-daily, *is* in fact a philosophical position. For those brought up in, or never having outgrown, the managerial paradigm, brute empiricism seems so natural somehow. It is the what-goes-without-saying (Barthes 1973) of marketing and consumer discourse. It is so dependable, so reliable, so entrenched, so inviolate, so commonsensical, so *obvious*. It is the ideology of the idle, the unthinking, the ignorant, the uninformed.

Now, you don't need me to remind you that the empire of empiricism is, if not exactly in decline, certainly heading for a fall. One only has to glance at the mainstream marketing and consumer research journals to realize that they con-tain virtually nothing of value. They are a malodorous morass of minor-twist research, formulaic papers, hair-splitting pedantry and leaden prose, unalloyed leaden prose, full-fathom-five prose, block-of-concrete-tied-round-the-ankles prose, tape-the-electrodes-to-my-testicles-and-give-me-5,000–volts-rather-than-write-like-that prose. The only purpose such publications serve, it seems to me, lies in advancing the academic careers of their perpetrators – I hesitate to call them "authors." Indeed, despite the recent and welcome rise of interpretive research perspectives, which tend to be more readable than most, even these, it pains me deeply to point out, are often less than inspirational. (Hit me with another shot of the juice, cyberdude, it's really quite invigorating.)

To take but a single example – an example, I hasten to add, that ranks among *the very best* of its type – consider Arnould and Price's (1993) much-cited celebra-tion of "River Magic." This may well have been a lead paper in the leading consumer research journal, and it is widely considered to be an exemplar of the interpretive research paradigm, but with the best will in the world, it is unspeak-ably tedious in places (cf. the "quantitative" discussions on pp. 39–40). Granted, these slabs of pabulum may represent a brilliantly bravura stroke of verisimilitude, where the ennui of the prose is punctuated by moments of astonishing insight, just like the white water rafting the authors endeavor to portray. However, a much more likely explanation is that their inclusion represents the extortionate textual tribute demanded by the miserly, not to say knuckle-dragging, intellectual gate-keepers of the journal in question.

Nevertheless, the question still has to be asked: does "River Magic" capture the magic of the river magic experience? And the answer, regrettably, is, no. The "River Magic" paper *tells* us about river magic, certainly, it simply doesn't *show* us any (see Booth 1983). Sadly, there is nothing magical, supernatural or even mildly thaumaturgic about Arnould and Price's ponderous piece. Although, to repeat, this paper ranks amongst the *very best* of the genre, it unfailingly reminds me of the rhetorical question posed about ethnography by literary critic Mary Louise Pratt

(1986: 33), "why do such interesting people, doing such interesting things, in such an interesting domain, produce such dull books and articles?"

Clearly, some people are going to be upset by my castigation of the marketing and consumer research corpus (you eyeballin' me, Arnould?). But, frankly, I don't care. As far as I am concerned, intellectual controversy and internecine conflict are good things on the whole and, in that respect at least, I am not alone. In a detailed analysis of the sociology of intellectual stagnation, which encompassed medieval Christendom, Hellenistic Greece, Han Dynasty China and the late Ottoman Empire, as well as our degraded postmodern times, Collins (1992: 77) reports that "The crucial conditions for creativity are those which sustain *multiple bases of intellectual conflict across a primary focus of attention*" (emphasis in original). Stagnation and mediocrity, by contrast, occur when there is a single dominant paradigm, when dissident voices are silenced and when easy consensus, rather than enraged confrontation, is the order of the day.

Collins, in fact, notes three forms of intellectual stagnation: *loss of cultural capital*, where old ideas are forgotten or abandoned; *dominance of the classics*, where past academic achievements remain unchallenged and unchallengable; and *technical refinement*, where intellectual activity does not stop but becomes increasingly esoteric, ethereal, inaccessible, incomprehensible (e.g. the proverbial "angels on the head of a pin" controversies of late–medieval Christendom). More significantly perhaps, Collins states that intellectual innovation and creativity are not enhanced – but substantially reduced – by the gradual break up of the "primary focus of attention" into smaller and smaller subfields, which appear to promise internal coherence and conflict avoidance yet inevitably fall prey to schismatic tendencies. Further subdivision duly ensues and the whole process of intellectual stagnation is thereby perpetuated.

It doesn't take a degree in rocket science to appreciate that these reflections are highly relevant to marketing and consumer research, though marketing majors, I grant you, might have trouble grasping the conceit. We are blessed with any number of senior scholarly citizens, curmudgeons one and all, who complain that the old ideas, the ideas of thirty years ago – *their* ideas – have been forgotten in the manic onward rush of the discipline or, worse, have been rediscovered without due and dutiful obeisance to the founding fathers (e.g. Baker 1995; Kotler 1994). Equally, you only have to approach a publisher with an idea for a completely new kind of marketing textbook, or submit an unconventionally written paper to one of the "leading" journals, to realize that marketing and consumer research is totally dominated by the so-called "classics," by the "this is the way we do things around here" mind-set, by the myopic "but that's not marketing" remark. And, as subscribers to *JMR*, *Marketing Science* and others too mystifying to mention can readily testify, technical refinement is not exactly in short supply in our thrusting, dynamic, innovative, imaginative, cutting-edge corner of the academy. If Collins is right, moreover, the continual fragmentation of the marketing discipline (e.g. the consumer research/marketing split, the impending heretical consumer research/ consumer research split, all with their tie-in journals, associations, newsletters and inherent instability), is only serving to perpetuate rather than alleviate the intellectual torpor into which our field has latterly sunk.

Coup de crisis

See what you've gone and done? See what you've made me do? See what's happened all because of your irrational fear of Darth Packard, Vance Vadar or whatever his name is? Thanks to you, I've gone and antagonized the entire marketing and consumer research community; I've upset some of the distinguished contributors to this landmark volume (Eric, Eric, Eric, tell me you're not angry, Eric) and now I'll never get published in *JMR*, *JCR*, *JM*, *MS* or anywhere else for that matter. In another couple of minutes I would have been into one of my foam-flecked, jowls-quivering, blood-vessel popping, eye-balls protruding, purple-faced postmodern harangues about the reason for reason, the rationale for rationality, the foundations of foundationalism, the reliability of reliability, the validity of validity, the universality of universality, my disinterest in disinterestedness, my objections to objectivity and the truth about truth. Lucky I managed to pull myself together in time. Christ, I'm hyperventilating.

Worst of all, buddy, we're almost out of space and it's all your fault. Look, can't you see we're right behind Hirschman and if we don't slow down fast we'll rear-end Beth (if you'll pardon the expression). Alternatively, we could just keep on driving out of this text – hey, the Thelma and Louise of consumer research – and leave an empty parking space where the chapter used to be. You've heard of blank verse? Well, this is blank prose or, rather, blank generation prose – sorry, make that slacker scholarship, X-scholarship, gonzo scholarship, dumb and dumber scholarship, Tweedledum and Tweedledumber scholarship, Drink me scholarship.

Tempting though it is to contribute a completely blank chapter – consisting, naturally, of sweet nothings – as an aestheticized, sagacious, erudite and entirely appropriate symbol of the crisis of representation that supposedly confronts us (can I put it on my Vita?; what shall I call the piece?: "Installation #1," "The text that dare not speak its name," "Brownian motions," perhaps?), I really think that we should take this final opportunity to lance the Packard boil, to pick the Packard pustule, to scratch the Packard scab before I'm forced, frankly, to figure with even more unmentionable body parts.

In seeking to unpack Packard (*yes!*), the crucial point is that, notwithstanding his overwrought invective and the ever-popular conspiracy theory connotations that have sustained the volume down the decades, *The Hidden Persuaders* focused attention on marketing and consumer research, elevated it to the status of an "issue" and, paradoxically, legitimized the illegitimate through its illegitimate legitimacy (*what?*). A more recent example of the same anomaly is the unexpected fillip that Nietzsche studies received as a result of Allan Bloom's (1987) anti-Freddy diatribe in *The Closing of the American Mind* (Schacht 1995). The same is true of postmodernism and, in a marketing context, interpretivism, where Shelby Hunt's late-1980s lock-up-your-daughters-or-your-livestock-at-least invective made it all the more attractive to tyro researchers, such as myself. Everyone in Hollywood knows, moreover, that there's nothing like a little outcry – or, ideally, a protest or two – to add a couple of extra zeros to the box office.

Analogously, the use of the word "crisis," an onomatopoetic alarm bell if ever there was one, serves primarily to draw academic attention to the issue at hand, be it "legitimacy," "education," "politics," "faith," "democracy" or, in our case, "representation" (see Marcus and Fischer 1986). It is a moot point whether there is a "real" crisis in consumer research, as defined earlier, and it really doesn't matter, at least not in our panic-stricken poststructuralist intellectual climate of hyperreality, heteroglossia and slippery signifiers. Short of remaining silent, we simply cannot escape the coils of representation, though even silence represents a form of anti-representational representation. As an, er, illustrious marketing scholar once pointed out in an incredibly important yet unaccountably overlooked publication, "No representation without taxation" – yeah, it's another one of my own but I gotta get something out of this chapter, if only a citation (Brown 1995c: 302) – "the output of most marketing research exercises actually comprises a representation (verbal delivery), of a representation (report, academic paper), of a representation (data analysis), of a representation (survey instrument), of a representation (sample), of a representation (respondent's response), of a representation (the researcher's belief that there is an issue worth exploring), of a representation (the textual context – extant publications etc. – from which this assumption derives)." Phew! Presumptuous, or what? Prodigal, or what? Preposterous, or what? Poppycock, that's what!!

What we are dealing with, then, is less a crisis of representation than a representation of crisis, albeit if representation really is in crisis, then our representation of the representation of crisis is also in crisis and any representation of the representation of the representation of crisis is equally crisis-prone and . . . (Hey, Stephen, haven't we been here before? Surely we passed that *mise en abyme* signpost a long way back. You're lost, godammit!) Be that as it may, and irrespective of the present parlous state of representation in marketing and consumer research, the very act of crying crisis has placed it firmly on the academic agenda. Some misanthropes, admittedly, may contend that the crisis-criers are seeking to draw attention to themselves, to further their own academic careers, to foment a palace rebellion and thence catapult themselves to positions of prominence within the marketing academy. However, as someone who has dropped the C-word in the past – now and then, occasionally, very rarely, hardly ever – I can assure you that my motives are entirely pure, utterly unselfish, totally disinterested, eminently altruistic and solely prompted by the greater good of our glorious discipline (move your ass, Phil, you're sitting in my chair).

Anywise, for far too long our field has studiously ignored representation *qua* representation; that is, the words and symbols on the page. For far too long, in Geertz's (1988) felicitous phrase, we have looked *through* the text rather than at it. For far too long we have accepted the positivistic dogma that research must be reported in a spare, exact, transparent, unadorned, rigorous, unassuming, objective, unpretentious, parsimonious prose – what Locke (1992) aptly describes as the "art of artless writing". For far too long we have denied the fact that *what we do*, as marketing and consumer researchers, is almost entirely literary or textually mediated (see you-know-who 1997). Again, this is not to suggest that the marketing intelligentsia are ignorant of these things. On the contrary, there are copious first-class commentaries and contributions – you know who they are, I don't need to cite them – but in many cases, too many cases, these papers tend to describe rather than demonstrate the importance of rhetoric, storytelling, creativity, poetics or whatever. There's nothing wrong with description, of course, or even prescription, but it's kinda hard to get excited over, say, "liberatory" postmodernism when the paper is written in ponderous academic prose (Firat and Venkatesh 1995).

If, in conclusion, it is necessary to cry crisis – however devalued the word, the concept, the very enunciation – in order to force our field to reflect on its tired, unimaginative, enervated, recondite, convention-bound modes of textual expression, then let us shout "crisis" from the academic rooftops. After all, we only really have to worry if someone tries to abandon scholarly standards altogether and writes in a trashy, blasphemous, proletarian, unprincipled, outrageous, egregiously offensive way. And that would never be allowed to happen.

Hey, buddy, how do I get to the interstate from here?

Post-script

Guess what? There's a little bit of time left on the parking meter and Hirschman's either caught up in the traffic or still trying to hail a cab. So, let me just elaborate briefly on this notion that marketing and consumer research are essentially literary endeavors. Although many academics like to think of themselves as scientists *manqué*, as the back-room boys behind the achievements of their managerial brethren, the brutal fact of the matter is that we are basically writers, authors, hacks, literary types, the chattering classes – albeit with a severe speech defect. What, you don't agree? Well, just think about it for a moment . . .

Isn't it true, for instance, that the vast bulk of marketing and consumer research output consists of works of literature? The companies, institutions, organizations, managers, salespersons, agents, households, shoppers, consumers, samples, surveys, interviews, attitudes, intentions, behaviors, concepts, models and theories that we encounter are *entirely textually mediated*. While they may ultimately correspond to some phenomena in the "real" world – though even that is debatable – these marketing phenomena only exist for us through several by no means transparent layers of textual tissue (published papers, submitted papers, data analysis, interview protocols, respondent representations, methodological guidelines, existing literature and so on). This is equally true of the pedagogic context, where much of what we do – and the metaphysics of presence notwithstanding – is essentially textual (handouts, overheads, lecture notes, textbooks and so on). To repeat the question, then, are we players in the literary game or not?

Now, I won't deny that it is going to be difficult for our discipline to reimagine itself as the domain, the preserve, the reserve, the – God help us – *breeding ground* of literary types, suspiciously effeminate literary types. As horny-handed, down-to-earth, no-nonsense para-practitioners, marketing academics like to think that they have better things to do with their time than lounge around in common rooms composing sonnets, spouting iambic pentameters and conducting analyses of emplotment in the papers of our principal man of letters, Shelby D. Hunt. While explications of imagery in Shakespeare, Milton, Shelley or Pound may serve some useful purpose – albeit I suspect the diehards of marketing science would deny us even that – it all seems so *excessive* when applied to the literary mediocrities of marketing and consumer research.

In this respect, however, marketing and consumer research has much to learn from anthropology, another discipline long accredited with pragmatic, matter-of-fact, workmanlike, commonsensical credentials. Faced with their infamous "crisis of representation," Marcus and Fischer (1986) declared an "experimental moment," where what counted as ethnographic writing was up for grabs. Some enthusiasts responded with more poetic, highly literary, anti-realist forms of postmodern expression, which teetered, as often as not, on the brink of obscurantism (e.g. Tyler 1986). Others sought to eliminate, in archetypal poststructuralist style, the author from the text by foregrounding the voices of the represented in a dialogic or polysemous manner, even though the authors always had the final, final say in the textual selection process (Crapanzano 1992). And yet others, in time-honored academic fashion, sat on the fence by passing comment on, and developing classifications of, the literary proclivities of their peers. Thus, to cite but the best known example, Van Maanen (1988) distinguished between "realist," "confessional" and "impressionistic" ethnographic tales, though he has since added several others including "dramatic," "critical," "self," "comedy," "hip-hop" and "fictional" ethnographies (Van Maanen 1995).

My point, then, is that by taking a leaf or two out of our anthropological colleagues' book, we too can write our way – as opposed to writing about writing our way – out of trouble, into trouble, double trouble, hubble, bubble toil and . . . come on, Beth, shake a leg.

Post-post-script

Jeez, what's keeping her? What will I write about now? Hmmm, I suppose you want an explanation of my title. You must have a pretty fair notion of "slacker scholarship" by now, but what's a "well wrought turn" when it's at home? Hell, I don't know; it just came to me and seemed singularly appropriate. Why must the title always correspond to the content? You've heard of automatic writing, haven't you (Yeats's *Second Coming*, for example)? Well, this is what I call semi-automatic writing, albeit a stream of semi-consciousness might be closer to the mark . . .

Never apologize, never explain, they say – but since you insist. I didn't try to develop this theme in the essay, I grant you, yet it seems to me that part of the problem with "crisis" is its essentially temporal nature (a decisive point in time etc.). The concept of "crisis," to my mind, is tainted with the Western progressivist worldview, a worldview that is out of step with the predominantly "spatial" ethos that, for many commentators, is *the* root metaphor of postmodernity. Thus, the word "turn" seems more apt than "crisis" somehow. It carries connotations of turning wheels, turns in the road, turns of phrase, turning one's hand to something, vaudville turns and so on (see Sherry 1991). However, I'm a sucker for anniversaries – another characteristic postmodern trait, according to Johnston (1991) – and as this year (1997) is not only Packard's fortieth but the fiftieth anniversary of literary theorist, Cleanth Brooks's (1947) celebrated book, *The Well Wrought Urn*, the allusive title appealed to my literary sensibilities. I do have them, you know, buried somewhere beneath the postmodern ordure. (I especially like the notion of "well wrought" since we are not only writers but wrighters – as in "wheelwright" – and hopefully righters as well. Actually, my original title was "over-wrought turn" but I reckoned that was a little too obscure. Well, that's my excuse and I'm sticking to it.)

Now, I know what the pedants among you are saying. Anniversaries? Temporal surely! Nothing spatial there, my lad. Cleanth Brooks? One of the New Critics, I think you'll find! Nothing postmodern about him, young man. Yeah, yeah, I know all that but there's this nostalgic propensity about postmodernism, and then there's Jameson's "perpetual present" and New Criticism is starting to make a comeback – neo-new criticism, I suppose you could call it (e.g. Blotner 1997; Spaulin and Fischer 1995; Winchell 1996). Look, I really don't want to go into all this; it's dangerous, digressive, disorientating, Spaghetti Junction stuff. I just can't be bothered. You can see now why I didn't want to explain myself and where "slacker scholarship" came from, can't you? Hey, Hirschman, hurry it up, for Christ's sake . . .

Post-post-post-script

Sorry, Beth, I can't wait any longer. I've got things to do, papers to write, people to pan, academics to antagonize, avenues to explore, ranges to ride, hills to climb, rhymes to reason, rocks to roll, metaphors to monger, crises to calm, turns to take, tropes to turn, money to burn, figures to forge, rivers to cross, dreams to chase, kites to fly, tears to cry, fish to fry, t(i)rades to ply, rules to break, breezes to shoot, sticks to shake, leaves to rake, finishes to fashion, escapes to attempt, exits to execute, craps to cut, ups to shut, offs to fuck.

Is that you, Professor Hirschman? What kept you? I'm getting kinda tired and emotional here.

References

Allen, G. (1994) *Harold Bloom: A Poetics of Conflict*, Hemel Hempstead: Harvester Wheatsheaf.

Anderson, P.F. (1983) "Marketing, Scientific Progress and Scientific Method," *Journal of Marketing*, 47, Fall: 18–31.

—— (1986) "On Method in Consumer Research: A Critical Relativist Perspective", *Journal of Consumer Research*, 13, September: 155–73.

—— (1989) "On Relativism and Interpretivism – with a Prolegomenon to the 'Why' Question," in E.C. Hirschman (ed.) *Interpretive Consumer Research*, Provo, UT: Association for Consumer Research, 10–23.

Arnould, E.J. and Price, L.L. (1993) "River Magic: Extraordinary Experience and the Extended Service Encounter," *Journal of Consumer Research*, 20, June: 24–45.

Aspinwall, L. (1958) "The Characteristics of Goods and Parallel Systems Theories" in E.J. Kelley and W. Lazer (eds) *Managerial Marketing*, Homewood, Ill: Richard D. Irwin, 434–50.

Ayto, J. (1990) *Dictionary of Word Origins*, New York, NY: Arcade Publishing.

Baker, M.J. (1995) "The Future of Marketing," in M.J. Baker (ed.) *Companion Encyclopedia of Marketing*, London: Routledge, 1003–18.

Bartels, R. (1962) *The Development of Marketing Thought*, Homewood, Ill: Richard D. Irwin.

Barthes, R. (1973 [1957]) "Myth Today," in R. Barthes (ed.) *Mythologies*, trans. A. Lavers, London: Paladin, 117–74.

Belk, R.W. (1987) "A Modest Proposal for Creating Verisimilitude in Consumer-information-processing Models and Some Suggestions for Establishing a Discipline to Study Consumer Behavior", in A.F. Firat, N. Dholakia and R.P. Bagozzi (eds) *Philosophical and Radical Thought in Marketing*, Lexington: Lexington Books, 361–72.

Bell, M.L. and Emory, C.W. (1971) "The Faltering Marketing Concept," *Journal of Marketing*, 35, October: 37–42.

Bennett, R.C. and Cooper, R.G. (1981) "The Misuse of Marketing: An American Tragedy," *Business Horizons*, 24, 6: 51–61.

Bloom, H. (1973) *The Anxiety of Influence: A Theory of Poetry*, Oxford: Oxford University Press.

Blotner, J. (1997) *Robert Penn Warren: A Biography*, New York, NY: Random House.

Booth, W.C. (1983) *The Rhetoric of Fiction*, 2nd edn, Harmondsworth: Penguin.

Brady, J. and Davis, I. (1993) "Marketing's Mid-Life Crisis," *McKinsey Quarterly*, 2: 17–28.

Brooks, C. (1947) *The Well Wrought Urn: Studies in the Structure of Poetry*, New York, NY: Harcourt Brace.

Brown, R.H. (1995) "Postmodern Representation, Postmodern Affirmation," in R.H. Brown (ed.) *Postmodern Representations: Truth, Power and Mimesis in the Human Sciences and Public Culture*, Urbana, Ill: University of Illinois Press, 1–19.

Brown, S. (1995a) "Life Begins at 40? Further Thoughts on Marketing's Mid-life Crisis," *Marketing Intelligence and Planning*, 13, 1: 4–17.

—— (1995b) *Postmodern Marketing*, London: Routledge.

—— (1995c) "Postmodern Marketing Research: No Representation Without Taxation," *Journal of the Market Research Society*, 37, 3: 287–310.

—— (1996) "Trinitarianism, the Eternal Evangel and the Three Eras Schema," in S. Brown, J. Bell and D. Carson (eds), *Marketing Apocalypse: Eschatology, Escapology and the Illusion of the End*, London: Routledge, 23–43.

—— (1997) *Postmodern Marketing Two: Telling Tales*, London: ITBP.

Campion, N. (1994) *The Great Year: Astrology, Millenarianism and History in the Western Tradition*, Harmondsworth: Arkana.

Collins, R. (1992) "On the Sociology of Intellectual Stagnation: The Late Twentieth Century in Perspective," in M. Featherstone (ed.) *Cultural Theory and Cultural Change*, London: Sage, 73–96.

Crapanzano, V. (1992) *Hermes' Dilemma and Hamlet's Desire: On the Epistemology of Interpretation*, Cambridge, MA: Harvard University Press.

Deleuze, G. and Guattari, F. (1988 [1980]) *A Thousand Plateaus: Capitalism and Schizophrenia*, trans. B. Massumi, London: The Athlone Press.

Denzin, N.K. (1995) "The Poststructural Crisis in the Social Sciences: Learning from James Joyce," in R.H. Brown (ed.) *Postmodern Representations: Truth, Power and Mimesis in the Human Sciences and Public Culture*, Urbana, Ill: University of Illinois Press, 38–59.

Dickens, D.R. and Fontana, A. (1994) "Postmodernism in the Social Sciences," in D.R. Dickens and A. Fontana (eds) *Postmodernism and Social Inquiry*, London: UCL Press, 1–22.

Eliade, M. (1989 [1954]) *The Myth of the Eternal Return: Cosmos and History*, Harmondsworth: Penguin.

Firat, A.F. and Venkatesh, A. (1995), "Liberatory Postmodernism and the Reenchantment of Consumption," *Journal of Consumer Research*, 22, December: 239–67.

Fisk, G. (1971) "The Role of Marketing Theory," in G. Fisk (ed.) *New Essays in Marketing Theory*, Boston, MA: Allyn and Bacon, 1–5.

Geertz, C. (1988) *Works and Lives: The Anthropologist as Author*, Stanford: Stanford University Press.

Hirschman, E.C. and Holbrook, M.B. (1992) *Postmodern Consumer Research: The Study of Consumption as Text*, Newbury Park, CA: Sage.

Hunt, S.D. (1984) "Should Marketing Adopt Relativism?," in P.F. Anderson and M.J. Ryan (eds) *Scientific Method in Marketing*, Chicago, Ill: American Marketing Association, 30–4.

—— (1989) "Naturalistic, Humanistic and Interpretive Inquiry: Challenges and Ultimate Potential," in E.C. Hirschman (ed.) *Interpretive Consumer Research*, Provo, UT: Association for Consumer Research, 185–98.

—— (1990) "Truth in Marketing Theory and Research," *Journal of Marketing*, 54, July: 1–15.

—— (1991) "Positivism and Paradigm Dominance in Consumer Research: Toward Critical Pluralism and Rapprochement," *Journal of Consumer Research*, 18, June: 32–44.

Johnston, W.M. (1991) *Celebrations: The Cult of Anniversaries in Europe and the United States*, New Brunswick: Transaction.

Kermode, F. (1967) *The Sense of an Ending: Studies in the Theory of Fiction*, New York, NY: Oxford University Press.

—— (1995) "Waiting for the End," in M. Bull (ed.) *Apocalypse Theory and the Ends of the World*, Oxford: Blackwell, 250–63.

Kotler, P. (1994) "Reconceptualising Marketing: An Interview with Philip Kotler," *European Management Journal*, 12, 4: 353–61.

LaCapra, D. (1985) *History and Criticism*, London: Cornell University Press.

Lifton, R.J. (1985) "The Image of the 'End of the World': A Psychohistorical View," in S. Friedländer, G. Holton, L. Marx, and E. Kolnikoff (eds) *Visions of Apocalypse: End or Rebirth?*, New York, NY: Holmes and Meier, 151–67.

Locke, D. (1992) *Science as Writing*, New Haven, Conn: Yale University Press.

Marcus, G.E. and Fischer, M.M.J. (1986) *Anthropology as Cultural Critique: An Experimental Moment in the Human Sciences*, Chicago, Ill: University of Chicago Press.

McDonald, M.H.B. (1994) "Marketing – A Mid-Life Crisis," *Marketing Business*, 30, May: 10–14.

Nehamas, A. (1985) *Nietzsche: Life as Literature*, Cambridge, MA: Harvard University Press.

Nietzsche, F. (1956 [1887]) *The Genealogy of Morals: An Attack*, trans. F. Golffing, New York, NY: Anchor Books.

—— (1961 [1885]) *Thus Spake Zarathustra*, trans. R.J. Hollingdale, Harmondsworth: Penguin.

Packard, V. (1957) *The Hidden Persuaders*, New York, NY: D. Mackay.

Pratt, M.L. (1986) "Fieldwork in Common Places," in J. Clifford and G.E. Marcus (eds) *Writing Culture: The Poetics and Politics of Ethnography*, Berkeley, CA: University of California Press, 27–50.

Ronell, A. (1994) *Finitude's Score: Essays for the End of the Millennium*, Lincoln, NB: University of Nebraska Press.

Schacht, R. (1995) *Making Sense of Nietzsche: Reflections Timely and Untimely*, Urbana, Ill: University of Illinois Press.

Sherry, J.F. (1991) "Postmodern Alternatives: The Interpretive Turn in Consumer Research," in T.S. Robertson and H.H. Kassarjian (eds) *Handbook of Consumer Research*, Englewood Cliffs, NJ: Prentice-Hall, 548–91.

Spaulin, W.J. and Fischer, M. (eds) (1995) *The New Criticism and Contemporary Literary Theory: Connections and Continuities*, New York, NY: Garland Publishing.

Tyler, S. (1986) "Post-modern Ethnography: From Document of the Occult to Occult Document," in J. Clifford and G.E. Marcus (eds) *Writing Culture: The Poetics and Politics of Ethnography*, Berkeley, CA: University of California Press, 122–40.

Van Maanen, J. (1988) *Tales of the Field: On Writing Ethnography*, Chicago, Ill: University of Chicago Press.

—— (1995) "An End to Innocence: the Ethnography of Ethnography," in J. Van Maanen (ed.) *Representation in Ethnography*, Thousand Oaks, CA: Sage, 1–35.

White, H. (1973) *Metahistory*, Baltimore: Johns Hopkins University Press.

Winchell, M.R. (1996) *Cleanth Brooks and the Rise of Modern Criticism*, Charlottesville, VA: University Press of Virginia.

14

AFTERWORDS: SOME REFLECTIONS ON THE MIND'S EYE

Elizabeth C. Hirschman

Some reflections on the mind's eye

My reflections on representation have been in process for almost twenty years, ever since I first started thinking about symbolism, images, and meaning as research topics. In one of my earliest efforts (Hirschman 1980), I speculated that all tangible objects are capable of carrying at least four layers of meaning:

1 *Direct sensory or iconic impressions*, such as color, shape, texture, size, weight, sound, taste and so forth, which I felt would be invariable across all humans.
2 *Idiosyncratic meanings*, which are associations due to unique, personal experiences with the object and which vary completely across people. For example, I associate the soupy song "Love is blue" with a certain boy I was dating at a certain place during a particular time in my life. Whenever I hear the song (fortunately, not often) I think of that boy, that place and that time – what cognitive psychologists would term autobiographical or episodic memory.
3 *Subcultural associations*, which are thoughts and images that are usually connected to an object by members of a given subculture. For example, growing up as a white girl in the southern United States, I have associations with the confederate flag and with the song "Dixie" that are probably quite different from those of a black girl growing up in the same place.
4 *Cultural associations*, which are thoughts and images associated with an object by most members of a given culture. For example, most Americans probably look upon Santa Claus, Mickey Mouse and Big Bird with affection.

Shortly after that time (1980), Morris Holbrook and I organized the Symbolic Consumption Conference at New York University. In preparing some papers for the conference, my thoughts on the role of symbolism and imagery in representation went a bit further. It dawned on me that we shared reality with other people only to the extent that we assigned similar meanings to objects in the natural

384

world. That is, two people could communicate with each other only to the extent that they shared the same set of symbolic associations about something. In contrast, they were isolated from each other to the extent that they perceived different meanings for the same thing (Hirschman 1981). (Of course, I was light years behind Sid Levy, Mikhail Bakhtin, Roland Barthes, Marshall Sahlins, and one thousand communications researchers, but for a woman with a Ph.D. in marketing, this was pretty good).

The next big breakthrough came in 1985 when I began reading Joseph Campbell's remarkable work on myth and archetypes (1968a; 1968b; 1974). I discovered that the motion pictures that had enthralled me since very early childhood were full of the same mythic imagery – heroes, monsters, villains, messiahs, witches, sorcerers and wise old men – identified by Campbell in ancient mythology. I sat down and watched the ten most popular motion pictures of all time (films like *Gone with the Wind*, *Star Wars*, and *ET*), and noticed for the first time a pantheon of archetypal images (Hirschman 1987).

It was a significant step for me to be able to relate the somewhat shallow ideas I had about a given character such as Han Solo or ET to the deeper meanings that Campbell assigned. Han Solo was no longer just the "good guy," but rather – in my mind's eye – the archetypal rogue-adventurer hero, akin to Odysseus and Hercules. Similarly, ET was no longer just a cute little space creature; I now recognized him as an archetypal messianic figure whose disciples were the children and whose antagonists (the scientists) were the Philistines or Romans. I suddenly became able to see images as metaphors, and this made possible an entire chain of analogic thought ("this is like this is like this is like this").

The mid-1980s were also a watershed time for consumer research as a whole. All hell had broken loose. As we look back now, over a decade later, we see what an extraordinary revolution in representation took place. David Mick's and Morris Holbrook's papers (Mick 1986; Holbrook and Grayson 1986) on semiotics and symbols were extremely important in outlining and illustrating, respectively, the importance and meaning of images. After that, a deluge of articles on literary criticism (Scott 1990, 1994a, and 1994b; Stern 1988a and 1988b), phenomenology (Thompson *et al.* 1989, 1990) and structuralism (Hirschman 1988) washed across the field and introduced novel ways of representing and reading consumer meanings in a variety of texts.

The over-privileging of the word

This is all bright and wonderful, but now I want to voice a criticism directed at myself as much as anyone else. I believe that we have become too enamored of and dependent on words – verbal or written text – in the research we conduct on meaning and symbolism and imagery and in the representation of our findings. With very few exceptions (and one of the major ones is the work of Linda Scott (1994a) on visual rhetoric), we shy away from dealing with non-written texts. As an example, let's consider my own procedure. If I conduct in-depth interviews with twenty consumers on a given topic, I take the interview tapes to be typed and work from the typed transcripts to do my analysis. I don't ask these consumers to express their ideas by drawing a picture or singing a song or making a meal or playing music or dancing. Nor do I as a researcher contemplate doing any of the above as a journal submission. I simply rely on their words and represent my own account in words, which limits both me and them tremendously. (Indeed, the only person I know who is doing multisensory, multimodal work is Jerry Zaltman, whose Z-met technique is innovative in its elicitation of the consumer's own imagery.)

Of course, when I attempt to communicate my interpretation to other researchers, I almost always rely on words to convey meaning. Once in a while I will use a photograph or videotape, but I have never used music or food or perfume or flowers or fabric or drawings.

I say this not because I honestly believe that tomorrow all of us will leap up and begin dancing, painting, composing and cooking to represent our research findings, but because I do think it is important for us to recognize the over-privileged nature of written or spoken language in what we do. Just as we once criticized our positivist colleagues for being confined by the tyranny of quantification – of insisting on translating phenomena into numbers and measurement before accepting it as having meaning – we are similarly enslaved by the tyranny of words. For many of us interpretive researchers, unless something is written it doesn't "count" as an interpretation.

There's more to meaning than words

Recently I have been working on a paper on human emotion with Barbara Stern. In doing research for the paper, I began reading studies in the neuroscience literature. There is an extraordinary revolution going on in that field fueled by recent advances in imaging technology – the capacity to "picture" areas of the brain. Using methods such as PET and MRI scanning, investigators can now identify the structures in the human brain that generate cognitions, emotions, and sensory images. And guess what? They are not all in the same place. Sensory images are constructed in a different way and located in a different place from linguistic elements such as word and sentences. These discoveries confirm earlier research dating from the 1920s, which found that people vary greatly in verbal fluency and sensory image-making. Whereas some people think primarily in words, others think primarily in visual and/or auditory images. Most of us combine the two when we think or iterate back and forth between the two.

Our translation capabilities suggest, to me at least, that we just cannot represent all of the meaning in a visual (or other sensory) image simply by using words to describe it. Our vocabulary for scent is especially impoverished. Further, a given internal or external sensory image – say a song or a whiff of perfume – may trigger related symbolic associations that evoke other sensory images, as well as verbal and cognitive associations. For example, if I play the song "Love is blue" in my head, I see visual images of myself dancing with that boyfriend, feel the warmth of a summer night in Atlanta, Georgia, smell beer and the boy's cologne, and have the cognition: "—— was a great guy, but I'm glad I didn't marry him. He was too short and had a real scratchy face."

All of these are highly personal and probably highly idiosyncratic meanings connected to the song. If pressed by an interpretive interviewer, I could probably come up with some subcultural and cultural associations as well. For example, in terms of subculture, I could mention that the song was playing at a college fraternity party, and in terms of culture, that it was an instrumental soft-rock recording by Paul Mauriat. But my words, though accurate, provide an incomplete account of the song's meaning. I cannot communicate accurately or fully the sensory images that are in my head and that are the biggest and most significant parts of the song's meaning to me. Unfortunately, I fear that we are often able to tap only the cognitive verbal portions of symbolic meaning because it is difficult to communicate what something "really" represents to another person. The texture of that song and its personal associations can only be represented by means that outstrip the capacities of printed words on a page, pictures, or even sounds – we currently have no way of representing smell, touch, or the sensation of bodies touching.

The collie and the land shark

I can give you a more recent example of the power of non-verbal representation by telling you the story of how my daughter Shannon got her dog, Charlie. Shortly after she turned three years old, Shannon announced to us that she wanted a brown, fluffy puppy. Our family had a long history of owning protection-type dogs: Rottweilers, Doberman pinschers, and German shepherds. But recently the protection-dog category seemed to be getting out of hand. There were numerous reports of children being attacked and mauled by pit bull terriers, Rottweilers, and Dobermans. Shannon is a big, active kid and I did not want to come home one day and find her bitten by her pet dog – or worse. (In conceptual terms, we could say that news stories about attacks by some protection dogs form much of the cultural discourse about this category.)

Because our family only had direct personal experience with this sort of dog, we had to rely entirely on indirect symbolic experience of other breeds. So we got out the encyclopedia and looked under DOGS for ideas. Toy dogs were too small; hunting dogs did not seem friendly; labradors and golden retrievers were too common and suburban – like Volvo stationwagons. And then, right there in the "working dog" group, we saw what we were looking for: a collie dog. It was fluffy, brown and white, large but not gigantic, and protective but not aggressive.

Since none of us had ever actually seen a real live collie dog, we relied almost entirely on the common cultural discourse (to use the current catch phrase) to attach meaning to the photo of the dog in the encyclopedia. And I realized that virtually all of our common cultural knowledge about collies – that is, what they represented – came from *Lassie,* the television series that made collies familiar to the American public. In my head I saw Lassie rescuing Timmy from a burning barn, fighting off a cougar and a wolf to save Timmy, leading Timmy out of a deep forest, saving a nest of baby ducks from a hawk, pulling Timmy out of a lake, and so forth. Mentally, I recast "Shannon" as "Timmy" and knew then that this was the right dog for us. We bought an eight-week-old collie puppy and named him Charlie. He's now six months old, weighs seventy-five pounds, and looks and acts just like Lassie.

This episode demonstrates two important points: first, collies truly are terrific dogs, and second, symbolic meaning can be represented and absorbed almost entirely by means of visual/sensory impressions. That is, Lassie's heroism was rarely *spoken about* in the television program but, rather, was nearly always *shown.* People came to understand what collies were – in other words, what they meant – more by watching the images than by hearing the dialogue. I believe that a tremendous amount of symbolic knowledge is represented and acquired by sensory transference of meaning from non-verbal or written texts.

Further, I also believe that visual and sensory images form the basis of our higher-level, abstract, cognitive constructions. Let me tell you another anecdotal tale. While I was searching for collie breeders from whom to buy a puppy for Shannon, I purchased several dog magazines and dog breeder directories. (I think I was probably also trying to make sure that collies were the right choice, as well. After all, there might be some new dog brand on the market of which I was not aware.)

These magazines and directories had pictures and written descriptions of hundreds of breeds, and I found myself turning page after page looking at each picture and the dog it represented. In the course of doing this, I discovered that the group of dogs that I had loosely categorized in my head as "protection dogs" had exploded in number and variety. There were no longer only German shepherds, Dobermans, and Rottweilers – the breeds with which I had direct, personal experience.

Instead, there had been enormous growth in a particular type of dog, a dog that had a certain physical look that was visible across multiple breeds. The German shepherds, Dobermans, and Rottweilers that I had grouped together mentally under the cognitive category of "protection dogs" did not physically resemble one another. For example, the German shepherd looks like a wolf, the Rottweiler like a bear, and the Doberman like a racehorse. What bound them together in my mind was the common behavioral attribute of being good guard dogs.

The new type of protection dog with which I was not personally familiar had a physical appearance that carried visually across several different breeds. These included the American pit bull terrier, the American Staffordshire terrier, the Argentine dogo, the cane corso, the alpha bulldog and the American bulldog. All of these breeds' visual representations featured a photograph of a short-haired, very muscular, medium to large dog, with a huge head dominated by a gaping mouth filled with teeth. The torso of the dog is wider at the chest, narrowing into a sharp

"V" toward the hips. The ears are often cropped very close to the head, which provides even more visual emphasis on the capacious jawline.

When I was looking at these visual images, I realized that I did not even need to read the written descriptions to form a new mental grouping for them: "land sharks." These clearly were dogs whose purpose was to pursue and bite their prey, probably another dog or a human. They were "Jaws-on-Paws," a pun that is also indicative of my thought processes as well. What I had done is connect the visual images of the dogs to the visual images of the great white shark in Spielberg's film *Jaws*. Indeed, when I looked at the pictures and listened closely to the sounds I was imagining, I could even hear John Williams's awesome theme music from the motion picture playing in my head: "boom-boom, boom-boom, boom-boom, da-da-da-da-da."

What is interesting about this anecdote (besides revealing my rich, strange fantasy life) is that, to my knowledge, I have never actually seen or touched a live shark or a live land-shark dog.[1] Virtually all of my knowledge about them comes from media representations such as motion pictures, television news reports, and dog advertisements. Indeed, my entire knowledge of collie dogs came from the same sources, since I had not laid eyes or ears or hands on a real one before I went to see Charlie and his parents for the first time. The gap between real life and representation leads me by a somewhat winding road to the last point I want to raise: "Who is Batman"?

"Who is Batman?"

Now I want to discuss the Big Problem I have with Jean Baudrillard and his notion of *hyperreality*. My understanding of Baudrillard's writings is that hyperreality occurs when the representations of objects become loosened from their iconic moorings to the actual object and become free-floating in the media – cyberspace or wherever – all the while morphing into phantom-like entities that are neither here nor there. Ordinary humans gazing on these phantasms mistake them for the Real Thing, or worse yet, imagine that they are the Real Thing, and therefore become addicted to an image instead of to a concrete object. Some social scientists believe that is bad for humans.

I take issue with this verdict on two counts. First, as I've already argued, much – perhaps almost all – of our knowledge of many real-world phenomena comes from just such hyperreal images. This has been true for our species ever since we were able to construct images (graven or otherwise) of real or imaginary creatures, people, or things. Prehistoric peoples' mental conceptions of gods and goddesses were carved or chiseled into stone, and in this way they made physically corporeal that which previously had only been ephemerally ideal. Other people could then observe this physical icon and mentally grasp what the idealized god looked like.

In contemporary culture, motion pictures serve the same function. They represent imagined things (such as space aliens) by conveying a visual and auditory sense of them. Further, videotape, film, and photographic images and sounds are all that most of us have as evidence that much of what we believe to be reality exists. For example, I have never seen President Bill Clinton, Madonna, Boris Yeltsin, Michael Jordan, O.J. Simpson, Queen Elizabeth II, Prince Charles, Hong Kong, China, Mt Everest, Russia, Bono, Paul McCartney, Stephen Hawking, or Bill Gates. I have never seen an Eskimo or a Laplander, a Maori or an Aborigine, a giant squid, an iceberg, or a volcano, except in secondary hyperreal images. Yet I believe that they exist and don't feel that I have been damaged by seeing these disconnected representations. (Of course, I could be wrong on both these counts.)

In addition, I can only know everyone and everything that perished before my time through the hyperreal detritus left behind: bones, portraits, photographs, blueprints, fossil impressions, and so forth. How else are we to know about dinosaurs, Karl Marx, Sigmund Freud, Marlene Dietrich, and Alexander the Great?

All of this brings me to my example of the complexity of discerning what is real and what is hyperreal. Let's consider the case of Batman and ask, "Who is Batman, really?" Batman began as a cartoon character in comic books written by Bob Kane during the 1940s and existed only as as a picture made out of ink and paper until the 1960s. In 1961 Batman was morphed into videotape images on the *Batman and Robin* television show, and the actor Adam West was the real person who portrayed the fictional character. In 1989 a motion picture appeared called *Batman*, which featured the actor Michael Keaton in the title role. Thus, at this point, another real man (Michael Keaton) had begun to impersonate the fictional character (Batman) via the hyperreal images of modern motion-picture photography.

In 1992 *Batman Returns* appeared – another motion picture starring Michael Keaton as the iconic representation of Batman. However, in 1995, as a result of contract disputes with Michael Keaton, actor Val Kilmer, also a real man[2], was cast as Batman in the film *Batman Forever*. But that Batman was not forever, for the next time Batman appeared to us in the flesh in the film *Batman and Robin* (1997), actor George Clooney was the real man inside the bat suit. This raises the existential question, "Who *is* Batman"?

The history of Batman's representations began with the image in Bob Kane's mind that led to his drawings in comic books. At this point, and in this medium, Batman came to have a physical presence and could begin to be surrounded with stories that endowed him with cultural meaning. Here he represents the warrior-hero archetypal figure that Campbell (1968a) so richly describes. Even though Batman was a mythic presence rather than a real, historic person, he was nonetheless a potent carrier of meaning.

The Batman concept first became associated with a real person during the 1960s, when the character was portrayed by an actor (Adam West) in a television series. In the succeeding generation, the concept has become associated with three different actors (Michael Keaton, Val Kilmer, and George Clooney) across a series of four motion pictures. Note that although each of these living human beings has portrayed Batman, none is "really" Batman. We are left with the reality that

Batman does not exist, except as a series of representations of a mental image that originated in one man's (Bob Kane's) mind.

That's about as hyperreal as one can get, and yet it is still possible for this fictional entity to have a rich, detailed, and impactful cultural heritage. And, I might add – given my current pro-visual/anti-verbal bias – much of what Batman represents to us resides in the visual experiences we have of him (and, as far as the four Batman films go, the powerful musical associations as well). Batman, like most archetypal warrior heroes, conveys most of his meaning by means of actions rather than words. He is not a profound orator and, in fact, in his most recent incarnation (George Clooney), Batman hardly has any dialogue!

Some closing thoughts

Well, for someone who has been thinking about the role of imagery in representation for almost twenty years, it should be pretty obvious that I haven't made a lot of progress! In fact, many days I feel that I am less sure of things now than I was back in 1980 when I first proposed the multilayered model of meaning. That model, born as it was during the reign of cognitive theory, very much reflected the hegemonic bias in favor of verbal conceptual associations – little sentences or phrases that were mentally stored as linkages to a central concept.

Since then, I've come to recognize in my own head what was formerly invisible in my theoretical formulations. That is, for me, much of meaning is composed of visual and auditory images, wordless pictures and sounds that for many of life's most important objects and events are the key symbolic elements. I wish I knew some way to project these images outward so that they would be accessible to others. I wish I knew some way that the people I've spoken to as informants could project their inner images outward to me so that they I could fully comprehend the meaning that they are trying to communicate with their words. I wish I knew some way to represent all of these inner images so that others could see what we mean.

Perhaps that is why I like going to the movies so much – because the images just pour off the screen and into my head. In my next life, I want to be a film-maker.

Notes

1 I'm lying a little bit here; I think I did see a red pit-bull-type dog in Pittsburgh, PA in 1978 but I did not stop to pet it.
2 I hope . . . I've only seen the hyperreal images of West, Keaton and Kilmer

References

Campbell, J. (1968a) *The Hero with a Thousand Faces*, Princeton: Princeton University Press.
—— (1968b) *Creative Mythology: The Masks of God*, New York: Penguin.
—— (1974) *The Mythic Image*, Princeton: Princeton University Press.
Hirschman, E.C. (1980) "Attributes of Attributes and Layers of Meaning," in J. Olson (ed.)

Advances in Consumer Research, vol. 8, Provo, UT: Association for Consumer Research, 1–6.

Hirschman, E.C. (1981) "Comprehending Symbolic Consumption: Three Theoretical Issues," in E.C. Hirschman and M.B. Holbrook (eds) *Symbolic Consumer Behavior*, New York: Association for Consumer Research, 4–6.

—— (1987) "Movies as Myths: An Interpretation of Motion Picture Mythology," in Jean Umiker-Sebeok (ed.) *Marketing and Semiotics: New Directions in the Study of Signs for Sale*, Berlin: Mouton de Gruyter, 335–74.

—— (1988) "The Ideology of Consumption: A Structural-Syntactical Analysis of *Dallas* and *Dynasty*," *Journal of Consumer Research*, 15,3: 344–59.

Holbrook, M.B. and Grayson, M.W. (1986) "The Semiology of Cinematic Consumption," *Journal of Consumer Research*, 13,3: 374–81.

Mick, D.G. (1986) "Consumer Research and Semiotics: Exploring the Morphology of Signs, Symbols, and Significance," *Journal of Consumer Research*, 13, 2: 196–213.

Scott, L.M. (1990) "Understanding Jingles and Needledrop: A Rhetorical Approach to Music in Advertising," *Journal of Consumer Research*, 17, 2: 223–36.

—— (1994a) "Images in Advertising: The Need for a Theory of Visual Rhetoric," *Journal of Consumer Research*, 21, 2: 252–73.

—— (1994b), "The Bridge from Text to Mind: Adapting Reader-Response Theory to Consumer Research," *Journal of Consumer Research*, 21, 3: 461–80.

Stern, B.B. (1988a) "How Does an Ad Mean? Language in Services Advertising," *Journal of Advertising*, 17 (Summer): 3–14.

—— (1988b) "Medieval Allegory: Roots of Advertising Strategy for the Mass Market," *Journal of Marketing*, 52, 3: 84–94.

—— (1989), "Literary Criticism and Consumer Research: Overview and Illustrative Analysis," *Journal of Consumer Research*, 16,3: 322–34.

Thompson, C.J., Locander, W.B., and Pollio, H.R. (1989) "Putting Consumer Experience Back into Consumer Research: The Philosophy and Method of Existential–Phenomenology," *Journal of Consumer Research*, 16,2: 133–46.

—— (1990) "The Lived Meaning of Free Choice: An Existential–Phenomenological Description of Everyday Consuming Experiences of Contemporary Married Women," *Journal of Consumer Research*, 17, 3: 346–61.

INDEX